EDITED BY CAROL McGUIRK

PENGUIN BOOKS

PENGUIN BOOKS

Published by the Penguin Group
Penguin Books Ltd, 80 Strand, London WC2R 0RL, England
Penguin Putnam Inc., 375 Hudson Street, New York, New York 10014, USA
Penguin Books Australia Ltd, 250 Camberwell Road, Camberwell, Victoria 3124, Australia
Penguin Books Canada Ltd, 10 Alcorn Avenue, Toronto, Ontario, Canada M4V 3B2
Penguin Books India (P) Ltd, 11 Community Centre, Panchsheel Park, New Delhi – 110 017, India
Penguin Books (NZ) Ltd, Cnr Rosedale and Airborne Roads, Albany, Auckland, New Zealand
Penguin Books (South Africa) (Pty) Ltd, 24 Sturdee Avenue, Rosebank 2196, South Africa

Penguin Books Ltd, Registered Offices: 80 Strand, London WC2R 0RL, England

www.penguin.com

First published 1993
19

'The Fornicator', 'To Alexander Findlater', 'When Princes and Prelates', 'Ode
to Spring', 'Kircudbright Grace', from James Kingsley, ed., *The Poems and Songs
of Robert Burns*, 3 vols., 1968, are reproduced by permission of Oxford
University Press

Typeset by Datix International Limited, Bungay, Suffolk
Printed in England by Clays Ltd, St Ives plc
Filmset in Monophoto Ehrhardt

ISBN-13: 978-0-140-42382-2

www.greenpenguin.co.uk

Penguin Books is committed to a sustainable future
for our business, our readers and our planet.
The book in your hands is made from paper
certified by the Forest Stewardship Council.

Contents

Preface

The standard scholarly edition, James Kinsley's monumental *Poems and Songs of Robert Burns* (Clarendon, 1968), collates all early versions of Burns's works – manuscript, transcript and printed – and arranges them in probable order of composition. I have followed a different approach in several respects. First, this edition is selective, printing a hundred texts (from Burns's more than six hundred poems and songs) and providing brief notes aimed more at sketching than exhaustively documenting wider contexts. Secondly, rather than offering the composite text that results from collation of multiple sources, I have tried to capture something of the experience of readers between 1786 and 1796 as they first encountered Burns's poems and songs as edited by his own hand: whenever possible, I have used as copy-text the first published form of most works. Finally, though I have, like Kinsley, arranged the texts in order of probable composition rather than (as in Henley and Henderson's Centenary edition, 1896–7) order of publication, I have sometimes differed from Kinsley in setting the chronology.

Specific differences are discussed in the notes, but there is one general matter of chronology that should be clarified here. Kinsley begins with work said to be written by the poet between the ages of fifteen and twenty-five (1774–84), followed by a second section of poems written between the ages of twenty-five and twenty-six (1784–5) and a third of work completed at the age of twenty-seven (1786). This creates a misleading impression of steady lyric output from Burns's adolescence; it also counts 1784 twice, setting barriers between 1784 and 1786, the period of Burns's real creative breakthrough. The 'early' work of Burns is best seen as produced in a blaze of creativity from about the age of twenty-four, the pace accelerating during the two years preceding the publication of his first collection, *Poems Chiefly in the Scottish Dialect* (1786). By the winter of 1785–6, Burns was working so quickly that chronology becomes less important than reflecting the near-simultaneity of some compositions. In a letter of 17 February 1786, the poet remarks that he has just completed 'The Ordination', 'Scotch Drink', 'The Cotter's Saturday Night', 'Address to the Deil', and 'The Twa Dogs'.

Burns began to write at fifteen, all sources agree. But he rewrote much of his juvenilia during the same period (1783-5) in which he was writing the poems for the Kilmarnock volume. Rather than seeing the poet's *First Commonplace Book* as the shrine for Burns's adolescent relics, I have assumed – noting the evidence it offers of a dramatic maturation of style between 1783 and 1785 – that it is better seen as the testing ground for the experiments in verse-form and 'voice' that culminated in the Kilmarnock edition (1786). Burns did write some version of 'Song Composed in August' (song 2 in Kinsley) at sixteen, for example, but a comparison between its mature diction and that of true juvenilia such as the charming but awkward 'O Once I Lov'd' suggests that he finished much later the accomplished song that we know. When revisions of early works seem likely to have been extensive, I have placed the text in the year in which it probably took its form as we know it.

The reason I have chosen the first published source as copy-text is that Burns seldom made substantive changes after first printing. (Exceptions, such as 'The Vision', are discussed in the notes.) His instinct when a new dimension for a completed text occurred to him was to write a new text, as with successive versions of 'Banks o' Doon', 'Duncan Gray', and 'Ca' the Yowes'. By contrast to such thorough re-castings, minor changes in subsequent printings of texts already published often seem the result not of new insight but of external pressure. In the review that established Burns's vogue in Edinburgh, Henry Mackenzie praised Burns's poems but deplored his lapses in diction and taste: 'Our Poet had, alas! no friends or companions from whom correction could be obtained. When we reflect on his rank in life ... we regret perhaps more than wonder, that delicacy should be so often offended in perusing a volume in which there is so much to interest and to please us.' Mackenzie's readers took to heart this call for 'correction', and Burns's revisions often reflect his half-hearted efforts to comply with the advice of such genteel but poem-deaf 'mentors' as Hugh Blair, Frances Dunlop, and George Thomson. (As their advice was invariably to anglicize, it is not surprising that the poet also begins to complain in his letters that he cannot write well in English, comments often quoted out of context to indicate Burns's discomfort with the language itself when what they suggest is the poet's distress at being instructed in it by self-appointed censors.) Burns made his best editorial decisions when the text was under his control and he worked undistracted by well-intentioned advice. And it was evidently before first publication that he gave most thought to defining his text for a general reader.

This final editing prior to first publication also makes the first published sources preferable to Burns's manuscripts as copy-texts. The poet's generosity in supplying friends and patrons with multiple manuscript copies of his work – even (as with the Glenriddell Manuscript) multi-volume compilations annotated and partly transcribed in his own hand – produced the multiple variants that form the basis for Kinsley's edition. Often the poet changed the text to personalize it for the recipient (and not always happily, as in the air-puffed version of 'Scots Wha Hae' sent to the Earl of Buchan). In this edition, I have assumed that, from the time of the *First Commonplace Book*, such play and variation in transcription produced an informal text and that the version Burns selected for publication is preferable.

Burns was, for instance, virtual editor of his first volume, *Poems Chiefly in the Scottish Dialect*, published by subscription at Kilmarnock in July 1786. In the two years preceding its publication, Burns, as mentioned, revised his juvenilia for his *First Commonplace Book* and also produced a quantity of new work, which he arranged for publication with an eye to consistency of speaker and tone. The presiding spirit of the Kilmarnock edition is not 'Rab the Ranter' as the folk of Mauchline knew him in 1786 – the parish rebel whose prospective father-in-law fainted on hearing the name of his pregnant daughter's betrothed. Burns's close friend of that period, David Sillar, described the poet in 1785–6: 'I recollect hearing his neighbours observe he had a great deal to say for himself, and that they suspected his *principles*. He wore the only tied hair in the parish; and in the church his plaid, which was of a particular colour, I think *fillemot*, he wrapped in a particular manner about his shoulders.' But the predominant speaker of the Kilmarnock edition is far less threatening: 'Robin' as a kindly rustic occasionally interrupted at the ploughing by the Scottish national muse. As he puts it (echoing Pope) in the 'anonymous' epigraph he provided for his volume: 'The Simple Bard, unbroke by rules of Art,/ He pours the wild effusions of the heart:/ And if inspir'd, 'tis Nature's pow'rs inspire;/ Hers all the melting thrill, and hers the kindling fire.'

With a canny eye to pleasing the regional audience of middling Scottish gentry and enlightened 'New Licht' liberals likely to hear of his volume – for there is no evidence Burns foresaw his instant success throughout Britain – the poet suppressed most of his satires and scatological works, including 'Holy Willie's Prayer', 'The Fornicator', and 'Love and Liberty'. In addition, the Kilmarnock volume's focus on poems 'chiefly' in Scottish led the poet to suppress some of his best early songs, which were written chiefly in English. Of dozens completed, only four lyrics were printed in the volume, which was predominantly narrative in focus. The continuing popularity of the poems first published at Kilmarnock – 'To a Mouse', 'The Cotter's Saturday Night', 'To a Louse', 'The Vision' – vindicates the poet's editorial judgement, but criticism still contends with the difficulty of seeing beyond this volume's largely sentimental focus to the total achievement of Burns's art. For while the Kilmarnock edition was a dazzling literary debut, it was also the source of the subsequent Burns myth. Of the hundred texts in the present edition, twenty-five were first printed in the volume published at Kilmarnock (which consisted of thirty-six poems in all). Because of their much greater length, however, they dominate this present edition – as they continue to dominate Burns's literary reputation.

The Edinburgh edition, likewise titled *Poems Chiefly in the Scottish Dialect*, appeared in April 1787 and is essentially an expanded Kilmarnock: Burns cut three epitaphs, but the main distinction of the Edinburgh edition is the fifteen poems and seven songs he added. Most variations between texts published in 1786 and 1787 show the poet's deference to Hugh Blair, who advised him on the edition (convincing Burns, for instance, that 'Love and Liberty' was unpublishable). The Kilmarnock edition is more forthright and plain-spoken – more like its author. In

'The Twa Dogs', for instance (first poem in both volumes), 'arse' (Kilmarnock) has been politely draped in dashes: 'a—' (Edinburgh). The Edinburgh text is used here only for poems and songs that first appeared there: notably 'Death and Dr Hornbook', a poem Burns never liked but that Blair (for once judging well) convinced him to include.

Burns sold the copyright of *Poems Chiefly in the Scottish Dialect* in 1787 to William Creech, an Edinburgh publisher he came to dislike. He barely looked over the proofs of the subsequent edition of 1793–4, to which he contributed only eight new works, reprinting several (notably 'Tam o' Shanter') completed after 1787 but first published in newspapers or periodicals. By 1793, Burns was absorbed in his song-revision work for two serial publications, James Johnson's *Scots Musical Museum* (1787–1803) and George Thomson's *Select Collection of Original Scottish Airs* (1793–1818). Like most editors, I have preferred *Scots Musical Museum* as copy-text for Burns's songs printed after 1787. Burns's songs had his nearly undivided creative attention after 1787 until his death in 1796, and James Johnson (who saw Burns as co-editor) reliably followed the poet's instructions. For songs not included in *Scots Musical Museum*, George Thomson's *Select Collection* has been consulted, but used only once as a copy-text. All but one of Thomson's volumes appeared after the poet's death, and the editor often changed both music and lyrics.

In descending order of most frequent use, the texts on which this edition relies are as follows: the Kilmarnock and (for the few texts appearing in book form first in 1787 or 1793–4) the two Edinburgh editions of *Poems Chiefly in the Scottish Dialect*; James Johnson's *Scots Musical Museum*; and J. C. Dick's *Songs of Robert Burns* (1903), which corrects both text and music of the later songs sent to *Select Collection*. For 'Love and Liberty' and 'Holy Willie's Prayer', major works suppressed during the poet's lifetime, I have used two editions of Burns's poems by Thomas Stewart printed in Glasgow in 1801 and 1802, reset from an earlier pamphlet series. Although unauthorized (Cadell and Davies of London held the copyright to Burns's work from 1800), Stewart's publications preserved several suppressed writings – apparently through manuscripts passed to Stewart by his uncle John Richmond, a crony of Burns's from Ayrshire (once Gavin

Hamilton's clerk) with whom the poet shared a flat at Baxter's Close in Edinburgh. Though Robert Cromek's *Reliques of Robert Burns* (1808) and James Currie's *Works of Robert Burns* (Liverpool, 1800) are not generally reliable (both editors bowdlerized the poet's texts), both men had access to unpublished manuscripts, and in a few instances their version has been used as copy-text. For fugitive posthumous publications not collected in earlier editions, copy-texts were taken from Henley and Henderson's Centenary edition (1896-7), Dick's *Songs of Robert Burns* (1903), and Kinsley's Clarendon edition (1968).

The copies of the Kilmarnock, the 1787 Edinburgh edition ('skinking' version) and the 1793-4 Edinburgh edition of *Poems Chiefly in the Scottish Dialect* microfilmed for use as copy-text are in the collections of the Houghton Library of Harvard University (shelf marks *EC75.B9375.786p, *EC75.B9375.786pb (A) and *EC75.B9375.786pn.v.2, respectively); I am grateful for permission to use them. The Houghton Library's copies of Johnson's *Scots Musical Museum* (1787-1803), Thomson's *Select Collection* (1801 reissue of the 1793 volume), Stewart's *Poems Ascribed to Robert Burns* (Glasgow, 1801), *Stewart's Edition of Burns's Poems* (Glasgow, 1802), and Currie's *Works of Robert Burns* (second edition; 1801) also are used with kind permission. For permission to use James Kinsley's text of three songs from *Merry Muses of Caledonia* and two poems ('To Alexander Findlater' and 'Kirkcudbright Grace') for which a reliable early printed source does not exist, I thank the Clarendon Press. Concentrated work on this edition during the summer of 1991 was made possible by the National Endowment for the Humanities and Harvard University, who funded a Summer Seminar on Blake and Rousseau. I am much indebted to the seminar's director, Leo Damrosch, and to fellow participants. A sabbatical leave from Florida Atlantic University in the autumn of 1992 considerably eased the final stages of revision. The supervisor of photography at FAU, William N. Watkins, provided generous help, transforming microfilm into legible photographs. I thank also my FAU colleagues Howard Pearce (whose keyboard has been on perpetual loan to this project since its inception) and Kenneth Keaton, for sharing his expertise in eighteenth-century music.

Copy-editing the work of Burns for modern readers presents

unique difficulties. His non-standard, protean vocabulary and spelling (he often spells the same word two or three different ways even within a single poem) can be confusing, yet are central to his vision and have not been altered here. Burns's discursive titles are also a distinctive feature of his early narrative work. Although a few such titles (e.g., 'The Auld Farmer's New-Year-Morning Salutation to his Auld Mare, Maggie, on Giving Her the Accustomed Ripp of Corn to Hansel in the New Year') are shortened for the Contents List, all are given in full above the text. The long 's' has been modernized, and eighteenth-century hyper-punctuation (as in the Kilmarnock title 'To a Mouse, on Turning her up in her Nest, with the Plough, November, 1785') has been trimmed. Like Jane Austen, Burns is prone to superfluous punctuation of possessives (her's; it's); this has been silently corrected.

A more perplexing editorial task was reconciling the inconsistency of typographical practices among the various copy-texts, especially italicizations, capitalizations, and dashes. The poet's numerous emphatic devices – asterisks, daggers, place-names spelled all in capitals, ironies underscored by italics – recall the flourishes and asterisks that embellish Burns's fair copies and letters and suggest that he never entirely lost his youthful affection for the typographical excesses of *Tristram Shandy*. Yet in the Kilmarnock edition (the most typographically eccentric copy-text) the typeface is unusually large and the lines set far apart: proportionally, Burns's emphases do not shout from the page as they would in a small paperbound edition such as this. For this reason, and because Burns simplified his printing instructions in later editions, I have printed all proper names in the usual manner (with initial capitals), even though Burns often (not always) printed place-names entirely in capitals. I have almost always retained italics, for they provide additional clarification of Burns's meaning by marking an idiom or coinage, or indicating ironic intention. In a few cases, too many italicized words in close proximity were distracting (in some Kilmarnock poems, for instance, Burns sets up a pattern of italicizing every single vernacular word). Italics truly marking ironic emphasis were kept in those cases, and vernacular words were printed in roman type. In doubtful cases I have kept to the copy-text. Henley and Henderson's Centenary edition, which entirely modernizes and repunctuates, provides fast-reading and admirably lucid texts that none the less seem overly homogenized, losing something of the poet's own voice.

Finally, to make the topical poems more accessible, I have spelled out all proper names and place-names which the poet cloaked in asterisks or dashes. For bawdy words, however, dashes have been kept for words the poet himself regarded as naughty enough invariably to require dashes, even in private letters. Such expressions as 'hell' and 'damned' have usually been spelled out when cloaked in the copy-text; the poet usually wrote such words in full.

In titling the songs, I have followed the copy-texts whenever possible; but James Johnson, who published the majority of Burns's songs, usually omitted titles, while George Thomson and the poet's posthumous editors were prone to substitution and invention. As may be seen from the eleven songs printed in his 1786 and 1787 *Poems*, Burns's own editorial practice was to title almost all his lyrics 'Song' or 'Fragment', providing above the text only the name of the air to which the lyrics are set. This illustrates Burns's modesty in seeing his lyrics as mere subordinate 'vehicles to the music'; but to follow his practice would frustrate the purposes of a Contents List: over a dozen entries would be identified only as 'Song'. I have used the initial phrase as the title of songs when they were left untitled in the copy-text, titled only 'Song', or 'Fragment', or given titles that are no longer used. When a phrase from a song's chorus is more famous than its title or opening line ('Auld lang syne', 'For a' that') it is given in parentheses in the Contents List. James Johnson's *Scots Musical Museum* furnished most of the musical texts for this edition, though Dick's *Songs of Robert Burns* furnished tunes for some dozen songs that either appeared without music in the copy text or appeared in Johnson or Thomson matched to the wrong tune. Thomson's *Select Collection* was used as the source for one song ('Logan Water'). The musical texts are printed in the notes for each song.

The notes will make sparing use of the standard commentary on Burns furnished by the poet's contemporaries and survivors. While reliable on the poet's early life, Burns's brother Gilbert – one of the major early sources for biographical information – may have done more damage to Burns's reputation than even the

Edinburgh literati or the song-editor Thomson. The evaluation of
his brother's character supplied by Gilbert in the narratives he
produced between 1797 and 1820 implies some unacknowledged
but pervasive resentment. (There was some coolness between
them in the final years of the poet's life – perhaps because Gilbert
refused to take over the lease of the farm at Ellisland, perhaps
because Robert resented Gilbert's inability to repay the 1788 loan
of some £180 of the proceeds from the Edinburgh edition.)
Unfortunately, the most voluble early informants on Burns are
among the most suspect. For all their occasionally Shandean
postures, Burns's letters furnish more reliable testimony, and the
notes have made extensive use of the excellent Ferguson/Roy
edition of *Letters of Robert Burns* (Clarendon, 1985).

I have appended a glossary rather than glossing each poem in
the margins. Glosses appearing on the same page detract from the
pleasure of initial encounter and are unnecessary given Burns's
careful training of the reader through repetition and context.
There is always something intrusive about a gloss, as an indignant
anonymous reviewer of the heavily glossed Centenary edition
noted in the *Edinburgh Evening News* in 1897: 'The poet's text is
flanked by innumerable . . . notes, just like a students' torchlight
procession escorted by mounted police . . . Even an Englishman,
one would presume, comprehends, or can guess, what "yon"
means. Mr Henley plants "yonder" carefully alongside whenever
the word appears. That it occurs on almost every page is nothing
to him.' My glossary is compiled from the meticulous, highly
detailed glossary Burns himself prepared for *Poems* 1787 (Edin-
burgh). I am grateful to my brother, Dr Donald McGuirk, Jr, for
his gift of a rare copy of the 1787 London edition of *Poems*: this
allowed me daily access to Burns's original glossary as I worked.
The poet's glosses have been supplemented by the glossaries of
other editions; here as elsewhere, James Kinsley's work was
invaluable. Prefixed to the glossary are excerpts from a guide to
Scots that first appeared in Allan Ramsay's *Poems* (1721); the
guide provides useful information on recognizing cognates (Scots
words differing only slightly in spelling or pronunciation from the
English).

This edition, in the selection of texts and the preparing of
notes, has presented Burns in terms of his individual poetic

achievement, his Scottish (and wider British/European) culture, and his historical era. A grasp of Scottish history is so important to understanding Burns that I have included a short outline of the series of separations and divisive 'unions' that preceded the eighteenth-century Scottish vernacular revival and that form one context for understanding the achievement – a cultural as well as a personal vindication – of Robert Burns. I hope, however, that readers may take from this collection a sense not only of Burns's sources and allusions but also of his continuing importance. Burns's power as an artist resides in his demotic yet idealizing poetic language: 'the only example in history,' said Emerson, 'of a language made classic through the genius of a single man.' It resides also in his peasant speakers, through whose richly indi- vidual voices (inverting the parodic moral of 'To a Louse') we are liberated to see 'the other' as we see ourselves. For no lyric poet so exploits our capacity for imaginative sympathy. Shelley, who had some stake in the matter, called poets the unacknowledged legislators of the world. If so, there is no amending the law as given by Robert Burns. With an entirely deceptive simplicity, he tells us who we are, by what we feel.

Table of Dates

1757   *15 December* Marriage of William Burnes or Burness
        (1721–84), originally of Kincardineshire, and Agnes
        Broun (1732–1820) of Maybole. Burnes, a head gardener
        at an estate, in 1750 had purchased a leasehold of seven
        and a half acres at Alloway and built the two-room
        cottage (one room for the family, one for the livestock)
        in which he and his wife set up house.

1759   *25 January* Robert Burns, eldest of seven children, is
        born in the cottage at Alloway in south-west Scotland.

1765   Robert and his brother Gilbert (1760–1827) are taught
        reading, writing, and English grammar by eighteen-
        year-old John Murdoch, a private school master shared
        by several village families. Murdoch later confessed to
        thinking Gilbert the more promising child: 'certainly if
        any person who knew the two boys had been asked
        which of them was most likely to court the Muses, he
        would surely never have guessed that Robert had a
        propensity of that kind.'

1766   William Burnes, borrowing £100 for stock, signs a
        twelve-year lease on Mount Oliphant, seventy Scots
        acres of farmland (ninety in English measure) later
        described by Gilbert as 'almost the very poorest soil I
        know of in a state of cultivation'. Robert and Gilbert
        continue their schooling with Murdoch at Alloway
        until he leaves the area in 1768.

1772   *summer* Attends Dalrymple school (largely to improve
        his penmanship) on alternate weeks with Gilbert: only
        one boy at a time can be spared for school.
            Gilbert wrote of the years at Mount Oliphant: 'To
        the buffettings of misfortune we could only oppose

hard labour and the most rigid economy. We lived very sparingly. For several years butchers' meat was a stranger in the house, while all the members of the family exerted themselves to the utmost of their strength, and rather beyond it, in the labours of the farm . . . To think of our father growing old (for he was now above fifty) broken down with the long continued fatigues of his life . . . these reflections produced in my brother's mind and mine sensations of the deepest distress. I doubt not but the hard labour and sorrow of this period of his life, was in a great measure the cause of that depression of spirits, with which Robert was so often afflicted through his whole life afterwards.'

1774   *autumn* Writes his first song ('O Once I Lov'd') for his partner in the harvest, either Nellie Kilpatrick or Nellie Blair. 'Thus with me,' he later wrote, 'began Love and Poesy.'

1775   *summer* Studies mathematics and surveying at Kirk-oswald; begins 'Song Composed in August' for Margaret Thomson, who lives next door to the school.

1777   William Burnes leases Lochlea farm near Tarbolton, 130 acres of good land at the ruinous rent of £130 – twenty shillings an acre. (Rent at Mount Oliphant, a smaller, poorer farm, was £45.) The family move from Mount Oliphant confident they will succeed at Lochlea.

1778–9   *winter* Attends dancing school in Tarbolton, causing a breach with his father, who has forbidden him to go. Probably during this year, William Burnes stops paying rent at Lochlea.

1780   Founds the Tarbolton Bachelor's Club with his brother Gilbert and five friends. Among the rules: 'Every man proper for a member of this Society, must have a frank, honest, open heart; above anything dirty or mean; and must be a professed lover of one or more of the female sex.'

1781   *4 July* Joins the Freemasons (Tarbolton lodge).
        summer Studies flax-dressing at Irvine: the poems and
        letters of this period suggest a severe depression.

1782   *1 January* During a drunken New Year's celebration
        the flax-dressing shop catches fire and burns to the
        ground. Burns leaves Irvine 'like a true poet, not worth
        a sixpence'.

1783   *January* Wins a prize of £3 for his flax-seed.
        April Begins to record and revise his juvenilia in his
        First Commonplace Book.
        17 May A writ of sequestration is issued against Wil-
        liam Burnes, seizing his property for eventual distribu-
        tion to creditors. Burnes appeals against the
        judgement.
        autumn As a refuge for the family in the event of their
        father's bankruptcy, the poet and Gilbert in their own
        names sub-lease Mossgiel (a 118-acre farm near the
        small town of Mauchline) from Gavin Hamilton, a
        family friend.

1784   *27 January* William Burnes wins the last of his appeals
        to the Court of Session, averting bankruptcy.
        13 February William Burnes dies of a 'phthisical con-
        sumption'. The family vacate Lochlea and move to
        Mossgiel.
        November? Meets Jean Armour, daughter of a mason
        and contractor in Mauchline.

1785   *22 May* Birth of Burns's first child Elizabeth ('dear-
        bought Bess'; d. 1817). The mother is Elizabeth Paton,
        a servant at Lochlea farm. The poet's mother rears her
        grandchild until 1796, when Betsey Paton (by then
        married) reclaims her.
        June Transcribes his first Scottish vernacular poem,
        'The Death and Dying Words of Poor Mailie', into the
        First Commonplace Book: it was begun at Lochlea farm
        several years earlier. (Early poems and songs of Burns
        were chiefly in English.)

28 October Death of John (b. 1769), the poet's brother.

1786   *January?* Books passage for Savannah-la-Mar (Jamaica) in the ship *Nancy*, hoping to escape a bleak future as a debt-ridden tenant farmer. The ship is scheduled to sail in late summer.

March Jean Armour's father, enraged at her betrothal to Burns and at her pregnancy, orders his lawyer (possibly Burns's friend Robert Aiken) to cut the couples' names out of their written agreement to marry. Jean is sent away to live with an uncle in Paisley. Furious at Jean's 'desertion', Burns courts Mary (perhaps Margaret) Campbell – Burns's name for her is 'Highland Mary' – a dairymaid who once worked as a nursemaid in Gavin Hamilton's house.

April Signs a letter 'Burnes' for the last time, henceforth using 'Burns'.

second Sunday in May Burns gives Highland Mary, probably as a token of their engagement, a two-volume Bible. She leaves Ayrshire for Greenock – in Burns's words 'to arrange matters among her friends for our projected change of life'.

July–August Appears at church on three Sundays to do public penance for fornication; Burns is allowed, however, to remain in his pew rather than stand with Jean in the 'place of repentance'.

22 July Tenancy of Mossgiel is transferred wholly to Gilbert Burns.

30 July Burns is in hiding from a writ issued by Jean Armour's father.

31 July Publication of *Poems Chiefly in the Scottish Dialect* at Kilmarnock. Three weeks later, of 612 copies printed (350 reserved for subscribers) only thirteen remain unsold.

1 September Postpones emigration to Jamaica.

3 September Jean Armour gives birth to twins, Jean (d. 1787) and Robert (d. 1857).

27 September Again postpones emigration.

end of autumn Mary Campbell dies of a fever and is buried in the West Highland Churchyard at Greenock. Shaken by her death and softened towards Jean Armour upon the birth of their twins, the poet decides not to emigrate but to seek a patron in Scotland.

29 November Arrives in Edinburgh with material for a new edition of his *Poems* and with hopes of securing patronage. Within weeks a favourable review of his poems by Henry Mackenzie appears in the fashionable periodical *The Lounger*; Burns is lionized as the 'heaven-taught ploughman'.

1787   *17 April* Publishes an enlarged edition of *Poems Chiefly in the Scottish Dialect* at Edinburgh. The list of 1,300 subscribers goes on for thirty-eight pages.

23 April Sells the copyright of *Poems Chiefly in the Scottish Dialect* for the sum Henry Mackenzie has suggested: 100 guineas.

5 May–1 June Tours the Border with Robert Ainsley.

22 May First volume of James Johnson's *Scots Musical Museum* is published in Edinburgh, including three songs by Burns.

June Tours the Western Highlands.

summer May (or Meg) Cameron, an Edinburgh servant, serves Burns with a writ demanding security for the support of their as-yet-unborn child. (She has exhausted a small amount the poet sent her in May.) Following Burns's compliance with the writ in mid-August (he keeps the document, inscribing it with two stanzas of bawdry), nothing further is said of her; an oblique statement in a letter by Burns, however, raises the possibility that she gave birth to stillborn triplets.

25 August–16 September Tours the Highlands again, accompanied by the irascible Edinburgh schoolmaster William Nichol.

October Tours Stirlingshire.

late October Returns to Edinburgh; sets to work revising songs for the second volume of *Scots Musical Museum*.

4 December Meets Agnes Craig M'Lehose, 'Nancy' in

'Ae Fond Kiss'. Married and the mother of three, she
has been separated some years from her husband, who
lives in Jamaica. Styling themselves 'Clarinda' and
'Sylvander', the two begin a heated flirtation, conducted
mostly through letters.

Jenny Clow, a servant of 'Clarinda's', bears Burns a
son that she refuses to allow him to raise. A letter of
1791 from Clarinda asking Burns's help for Jenny
Clow, then dying (probably of consumption), makes no
mention of the infant, but recent research by James
Mackay has shown that he survived and prospered.

1788   *14 February* Second volume of *Scots Musical Museum*
is published, including thirty-two songs by Burns,
among them 'Rattlin, Roarin Willie' and 'O'er the
Water to Charlie'.

February Considers the lease of Ellisland, a farm in
Dumfriesshire, on a brief visit to the area.

3 March Under Burns's protection, her family having
cast her off, Jean Armour gives birth to twin girls who
die within the month. The poet, entangled with 'Clar-
inda', remains reluctant to acknowledge Jean Armour
as his wife, although Scottish law (defining even spoken
agreement to marry as conferring conjugal rights and
obligations) would view their written agreement of
spring 1786 as binding, legitimizing any children.

The poet, some of whose closest friends were law-
yers, must have received bad legal advice on a matter
that in his eyes was settled by the mutilation of the
original agreement by Jean's angry father, his bach-
elor's certificate issued by his parish following his
public penance, and (most importantly) by her drawing
back from their engagement during the summer of 1786,
just before the sensational success of his *Poems*. (Burns
ascribed Jean's later efforts at reconciliation to her
father's interest in securing part of the profits.)

April Acknowledges Jean Armour as his wife, probably
after a final unsuccessful attempt to win 'Clarinda' and
a hint from the Board of Excise that an appointment

would be more likely if he settled down. In a letter to his song-editor Johnson he writes that 'I am so enamoured with a certain girl's prolific twin-bearing merit, that I have given her a *legal* title to the best blood in my body; and so farewell Rakery!'

May Lends his brother Gilbert £180, perhaps half the proceeds of *Poems Chiefly in the Scottish Dialect*, a sum not repaid (principal or interest) until 1820, when Gilbert reimburses the estate using the proceeds from his own edition of his brother's poems.

June Moves to Dumfriesshire to build a house at Ellisland, a farm for which he has signed a seventy-six-year lease; writes 'Of a' the Airts' for absent Jean, who joins him in December.

14 July Is commissioned as an Exciseman, a position originally intended merely to supplement income generated by the farm and dairy at Ellisland.

1789   *18 August* Birth of his favourite son, Francis Wallace (d. 1803). Several years later in a letter to 'Frank's' godmother, the poet wrote: 'I look on your little Namesake to be my chef d'oeuvre in that species of manufacture, as I look on 'Tam o' Shanter' to be my standard performance in the Poetical line. 'Tis true, both the one & the other discover a spice of roguish waggery that might perhaps be as well spared; but then they also shew in my opinion a force of genius & a finishing polish that I despair of ever excelling.'

1790   *winter* Suffers a long illness; becomes sure that Ellisland will never become profitable; begins to consider a full-time career 'grinding the faces of the publican and sinner on the merciless wheel of the Excise'.

February Third volume of *Scots Musical Museum* is published, including forty songs by Burns, among them 'John Anderson my Jo', 'Tam Glen', and 'Farewell to the Highlands'.

24 July Death of William (b. 1767), the poet's brother.

1 December Completes 'Tam o' Shanter'.

1791   *31 March* A daughter Elizabeth (d. 1873) is born to
Helen Anne Park, niece (or perhaps second cousin) of
the proprietress of the Globe Inn, Dumfries. 'Anna'
Park inspired 'Yestreen I Had a Pint o' Wine', the
love-song Burns considered his best. She left Dumfries
to begin a new life elsewhere, or possibly died in
childbirth. Jean nurses the infant Elizabeth along with
one of her own sons, born nine days later.
9 April A son, William Nichol (d. 1872), is born to
Jean at Ellisland.
10 September Gives up the lease on Ellisland for full-
time work as an Exciseman.
late autumn? Moves with Jean and four children to a
three-room, second-floor flat in the town of Dumfries.
In later life, Jean recalled their town routine: 'Burns
was not an early riser, excepting when he had something
particular to do in the way of his profession . . . The
family breakfasted at nine. If he lay long in bed awake,
he was always reading. At all meals he had a book
beside him at the table. He did his work in the forenoon
and was seldom engaged professionally in the evening.
Dined at two o'clock when he dined at home. Was fond
of plain things, and hated tarts, pies and puddings.
When at home in the evening, he employed his time in
writing and reading, with the children playing about
him. Their prattle never disturbed him.'

1792   *August* Fourth volume of *Scots Musical Museum* is
published, including forty-seven songs by Burns,
among them 'The Banks o' Doon', 'Ae Fond Kiss', and
'Afton Water'. (Kinsley, perhaps counting material col-
lected as well as revised, numbered sixty songs by
Burns in the volume.)
September Begins contributing songs to George Thom-
son's *Select Collection of Original Scottish Airs*.
21 November A daughter (his third to be named Eliza-
beth; d. 1795) is born to Jean.
December Civil unrest in Dumfries; the poet is almost

dismissed from his Excise post for pro-revolutionary
statements.

1793   *February* William Creech, who now owns the copyright,
issues a new edition of *Poems Chiefly in the Scottish
Dialect*, expanded to two volumes. The poet, absorbed
in song-writing and work for the Excise, has not been
much consulted about the edition and becomes indig-
nant with Creech over a delay in receiving his copies.

May First volume of Thomson's *Select Collection* ap-
pears, containing seven new songs by Burns.

19 May Moves his family to larger quarters, a rented
house in Mill Street, Dumfries. During the 1830s, the
poet's eldest son described the family's life at Mill
Street for the editor Robert Chambers: 'his father and
mother led a life that was comparatively genteel. They
always had a maid-servant, and sat in their parlour.
That apartment, together with two bedrooms, was well
furnished and carpeted; and when good company assem-
bled, which was often the case, the hospitable board
which they surrounded was of a patrician mahogany.
There was much rough comfort in the house ... for
the poet received many presents of jam and country
produce from the rural gentlefolk, besides occasional
barrels of oysters from Hill, Cunningham, and other
friends in town; so that [the poet] possibly was as much
envied by some of his neighbours as he has since been
pitied by the general body of his countrymen.'

July–August Tours Galloway with John Syme; writes
'Robert Bruce's March to Bannockburn' ('Scots Wha
Hae').

1794   *12 August* A son, James Glencairn Burns (d. 1865), is
born.

December Is appointed acting supervisor of the Excise.

1795   *January* Joins the Dumfries Volunteers.

September Death of his daughter Elizabeth shortly
before her third birthday.

December Seriously ill, unable to work.

1796   *21 July* Dies in Dumfries of chronic bacterial infection
           starting probably in his teens: endocarditis or rheumatic
           fever according to most biographies; brucellosis accord-
           ing to Fowler's (1988).
           25 July Is buried with full military honours despite his
           dying request for a simple funeral. On this day, Jean
           gives birth to Maxwell (d. 1799), a son named after the
           family physician.
               Jean (d. 1834) survives her husband nearly forty
           years. Only three of their nine children – all sons –
           survive to adulthood. (The two illegitimate daughters
           reared in the family also survive past their teens, as
           does the poet's son by Jenny Clow.)
           December Fifth volume of *Scots Musical Museum* is
           published, including thirty-seven songs by Burns,
           among them 'Auld Lang Syne'.

Further Reading and Recordings

Editions and Reference

Ashmead, John, and John Davison, *Songs of Robert Burns*, New York: Garland, 1988.

Dick, James C., *Songs of Robert Burns*, 1903; reprinted Hatboro, Pa: Folklore Associates, 1962.

Kinsley, James, *The Poems and Songs of Robert Burns*, 3 vols., Oxford: Clarendon, 1968.

Lindsay, Maurice, *The Burns Encyclopedia*, 3rd edition, New York: St Martin's, 1980.

Low, Donald, ed., *Robert Burns: The Critical Heritage*, London: Routledge and Kegan Paul, 1974.

The Songs of Robert Burns, London: Routledge, 1993.

Roy, G. Ross, and J. DeLancey Ferguson, *The Letters of Robert Burns*, 2 vols., Oxford: Clarendon, 1985.

Criticism, Biography, Background

Bentman, Raymond, *Robert Burns*, Boston: G. K. Hall, 1987.

Brown, Hilton, *There Was a Lad: An Essay on Robert Burns*, London: Hamish Hamilton, 1949.

Crawford, Thomas, *Burns: A Study of the Poems and Songs*, Edinburgh: Oliver and Boyd, 1960.

Daiches, David, *The Paradox of Scottish Culture: The Eighteenth Century Experience*, London: Oxford, 1964.

Fergusson, DeLancey, *Pride and Passion: Robert Burns*, New York: Oxford, 1939.

Mackay, James, *A Biography of Robert Burns*, Edinburgh: Mainstream, 1992.

Recordings

McColl, Ewan, *Songs of Robert Burns*, Folkways: 1959.
Redpath, Jean, and Serge Hovey, *The Songs of Robert Burns*, 7 vols., Philo Records: 1976–89.
Various Artists, *The Complete Songs of Robert Burns*, In association with the Robert Burns Federation, 6 vols., Linn CD: 1995.

O Once I Lov'd

(TUNE: I AM A MAN UNMARRIED (NOT EXTANT))

O once I lov'd a bonny lass
    Ay and I love her still
And whilst that virtue warms my breast
    I'll love my handsome Nell.
5   Fal lal de dal &c.

As bonny lasses I hae seen,
    And mony full as braw;
But for a modest gracefu' mien,
    The like I never saw.

10 A bonny lass I will confess
    Is pleasant to the e'e;
But without some better qualities
    She's no a lass for me.

But Nelly's looks are blythe and sweet,
15   And what is best of a',
Her reputation is compleat
    And fair without a flaw.

She dresses ay sae clean and neat,
    Both decent and genteel;
20 And then there's something in her gate
    Gars ony dress look weel.

A gaudy dress and gentle air
    May slightly touch the heart;
But it's innocence and modesty
25   That polisses the dart.

'Tis this in Nelly pleases me;
    'Tis this inchants my soul;
For absolutely in my breast
    She reigns without controul.

            Finis

Behind Yon Hills Where Lugar Flows

(TUNE: MY NANIE, O)

Behind yon hills where Lugar flows,
 'Mang moors an' mosses many, O,
The wintry sun the day has clos'd,
 And I'll awa to Nanie, O.

5 The westlin wind blaws loud an' shill;
 The night's baith mirk and rainy, O;
But I'll get my plaid an' out I'll steal,
 An' owre the hill to Nanie, O.

My Nanie's charming, sweet an' young;
10 Nae artfu' wiles to win ye, O:
May ill befa' the flattering tongue
 That wad beguile my Nanie, O.

Her face is fair, her heart is true,
 As spotless as she's bonie, O;
15 The op'ning gowan, wat wi' dew,
 Nae purer is than Nanie, O.

A country lad is my degree,
 An' few there be that ken me, O;
But what care I how few they be,
20 I'm welcome ay to Nanie, O.

My riches a's my penny-fee,
 An' I maun guide it cannie, O;
But warl's gear ne'er troubles me,
 My thoughts are a', my Nanie, O.

25 Our auld Guidman delights to view
 His sheep an' kye thrive bonie, O;
But I'm as blythe that hauds his pleugh,
 An' has nae care but Nanie, O.

Come weel come woe, I care na by,
30   I'll tak what Heav'n will sen' me, O:
Nae ither care in life have I,
     But live, an' love my Nanie, O.

Mary Morison

(TUNE: DUNCAN DAVISON)

O Mary, at thy window be,
     It is the wish'd, the trysted hour;
Those smiles and glances let me see,
     That make the miser's treasure poor:
5   How blythly wad I bide the stoure,
     A weary slave frae sun to sun;
Could I the rich reward secure,
     The lovely Mary Morison.

Yestreen when to the trembling string
10   The dance gaed thro' the lighted ha',
To thee my fancy took its wing,
     I sat, but neither heard nor saw:
Tho' this was fair, and that was braw,
     And yon the toast of a' the town,
15   I sigh'd, and said amang them a',
     'Ye are na Mary Morison.'

O Mary, canst thou wreck his peace,
     Wha for thy sake wad gladly die!
Or canst thou break that heart of his,
20   Whase only faut is loving thee.
If love for love thou wilt na gie,
     At least be pity to me shown;
A thought ungentle canna be
     The thought o' Mary Morison.

It Was Upon a Lammas Night

(TUNE: CORN RIGS ARE BONIE)

It was upon a Lammas night,
  When corn rigs are bonie,
Beneath the moon's unclouded light,
  I held awa to Annie:
5 The time flew by, wi' tentless heed,
  Till 'tween the late and early;
Wi' sma' persuasion she agreed,
  To see me thro' the barley.

The sky was blue, the wind was still,
10 The moon was shining clearly;
I set her down, wi' right good will,
  Amang the rigs o' barley:
I ken't her heart was a' my ain;
  I lov'd her most sincerely;
15 I kiss'd her owre and owre again,
  Amang the rigs o' barley.

I lock'd her in my fond embrace;
  Her heart was beating rarely:
My blessings on that happy place,
20 Amang the rigs o' barley!
But by the moon and stars so bright,
  That shone that hour so clearly!
She ay shall bless that happy night,
  Amang the rigs o' barley.

25 I hae been blythe wi' comrades dear;
  I hae been merry drinking;
I hae been joyfu' gath'rin gear;
  I hae been happy thinking;
But a' the pleasures e'er I saw,
30 Tho' three times doubl'd fairly,
That happy night was worth them a',
  Amang the rigs o' barley.

Corn rigs, an' barley rigs,
  An' corn rigs are bonie:
35   I'll ne'er forget that happy night
  Amang the rigs wi' Annie.

Song Composed in August

(TUNES: I HAD A HORSE, I HAD NAE MAIR; PORT
GORDON)

Now westlin winds, and slaught'ring guns
  Bring Autumn's pleasant weather;
And the moorcock springs, on whirring wings,
  Amang the blooming heather:
5 Now waving grain, wide o'er the plain,
  Delights the weary farmer;
And the moon shines bright, when I rove at night,
  To muse upon my charmer.

The partridge loves the fruitful fells;
10   The plover loves the mountains;
The woodcock haunts the lonely dells;
  The soaring hern the fountains:
Thro' lofty groves, the cushat roves,
  The path of man to shun it;
15 The hazel bush o'erhangs the thrush,
  The spreading thorn the linnet.

Thus ev'ry kind their pleasure find,
  The savage and the tender;
Some social join, and leagues combine;
20   Some solitary wander;
Avaunt, away! the cruel sway,
  Tyrannic man's dominion;
The sportsman's joy, the murd'ring cry,
  The flutt'ring, gory pinion!

25 But Peggy dear, the ev'ning's clear,
        Thick flies the skimming swallow;
    The sky is blue, the fields in view,
        All fading-green and yellow:
    Come let us stray our gladsome way,
30   And view the charms of nature;
    The rustling corn, the fruited thorn,
        And ev'ry happy creature.

    We'll gently walk, and sweetly talk,
        Till the silent moon shine clearly;
35 I'll grasp thy waist, and fondly prest,
        Swear how I love thee dearly:
    Not vernal show'rs to budding flow'rs,
        Not autumn to the farmer,
    So dear can be, as thou to me,
        My fair, my lovely charmer!

John Barleycorn*
A Ballad

(TUNES: COLD AND RAW; LULL ME BEYOND THEE)

    There was three kings into the east,
        Three kings both great and high,
    And they hae sworn a solemn oath
        John Barleycorn should die.

5   They took a plough and plough'd him down,
        Put clods upon his head,
    And they hae sworn a solemn oath
        John Barleycorn was dead.

* This is partly composed on the plan of an old song known by the same name.
[RB]

But the chearful spring came kindly on,
10   And show'rs began to fall;
John Barleycorn got up again,
     And sore surpris'd them all.

The sultry suns of summer came,
     And he grew thick and strong,
15   His head weel arm'd wi' pointed spears,
     That no one should him wrong.

The sober autumn enter'd mild,
     When he grew wan and pale;
His bending joints and drooping head
20   Show'd he began to fail.

His colour sicken'd more and more,
     He faded into age;
And then his enemies began
     To show their deadly rage.

25   They've taen a weapon, long and sharp,
     And cut him by the knee;
Then ty'd him fast upon a cart,
     Like a rogue for forgerie.

They laid him down upon his back,
30   And cudgell'd him full sore;
They hung him up before the storm,
     And turn'd him o'er and o'er.

They filled up a darksome pit
     With water to the brim,
35   They heaved in John Barleycorn,
     There let him sink or swim.

They laid him out upon the floor,
     To work him farther woe,
And still, as signs of life appear'd,
40   They toss'd him to and fro.

They wasted, o'er a scorching flame,
 The marrow of his bones;
But a miller us'd him worst of all,
 For he crush'd him between two stones.

45 And they hae taen his very heart's blood,
 And drank it round and round;
And still the more and more they drank,
 Their joy did more abound.

John Barleycorn was a hero bold,
50 Of noble enterprise,
For if you do but taste his blood,
 'Twill make your courage rise.

'Twill make a man forget his woe;
 'Twill heighten all his joy:
55 'Twill make the widow's heart to sing,
 Tho' the tear were in her eye.

Then let us toast John Barleycorn,
 Each man a glass in hand;
And may his great posterity
60 Ne'er fail in old Scotland!

The Death and Dying Words of Poor Mailie, the Author's Only Pet Yowe, an Unco' Mournfu' Tale

As *Mailie*, an' her lambs thegither,
Was ae day nibbling on the tether,
Upon her cloot she coost a hitch,
An' owre she warsl'd in the ditch:
5 There, groaning, dying, she did ly,
When *Hughoc* he cam doytan by.

* A neibor herd-callan. [RB]

Wi' glowrin een, an' lifted han's,
Poor *Hughoc* like a statue stan's;
He saw her days were near-hand ended,
10   But, waes my heart! he could na mend it!
He gaped wide, but naething spak,
At length poor *Mailie* silence brak.

'O thou, whase lamentable face
Appears to mourn my woefu' case!
15   My *dying words* attentive hear,
An' bear them to my *Master* dear.

'Tell him, if e'er again he keep
As muckle gear as buy a *sheep*,
O, bid him never tye them mair,
20   Wi' wicked strings o' hemp or hair!
But ca them out to park or hill,
An' let them wander at their will:
So, may his flock increase an' grow
To *scores* o' lambs, and *packs* of woo'.

25   'Tell him, he was a Master kin',
An' ay was guid to me an' mine;
An' now my *dying* charge I gie him,
My helpless *lambs*, I trust them wi' him.

'O, bid him save their harmless lives,
30   Frae dogs an' tods, an' butchers' knives!
But gie them guid *cow-milk* their fill,
Till they be fit to fend themsel;
And tent them duely, e'en an' morn,
Wi' taets o' *hay* an' ripps o' *corn*.

35   'An' may they never learn the gaets,
Of ither vile, wanrestfu' *Pets*!
To slink thro' slaps, an' reave an' steal,
At stacks o' pease, or stocks o' kail.
So may they, like their great *forbears*,
40   For monie a year come thro' the sheers:
So *wives* will gie them bits o' bread,
And *bairns* greet for them when they're dead.

'My poor *toop-lamb*, my son an' heir,
O, bid him breed him up wi' care!
45   An' if he live to be a beast,
To pit some havins in his breast!
An' warn him, what I winna name,
To stay content wi *yowes* at hame;
An' no to rin an' wear his cloots,
50   Like ither, menseless, graceless brutes.

'An' niest my *yowie*, silly thing,
Gude keep thee frae a *tether string*!
O, may thou ne'er forgather up,
Wi' onie blastet, moorlan *toop*;
55   But ay keep mind to moop an' mell,
Wi' sheep o' credit like thysel!

'And now, *my bairns*, wi' my last breath,
I lea'e my blessin wi' you baith:
An' when ye think upo' your Mither,
60   Mind to be kind to ane anither.

'Now, honest *Hughoc*, dinna fail;
To tell my Master a' my tale;
An' bid him burn this cursed *tether*,
An' for thy pains thou'se get my blather.'

65   This said, poor *Mailie* turn'd her head,
An' clos'd her een amang the dead!

Poor Mailie's Elegy

Lament in rhyme, lament in prose,
Wi' saut tears trickling down your nose;
Our *Bardie's* fate is at a close,
          Past a' remead!
5   The last, sad cape-stane of his woes;
          Poor Mailie's dead!

It's no the loss o' warl's gear,
That could sae bitter draw the tear,
Or make our *Bardie*, dowie, wear
        The mourning weed:
10 He's lost a friend and neebor dear,
        In *Mailie* dead.

Thro' a' the town she trotted by him;
A lang half-mile she could descry him;
15 Wi' kindly bleat, when she did spy him,
        She ran wi' speed:
A friend mair faithfu' ne'er came nigh him,
        Than *Mailie* dead.

I wat she was a *sheep* o' sense,
20 An' could behave hersel wi' mense:
I'll say't, she never brak a fence,
        Thro' thievish greed.
Our *Bardie*, lanely, keeps the spence
        Sin' *Mailie's* dead.

25 Or, if he wanders up the howe,
Her living image in *her yowe*,
Comes bleating till him, owre the knowe,
        For bits o' bread;
An' down the briny pearls rowe
30   For *Mailie* dead.

She was nae get o' moorlan tips,
Wi' tauted ket, an' hairy hips;
For her forbears were brought in ships,
        Frae 'yont the Tweed:
35 A bonier *fleesh* ne'er cross'd the clips
        Than *Mailie's* dead.

Wae worth that man wha first did shape,
That vile, wanchancie thing – *a raep*!
It maks guid fellows girn an' gape,
40   Wi' chokin dread;
An' *Robin's* bonnet wave wi' crape
        For *Mailie* dead.

O, a' ye *Bards* on bonie Doon!
An' wha on Aire your chanters tune!
45   Come, join the melancholious croon
     O' *Robin's* reed!
His heart will never get aboon!
     His *Mailie's* dead!

My Father Was a Farmer

(TUNE: THE WEAVER AND HIS SHUTTLE, O)

My father was a farmer upon the Carrick border, O
And carefully he bred me in decency and order, O
He bade me act a manly part, though I had ne'er a
     farthing, O
For without an honest manly heart, no man was worth
     regarding, O.

5   Then out into the world my course I did determine, O
Tho' to be rich was not my wish, yet to be great was
     charming, O
My talents they were not the worst; nor yet my
     education, O
Resolv'd was I, at least to try, to mend my situation, O.

In many a way, and vain essay, I courted fortune's favor, O
10   Some cause unseen still stept between to frustrate each
     endeavour, O
Sometimes by foes I was o'erpower'd; sometimes by friends
     forsaken, O
And when my hope was at the top, I still was worst
     mistaken, O.

Then sore harass'd, and tir'd at last, with fortune's vain
     delusion, O
I dropt my schemes, like idle dreams, and came to this
     conclusion, O
15   The past was bad, the future hid; its good or ill untryed, O
But the present hour was in my pow'r, and so I would
     enjoy it, O.

No help, nor hope, nor view had I; nor person to befriend
    me, O
So I must toil, and sweat and moil, and labor to sustain
    me, O
To plough and sow, to reap and mow, my father bred me
    early, O
20 For one, he said, to labor bred, was a match for fortune
    fairly, O.

Thus all obscure, unknown, and poor, thro' life I'm doom'd
    to wander, O
Till down my weary bones I lay in everlasting slumber, O
No view nor care, but shun whate'er might breed me pain
    or sorrow, O
I live today, as well's I may, regardless of tomorrow, O.

25 But cheerful still, I am as well, as a monarch in a palace, O
Tho' fortune's frown still hunts me down, with all her
    wonted malice, O
I make indeed, my daily bread, but ne'er can make it
    farther, O
But as daily bread is all I need, I do not much regard
    her, O.

When sometimes by my labor I earn a little money, O
30 Some unforseen misfortune comes generally upon me, O
Mischance, mistake, or by neglect, or my good-natur'd
    folly, O
But come what will, I've sworn it still, I'll ne'er be
    melancholy, O.

All you who follow wealth and power with unremitting
    ardor, O
The more in this you look for bliss, you leave your view
    the farther, O
35 Had you the wealth Potosi boasts, or nations to adore
    you, O
A cheerful honest-hearted clown I will prefer before
    you, O.

Epitaph on My Own Friend, and My Father's Friend, William Muir of Tarbolton Mill

An honest man here lies at rest,
As e'er God with his image blest:
The friend of man, the friend of truth,
The friend of age, and guide of youth:
5 Few hearts like his with virtue warm'd,
Few heads with knowledge so inform'd:
If there's another world, he lives in bliss;
If there is none, he made the best of this.

Green Grow the Rashes. A Fragment

(TUNE: GREEN GROWS THE RASHES)

CHORUS

Green grow the rashes, O;
Green grow the rashes, O;
The sweetest hours that e'er I spend,
Are spent amang the lasses, O.

5 There's nought but care on ev'ry han',
In ev'ry hour that passes, O:
What signifies the life o' man,
An' 'twere na for the lasses, O?
Green grow, &c.

10 The warly race may riches chase,
An' riches still may fly them, O;
An' tho' at last they catch them fast,
Their hearts can ne'er enjoy them, O.
Green grow, &c.

15 But gie me a canny hour at e'en,
        My arms about my Dearie, O;
An' warly cares, an' warly men,
        May a' gae tapsalteerie, O!
                Green grow, &c.

20 For you sae douse, ye sneer at this,
        Ye're nought but senseless asses, O:
The wisest Man the warl' saw,
        He dearly lov'd the lasses, O.
                Green grow, &c.

25 Auld Nature swears, the lovely Dears
        Her noblest work she classes, O:
Her prentice han' she try'd on man,
        An' then she made the lasses, O.
                Green grow, &c.

Epistle to Davie, a Brother Poet

                        January –

While winds frae off Ben Lomond blaw,
And bar the doors wi' driving snaw,
        And hing us owre the ingle,
I set me down, to pass the time,
5 And spin a verse or twa o' rhyme,
        In hamely, *westlin* jingle.
While frosty winds blaw in the drift,
        Ben to the chimla lug,
I grudge a wee the *Great-folk's* gift,
10   That live sae bien an' snug:
                I tent less, and want less
                        Their roomy fire-side;
                But hanker, and canker,
                        To see their cursed pride.

15   It's hardly in a body's pow'r,
    To keep, at times, frae being sour,
        To see how things are shar'd;
    How *best o' chiels* are whyles in want,
    While *coofs* on countless thousands rant,
20   And ken na how to wair't:
    But Davie lad, ne'er fash your head,
      Though we hae little gear,
    We're fit to earn our daily bread,
      As lang's we're hale and fier:
25   'Mair spier na, nor fear na,'*
        Auld age ne'er mind a feg;
      The last o't, the warst o't,
        Is only but to beg.

    To lye in kilns and barns at e'en,
30   When banes are craz'd, and bluid is thin,
      Is, doubtless, great distress!
    Yet then *content* could make us blest;
    Ev'n then, sometimes we'd snatch a taste
      Of truest happiness.
35   The honest heart that's free frae a'
      Intended fraud or guile,
    However Fortune kick the ba',
      Has ay some cause to smile:
      And mind still, you'll find still,
40   A comfort this nae sma';
      Nae mair then, we'll care then,
        Nae *farther* we can *fa'*.

    What tho', like commoners of air,
    We wander out, we know not where,
45   But either house or hal'?
    Yet *Nature's* charms, the hills and woods,
    The sweeping vales, and foaming floods,
      Are free alike to all.

* Ramsay. [RB]

In days when daisies deck the ground,
50   And blackbirds whistle clear,
With honest joy, our hearts will bound,
    To see the *coming* year:
        On braes when we please then,
        We'll sit and *sowth* a tune;
55   Syne *rhyme* till't, we'll time till't,
        And sing't when we hae done.

It's no in titles nor in rank;
It's no in wealth like *Lon'on Bank*,
    To purchase peace and rest;
60   It's no in makin muckle, mair:
It's no in books, it's no in lear,
    To make us truly blest:
If happiness hae not her seat
    And center in the breast,
65   We may be wise, or rich, or great,
    But never can be blest:
        Nae treasures, nor pleasures
        Could make us happy lang;
        The *heart* ay's the part ay,
70   That makes us right or wrang.

Think ye, that sic as you and I,
Wha drudge and drive thro' wet and dry,
    Wi' never-ceasing toil;
Think ye, are we less blest than they,
75   Wha scarcely tent us in their way,
    As hardly worth their while?
Alas! how aft, in haughty mood,
    God's creatures they oppress!
Or else, neglecting a' that's guid,
80   They riot in excess!
        Baith careless, and fearless,
        Of either Heaven or Hell;
        Esteeming, and deeming,
        It a' an idle tale!

85 Then let us chearfu' acquiesce;
Nor make our scanty pleasures less,
 By pining at our state:
And, even should misfortunes come,
I here wha sit, hae met wi' some,
90 An's thankfu' for them yet.
They gie the wit of Age to Youth;
 They let us ken oursel;
They make us see the naked truth,
 The *real* guid and ill.
95   Tho' losses, and crosses,
   Be lessons right severe,
  There's wit there, ye'll get there,
   Ye'll find nae other where.

But tent me, Davie, *Ace o' Hearts*!
100 (To say aught less wad wrang the *cartes*,
 And flatt'ry I detest)
This life has joys for you and I;
And joys that riches ne'er could buy;
 And joys the very best.
105 There's a' the pleasures o' the heart,
 The Lover and the Frien';
Ye hae your Meg, your dearest part,
 And I my darling Jean!
  It warms me, it charms me,
110   To mention but her *name*:
  It heats me, it beets me,
   And sets me a' on flame!

O, all ye Pow'rs who rule above!
O Thou, whose very Self art *love*!
115 Thou know'st my words sincere!
The life blood streaming thro' my heart,
Or my more dear Immortal part,
 Is not more fondly dear!
When heart-corroding care and grief
120 Deprive my soul of rest,
Her dear idea brings relief,
 And solace to my breast.

Thou Being, All-seeing,
   O hear my fervent pray'r!
125   Still take her, and make her,
   Thy most peculiar care!

All hail! ye tender feelings dear!
The smile of love, the friendly tear,
   The sympathetic glow!
130 Long since, this world's thorny ways
Had number'd out my weary days,
   Had it not been for you!
Fate has still blest me with a friend,
   In ev'ry care and ill;
135 And oft a more *endearing* band,
   A *tye* more tender still.
      It lightens, it brightens,
         The tenebrific scene,
      To meet with, and greet with,
140   My Davie or my Jean!

O, how that *name* inspires my style!
The words come skelpan, rank and file,
   Amaist before I ken!
The ready measure rins as fine,
145 As *Phoebus* and the famous *Nine*
   Were glowran owre my pen.
My spavet *Pegasus* will limp,
   Till ance he's fairly het;
And then he'll hilch, and stilt, and jimp,
150   And rin an unco fit:
      But least then, the beast then,
         Should rue this hasty ride,
      I'll light now, and dight now,
         His sweaty, wizen'd hide.

Holy Willie's Prayer

'And send the Godly in a pet to pray –' Pope

O Thou, wha in the heavens dost dwell,
Wha, as it pleases best thysel',
Sends ane to heaven and ten to hell,
                    A' for thy glory,
5   And no for ony guid or ill
                    They've done afore thee!

I bless and praise thy matchless might,
Whan thousands thou hast left in night,
That I am here afore thy sight,
10   For gifts an' grace,
A burnin' an' a shinin' light,
                    To a' this place.

What was I, or my generation,
That I should get such exaltation,
15 I wha deserve sic just damnation,
                    For broken laws,
Five thousand years ere my creation,
                    Thro' Adam's cause.

When frae my mither's womb I fell,
20 Thou might ha'e plunged me in hell,
To gnash my gums, to weep and wail,
                    In burnin' lake,
Whar damned devils roar and yell,
                    Chain'd to a stake.

25 Yet I am here a chosen sample,
To show thy grace is great an' ample;
I'm here a pillar in thy temple,
                    Strong as a rock,
A guide, a buckler, an' example
30   To a' thy flock.

But yet, O Lord! confess I must,
At times I'm fash'd wi' fleshly lust
An' sometimes too, wi' warldly trust,
         Vile Self gets in;
35 But thou remembers we are dust,
         Defil'd in sin.

O Lord! yestreen, thou kens, wi' Meg –
Thy pardon I sincerely beg –
O may't ne'er be a living plague
         To my dishonor!
40
An' I'll ne'er lift a lawless leg
         Again upon her.

Besides, I farther maun avow –
Wi' Leezie's lass, three times, I trow –
45 But, Lord, that Friday I was fou,
         When I cam near her,
Or else, thou kens, thy servant true
         Wad never steer her.

Maybe thou lets this fleshly thorn
50 Buffet thy servant e'en and morn,
Lest he owre proud and high should turn
         That he's sae gifted:
If sae, thy han' maun e'en be borne
         Until thou lift it.

55 Lord, bless thy Chosen in this place,
For here thou has a chosen race!
But God confound their stubborn face
         An' blast their name,
Wha bring thy elders to disgrace
60   An' open shame!

Lord mind Gaun Hamilton's deserts,
He drinks, an' swears, an' plays at carts,
Yet has sae mony takin' arts,
         Wi' great an' sma'
65 Frae God's ain priest the people's hearts
         He steals awa'.

An' whan we chasten'd him therefore,
Thou kens how he bred sic a splore,
As set the warld in a roar
70   O laughin' at us;
Curse thou his basket and his store,
                     Kail an' potatoes.

Lord hear my earnest cry an' pray'r
Against that presbyt'ry o' Ayr;
75 Thy strong right hand, Lord make it bare,
                     Upo' their heads,
Lord weigh it down, and dinna spare,
                     For their misdeeds.

O Lord my God, that glib-tongu'd Aiken,
80 My very heart an' soul are quakin',
To think how we stood, sweatin', shakin',
                     An' pissed wi' dread,
While Auld wi' hingin lip gaed sneakin',
                     And hid his head.

85 Lord in the day of vengeance try him,
Lord visit them wha did employ him,
And pass not in thy mercy by 'em,
                     Nor hear their prayer;
But for thy people's sake destroy 'em,
90   And dinna spare.

But Lord remember me and mine
Wi' mercies temp'ral and divine,
That I for gear and grace may shine,
                     Excell'd by nane,
95   An' a' the glory shall be thine,
                     Amen, Amen.

Death and Dr Hornbook. A True Story

Some books are lies frae end to end,
And some great lies were never penn'd:
Ev'n ministers they hae been kenn'd,
    In holy rapture,
5 Great lies and nonsense baith to vend,
     And nail't wi' Scripture.

But this that I am gaun to tell,
Which lately on a night befel,
Is just as true's the Deil's in hell,
10   Or Dublin city:
That e'er he nearer comes oursel
    'S a muckle pity.

The clachan yill had made me canty,
I was na fou, but just had plenty;
15 I stacher'd whyles, but yet took tent ay
    To free the ditches;
An' hillocks, stanes, and bushes kenn'd ay
    Frae ghaists an' witches.

The rising moon began to glowr
20 The distant Cumnock hills out–owre;
To count her horns, wi' a' my pow'r,
    I set mysel,
But whether she had three or four,
    I cou'd na tell.

25 I was come round about the hill,
And todlin down on Willie's mill,
Setting my staff wi' a' my skill,
     To keep me sicker;
Tho' leeward whyles, against my will,
     I tóok a bicker.

30

I there wi' *Something* does forgather,
That pat me in an eerie swither;
An awfu' scythe, out-owre ae shouther,
              Clear-dangling, hang;
35 A three-tae'd leister on the ither
              Lay, large an' lang.

In stature seem'd lang Scotch ells twa,
The queerest shape that e'er I saw,
For fient a wame it had ava,
40   And then its shanks,
They were as thin, as sharp an' sma'
              As cheeks o' branks.

'Guid-een,' quo' I; 'Friend! hae ye been mawin,
When ither folk are busy sawing*?'
45 It seem'd to mak a kind o' stan',
              But naething spak;
At length, says I, 'Friend, whare ye gaun,
              Will ye go back?'

It spak right howe – 'My name is *Death*,
50 But be na' fley'd.' – Quoth I, 'Guid faith,
Ye're maybe come to stap my breath;
              But tent me, billie;
I red ye weel, take care o' skaith,
              See, there's a gully!'

55 'Gudeman,' quo' he, 'put up your whittle,
I'm no design'd to try its mettle;
But if I did, I wad be kittle
              To be mislear'd,
I wad na' mind it, no that spittle
60   Out-owre my beard.'

'Weel, weel!' says I, 'a bargain be't;
Come, gie's your hand, an' sae we're gree't;
We'll ease our shanks an' tak a seat,

* This rencounter happened in seed-time 1785. [RB]

Come, gie's your news!

65 This while* ye hae been mony a gate,
At mony a house.'

'Ay, ay!' quo' he, an' shook his head,
'It's e'en a lang, lang time indeed
Sin I began to nick the thread,
70 An' choke the breath:
Folk maun do something for their bread,
And sae maun *Death*.

'Sax thousand years are near hand fled
Sin' I was to the butching bred,
75 And mony a scheme in vain's been laid,
To stap or scar me;
Till ane *Hornbook*'s† ta'en up the trade,
And faith, he'll waur me.

'Ye ken *Jock Hornbook* i' the clachan,
80 Deil mak his king's-hood in a spleuchan!
He's grown sae weel acquaint wi' *Buchan*,‡
And ither chaps,
The weans haud out their fingers laughing,
And pouk my hips.

85 'See, here's a scythe, and there's a dart,
They hae pierc'd mony a gallant heart;
But Doctor *Hornbook*, wi' his art
And cursed skill,
Has made them baith no worth a f-rt,
90 Damn'd haet they'll kill!

''Twas but yestreen, nae farther gaen,
I threw a noble throw at ane;
Wi' less, I'm sure, I've hundreds slain;

---

* An epidemical fever was then raging in that country. [RB]
† This gentleman, Dr Hornbook, is, professionally, a brother of the sovereign Order of the Ferula; but, by intuition and inspiration, is at once an Apothecary, Surgeon, and Physician. [RB]
‡ Buchan's Domestic Medicine. [RB]

But deil-ma-care!
95 It just play'd dirl on the bane,
But did nae mair.

'*Hornbook* was by, wi' ready art,
And had sae fortify'd the part,
That when I looked to my dart,
100   It was sae blunt,
Fient haet o't wad hae pierc'd the heart
Of a kail-runt.

'I drew my scythe in sic a fury,
I nearhand cowpit wi' my hurry,
105 But yet the bauld *Apothecary*
Withstood the shock;
I might as weel hae try'd a quarry
O' hard whin-rock.

'Ev'n them he canna get attended,
110 Altho' their face he ne'er had kend it,
Just sh-t in a kail-blade and send it,
As soon's he smells 't
Baith their disease, and what will mend it,
At once he tells 't.

115 'And then a' doctor's saws and whittles,
Of a' dimensions, shapes, an' mettles,
A' kinds o' boxes, mugs, an' bottles,
He's sure to hae;
Their Latin names as fast he rattles
120   As A B C.

'Calces o' fossils, earths, and trees;
True sal-marinum o' the seas;
The farina of beans and pease,
He has't in plenty;
125 Aqua-fontis, what you please,
He can content ye.

'Forbye some new, uncommon weapons,
Urinus spiritus of capons;
Or mite-horn shavings, filings, scrapings,

130   Distill'd *per se*;
Sal-alkali o' midge-tail clippings,
     And mony mae.'

'Waes me for *Johnny Ged's Hole** now,'
Quoth I, 'if that thae news be true!
135 His braw calf-ward whare gowans grew,
     Sae white an' bonie,
Nae doubt they'll rive it wi' the plew;
     They'll ruin *Johnie*!'

The creature grain'd an eldritch laugh,
140 And says, 'Ye needna yoke the pleugh,
Kirk-yards will soon be till'd eneugh,
     Tak ye nae fear:
They'll a' be trench'd wi' mony a sheugh,
     In twa-three year.

145 'Where I kill'd ane, a fair strae-death,
By loss o' blood, or want o' breath,
This night I'm free to tak my aith,
     That *Hornbook*'s skill
Has clad a score i' their last claith,
150   By drap and pill.

'An honest wabster to his trade,
Whase wife's twa nieves were scarce weel-bred,
Gat tippence-worth to mend her head,
     When it was sair;
155 The wife slade cannie to her bed,
     But ne'er spak mair.

'A countra laird had ta'en the batts,
Or some curmurring in his guts,
His only son for *Hornbook* sets,
160   And pays him well,
The lad, for twa guid gimmer-pets,
     Was laird himsel.

---

* The grave-digger. [RB]

'A bonie lass, ye kend her name,
Some ill-brewn drink had hov'd her wame,
165 She trusts hersel, to hide the shame,
    In *Hornbook*'s care;
Horn sent her aff to her lang hame,
    To hide it there.

'That's just a swatch o' *Hornbook*'s way,
Thus goes he on from day to day,
170 Thus does he poison, kill, an' slay,
    An's weel pay'd for't;
Yet stops me o' my lawfu' prey,
    Wi' his damn'd dirt!

175 'But hark! I'll tell you of a plot,
Tho' dinna you be speakin o't;
I'll nail the self-conceited sot,
    As dead's a herrin:
Niest time we meet, I'll wad a groat,
180   He gets his fairin!'

But just as he began to tell,
The auld kirk-hammer strak the bell
Some wee, short hour ayont the twal,
    Which rais'd us baith:
185 I took the way that pleas'd mysel,
    And sae did *Death*.

When First I Came to Stewart Kyle

(TUNE: I HAD A HORSE, I HAD NAE MAIR)

When first I came to Stewart Kyle
 My mind it was nae steady,
Where e'er I gaed, where e'er I rade,
 A mistress still I had ay:
But when I came roun' by Mauchlin town,
 Not dreadin' any body,
My heart was caught before I thought
 And by a Mauchlin lady –

Epistle to John Lapraik, an Old Scotch Bard

April 1st, 1785

While briers an' woodbines budding green,
An' paitricks scraichan loud at e'en,
And morning poossie whiddan seen,
           Inspire my Muse,
5 This freedom, in an *unknown* frien',
           I pray excuse.

On Fasteneen we had a rockin,
To ca' the crack and weave our stockin;
And there was muckle fun and jokin,
10   Ye need na doubt;
At length we had a hearty yokin,
           At *sang about*.

There was ae sang, amang the rest,
Aboon them a' it pleas'd me best,
15 That some kind husband had addrest,
           To some sweet wife:
It thirl'd the heart-strings thro' the breast,
           A' to the life.

I've scarce heard ought describ'd sae weel,
20 What gen'rous, manly bosoms feel;
Thought I, 'Can this be Pope, or Steele,
           Or Beattie's wark';
They tald me 'twas an odd kind chiel
           About Muirkirk.

25 It pat me fidgean-fain to hear't,
And sae about him there I spier't;
Then a' that kent him round declar'd,
           He had *ingine*,
That nane excell'd it, few cam near't,
30   It was sae fine.

That set him to a pint of ale,
An' either douse or merry tale,
Or rhymes an' sangs he'd made himsel,
                    Or witty catches,
35   'Tween Inverness and Tiviotdale,
                    He had few matches.

Then up I gat, and swoor an aith,
Tho' I should pawn my pleugh an' graith,
Or die a cadger pownie's death,
40   At some dyke-back,
A pint an' gill I'd gie them baith,
                    To hear your crack.

But first an' foremost, I should tell,
Amaist as soon as I could spell,
45   I to the *crambo-jingle* fell,
                    Tho' rude an' rough
Yet crooning to a body's sel,
                    Does weel eneugh.

I am nae *Poet*, in a sense,
50   But just a *Rhymer* like by chance,
An' hae to learning nae pretence,
                    Yet, what the matter?
Whene'er my Muse does on me glance,
                    I jingle at her.

55   Your critic-folk may cock their nose,
And say, 'How can you e'er propose,
You, wha ken scarcely *verse* frae *prose*,
                    To mak a *sang*?'
But by your leaves, my learned foes,
60   Ye're maybe wrang.

What's a' your jargon o' your schools,
Your Latin names for horns an' stools;
If honest Nature made you fools,
                    What sairs your Grammars?
65   Ye'd better taen up spades and shools,
                    Or knappin-hammers.

A set o' dull, conceited hashes,
Confuse their brains in colledge-classes!
They *gang in* stirks, and *come out* asses,
70   Plain truth to speak;
An' syne they think to climb Parnassus
                    By dint o' Greek!

Gie me ae spark o' Nature's fire,
That's a' the learning I desire;
75 Then tho' I drudge thro' dub an' mire
                    At pleugh or cart,
My Muse, tho' hamely in attire,
                    May touch the heart.

O for a spunk o' Allan's glee,
80 Or Fergusson's, the bauld an' slee,
Or bright Lapraik's, my friend to be,
                    If I can hit it!
That would be *lear* eneugh for me,
                    If I could get it.

85 Now, Sir, if ye hae friends enow,
Tho' *real friends* I b'lieve are few,
Yet, if your catalogue be fow,
                    I'se no insist;
But gif ye want ae friend that's true,
90   I'm on your list.

I winna blaw about mysel,
As ill I like my fauts to tell;
But friends an' folk that wish me well,
                    They sometimes roose me;
95 Tho' I maun own, as monie still,
                    As far abuse me.

There's ae *wee faut* they whiles lay to me;
I like the lasses – Gude forgie me!
For monie a plack they wheedle frae me,
100   At dance or fair:
Maybe some *ither thing* they gie me
                    They weel can spare.

But Mauchline Race or Mauchline Fair,
I should be proud to meet you there;
105   We'se gie a night's discharge to *care*,
                If we forgather,
An' hae a swap o' *rhymin-ware*,
                Wi' ane anither.

The *four-gill chap*, we'se gar him clatter,
110   An' kirs'n him wi' reekin water;
Syne we'll sit down an' tak our whitter,
                To chear our heart;
An' faith, we'se be acquainted better
                Before we part.

115   Awa ye selfish, warly race,
Wha think that havins, sense an' grace,
Ev'n love and friendship should give place
                To *catch-the-plack!*
I dinna like to see your face,
120   Nor hear your crack.

But ye whom social pleasure charms,
Whose hearts the *tide of kindness* warms,
Who hold your *being* on the terms,
                'Each aid the others,'
125   Come to my bowl, come to my arms,
                My friends, my brothers!

But to conclude this lang epistle,
As my auld pen's worn to the grissle;
Twa lines frae you wad gar me fissle,
130   Who am, most fervent,
While I can either sing, or whissle,
                Your friend and servant.

To the Same
April 21st, 1785

While new-ca'd kye rowte at the stake,
An' pownies reek in pleugh or braik,
This hour on e'enin's edge I take,
        To own I'm debtor,
5 To honest-hearted, auld Lapraik,
        For his kind *letter*.

Forjesket sair, with weary legs,
Rattlin the corn out-owre the rigs,
Or dealing thro' amang the naigs
10   Their ten-hours bite,
My awkart Muse sair pleads and begs,
        I would na write.

The tapetless, ramfeezl'd hizzie,
She's saft at best an' something lazy,
15 Quo' she, 'Ye ken we've been sae busy
        This month an' mair,
That trouth, my head is grown right dizzie,
        An' something sair.'

Her dowf excuses pat me mad;
20 'Conscience,' says I, 'ye thowless jad!
I'll write, an' that a hearty blaud,
        This vera night;
So dinna ye affront your trade,
        But rhyme it right.

25 'Shall bauld Lapraik, the *king o' hearts*,
Tho' mankind were a *pack o' cartes*,
Roose you sae weel for your deserts,
        In terms sae friendly,
Yet ye'll neglect to shaw your parts
30   An' thank him kindly?'

Sae I gat paper in a blink,
An, down gaed *stumpie* in the ink:
Quoth I, 'Before I sleep a wink,
    I vow I'll close it;
35 An' if ye winna mak it clink,
    By Jove I'll prose it!'

Sae I've begun to scrawl, but whether
In rhyme, or prose, or baith thegither,
Or some hotch-potch that's rightly neither,
    Let time mak proof;
40 But I shall scribble down some blether
    Just clean aff-loof.

My worthy friend, ne'er grudge an' carp,
Tho' Fortune use you hard an' sharp;
45 Come, kittle up your moorlan harp
    Wi' gleesome touch!
Ne'er mind how Fortune waft and warp;
    She's but a b-tch.

She's gien me monie a jirt an' fleg,
50 Sin' I could striddle owre a rig;
But by the Lord, tho' I should beg
    Wi' lyart pow,
I'll laugh, an' sing, an' shake my leg,
    As lang's I dow!

55 Now comes the sax an' twentieth simmer,
I've seen the bud upo' the timmer,
Still persecuted by the limmer
    Frae year to year;
But yet, despite the kittle kimmer,
60   *I, Rob, am here.*

Do ye envy the city-gent,
Behind a kist to lie an' sklent,
Or, purse-proud, big wi' cent per cent,
    An' muckle wame,
65 In some bit Brugh to represent
    A Baillie's name?

Or is't the paughty, feudal *Thane*,
Wi' ruffl'd sark an' glancin cane,
Wha thinks himsel nae *sheep-shank bane*,
70   But lordly stalks,
While caps an' bonnets aff are taen,
             As by he walks?

'O Thou wha gies us each guid gift!
Gie me o' *wit* an' *sense* a lift,
75 Then turn me, if Thou please, *adrift*,
             Thro' Scotland wide;
Wi' *cits* nor *lairds* I wadna shift,
             In a' their pride!'

Were this the charter o' our state,
80 'On pain o' hell be rich an' great,'
Damnation then would be our fate,
             Beyond remead;
But, thanks to *Heav'n*, that's no the gate
             We learn our *creed*.

85 For thus the royal Mandate ran,
When first the human race began,
'The social, friendly, honest man,
             Whate'er he be,
'Tis *he* fulfils *great Nature's plan*,
90   And none but *he*.'

O Mandate, glorious and divine!
The followers o' the ragged Nine,
Poor, thoughtless devils! yet may shine
             In glorious light,
95 While sordid sons o' Mammon's line
             Are dark as night!

Tho' here they scrape, an' squeeze, an' growl,
Their worthless nievefu' of a soul,
May in some future carcase howl,
90   The forest's fright;
Or in some day-detesting owl
             May shun the light.

Then may Lapraik and Burns arise,
To reach their native, kindred skies,
95   And *sing* their pleasures, hopes and joys,
                    In some mild sphere,
Still closer knit in friendship's ties
                    Each passing year!

To William Simson, Ochiltree

May – 1785

I gat your letter, winsome Willie;
Wi' gratefu' heart I thank you brawlie;
Tho' I maun say't, I wad be silly,
                    An' unco vain,
5   Should I believe, my coaxin billie,
                    Your flatterin strain.

But I'se believe ye kindly meant it,
I sud be laith to think ye hinted
Ironic satire, sidelins sklented,
10   On my poor Musie;
Tho' in sic phraisin terms ye've penn'd it,
                    I scarce excuse ye.

My senses wad be in a creel,
Should I but dare a *hope* to speel,
15   Wi' Allan, or wi' Gilbertfield,
                    The braes o' fame;
Or Fergusson, the writer-chiel,
                    A deathless name.

(O Fergusson! thy glorious parts,
20   Ill suited law's dry, musty arts!
My curse upon your whunstane hearts,
                    Ye Enbrugh Gentry!
The tythe o' what ye waste at cartes
                    Wad stow'd his pantry!)

25   Yet when a tale comes i' my head,
Or lasses gie my heart a screed,
As whiles they're like to be my dead,
          (O sad disease!)
I kittle up my *rustic reed*;
30   It gies me ease.

Auld Coila, now, may fidge fu' fain,
She's gotten *Bardies* o' her ain,
Chiels wha their chanters winna hain,
          But tune their lays,
35   Till echoes a' resound again
          Her weel-sung praise.

Nae *Poet* thought her worth his while,
To set her name in measur'd style;
She lay like some unkend-of isle
          Beside New Holland,
40   Or whare wild-meeting oceans boil
          Besouth Magellan.

Ramsay and famous Fergusson
Gied Forth and Tay a lift aboon;
45   Yarrow an' Tweed, to monie a tune,
          Owre Scotland rings,
While Irwin, Lugar, Aire an' Doon,
          Naebody sings.

Th' Illissus, Tiber, Thames an' Seine,
50   Glide sweet in monie a tunefu' line;
But Willie set your fit to mine,
          An' cock your crest,
We'll gar our streams an' burnies shine
          Up wi' the best.

55   We'll sing auld Coila's plains an' fells,
Her moors red-brown wi' heather bells,
Her banks an' braes, her dens an' dells,
          Where glorious Wallace
Aft bure the gree, as story tells,
60   Frae Suthron billies.

At Wallace' name, what Scottish blood,
But boils up in a spring-tide flood!
Oft have our fearless fathers strode
          By Wallace' side,
65   Still pressing onward, red-wat-shod,
          Or glorious dy'd!

O sweet are Coila's haughs an' woods,
When lintwhites chant amang the buds,
And jinkin hares, in amorous whids,
70   Their loves enjoy,
While thro' the braes the cushat croods
          With wailfu' cry!

Ev'n winter bleak has charms to me,
When winds rave thro' the naked tree;
75   Or frosts on hills of Ochiltree
          Are hoary gray;
Or blinding drifts wild-furious flee,
          Dark'ning the day!

O Nature! a' thy shews an' forms
80   To feeling, pensive hearts hae charms!
Whether the Summer kindly warms,
          Wi' life an' light,
Or Winter howls, in gusty storms,
          The lang, dark night!

85   The *Muse*, nae *Poet* ever fand her,
Till by himsel he learn'd to wander,
Adown some trottin burn's meander,
          An' no think lang;
O sweet, to stray an' pensive ponder
90   A heart-felt sang!

The warly race may drudge an' drive,
Hog-shouther, jundie, stretch an' strive,
Let me fair Nature's face descrive,
          And I, wi' pleasure,
95   Shall let the busy, grumbling hive
          Bum owre their treasure.

Fareweel, 'my rhyme-composing' brither!
We've been owre lang unkenn'd to ither:
Now let us lay our heads thegither,
        In love fraternal:
May *Envy* wallop in a tether,
        Black fiend, infernal!

While Highlandmen hate tolls an' taxes;
While moorlan herds like guid, fat braxies;
While Terra firma, on her axis,
        Diurnal turns,
Count on a friend, in faith an' practice,
        In Robert Burns.

POSTSCRIPT

My memory's no worth a preen;
I had amaist forgotten clean,
Ye bad me write you what they mean
        By this *new-light*,*
'Bout which our *herds* sae aft hae been
        Maist like to fight.

In days when mankind were but callans,
At grammar, logic, an' sic talents,
They took nae pains their speech to balance,
        Or rules to gie,
But spak their thoughts in plain, braid lallans,
        Like you or me.

In thae auld times, they thought the Moon,
Just like a sark, or pair o' shoon,
Woor by degrees, till her last roon
        Gaed past their viewin,
An' shortly after she was done
        They gat a new ane.

* A cant-term for those religious opinions, which Dr Taylor of Norwich has defended so strenuously. [RB]

This past for certain, undisputed;
It ne'er cam i' their heads to doubt it,
Till chiels gat up an' wad confute it,
130   An' ca'd it wrang;
An' muckle din there was about it,
                    Baith loud an' lang.

Some *herds*, weel-learn'd upo' the beuk,
Wad threap auld folk the thing misteuk;
135 For 'twas the *auld moon* turn'd a newk
                    An' out o' sight,
An' backlins-comin, to the leuk,
                    She grew mair bright.

This was deny'd, it was affirm'd;
140 The *herds* an' *hissels* were alarm'd;
The rev'rend gray-beards rav'd an' storm'd,
                    That beardless laddies
Should think they better were inform'd,
                    Than their auld dadies.

145 Frae less to mair it gaed to sticks;
Frae words an' aiths to clours an' nicks;
And monie a fallow gat his licks,
                    Wi' hearty crunt;
And some, to learn them for their tricks,
150   Were hang'd an' brunt.

This game was play'd in monie lands,
An' *auld-light* caddies bure sic hands,
That faith, the youngsters took the sands
                    Wi' nimble shanks,
155 Till Lairds forbad, by strict commands,
                    Sic bluidy pranks.

But *new-light herds* gat sic a cowe,
Folk thought them ruin'd stick-an-stowe,
Till now amaist on ev'ry *knowe*
160   Ye'll find ane plac'd;
An' some, their *New-light* fair avow,
                    Just quite barefac'd.

Nae doubt the *auld-light flocks* are bleatan;
Their zealous *herds* are vex'd an' sweatan;
165   Mysel, I've ev'n seen them greetan
         Wi' girnan spite,
To hear the Moon sae sadly lie'd on
         By word an' write.

But shortly they will cowe the louns!
170   Some *auld-light herds* in neebor towns
Are mind't, in things they ca' *balloons*,
         To tak a flight,
And stay ae month amang the Moons
         An' see them right.

175   Guid observation they will gie them;
And when the auld Moon's gaun to lea'e them,
The hindmost *shaird*, they'll fetch it wi' them,
         Just i' their pouch,
And when the *new-light* billies see them,
180   I think they'll crouch!

Sae, ye observe that a' this clatter
Is naething but a 'moonshine matter';
But tho' dull *prose-folk* latin splatter
         In logic tulzie,
185   I hope we *Bardies* ken some better
         Than mind suc brulzie.

The Vision

DUAN FIRST*

The sun had clos'd the *winter-day*,
The Curlers quat their roaring play,
And hunger'd maukin taen her way

---

* Duan, a term of Ossian's for the different divisions of a digressive Poem. See his Cath-Loda, Vol. 2 of M'Pherson's Translation. [RB]

To kail-yards green,
5   While faithless snaws ilk step betray
Whare she has been.

The thresher's weary *flingin-tree*,
The lee-lang day had tir'd me;
And when the day had clos'd his e'e,
10   Far i' the west,
Ben i' the spence, right pensivelie,
I gaed to rest.

There, lanely, by the ingle-cheek,
I sat and ey'd the spewing reek,
15   That fill'd, wi' hoast-provoking smeek,
The auld, clay biggin;
And heard the restless rattons squeak
About the riggin.

All in this mottie, misty clime,
20   I backward mus'd on wasted time,
How I had spent my *youthfu' prime*,
An' done nae-thing,
But stringing blethers up in rhyme
For fools to sing.

25   Had I to guid advice but harket,
I might, by this, hae led a market,
Or strutted in a bank and clarket
My cash-account;
While here, half-mad, half-fed, half-sarket,
30   Is a' th' amount.

I started, mutt'ring blockhead! coof!
And heav'd on high my wauket loof,
To swear by a' yon starry roof,
Or some rash aith,
35   That I henceforth would be *rhyme-proof*
Till my last breath –

When click! the string the snick did draw;
And jee! the door gaed to the wa';
And by my ingle-lowe I saw,
40   Now bleezan bright,
A tight, outlandish Hizzie, braw,
                          Come full in sight.

Ye need na doubt, I held my whisht;
The infant aith, half-form'd, was crusht;
45   I glowr'd as eerie's I'd been dusht,
                          In some wild glen;
When sweet, like *modest Worth*, she blusht,
                          And stepped ben.

Green, slender, leaf-clad holly-boughs
50   Were twisted, gracefu', round her brows,
I took her for some Scottish Muse,
                          By that same token;
And come to stop those reckless vows,
                          Would soon been broken.

55   A 'hare-brain'd, sentimental trace'
Was strongly marked in her face;
A wildly-witty, rustic grace
                          Shone full upon her;
Her *eye*, ev'n turn'd on empty space,
60   Beam'd keen with *Honor*.

Down flow'd her robe, a tartan sheen,
Till half a leg was scrimply seen;
And such a leg! my Bess, I ween,
                          Could only peer it;
65   Sae straught, sae taper, tight and clean,
                          Nane else came near it.

Her mantle large, of greenish hue,
My gazing wonder chiefly drew;
Deep lights and shades, bold-mingling, threw
70   A lustre grand;
And seem'd, to my astonish'd view,
                          A well-known land.

Here, rivers in the sea were lost;
There, mountains to the skies were tost:
75 Here, tumbling billows mark'd the coast,
                        With surging foam;
There, distant shone Art's lofty boast
                        The lordly dome.

Here, Doon pour'd down his far-fetch'd floods;
80 There, well-fed Irwine stately thuds:
Auld, hermit Aire staw thro' his woods,
                        On to the shore;
And many a lesser torrent scuds,
                        With seeming roar.

85 Low, in a sandy valley spread,
An ancient Borough rear'd her head;
Still, as in *Scottish story* read,
                        She boasts a *Race*,
To ev'ry nobler virtue bred,
90   And polish'd grace.

DUAN SECOND

With musing-deep, astonish'd stare,
I view'd the heavenly-seeming *Fair*;
A whisp'ring *throb* did witness bear
                        Of kindred sweet,
95 When with an elder Sister's air
                        She did me greet.

'All hail! *my own* inspired Bard!
In me thy native Muse regard!
Nor longer mourn thy fate is hard,
100   Thus poorly low!
I come to give thee such *reward*,
                        As *we* bestow.

'Know, the great *Genius* of this Land,
Has many a light, aerial band,
105 Who, all beneath his high command,
    Harmoniously,
As *Arts* or *Arms* they understand,
    Their labors ply.

'They Scotia's Race among them share;
110 Some fire the Sodger on to dare;
Some rouse the Patriot up to bare
    Corruption's heart:
Some teach the Bard, a darling care,
    The tuneful Art.

115 ''Mong swelling floods of reeking gore,
They ardent, kindling spirits pour;
Or mid the venal Senate's roar,
    They, sightless, stand,
To mend the honest *Patriot-lore*,
120   And grace the hand.

'Hence, Fullarton, the brave and young;
Hence, Dempster's truth-prevailing tongue;
Hence, sweet harmonious Beattie sung
    His "Minstrel lays";
125 Or tore, with noble ardour stung,
    The *Sceptic's* bays.

'To lower Orders are assign'd,
The humbler ranks of human-kind,
The rustic Bard, the lab'ring Hind,
130   The Artisan;
All chuse as various they're inclin'd,
    The various man.

'When yellow waves the heavy grain,
The threat'ning *storm*, some strongly rein;
135 Some teach to meliorate the plain,
    With *tillage-skill*;
And some instruct the Shepherd-train,
    Blythe o'er the hill.

'Some hint the Lover's harmless wile;
140 Some grace the Maiden's artless smile;
Some soothe the Lab'rer's weary toil,
                              For humble gains,
And make his *cottage-scenes* beguile
                              His cares and pains.

145 'Some, bounded to a district-space,
Explore at large Man's *infant race*,
To mark the embryotic trace,
                              Of *rustic Bard*;
And careful note each op'ning grace,
150   A guide and guard.

'*Of these am I* – Coila my name;
And this district as mine I claim,
Where once the Campbells, chiefs of fame,
                              Held ruling pow'r:
155 I mark'd thy embryo-tuneful flame,
                              Thy natal hour.

'With future hope, I oft would gaze,
Fond, on thy little, early ways,
Thy rudely-caroll'd, chiming phrase,
160   In uncouth rhymes,
Fir'd at the simple, artless lays
                              Of other times.

'I saw thee seek the sounding shore,
Delighted with the dashing roar;
165 Or when the North his fleecy store
                              Drove thro' the sky,
I saw grim Nature's visage hoar,
                              Struck thy young eye.

'Or when the deep-green-mantl'd Earth,
170 Warm-cherished ev'ry floweret's birth,
And joy and music pouring forth,
                              In ev'ry grove,
I saw thee eye the gen'ral mirth
                              With boundless love.

175 'When ripen'd fields, and azure skies,
Call'd forth the Reaper's rustling noise,
I saw thee leave their ev'ning joys,
          And lonely stalk,
To vent thy bosom's swelling rise,
180   In pensive walk.

'When *youthful love*, warm-blushing, strong,
Keen-shivering shot thy nerves along,
Those accents, grateful to thy tongue,
          The adored *Name*,
185 I taught thee how to pour in song,
          To soothe thy flame.

'I saw thy pulse's maddening play,
Wild-send thee Pleasure's devious way,
Misled by Fancy's *meteor-ray*,
190   By Passion driven;
But yet the *light* that led astray,
          Was *light* from Heaven.

'I taught thy manners-painting strains,
The *loves*, the *ways* of simple swains,
195 Till now, o'er all my wide domains,
          Thy fame extends;
And some, the pride of Coila's plains,
          Become thy friends.

'Thou canst not learn, nor can I show,
200 To paint with Thomson's landscape-glow;
Or wake the bosom-melting throe,
          With Shenstone's art;
Or pour, with Gray, the moving flow,
          Warm on the heart.

205 'Yet all beneath th' unrivall'd Rose,
The lowly Daisy sweetly blows;
Tho' large the forest's Monarch throws
          His army shade,
Yet green the juicy Hawthorn grows,
210   Adown the glade.

'Then never murmur nor repine;
Strive in thy *humble sphere* to shine;
And trust me, not *Potosi's mine*,
                              Nor *Kings' regard*,
215 Can give a bliss o'ermatching thine,
                              A rustic Bard.

'To give my counsels all in one,
Thy tuneful-flame still careful fan;
Preserve the *dignity of Man*,
220   With Soul erect;
And trust, the Universal Plan
                              Will all protect.

'*And wear thou this*' – She solemn said,
And bound the *Holly* round my head:
225 The polish'd leaves, and berries red,
                              Did rustling play;
And, like a passing thought, she fled,
                              In light away.

A Poet's Welcome to His Love-Begotten Daughter; The First Instance that Entitled Him to the Venerable Appellation of Father

Thou's welcome wean, mischanter fa' me,
If thoughts o' thee, or yet thy Mamie,
Shall ever daunton me, or awe me,
                              My sweet wee lady,
5   Or if I blush when thou shalt ca' me
                              Tit-ta or daddy.

What tho' they ca' me fornicator,
An' tease my name in kintry clatter:
The mair they tauk I'm kent the better,
10   E'en let them clash;
An auld wife's tongue's a feckless matter
                              To gie ane fash.

Welcome, my bonie, sweet, wee dochter!
Tho' ye come here a wee unsought for,
15   And tho' your comin I hae fought for
                Baith kirk and queir;
Yet, by my faith, ye're no unwrought for –
                That I shall swear!

Wee image of my bonny Betty,
20   I fatherly will kiss and daut thee,
As dear an' near my heart I set thee
                Wi' as gude will
As a' the priests had seen me get thee
                That's out o' hell.

25   Sweet fruit o' mony a merry dint,
My funny toil is no a' tint;
Tho' ye came to the warl asklent,
                Which fools may scoff at;
In my last plack thy part's be in't,
30   The better ha'f o't.

Tho' I should be the waur bestead,
Thou's be as braw and bienly clad,
And thy young years as nicely bred
                Wi' education,
35   As onie brat o' wedlock's bed
                In a' thy station.

Gude grant that thou may ay inherit
Thy mither's looks, and gracefu' merit;
An' thy poor worthless dady's spirit,
40   Without his failins,
'Twill please me mair to see thee heir it
                Than stocket mailens.

An' if thou be what I wad ha'e thee,
An' tak the counsel I sall gi'e thee,
45   A lovin' father I'll be to thee,
                If thou be spar'd;
Thro' a' thy childish years I'll e'e thee,
                An' think't weel war'd.

The Fornicator. A New Song

(TUNE: CLOUT THE CALDRON)

Ye jovial boys who love the joys,
    The blissful joys of lovers;
Yet dare avow with dauntless brow,
    When th' bonie lass discovers;
5   I pray draw near and lend an ear,
    And welcome in a frater,
For I've lately been on quarantine,
    A proven Fornicator.

Before the congregation wide
10   I pass'd the muster fairly,
My handsome Betsey by my side,
    We gat our ditty rarely;
But my downcast eye by chance did spy
    What made my lips to water,
15 Those limbs so clean where I, between,
    Commenc'd a Fornicator.

With rueful face and signs of grace
    I pay'd the buttock-hire,
The night was dark and thro' the park
20   I could not but convoy her;
A parting kiss, what could I less,
    My vows began to scatter,
My Betsey fell – lal de dal lal lal,
    I am a Fornicator.

25 But for her sake this vow I make,
    And solemnly I swear it,
That while I own a single crown,
    She's welcome for to share it;
And my roguish boy his mother's joy,
30   And the darling of his pater,
For him I boast my pains and cost,
    Although a Fornicator.

Ye wenching blades whose hireling jades
   Have tipt you off blue-boram,
35 I tell ye plain, I do disdain
   To rank you in the quorum;
But a bonie lass upon the grass
   To teach her *esse mater*;
And no reward but for regard,
40   O that's a Fornicator.

Your warlike kings and heroes bold,
   Great captains and commanders;
Your mighty Cèsars fam'd of old,
   And conquering Alexanders;
45 In fields they fought and laurels bought
   And bulwarks strong did batter,
And still they grac'd our noble list
   And ranked Fornicator!

The Rantin Dog the Daddie O't

(TUNE: WHARE WAD BONIE ANNIE LIE)

O wha my babie-clouts will buy,
O wha will tent me when I cry;
Wha will kiss me where I lie;
   The rantin dog the daddie o't.

5 O wha will own he did the faut,
O wha will buy the groanin maut,
O wha will tell me how to ca't,
   The rantin dog the daddie o't.

When I mount the Creepie-chair,
10 Wha will sit beside me there,
Gie me Rob, I'll seek nae mair,
   The rantin dog the daddie o't.

Wha will crack to me my lane;
Wha will mak me fidgin fain;
15 Wha will kiss me o'er again;
   The rantin dog the daddie o't.

Address to the Unco Guid, or the Rigidly Righteous

My son, these maxims make a rule,
And lump them ay thegither;
The Rigid Righteous *is a fool,*
The Rigid Wise *anither;*
The cleanest corn that e'er was dight
May hae some pyles o' caff in;
So ne'er a fellow-creature slight
For random fits o' daffin.
Solomon. – Eccles. 7: 1–6

O ye wha are sae guid yoursel,
    Sae pious and sae holy,
Ye've nought to do but mark and tell
    Your neebours' fauts and folly!
5   Whase life is like a weel-gaun mill,
    Supply'd wi' store o' water,
The heaped happer's ebbing still,
    And still the clap plays clatter.

Hear me, ye venerable core,
10   As counsel for poor mortals,
That frequent pass douce Wisdom's door
    For glaikit Folly's portals;
I, for their thoughtless, careless sakes
    Would here propone defences,
15   Their donsie tricks, their black mistakes,
    Their failings and mischances.

Ye see your state wi' theirs compar'd,
    And shudder at the niffer,
But cast a moment's fair regard
20   What maks the mighty differ;
Discount what scant occasion gave,
    That purity ye pride in,
And (what's aft mair than a' the lave)
    Your better art o' hiding.

25 Think, when your castigated pulse
  Gies now and then a wallop,
What ragings must his veins convulse,
  That still eternal gallop:
Wi' wind and tide fair i' your tail,
30 Right on ye scud your sea-way;
But in the teeth o' baith to sail,
  It maks an unco leeway.

See Social-life and Glee sit down,
  All joyous and unthinking,
35 Till, quite transmugrify'd, they're grown
  Debauchery and Drinking:
O would they stay to calculate
  Th' eternal consequences;
Or your more dreaded hell to state,
40 Damnation of expences!

Ye high, exalted, virtuous Dames,
  Ty'd up in godly laces,
Before ye gie poor *Frailty* names,
  Suppose a change o' cases;
45 A dear-lov'd lad, convenience snug,
  A treacherous inclination –
But, let me whisper in your lug,
  Ye're aiblens nae temptation.

Then gently scan your brother Man,
50 Still gentler sister Woman;
Tho' they may gang a kennin wrang,
  To step aside is human:
One point must still be greatly dark,
  The moving *Why* they do it;
55 And just as lamely can ye mark,
  How far perhaps they rue it.

Who made the heart, 'tis *He* alone
  Decidedly can try us,
He knows each chord its various tone,
60 Each spring its various bias:

Then at the balance let's be mute,
 We never can adjust it;
What's *done* we partly may compute,
 But know not what's *resisted*.

Man Was Made to Mourn. A Dirge

(TUNE: PEGGY BAWN)

When chill November's surly blast
 Made fields and forests bare,
One ev'ning, as I wander'd forth,
 Along the banks of Aire,
5 I spy'd a man, whose aged step
 Seem'd weary, worn with care;
His face was furrow'd o'er with years,
 And hoary was his hair.

Young stranger, whither wand'rest thou?
10 Began the rev'rend Sage;
Does thirst of wealth thy step constrain,
 Or youthful pleasure's rage?
Or haply, prest with cares and woes,
 Too soon thou hast began,
15 To wander forth, with me, to mourn
 The miseries of Man.

The sun that overhangs yon moors,
 Out-spreading far and wide,
Where hundreds labour to support
20 A haughty lordling's pride;
I've seen yon weary winter-sun
 Twice forty times return;
And ev'ry time has added proofs,
 That Man was made to mourn.

25   O Man! while in thy early years,
        How prodigal of time!
     Mispending all thy precious hours,
        Thy glorious, youthful prime!
     Alternate follies take the sway;
30   Licentious passions burn;
     Which tenfold force gives Nature's law,
        That Man was made to mourn.

     Look not alone on youthful prime,
        Or manhood's active might;
35   Man then is useful to his kind,
        Supported is his right:
     But see him on the edge of life,
        With cares and sorrows worn,
     Then age and want, Oh! ill-match'd pair!
40   Show Man was made to mourn.

     A few seem favourites of Fate,
        In pleasure's lap carest;
     Yet think not all the Rich and Great,
        Are likewise truly blest.
45   But Oh! what crouds in ev'ry land,
        All wretched and forlorn,
     Thro' weary life this lesson learn,
        That Man was made to mourn!

     Many and sharp the num'rous ills
50   Inwoven with our frame!
     More pointed still we make ourselves,
        Regret, remorse and shame!
     And Man, whose heav'n-erected face,
        The smiles of love adorn,
55   Man's inhumanity to Man
        Makes countless thousands mourn!

See yonder poor, o'erlabour'd wight,
    So abject, mean and vile,
Who begs a brother of the earth
60   To give him leave to toil;
And see his lordly *fellow-worm*,
    The poor petition spurn,
Unmindful, tho' a weeping wife,
    And helpless offspring mourn.

65 If I'm design'd yon lordling's slave,
    By Nature's law design'd,
Why was an independent wish
    E'er planted in my mind?
If not, why am I subject to
70   His cruelty, or scorn?
Or why has Man the will and pow'r
    To make his fellow mourn?

Yet let not this too much, my son,
    Disturb thy youthful breast:
75 This partial view of human-kind
    Is surely not the *last*!
The poor, oppressed, honest man
    Had never, sure, been born,
Had there not been some recompense
80   To comfort those that mourn!

O Death! the poor man's dearest friend,
    The kindest and the best!
Welcome the hour, my aged limbs
    Are laid with thee at rest!
85 The great, the wealthy fear thy blow,
    From pomp and pleasure torn;
But Oh! a blest relief for those
    That weary-laden mourn!

The Holy Fair

A robe of seeming truth and trust
  Hid crafty observation;
And secret hung, with poison'd crust,
  The dirk of defamation:
A mask that like the gorget show'd,
  Dye-varying, on the pigeon;
And for a mantle large and broad,
  He wrapt him in Religion.
          Hypocrisy a-la-Mode

Upon a simmer Sunday morn,
  When Nature's face is fair,
I walked forth to view the corn,
  And snuff the callor air.
5   The rising sun, owre Galston muirs,
  Wi' glorious light was glintan;
The hares were hirplan down the furrs,
  The lav'rocks they were chantan
          Fu' sweet that day.

10   As lightsomely I glowr'd abroad,
  To see a scene sae gay,
Three hizzies, early at the road,
  Cam skelpan up the way.
Twa had manteeles o' dolefu' black,
15   But ane wi' lyart lining;
The third, that gaed a wee a-back,
  Was in the fashion shining
          Fu' gay that day.

The *twa* appear'd like sisters twin,
20   In feature, form an' claes;
Their visage wither'd, lang an' thin,
     As sour as ony slaes:
The *third* cam up, hap-step-an'-loup,
     As light as ony lambie,
25 An' wi' a curchie low did stoop,
     As soon as e'er she saw me,
            Fu' kind that day.

Wi' bonnet aff, quoth I, 'Sweet lass,
     I think ye seem to ken me;
30 I'm sure I've seen that bonie face,
     But yet I canna name ye.'
Quo' she, an laughan as she spak,
     An' taks me by the han's,
'Ye, for my sake, hae gien the feck
35   Of a' the *ten comman*'s
            A screed some day.

'My name is Fun – your cronie dear,
     The nearest friend ye hae;
An' this is Superstition here,
40   An' that's Hypocrisy.
I'm gaun to Mauchline *holy fair*,
     To spend an hour in daffin:
Gin ye go there, yon runkl'd pair,
     We will get famous laughin
45   At them this day.'

Quoth I, 'With a' my heart I'll do't;
     I'll get my Sunday's sark on,
An' meet you on the holy spot;
     Faith, we'se hae fine remarkin!'
50 Then I gaed hame at crowdie-time,
     An' soon I made me ready;
For roads were clad, frae side to side,
     Wi' monie a wearie body,
            In droves that day.

55 Here, farmers gash, in ridin graith,
        Gaed hoddan by their cotters;
    There, swankies young, in braw braid-claith,
        Are springan owre the gutters.
    The lasses, skelpan barefit, thrang,
60   In silks and scarlets glitter;
    Wi' *sweet-milk cheese*, in mony a whang,
        An' *farls*, bak'd wi' butter,
                    Fu' crump that day.

    When by the *plate* we set our nose,
65   Weel heaped up wi' ha'pence,
    A greedy glowr *black-bonnet* throws,
        An' we maun draw our tippence.
    Then in we go to see the show,
        On ev'ry side they're gath'ran;
70 Some carryan dails, some chairs an' stools,
        An' some are busy bleth'ran
                    Right loud that day.

    Here stands a shed to fend the show'rs,
        An' screen our countra gentry;
75 There *racer Jess*, an' twathree wh-res,
        Are blinkan at the entry.
    Here sits a raw o' tittlan jads,
        Wi' heaving breasts an' bare neck;
    And there a batch o' Wabster lads,
80   Blackguarding from Kilmarnock
                    For *fun* this day.

    Here, some are thinkan on their sins,
        An' some upo' their claes;
    Ane curses feet that fyl'd his shins,
85   Anither sighs an' prays:
    On this hand sits an *Elect* swatch,
        Wi' screw'd-up, grace-proud faces;
    On that, a set o' chaps, at watch,
        Thrang winkan on the lasses
90   To *chairs* that day.

O happy is that man, an' blest!
   Nae wonder that it pride him!
Whase ain dear lass, that he likes best,
   Comes clinkan down beside him!
95 Wi' arm repos'd on the *chair-back*,
   He sweetly does compose him;
Which, by degrees, slips round her *neck*
   An's loof upon her *bosom*
            Unkend that day.

100 Now a' the congregation o'er
   Is silent expectation;
For Sawney speels the holy door,
   Wi' tidings of salvation.
Should *Hornie*, as in ancient days,
105   'Mang sons o' God present him,
The vera sight o' Moodie's face,
   To's ain *het hame* had sent him
            Wi' fright that day.

Hear how he clears the points o' faith
110   Wi' rattlin an' thumpin!
Now meekly calm, now wild in wrath,
   He's stampan, an he's jumpan!
His lengthen'd chin, his turn'd up snout,
   His eldritch squeel an' gestures,
115 O how they fire the heart devout,
   Like *cantharidian* plaisters
            On sic a day!

But hark! the *tent* has chang'd its voice;
   There's peace an' rest nae langer;
120 For a' the *real judges* rise,
   They canna sit for anger.
Smith opens out his cauld harangues,
   On *practice* and on *morals*;
An' aff the *godly* pour in thrangs,
125   To gie the jars an' barrels
           A lift that day.

What signifies his barren shine,
   Of *moral pow'rs* an' *reason?*
His English style, an' gesture fine,
130   Are a' clean out o' season.
Like Socrates or Antonine,
   Or some auld pagan heathen,
The *moral man* he does define,
   But ne'er a word o' *faith* in
135   That's right this day.

In guid time comes an antidote
   Against sic poosion'd nostrum;
For Peebles, frae the water-fit,
   Ascends the *holy rostrum*:
140 See, up he's got the word o' God,
   An' meek an' mim has view'd it,
While Common Sense has taen the road,
   An' aff, an' up the Cowgate
           Fast, fast this day.

145 Wee Miller neist, the guard relieves,
   An' Orthodoxy raibles,
Tho' in his heart he weel believes,
   An' thinks it auld wives' fables:
But faith! the birkie wants a *Manse*,
150   So, cannilie he hums them;
Altho' his carnal Wit an' Sense
   Like hafflins-wise o'ercomes him
          At times that day.

Now, butt an' ben, the change-house fills,
155   Wi' yill-caup Commentators:
Here's crying out for bakes an' gills,
   An' there the pint-stowp clatters;
While thick an' thrang, an' loud an' lang,
   Wi' *Logic*, an' wi' *Scripture*,
160 They raise a din that in the end,
   Is like to breed a rupture
         O' wrath that day.

Leeze me on Drink! it gies us mair
 Than either school or colledge:
165 It kindles wit, it waukens lear,
 It pangs us fou o' knowledge.
Be't *whisky-gill* or *penny-wheep*,
 Or ony stronger potion,
It never fails, on drinkin deep,
170 To kittle up our *notion*,
  By night or day.

The lads and lasses, blythely bent
 To mind baith *saul* an' *body*,
Sit round the table, weel content,
175 An' steer about the *toddy*.
On this ane's dress, an' that ane's leuk,
 They're makin observations;
While some are cozie i' the neuk,
 An' forming *assignations*
180 To meet some day.

But now the Lord's ain trumpet touts,
 Till a' the hills are rairan,
An' echos back return the shouts;
 Black Russel is na spairan:
185 His piercin words, like Highlan swords,
 Divide the joints an' marrow;
His talk o' Hell, where devils dwell,
 Our vera *'sauls does harrow'
  Wi' fright that day!

190 A vast, unbottom'd, boundless *Pit*,
 Fill'd fou o' *lowan brunstane*,
Whase raging flame, an' scorching heat,
 Wad melt the hardest whun-stane!
The *half asleep* start up wi' fear,
195 An' think they hear it roaran,
When presently it does appear,
 'Twas but some neebor *snoran*
  Asleep that day.

* Shakespeare's Hamlet. [RB]

'Twad be owre lang a tale to tell,
200   How monie stories past,
An' how they crouded to the yill,
    When they were a' dismist:
How drink gaed round, in cogs an' caups,
    Amang the furms an' benches;
205 An' cheese an' bread, frae women's laps,
    Was dealt about in lunches,
            An' dawds that day.

In comes a gawsie, gash Guidwife,
    An' sits down by the fire,
210 Syne draws her *kebbuck* an' her knife;
    The lasses they are shyer.
The auld Guidmen, about the *grace*,
    Frae side to side they bother,
Till some ane by his bonnet lays,
215   And gies them't, like a *tether*,
            Fu' lang that day.

Waesucks! for him that gets nae lass,
    Or lasses that hae naething!
Sma' need has he to say a grace,
220   Or melvie his braw claithing!
O Wives be mindfu', ance yourself,
    How bonie lads ye wanted,
An' dinna, for a *kebbuck-heel*,
    Let lasses be affronted
225   On sic a day!

Now Clinkumbell, wi' rattlan tow,
    Begins to jow an' croon;
Some swagger hame, the best they dow,
    Some wait the afternoon.
230 At slaps the billies halt a blink,
    Till lasses strip their shoon:
Wi' *faith* an' *hope*, an' *love* an' *drink*,
    They're a' in famous tune
            For crack that day.

235   How monie hearts this day converts,
      O' sinners and o' lasses!
  Their hearts o' stane, gin night are gane,
      As saft as ony flesh is.
  There's some are fou o' *love divine*;
240   There's some are fou o' *brandy*;
  An' monie jobs that day begin,
      May end in *Houghmagandie*
           Some ither day.

To the Rev. John M'Math, Inclosing a Copy of Holy Willie's Prayer, Which He Had Requested

Sept. 17th, 1785

While at the stook the shearers cow'r
To shun the bitter blaudin' show'r,
Or in gulravage rinnin scow'r
      To pass the time,
5   To you I dedicate the hour
      In idle rhyme.

My musie, tir'd wi' mony a sonnet
On gown, an' ban', an' douse black bonnet,
Is grown right eerie now she's done it,
10   Lest they should blame her,
An' rouse their holy thunder on it
      And anathem her.

I own, 'twas rash, an' rather hardy,
That I, a simple countra bardie,
15   Shou'd meddle wi' a pack sae sturdy,
      Wha, if they ken me,
Can easy, wi' a single wordie,
      Louse hell upon me.

But I gae mad at their grimaces,
20   Their sighan, cantan, grace-prood faces,
Their three-miles prayers, an' hauf-mile graces,
                    Their raxan conscience,
Whase greed, revenge, an' pride disgraces
                    Waur nor their nonsense.

25   There's *Gaun*, miska't waur than a beast,
Wha has mair honor in his breast,
Than mony scores as guid's the priest
                    Wha sae abus't him;
An' may a bard no crack his jest
30   What way they've use't him?

See him, the poor man's friend in need,
The gentleman in word an' deed,
An' shall his fame an' honor bleed
                    By worthless skellums,
35   An' not a muse erect her head
                    To cowe the blellums?

O Pope, had I thy satire's darts
To gie the rascals their deserts,
I'd rip their rotten, hollow hearts,
                    An' tell aloud
40   Their jugglin' hocus pocus arts
                    To cheat the crowd.

God knows, I'm no the thing I shou'd be,
Nor am I even the thing I cou'd be,
45   But twenty times, I rather wou'd be
                    An atheist clean,
Than under gospel colors hid be
                    Just for a screen.

An honest man may like a glass,
50   An honest man may like a lass,
But mean revenge, an' malice fause
                    He'll still disdain,
An' then cry zeal for gospel laws,
                    Like some we ken.

55   They take religion in their mouth;
     They talk o' mercy, grace, an' truth,
     For what? to gie their malice skouth
                    On some puir wight,
     An' hunt him down, o'er right an' ruth,
60   To ruin streight.

     All hail, religion! maid divine!
     Pardon a muse sae mean as mine,
     Who in her rough, imperfect line
                    Thus daurs to name thee;
65   To stigmatize false friends of thine
                    Can ne'er defame thee.

     Tho' blotch't an' foul wi' mony a stain,
     An' far unworthy of thy train,
     With trembling voice I tune my strain
70   To join with those,
     Who boldly dare thy cause maintain
                    In spite of foes:

     In spite o' crowds, in spite o' mobs,
     In spite of undermining jobs,
75   In spite o' dark banditti stabs
                    At worth an' merit,
     By scoundrels, even wi' holy robes,
                    But hellish spirit.

     O Ayr, my dear, my native ground,
80   Within thy presbytereal bound
     A candid lib'ral band is found
                    Of public teachers,
     As men, as christians too renown'd
                    An' manly preachers.

85   Sir, in that circle you are nam'd,
     Sir, in that circle you are fam'd;
     An' some, by whom your doctrine's blam'd,
                    (Which gies you honor)
     Ev'n Sir, by them your heart's esteem'd,
90   An' winning manner.

Pardon this freedom I have ta'en,
An' if impertinent I've been,
Impute it not, good Sir, in ane
    Whase heart ne'er wrang'd ye,
95 But to his utmost would befriend
    Ought that belang'd ye.

To a Mouse
On Turning Her up in Her Nest with the Plough, November 1785

Wee, sleeket, cowran, tim'rous *beastie*,
O, what a panic's in thy breastie!
Thou need na start awa sae hasty,
    Wi' bickering brattle!
5 I wad be laith to rin an' chase thee,
    Wi' murd'ring *pattle*!

I'm truly sorry Man's dominion
Has broken Nature's social union,
An' justifies that ill opinion,
10   Which makes thee startle,
At me, thy poor, earth-born companion,
    An' *fellow-mortal*!

I doubt na, whyles, but thou may thieve;
What then? poor beastie, thou maun live!
15 A *daimen-icker* in a *thrave*
    'S a sma' request:
I'll get a blessin wi' the lave,
    An' never miss't!

Thy wee-bit *housie*, too, in ruin!
20 It's silly wa's the win's are strewin!
An' naething, now, to big a new ane,
    O' foggage green!
An' bleak December's winds ensuin,
    Baith snell an' keen!

25   Thou saw the fields laid bare an' wast,
     An' weary Winter comin fast,
     An' cozie here, beneath the blast,
                         Thou thought to dwell,
     Till crash! the cruel *coulter* past
30   Out thro' thy cell.

     That wee-bit heap o' leaves an' stibble,
     Has cost thee monie a weary nibble!
     Now thou's turn'd out, for a' thy trouble,
                         But house or hald,
35   To thole the Winter's sleety dribble,
                         An' *cranreuch* cauld!

     But Mousie, thou art no thy-lane,
     In proving *foresight* may be vain:
     The best laid schemes o' *Mice* an' *Men*,
40   Gang aft agley,
     An' lea'e us nought but grief an' pain,
                         For promis'd joy!

     Still, thou art blest, compar'd wi' *me*!
     The *present* only toucheth thee:
45   But Och! I *backward* cast my e'e,
                         On prospects drear!
     An' *forward*, tho' I canna *see*,
                         I *guess* an' *fear*!

Love and Liberty. A Cantata

RECITATIVO

When lyart leaves bestrow the yird,
Or wavering like the *Bauckie-bird,
    Bedim cauld Boreas' blast;
When hailstanes drive wi' bitter skyte,
5   And infant frosts begin to bite,
    In hoary cranreuch drest;
Ae night at e'en a merry core
    O' randie, gangrel bodies,
In Poosie-Nansie's held the splore,
10   To drink their orra duddies:
            Wi' quaffing and laughing,
                They ranted an' they sang;
            Wi' jumping an' thumping
                The vera girdle rang.

15   First, neist the fire, in auld red rags,
Ane sat; weel brac'd wi' mealy bags,
    And knapsack a' in order;
His doxy lay within his arm,
Wi' usquebae an' blankets warm,
20   She blinket on her sodger:
An' ay he gives the tozie drab
    The tither skelpin' kiss,
While she held up her greedy gab
    Just like an aumos dish.
25   Ilk smack still, did crack still,
            Just like a cadger's whip,
        Then staggering an' swaggering
            He roar'd this ditty up —

* The old Scotch name for the Bat. [RB]

BURNS

W. Weir delt   R. Scott sculp.

Glasgow, Printed for Stewart and Meikie, Booksellers, 1800.

THE

JOLLY BEGGARS;

OR,

TATTERDEMALLIONS.

A CANTATA.

BY ROBERT BURNS,
THE AYRSHIRE POET.

To which are added,
LINES ON WRANGLING,

THE WISH,

AND

THE LADY'S CHOICE.

Here's to budgets, bags, and wallets!
Here's to all the wandering train!
Here's our ragged brats and callets!
One and all cry out, Amen!

GLASGOW:
PRINTED BY CHAPMAN & LANG, TRONGATE,
For Stewart & Meikle.

1799

Title page and frontispiece of Stewart and Meikle's rare tract, the first publication of 'Love and Liberty' (Glasgow, 1799). The tract bears a title of the editors' contrivance. The engraving by W. Weir reflects the poet's contemporary reputation as a dangerous man – a view that later nineteenth-century bardolatry softened into myth. (Reproduced by permisson of The Mitchell Library, Glasgow.)

AIR
TUNE: SOLDIER'S JOY

I am a son of Mars who have been in many wars,
30   And show my cuts and scars wherever I come;
This here was for a wench, and that other in a trench,
When welcoming the French at the sound of the drum.
                    Lal de daudle, &c.

My prenticeship I past where my leader breath'd his last,
35   When the bloody die was cast on the heights of Abram;
I served out my trade when the gallant game was play'd,
And the Moro low was laid at the sound of the drum.
                    Lal de daudle, &c.

I lastly was with Curtis, among the *floating batt'ries*,
40   And there I left for witness an arm and a limb;
Yet let my country need me, with Elliot to head me,
I'd clatter on my stumps at the sound of a drum.
                    Lal de daudle, &c.

And now tho' I must beg with a wooden arm and leg,
45   And many a tatter'd rag hanging over my bum,
I'm as happy with my wallet, my bottle and my callet,
As when I us'd in scarlet to follow a drum.

                    Lal de daudle, &c.

What tho' with hoary locks, I must stand the winter
    shocks,
50   Beneath the woods and rocks oftentimes for a home,
When the tother bag I sell, and the tother bottle tell,
I could meet a troop of hell at the sound of a drum.

                    Lal de daudle, &c.

RECITATIVO

He ended; and the kebars sheuk,
55   Aboon the chorus roar;
While frighted rattons backward leuk,
    And seek the benmost bore:

A fairy Fiddler frae the neuk,
    He skirl'd out encore!
60   But up arose the martial Chuck,
    And laid the loud uproar.

AIR

TUNE: SOLDIER LADDIE

I once was a maid, tho' I cannot tell when, — And still my delight is in proper young men; Some one of a troop of dragoons was my daddie; No wonder I'm fond of a sodger laddie.

CHORUS

Sing, lal de lal, sing, lal de lal, sing, lal de lal, sing lal de lal, sing, lal de lal, sing, lal de lal, sing, lal de lal, sing, lal de lal, sing, lal de lal, sing, lal de lal, sing, lal de lal.

I once was a maid, tho' I cannot tell when,
And still my delight is in proper young men;
Some one of a troop of dragoons was my daddie,
65   No wonder I'm fond of a sodger laddie.
            Sing, Lal de lal, &c.

The first of my loves was a swaggering blade,
To rattle the thundering drum was his trade;
His leg was so tight, and his cheek was so ruddy,
70   Transported I was with my sodger laddie.
            Sing, Lal de lal, &c.

But the godly old chaplain left him in the lurch,
The sword I forsook for the sake of the church;
He ventur'd the *soul*, and I risked the *body*,
75 'Twas then I prov'd false to my sodger laddie.
       Sing, Lal de lal, &c.

Full soon I grew sick of my sanctified sot,
The regiment *at large* for a *husband* I got;
From the gilded Spontoon to the Fife I was ready,
80 I asked no more but a sodger laddie.
       Sing, Lal de lal, &c.

But the peace it reduc'd me to beg in despair,
Till I met my old boy at a Cunningham fair;
His *rags regimental* they flutter'd so gaudy,
85 My heart it rejoic'd at a sodger laddie.
       Sing, Lal de lal, &c.

And now I have liv'd – I know not how long,
And still I can join in a cup or a song;
But whilst with both hands I can hold the glass steady,
90 Here's to thee, my hero, my sodger laddie.
       Sing, Lal de lal, &c.

RECITATIVO

Then neist outspak a raucle Carlin,
Wha kent fu' weel to cleek the sterling,
For mony a pursie she had hooked,
95 And had in mony a well been douked.
Her love had been a Highland laddie,
But weary fa' the waefu' woodie!
Wi' sighs and sobs she thus began
To wail her braw John Highlandman.

AIR

TUNE: O AN YE WERE DEAD GUIDMAN

100   A Highland lad my love was born,
      The Lalland laws he held in scorn;
      But he still was faithfu' to his clan,
      My gallant, braw John Highlandman.

          Sing hey my braw John Highlandman!
105   Sing ho my braw John Highlandman!
          There's not a lad in a' the lan'
          Was match for my John Highlandman.

      With his philibeg an' tartan plaid,
      An' gude claymore down by his side,
110   The ladies' hearts he did trepan,
      My gallant, braw John Highlandman.
                    Sing hey, &c.

We rang'd a' from Tweed to Spey,
An' liv'd like lords and ladies gay:
115 For a Lalland face he feared none,
My gallant, braw John Highlandman.
                    Sing hey, &c.

They banish'd him beyond the sea,
But ere the bud was on the tree,
120 Adown my cheeks the pearls ran,
Embracing my John Highlandman.
                    Sing hey, &c.

But Oh! they catch'd him at the last,
And bound him in a dungeon fast;
125 My curse upon them every one,
They've hang'd my braw John Highlandman.
                    Sing hey, &c.

And now a widow, I must mourn
The pleasures that will ne'er return;
130 No comfort but a hearty can,
When I think on John Highlandman.
                    Sing hey, &c.

RECITATIVO

A pygmy Scraper wi' his fiddle,
Wha us'd to trysts an' fairs to driddle,
135 Her strappan limb an' gausy middle
                    He reach'd nae higher,
Had hol'd his heartie like a riddle,
                    An' blawn't on fire.

Wi' hand on hainch, an' upward e'e,
140 He croon'd his gamut, one, two, three,
Then in an Arioso key,
                    The wee Apollo
Set off wi' Allegretto glee
                    His giga solo.

AIR

TUNE: WHISTLE OWRE THE LAVE O'T

Moderately

Let me ryke up to dight that tear, An' go wi' me an' be my dear, An' then your ev-ry care an' fear May whis-tle owre the lave o't.

CHORUS

I am a— fid-dler to my trade, An' a' the tunes that e'er I play'd, The sweet-est still to wife or maid Was— whis-tle owre the lave o't.

145   Let me ryke up to dight that tear,
      An' go wi' me an' be my dear,
      An' then your every care an' fear
          May whistle owre the lave o't.

Chorus
          I am a fiddler to my trade,
150   An' a' the tunes that e'er I play'd,
          The sweetest still to wife or maid,
                  Was whistle owre the lave o't.

      At kirns an' weddins we'se be there,
      And O! sae nicely's we will fair;
155   We'll bouse about till Daddie Care
              Sing, whistle owre the lave o't.
                          I am, &c.

Sae merrily's the banes we'll pyke,
An' sun oursells about the dyke,
160   An' at our leisure when ye like,
        We'll whistle owre the lave o't.
                I am, &c.

But bless me wi' your heav'n o' charms,
An' while I kittle hair on thairms,
165   *Hunger*, *Cauld*, an' a' sic harms,
        May whistle owre the lave o't.
                I am, &c.

RECITATIVO

Her charms had struck a sturdy Caird,
    As weel as poor Gutscraper;
170   He taks the Fiddler by the beard,
        An' draws a roosty rapier. –
He swoor by a' was swearing worth,
    To speet him like a pliver,
Unless he would from that time forth,
175   Relinquish her for ever.

Wi' ghastly e'e, poor Tweedle-dee
    Upon his hunkers bended,
An' pray'd for grace wi' ruefu' face,
    An' so the quarrel ended.
180   But tho' his little heart did grieve,
        When round the Tinkler prest her,
He feign'd to snirtle in his sleeve,
        When thus the Caird address'd her.

AIR

TUNE: CLOUT THE CAUDRON

Lively

My bo - ny lass, I work in brass, A tink - ler is my sta - tion; I've
tra - vell'd round all Chris-tian ground In this my oc - cu - pa - tion. I've
ta'en the gold, an' been en - roll'd In many a no - ble— squad - ron; But
vain they search'd, when off I march'd To— go an' clout the— caud - ron.

My bonny lass I work in brass,
185   A Tinkler is my station;
I've travell'd round all Christian ground
    In this my occupation.
I've ta'en the gold an' been enroll'd
    In many a noble squadron;
190   But vain they search'd, when off I march'd
    To go an' clout the caudron.
          I've ta'en the gold, &c.

Despise that shrimp, that wither'd imp,
    Wi' a' his noise an' caprin',
195   An' tak a share wi' those that bear
    The *budget* an' the *apron*.
An' *by* that stowp! my faith an' houpe,
    An' *by* that dear *Keilbaigie,
If e'er ye want, or meet wi' scant,
200   May I ne'er weet my craigie.
          An' by that stowp, &c.

---

* A peculiar sort of Whisky so called; a great favourite with Poosie Nansie's clubs. [RB]

RECITATIVO

The Caird prevail'd – th' unblushing fair
    In his embraces sunk,
Partly wi' Love o'ercome sae sair,
205   An' partly she was drunk.
Sir Violino with an air,
    That show'd a man o' spunk,
Wish'd *unison* between the pair,
    An' made the bottle clunk
210   To their health that night.

But hurchin Cupid shot a shaft
    That played a dame a shavie,
The fiddler rak'd her *fore and aft*,
    Behint the chicken cavie.
215 Her lord a wight o' *Homer's craft,
    Tho' limpan wi' the spavie,
He hirpl'd up, and lap like daft,
    An' shor'd them Dainty Davie
           O' *boot* that night.

220 He was a care-defying blade
    As ever Bacchus listed,
Tho' Fortune sair upon him laid,
    His heart she ever miss'd it.
He had no wish but – to be glad,
225   Nor want but – when he thristed;
He hated nought but – to be sad,
    And thus the Muse suggested,
           His sang that night.

* Homer is allowed to be the oldest ballad singer on record. [RB]

AIR
TUNE: FOR A' THAT, AN' A' THAT

I am a Bard of no regard,
230   Wi' gentle folks, an' a' that;
But *Homer-like*, the glowran byke,
     Frae town to town I draw that.

Chorus
     For a' that, an' a' that,
        An' twice as muckle's a' that;
235   I've lost but ane, I've twa behin',
     I've *wife eneugh* for a' that.

I never drank the Muse's *stank*,
     Castalia's burn, an' a' that;
But there it streams, and richly reams,
240   My *Helicon* I ca' that.
     For a' that, &c.

Great love I bear to a' the fair,
     Their humble slave, an' a' that;
But lordly will, I hold it still
245   A mortal sin to thraw that.
     For a' that, &c.

In raptures sweet, this hour we meet,
  Wi' mutual love an' a' that;
But for how lang the *flie may stang*,
250 Let *inclination* law that.
    For a' that, &c.

Their tricks and craft have put me daft,
  They've ta'en me in, an' a' that;
But clear your decks, an' here's the sex!
  I like the jads for a' that.

    For a' that, an' a' that,
      An' twice as muckle's a' that;
    My *dearest bluid*, to do them guid,
      They're welcome till't for a' that.

RECITATIVO

260 So sung the bard – and Nansie's wa's
    Shook with a thunder of applause,
  Re-echo'd from each mouth;
    They toom'd their pocks, an' pawn'd their duds,
  They scarcely left to coor their fuds,
265   To quench their lowan drouth.
  Then owre again, the jovial thrang,
    The poet did request,
  To lowse his pack an' wale a sang,
    A ballad o' the best.
270   He rising, rejoicing,
          Between his twa *Deborahs*,
        Looks round him, an' found them
          Impatient for the chorus.

AIR

TUNE: JOLLY MORTALS FILL YOUR GLASSES

See the smok - ing bowl be - fore us, Mark our jo - vial rag - ged ring!

Round and round take up the chor - us, And in rap - tures let us sing, –

   See! the smoking bowl before us,
275   Mark our jovial ragged ring!
   Round and round take up the chorus,
      And in raptures let us sing.

Chorus
      A fig for those by law protected!
         Liberty's a glorious feast!
280   Courts for cowards were erected,
         Churches built to please the priest.

   What is title? what is treasure?
      What is reputation's care?
   If we lead a life of pleasure,
285   'Tis no matter *how* or *where*!
            A fig, &c.

   With the ready trick and fable,
      Round we wander all the day;
   And at night, in barn or stable,
290   Hug our doxies on the hay.
            A fig, &c.

   Does the train-attended *carriage*
      Thro' the country lighter rove?
   Does the sober bed of *marriage*
295   Witness brighter scenes of love?
            A fig, &c.

Life is all a *variorum*,
    We regard not how it goes;
Let them cant about *decorum*
300   Who have characters to lose.
          A fig, &c.

Here's to budgets, bags and wallets!
    Here's to all the wandering train!
Here's our ragged *brats* and *callets*!
305   One and all cry out, Amen!

      A fig for those by law protected!
        Liberty's a glorious feast!
      Courts for cowards were erected,
        Churches built to please the priest.

To a Louse
On Seeing One on a Lady's Bonnet at Church

Ha! whare ye gaun, ye crowlan ferlie!
Your impudence protects you sairly:
I canna say but ye strunt rarely,
      Owre *gawze* and *lace*;
5 Tho' faith, I fear ye dine but sparely,
      On sic a place.

Ye ugly, creepan, blastet wonner,
Detested, shunn'd, by saunt an' sinner,
How daur ye set your fit upon her,
10   Sae fine a *Lady*!
Gae somewhere else and seek your dinner,
      On some poor body.

Swith, in some beggar's haffet squattle;
There ye may creep, and sprawl, and sprattle,
15 Wi' ither kindred, jumping cattle,
      In shoals and nations;
Whare *horn* nor *bane* ne'er daur unsettle,
      Your thick plantations.

Now haud you there, ye're out o' sight,
20   Below the fatt'rels, snug and tight,
Na faith ye yet! ye'll no be right,
                    Till ye've got on it,
The vera tapmost, towrin height
                    O' *Miss's bonnet*.

25   My sooth! right bauld ye set your nose out,
As plump an' gray as onie grozet:
O for some rank, mercurial rozet,
                    Or fell, red smeddum,
I'd gie you sic a hearty dose o't,
30   Wad dress your droddum!

I wad na been surpriz'd to spy
You on an auld wife's *flainen toy*;
Or aiblins some bit duddie boy,
                    On's *wylecoat*;
35   But Miss's fine *Lunardi*, fye!
                    How daur ye do't?

O Jenny dinna toss your head,
An' set your beauties a' abread!
Ye little ken what cursed speed
40   The blastie's makin,
Thae *winks* and *finger-ends*, I dread,
                    Are notice takin!

O wad some Pow'r the giftie gie us
To see oursels as others see us!
45   It wad frae monie a blunder free us
                    An' foolish notion:
What airs in dress an' gait wad lea'e us,
                    And ev'n Devotion!

The Author's Earnest Cry and Prayer, to the Right
Honorable and Honorable, the Scotch
Representatives in the House of Commons*

Dearest of Distillations last and best! –
How art thou lost! –
Parody on Milton

Ye Irish lords, ye knights an' squires,
Wha represent our Brughs an' Shires
An' dousely manage our affairs
        In Parliament,
5 To you a simple Bardie's pray'rs
        Are humbly sent.

Alas! my roupet Muse is haerse!
Your Honor's hearts wi' grief 'twad pierce,
To see her sittan on her arse
10   Low i' the dust,
An' scriechan out prosaic verse,
        An' like to brust!

Tell them wha hae the chief direction,
Scotland an' *me's* in great affliction,
15 E'er sin' they laid that curst restriction
        On Aquavitae;
An' rouse them up to strong conviction,
        An' move their pity.

Stand forth and tell yon Premier Youth,
20 The honest, open, naked truth:
Tell him o' mine an' Scotland's drouth,
        His servants humble:
The muckle devil blaw you south,
        If ye dissemble!

---

* This was wrote before the Act anent the Scotch distilleries, of session 1786; for
which Scotland and the Author return their most grateful thanks. [RB]

25   Does ony *great man* glunch an' gloom?
      Speak out an' never fash your thumb.
      Let *posts* an' *pensions* sink or swoom
                Wi' them wha grant them:
      If honestly they canna come,
30   Far better want them.

      In gath'rin votes you were na slack,
      Now stand as tightly by your tack:
      Ne'er claw your lug, an' fidge your back,
                An' hum an' haw,
35   But raise your arm, an' tell your crack
                Before them a'.

      Paint Scotland greetan owre her thrissle;
      Her *mutchkin stowp* as toom's a whissle;
      An' damn'd Excise-men in a bussle,
40   Seizan a *Stell*,
      Triumphant crushan't like a muscle
                Or laimpet shell.

      Then on the tither hand present her,
      A blackguard *Smuggler*, right behint her,
45   An' cheek-for-chow, a chuffie *Vintner*,
                Colleaguing join,
      Picking her pouch as bare as Winter,
                Of a' kind coin.

      Is there, that bears the name o' Scot,
50   But feels his heart's bluid rising hot,
      To see his poor, auld Mither's *pot*,
                Thus dung in staves,
      An' plunder'd o' her hindmost groat,
                By gallows knaves?

55   Alas! I'm but a nameless wight,
      Trode i' the mire out o' sight!
      But could I like Montgomeries fight,
                Or gab like Boswell,
      There's some *sark-necks* I wad *draw* tight,
60   An' *tye* some *hose* well.

God bless your Honors, can ye see't,
The kind, auld, cantie Carlin greet,
An' no get warmly to your feet,
   An' gar them hear it,
65 An' tell them, with a patriot-heat,
    Ye winna bear it?

Some o' you nicely ken the laws,
To round the period an' pause,
And with rhetoric clause on clause
70   To mak harangues;
Then echo thro' Saint Stephens wa's
    Auld Scotland's wrangs.

Dempster, a true-blue Scot I'se warran;
Thee, aith-detesting, chaste Kilkerran;
75 An' that glib-gabbet Highland Baron,
    The Laird o' Graham;
And ane, a chap that's damn'd auldfarran,
    Dundas his name.

Erskine, a spunkie norland billie;
80 True Campbells, Frederick an' Ilay;
An' Liviston, the bauld Sir Willie;
    An' monie ithers,
Whom auld Demosthenes or Tully
    Might own for brithers.

85 Arouse my boys! exert your mettle,
To get auld Scotland back her *kettle*!
Or faith! I'll wad my new pleugh-pettle,
    Ye'll see't or lang,
She'll teach you, wi' a reekan whittle,
90   Anither sang.

This while she's been in crankous mood,
Her *lost Militia* fir'd her bluid;
(Deil na they never mair do guid,
    Play'd her that pliskie!)
95 An' now she's like to rin red-wud
    About her *Whisky*.

An' Lord! if ance they pit her till't,
Her tartan petticoat she'll kilt,
An' durk an' pistol at her belt,
100   She'll tak the streets,
An' rin her whittle to the hilt,
                    I' th' first she meets!

For God-sake, Sirs! then speak her fair,
An' straik her cannie wi' the hair,
105 An' to the *muckle house* repair,
                    Wi' instant speed,
An' strive, wi' a' your Wit an' Lear,
                    To get remead.

Yon ill-tongu'd tinkler, Charlie Fox,
110 May taunt you wi' his jeers an' mocks;
But gie him't het, my hearty cocks!
                    E'en cowe the cadie!
An' send him to his dicing box,
                    An' sportin lady.

115 Tell yon guid bluid o' auld Boconnock's,
I'll be his debt twa mashlum bonnocks,
An' drink his health in auld *Nanse Tinnock's
                    Nine times a week,
If he some scheme, like tea an' winnocks,
120   Wad kindly seek.

Could he some *commutation* broach,
I'll pledge my aith in guid braid Scotch,
He need na fear their foul reproach
                    Nor erudition,
125 Yon mixtie-maxtie, queer hotch-potch,
                    The *Coalition*.

Auld Scotland has a raucle tongue;
She's just a devil wi' a rung;
An' if she promise auld or young

* A worthy old Hostess of the Author's in Mauchline, where he sometimes studies
Politics over a glass of guid auld Scotch Drink. [RB]

130   To tak their part,
Tho' by the neck she should be strung,
                She'll no desert.

And now, ye chosen Five and Forty,
May still your Mither's heart support ye;
135 Then, tho' a *Minister* grow dorty,
                An' kick your place,
Ye'll snap your fingers, poor an' hearty,
                Before his face.

God bless your Honors, a' your days,
140 Wi' sowps o' kail and brats o' claise,
In spite o' a' the thievish kaes
                That haunt St *Jamie*'s!
Your humble Bardie sings an' prays
                While *Rab* his name is.

POSTSCRIPT

145 Let half-starv'd slaves in warmer skies,
See future wines, rich-clust'ring, rise;
Their lot auld Scotland ne'er envies,
                But blythe an' frisky,
She eyes her freeborn, martial boys,
150   Tak aff their Whisky.

What tho' their Phoebus kinder warms,
While Fragrance blooms an' Beauty charms!
When wretches range, in famish'd swarms,
                The scented groves,
155 Or hounded forth, *dishonor* arms
                In hungry droves.

Their *gun's* a burden on their shouther;
They downa bide the stink o' *powther*;
Their bauldest thought's a hank'ring swither,
160   To stan' or rin,
Till skelp – a shot – they're aff, a' throw'ther,
                To save their skin.

But bring a Scotchman frae his hill,
Clap in his cheek a *Highland gill*,
165   Say, such is Royal George's will,
                    An' there's the foe,
He has nae thought but how to kill
                    Twa at a blow.

No cauld, faint-hearted doubtings tease him;
170   Death comes, wi' fearless eye he sees him;
Wi' bluidy han' a welcome gies him;
                    An' when he fa's,
His latest draught o' breathin lea'es him
                    In faint huzzas.

175   Sages their solemn een may steek,
An' raise a philosophic reek,
An' physically causes seek,
                    In *clime* an' *season*,
But tell me *Whisky's* name in Greek,
180   I'll tell the reason.

Scotland, my auld, respected Mither!
Tho' whyles ye moistify your leather,
Till whare ye sit, on craps o' heather,
                    Ye tine your dam;
185   FREEDOM and WHISKY gang thegither,
                    Tak aff your *dram*!

The Twa Dogs. A Tale

'Twas in that place o' Scotland's isle,
That bears the name o' auld king Coil,
Upon a bonie day in June,
When wearing thro' the afternoon,
5   *Twa Dogs*, that were na thrang at hame,
Forgather'd ance upon a time.

The first I'll name, they ca'd him Caesar,
Was keepet for His Honor's pleasure;
His hair, his size, his mouth, his lugs,
10   Shew'd he was nane o' Scotland's dogs,
But whalpet some place far abroad,
Where sailors gang to fish for cod.

His locked, letter'd, braw brass-collar
Shew'd him the *gentleman* an' *scholar*;
15   But tho' he was o' high degree,
The fient a pride na pride had he,
But wad hae spent an hour caressan,
Ev'n wi' a Tinkler-gipsey's *messan*:
At kirk or market, mill or smiddie,
20   Nae tawted *tyke*, tho' e'er sae duddie,
But he wad stan't, as glad to see him,
An' stroan't on stanes an' hillocks wi' him.

The tither was a *ploughman's collie*,
A rhyming, ranting, raving billie,
25   Wha for his friend an' comrade had him,
And in his freaks had *Luath* ca'd him,
After some dog in *Highland sang,
Was made lang syne, lord knows how lang.

He was a gash an' faithfu' *tyke*,
30   As ever lap a sheugh or dyke.
His honest, sonsie, baws'nt face,
Ay gat him friends in ilka place;
His breast was white, his towsie back,
Weel clad wi' coat o' glossy black;
35   His gawsie tail, wi' upward curl,
Hung owre his hurdies wi' a swirl.

* Cuchullin's dog in Ossian's Fingal. [RB]

Nae doubt but they were fain o' ither,
An' unco pack an' thick thegither;
Wi' social nose whyles snuff'd an' snowket;
40 Whiles mice and modewurks they howket;
Whyles scour'd awa in lang excursion,
An' worry'd ither in diversion;
Till tir'd at last wi' mony a farce,
They set them down upon their arse,
45 An' there began a lang digression
About the *lords o' the creation.*

CAESAR

I've aften wonder'd, honest Luath,
What sort o' life poor dogs like you have;
An' when the *gentry* life I saw,
50 What way *poor bodies* liv'd ava.

Our *Laird* gets in his racked rents,
His coals, his kane, an' a' his stents:
He rises when he likes himsel;
His flunkies answer at the bell;
55 He ca's his coach; he ca's his horse;
He draws a bonie, silken purse
As lang's my tail, whare thro' the steeks,
The yellow letter'd *Geordie* keeks.

Frae morn to een it's nought but toiling,
60 At baking, roasting, frying, boiling;
An' tho' the gentry first are steghan,
Yet e'en the *ha' folk* fill their peghan
Wi' sauce, ragouts, and suc like trashtrie,
That's little short o' downright wastrie.
65 Our Whipper-in, wee blastiet wonner,
Poor, worthless elf, it eats a dinner,
Better than ony *Tenant-man*
His Honor has in a' the lan':
And what poor *Cot-folk* pit their painch in,
70 I own it's past my comprehension.

LUATH

Trowth, Caesar, whyles they're fash't enough;
A *Cotter* howkan in a sheugh,
Wi' dirty stanes biggan a dyke,
Bairan a quarry, an' sic like,
75 Himsel, a wife, he thus sustains,
A smytrie o' wee, duddie weans,
An' nought but his han'-duark, to keep
Them right an' tight in thack an' raep.

An' when they meet wi' sair disasters,
80 Like loss o' health or want o' masters,
Ye maist wad think, a wee touch langer,
An' they maun starve o' cauld and hunger:
But how it comes, I never kent yet,
They're maistly wonderfu' contented;
85 An' buirdly chiels, and clever hizzies,
Are bred in sic a way as this is.

CAESAR

But then, to see how ye're negleket,
How huff'd, an' cuff'd, an' disrespeket!
Lord man, our gentry care as little
90 For *delvers*, *ditchers*, an sic cattle;
They gang as saucy by poor folk,
As I wad by a stinkan brock.

I've notic'd, on our Laird's *court-day*,
An' mony a time my heart's been wae,
95 Poor *tenant bodies*, scant o' cash,
How they maun thole a *factor's* snash;
He'll stamp an' threaten, curse an' swear,
He'll *apprehend* them, *poind* their gear;
While they maun stan', wi' aspect humble,
100 An' hear it a', an' fear an' tremble!

I see how folk live that hae riches;
But surely poor-folk maun be wretches!

LUATH

They're no sae wretched's ane wad think;
Tho' constantly on poortith's brink,
105 They're sae accustom'd wi' the sight,
The view o't gies them little fright.

Then chance and fortune are sae guided,
They're ay in less or mair provided;
An' tho' fatigu'd wi' close employment,
110 A blink o' rest's a sweet enjoyment.

The dearest comfort o' their lives,
Their grushie weans an' faithfu' wives;
The *prattling things* are just their pride,
That sweetens a' their fire-side.

115 An' whyles twalpennie-worth o' *nappy*
Can mak the bodies unco happy;
They lay aside their private cares,
To mind the Kirk and State affairs;
They'll talk o' *patronage* an' *priests*,
120 Wi' kindling fury i' their breasts,
Or tell what new taxation's comin,
An' ferlie at the folk in Lon'on.

As bleak-fac'd Hallowmass returns,
They get the jovial, rantan *Kirns*,
125 When *rural life*, of ev'ry station,
Unite in common recreation;
Love blinks, Wit slaps, an' social Mirth
Forgets there's *care* upo' the earth.

That *merry day* the year begins,
130 They bar the door on frosty win's;
The nappy reeks wi' mantling ream,
An' sheds a heart–inspiring steam;
The luntan pipe, an' sneeshin mill,
Are handed round wi' right guid will;
135 The cantie auld folks, crackan crouse,
The young anes rantan thro' the house –
My heart has been sae fain to see them,
That I for joy hae barket wi' them.

Still it's owre true that ye hae said,
140 Sic game is now owre aften play'd;
There's monie a creditable *stock*
O' decent, honest, fawsont folk,
Are riven out baith root an' branch,
Some rascal's pridefu' greed to quench,
145 Wha thinks to knit himself the faster
In favor wi' some *gentle Master*,
Wha aiblens thrang a *parliamentin*,
For Britain's guid his saul indentin –

CAESAR

Haith lad, ye little ken about it;
150 *For Britain's guid!* guid faith! I doubt it.
Say rather, gaun as Premiers lead him,
An' saying *aye* or *no*'s they bid him:
At operas an' plays parading,
Mortgaging, gambling, masquerading:
155 Or maybe in a frolic daft,
To Hague or Calais takes a waft,
To make a *tour* an' tak a whirl,
To learn *bon ton* an' see the worl'.

There at Vienna or Versailles,
160 He rives his father's auld entails,
Or by Madrid he takes the rout,
To thrum *guittars* an' fecht wi' nowt;
Or down *Italian vista* startles,
Wh-re-hunting amang groves o' myrtles:
165 Then bowses drumlie *German-water*,
To mak himsel look fair and fatter,
An' purge the bitter ga's an' cankers,
O' curst *Venetian* bores and chancres.

For Britain's guid! for her destruction!
170 Wi' dissipation, feud an' faction!

LUATH

Hech man! dear sirs! is that the gate,
They waste sae mony a braw estate!
Are we sae foughten and harass'd
For gear to gang that gate at last!

175   O would they stay aback frae courts,
An' please themsels wi' countra sports,
It wad for ev'ry ane be better,
The *Laird*, the *Tenant*, an' the *Cotter*!
For thae frank, rantan, ramblan billies,
180   Fient haet o' them's ill-hearted fellows;
Except for breakin o' their timmer,
Or speakin lightly o' their *Limmer*,
Or shootin of a hare or moorcock,
The ne'er-a-bit they're ill to poor folk.

185   But will ye tell me, master Caesar,
Sure *great folk*'s life's a life o' pleasure?
Nae cauld nor hunger e'er can steer them,
The vera thought o't need na fear them.

CAESAR

Lord man, were ye but whyles where I am,
190   The *gentles* ye wad neer envy them!

It's true, they need na starve or sweat,
Thro' Winter's cauld, or Summer's heat;
They've nae sair-wark to craze their banes,
An' fill *auld-age* wi' grips an' granes;
195   But *human-bodies* are sic fools,
For a' their colledges an' schools,
That when nae *real* ills perplex them,
They *mak* enow themsels to vex them;
An' ay the less they hae to sturt them,
200   In like proportion, less will hurt them.

A country fellow at the pleugh,
His *acre's* till'd, he's right eneugh;
A country girl at her wheel,
Her *dizzen's* done, she's unco weel;
205   But Gentlemen, an' Ladies warst,
Wi' ev'n down *want o' wark* are curst.
They loiter, lounging, lank an' lazy;
Tho' deil-haet ails them, yet uneasy;
Their days, insipid, dull an' tasteless,
210   Their nights, unquiet, lang an' restless.

An ev'n their sports, their balls an' races,
Their galloping thro' public places,
There's sic parade, sic pomp an' art,
The joy can scarcely reach the heart.

215   The *Men* cast out in *party-matches*,
Then sowther a' in deep debauches.
Ae night, they're mad wi' drink an' wh-ring,
Niest day their life is past enduring.

The *Ladies* arm-in-arm in clusters,
220   As great an' gracious a' as sisters;
But hear their *absent thoughts* o' ither,
They're a run deils an' jads thegither.
Whyles, owre the wee bit cup an' platie,
They sip the *scandal-potion* pretty;
225   Or lee-lang nights, wi' crabbet leuks,
Pore owre the devil's *pictur'd beuks*;
Stake on a chance a farmer's stackyard,
An' cheat like ony *unhang'd blackguard*.

There's some exceptions, man an' woman;
230   But this is Gentry's life in common.

By this, the sun was out o' sight,
An' darker gloamin brought the night:
The *bum-clock* humm'd wi' lazy drone,
The kye stood rowtan i' the loan;
235   When up they gat an' shook their lugs,
Rejoic'd they were na *men* but *dogs*;
An' each took off his several way,
Resolv'd to meet some ither day.

The Cotter's Saturday Night

INSCRIBED TO R. AIKEN, ESQ.

Let not Ambition mock their useful toil,
Their homely joys, and destiny obscure;
Nor Grandeur hear, with a disdainful smile,
The short and simple annals of the Poor.
                                            Gray

My lov'd, my honor'd, much respected friend,
    No mercenary Bard his homage pays;
With honest pride, I scorn each selfish end,
    My dearest meed, a friend's esteem and praise:
5   To you I sing, in simple Scottish lays,
    The *lowly train* in life's sequester'd scene;
The native feelings strong, the guileless ways,
    What Aiken in a *cottage* would have been;
Ah! tho' his worth unknown, far happier there I ween!

10 November chill blaws loud wi' angry sugh;
    The short'ning winter-day is near a close;
The miry beasts retreating frae the pleugh;
    The black'ning trains o' craws to their repose:
The toil-worn Cotter frae his labor goes,
15   *This night* his weekly moil is at an end,
Collects his *spades*, his *mattocks* and his *hoes*,
    Hoping the *morn* in ease and rest to spend,
And weary, o'er the moor, his course does hameward bend.

At length his lonely *Cot* appears in view,
20   Beneath the shelter of an aged tree;
The expectant *wee-things*, toddlan, stacher through
    To meet their *Dad*, wi' flichterin noise and glee.
His wee-bit ingle, blinkan bonilie,
    His clean hearth-stane, his thriftie *Wifie's* smile,
25 The *lisping infant*, prattling on his knee,
    Does a' his weary *kiaugh* and care beguile,
And makes him quite forget his labor and his toil.

Belyve, the *elder bairns* come drapping in,
　　At *service* out, amang the farmers roun';
30　Some ca' the pleugh, some herd, some tentie rin
　　A cannie errand to a neebor town:
Their eldest hope, their *Jenny*, woman-grown,
　　In youthfu' bloom, love sparkling in her e'e,
Comes hame, perhaps, to shew a braw new gown,
35　Or deposite her sair-won penny-fee,
To help her *Parents* dear, if they in hardship be.

Wi' joy unfeign'd, *brothers* and *sisters* meet,
　　And each for other's weelfare kindly spiers:
The social hours, swift-wing'd, unnotic'd fleet;
40　Each tells the uncos that he sees or hears;
The Parents partial eye their hopeful years;
　　Anticipation forward points the view;
The *Mother*, wi' her needle and her sheers,
　　Gars auld claes look amaist as weel's the new;
45　The *Father* mixes a' wi' admonition due.

Their Master's and their Mistress's command,
　　The *younkers* a' are warned to obey;
And mind their labors wi' an eydent hand,
　　And ne'er, tho' out o' sight, to jauk or play:
50　'And O! be sure to fear the Lord alway!
　　And mind your *duty*, duely, morn and night!
Lest in temptation's path ye gang astray,
　　Implore His *counsel* and assisting *might*:
They never sought in vain that sought the Lord aright.'

55　But hark! a rap comes gently to the door;
　　Jenny, wha kens the meaning o' the same,
Tells how a neebor lad came o'er the moor,
　　To do some errands, and convoy her hame.
The wily Mother sees the *conscious flame*
60　Sparkle in *Jenny's* e'e, and flush her cheek,
With heart-struck, anxious care enquires his name,
　　While *Jenny* hafflins is afraid to speak;
Weel-pleas'd the Mother hears, it's nae wild,
　　　　worthless *Rake*.

With kindly welcome, *Jenny* brings him ben;
65   A *strappan youth*; he takes the Mother's eye;
Blythe *Jenny* sees the *visit's* no ill taen;
    The Father cracks of horses, pleughs and kye.
The *Youngster's* artless heart o'erflows wi' joy,
    But blate and laithfu', scarce can weel behave;
70   The Mother, wi' a woman's wiles, can spy
    What makes the *youth* sae bashfu' and sae grave;
Weel-pleas'd to think her *bairn's* respected like the lave.

O happy love! where love like this is found!
    O heart-felt raptures! bliss beyond compare!
75   I've paced much this weary, *mortal round*,
    And sage Experience bids me this declare –
    'If Heaven a draught of heavenly pleasure spare,
    One *cordial* in this melancholy *Vale*,
    'Tis when a youthful, loving, *modest* pair,
80   In other's arms, breathe out the tender tale,
Beneath the milk-white thorn that scents the ev'ning gale.'

Is there, in human form, that bears a heart –
    A Wretch! a Villain! lost to love and truth!
That can, with studied, sly, ensnaring art,
85   Betray sweet Jenny's unsuspecting youth?
Curse on his perjur'd arts! dissembling smooth!
    Are *Honor*, *Virtue*, *Conscience*, all exil'd?
Is there no pity, no relenting ruth,
    Points to the parents fondling o'er their child?
90   Then paints the *ruin'd Maid*, and *their* distraction wild!

But now the supper crowns their simple board,
    The healsome *porritch*, chief of Scotia's food:
The soupe their *only Hawkie* does afford,
    That 'yont the hallan snugly chows her cood:
95   The *Dame* brings forth, in complimental mood,
    To grace the lad, her weel-hain'd kebbuck, fell,
And aft he's prest, and aft he ca's it guid;
    The frugal *Wifie*, garrulous, will tell,
How 'twas a towmond auld, sin' lint was i' the bell.

100 The chearfu' supper done, wi' serious face,
　　They, round the ingle, form a circle wide;
　The Sire turns o'er, with patriarchal grace,
　　The big *ha'-Bible*, ance his *Father's* pride:
　His bonnet rev'rently is laid aside,
105　　His *lyart haffets* wearing thin and bare;
　Those strains that once did sweet in Zion glide,
　　He wales a portion with judicious care;
　'*And let us worship God*!' he says with solemn air.

　They chant their artless notes in simple guise;
110　　They tune their *hearts*, by far the noblest aim:
　Perhaps *Dundee's* wild warbling measures rise,
　　Or plaintive *Martyrs*, worthy of the name;
　Or noble *Elgin* beets the heaven-ward flame,
　　The sweetest far of Scotia's holy lays:
115 Compar'd with these, *Italian trills* are tame;
　　The tickl'd ears no heart-felt raptures raise;
　Nae unison hae they, with our Creator's praise.

　The priest-like Father reads the sacred page,
　　How *Abram* was the Friend of God on high;
120 Or, *Moses* bade eternal warfare wage,
　　With *Amalek's* ungracious progeny;
　Or how the *royal Bard* did groaning lye,
　　Beneath the stroke of Heaven's avenging ire;
　Or *Job's* pathetic plaint, and wailing cry;
125　　Or rapt *Isaiah's* wild, seraphic fire;
　Or other *Holy Seers* that tune the *sacred lyre*.

　Perhaps the *Christian volume* is the theme,
　　How *guiltless blood* for *guilty man* was shed;
　How He, who bore in heaven the second name,
130　　Had not on earth whereon to lay His head;
　How His first *followers* and *servants* sped;
　　The *precepts sage* they wrote to many a land:
　How *he*, who lone in *Patmos* banished,
　　Saw in the sun a mighty angel stand;
135 And heard great *Bab'lon's* doom pronounc'd by
　　　Heaven's command.

Then kneeling down to Heaven's Eternal King,
    The *Saint*, the *Father*, and the *Husband* prays:
Hope 'springs exultant on triumphant wing,'*
    That *thus* they all shall meet in future days:
140 There, ever bask in *uncreated rays*,
    No more to sigh, or shed the bitter tear,
Together hymning their Creator's praise,
    In *such society*, yet still more dear;
While circling time moves round in an eternal sphere.

145 Compar'd with *this*, how poor Religion's pride,
    In all the pomp of *method*, and of *art*,
When men display to congregations wide,
    Devotion's ev'ry grace, except the *heart*!
The Power, incens'd, the pageant will desert,
150   The pompous strain, the sacerdotal stole;
But haply, in some *cottage* far apart,
    May hear, well pleas'd, the language of the *soul*;
And in His *Book of Life* the inmates poor enroll.

Then homeward all take off their sev'ral way;
155   The youngling *cottagers* retire to rest:
The parent-pair their *secret homage* pay,
    And proffer up to Heaven the warm request,
That He who stills the *raven's* clam'rous nest,
    And decks the *lily* fair in flow'ry pride,
160 Would, in the way *His Wisdom* sees the best,
    For *them* and for their *little ones* provide;
But chiefly, in their hearts with *Grace divine* preside.

From scenes like these, old Scotia's grandeur springs,
    That makes her lov'd at home, rever'd abroad:
165 Princes and lords are but the breath of kings,
    'An honest man's the noblest work of God.'
And *certes*, in fair virtue's heavenly road,
    The *Cottage* leaves the *Palace* far behind:
What is a lordling's pomp? a cumbrous load,
170   Disguising oft the *wretch* of human kind,
Studied in arts of Hell, in wickedness refin'd!

* Pope's Windsor Forest. [RB]

O Scotia! my dear, my native soil!
 For whom my warmest wish to heaven is sent!
Long may thy hardy sons of *rustic toil*,
175 Be blest with health, and peace, and sweet content!
And O may Heaven their simple lives prevent
 From *luxury's* contagion, weak and vile!
Then howe'er *crowns* and *coronets* be rent,
 A *virtuous populace* may rise the while,
180 And stand a wall of fire around their much-lov'd Isle.

O Thou! who pour'd the *patriotic tide*,
 That stream'd thro' great, unhappy Wallace' heart;
Who dar'd to, nobly, stem tyrannic pride,
 Or *nobly die*, the second glorious part:
185 (The Patriot's God, peculiarly thou art,
 His *friend, inspirer, guardian* and *reward*!)
O never, never Scotia's realm desert,
 But still the *Patriot*, and the *Patriot-Bard*,
In bright succession raise, her *Ornament* and *Guard*!

*The Auld Farmer's New-Year-Morning Salutation
to His Auld Mare, Maggie, on Giving Her the
Accustomed Ripp of Corn to Hansel in the New-
Year*

A *Guid New-year* I wish you Maggie!
Hae, there's a ripp to thy auld baggie;
Tho' thou's howe-backet, now, an' knaggie,
    I've seen the day,
5 Thou could hae gaen like ony staggie
     Out owre the lay.

Tho' now thou's dowie, stiff an' crazy,
And thy auld hide as white's a daisie,
I've seen thee dappl't, sleek an' glaizie,
    A bonie gray:
10 He should been tight that daur't to *raize* thee,
     Ance in a day.

Thou ance was i' the foremost rank,
A *filly* buirdly, steeve an' swank,
15   An' set weel down a shapely shank,
                    As e'er tread yird;
An' could hae flown out owre a stank,
                    Like onie bird.

It's now some nine-an'-twenty-year,
20   Sin' thou was my *Guidfather's meere*;
He gied me thee, o' tocher clear,
                    An' fifty mark;
Tho' it was sma', 'twas *weel-won* gear,
                    An' thou was stark.

25   When first I gaed to woo my *Jenny*,
Ye then was trottan wi' your Minnie:
Tho' ye was trickie, slee an' funnie,
                    Ye ne'er was donsie;
But hamely, tawie, quiet an' cannie,
30   An' unco sonsie.

That *day*, ye pranc'd wi' muckle pride,
When ye bure hame my bonie *Bride*:
An' sweet an' gracefu' she did ride
                    Wi' maiden air!
35   Kyle-Stewart I could bragged wide,
                    For sic a *pair*.

Tho' now ye dow but hoyte and hoble,
An' wintle like a saumont-coble,
That day, ye was a jinker noble,
40   For heels an' win'!
An' ran them till they a' did wauble,
                    Far, far behin'!

When thou an' I were young an' skiegh,
An' *stable-meals* at Fairs were driegh,
45   How thou wad prance, an' snore, an' scriegh,
                    An' tak the road!
Towns-bodies ran, an' stood abiegh,
                    An' ca't thee mad.

When thou was corn't, an' I was mellow,
50 We took the road ay like a swallow:
At *Brooses* thou had ne'er a fellow,
                  For pith an' speed;
But ev'ry tail thou pay't them hollow,
                  Whare'er thou gaed.

55 The sma', droot-rumpl't, hunter cattle,
Might aiblens waur't thee for a brattle;
But *sax Scotch mile*, thou try't their mettle,
                  And gart them whaizle:
Nae whip nor spur, but just a wattle
60   O' saugh or hazle.

Thou was a noble *Fittie-lan'*,
As e'er in tug or tow was drawn!
Aft thee an' I, in aught hours gaun,
                  On guid March-weather,
65 Hae turn'd *sax-rood* beside our han',
                  For days thegither.

Thou never braing't, an' fetch't, an' fliskit,
But thy *auld tail* thou wad hae whisket,
An' spread abreed thy weel-fill'd *brisket*,
70   Wi' pith an' pow'r,
Till sprittie knowes wad rair't an' risket,
                  An' slypet owre.

When frosts lay lang, an' snaws were deep,
An' threaten'd *labor* back to keep,
75 I gied thy *cog* a wee-bit heap
                  Aboon the timmer;
I ken'd my *Maggie* wad na sleep
                  For that, or Simmer.

In *cart* or *car* thou never reestet;
80 The steyest brae thou wad hae fac'd it;
Thou never lap, an' sten't, an' breastet,
                  Then stood to blaw;
But just thy step a wee thing hastet,
                  Thou snoov't awa.

85   My pleugh is now thy *bairn-time* a';
     Four gallant brutes, as e'er did draw;
     Forby sax mae, I've sell't awa,
                         That thou hast nurst:
     They drew me thretteen pund an' twa,
90   The vera warst.

     Monie a sair daurk we twa hae wrought,
     An' wi' the weary warl' fought!
     An' monie an' *anxious day*, I thought
                         We wad be beat!
95   Yet here to *crazy Age* we're brought,
                         Wi' something yet.

     An' think na, my auld, trusty *Servan*',
     That now perhaps thou's less deservin,
     An' thy *auld days* may end in starvin',
100   For my last fow,
     A heapet *stimpart*, I'll reserve ane
                         Laid by for you.

     We've worn to crazy years thegither;
     We'll toyte about wi' ane anither;
105 Wi' tentie care I'll flit thy tether,
                         To some hain'd rig,
     Where ye may nobly rax your leather,
                         Wi sma' fatigue.

To James Smith

Friendship, mysterious cement of the soul!
Sweet'ner of Life, and solder of Society!
I owe thee much –
                    Blair

Dear Smith, the sleest, pawkie thief,
That e'er attempted stealth or rief,
Ye surely hae some warlock-breef
                    Owre human hearts;
5   For ne'er a bosom yet was prief
                    Against your arts.

For me, I swear by sun an' moon,
And ev'ry star that blinks aboon,
Ye've cost me twenty pair o' shoon
10   Just gaun to see you;
And ev'ry ither pair that's done,
                    Mair taen I'm wi' you.

That auld, capricious carlin, *Nature*,
To mak amends for scrimpet stature,
15   She's turn'd you off, a human-creature
                    On her *first* plan,
And in her freaks, on ev'ry feature,
                    She's wrote, *the Man*.

Just now I've taen the fit o' rhyme,
20   My barmie noddle's working prime,
My fancy yerket up sublime,
                    Wi' hasty summon:
Hae ye a leisure-moment's time
                    To hear what's comin?

25   Some rhyme a neebor's name to lash;
Some rhyme (vain thought!) for needfu' cash;
Some rhyme to court the countra clash,
                    An' raise a din;
For me, an *aim* I never fash;
30   I rhyme for *fun*.

The star that rules my luckless lot,
Has fated me the russet coat,
An' damn'd my fortune to the groat;
    But, in requit,
35 Has blest me with a *random-shot*
     O' countra wit.

This while my notion's taen a sklent,
To try my fate in guid, black *prent*;
But still the mair I'm that way bent,
40   Something cries, 'Hoolie!'
I red you, honest man, tak tent!
    Ye'll shaw your folly.

'There's ither Poets, much your betters,
Far seen in *Greek*, deep men o' *letters*,
45 Hae thought they had ensur'd their debtors,
    A' future ages;
Now moths deform in shapeless tatters,
    Their unknown pages.'

Then farewel hopes of laurel-boughs,
50 To garland my poetic brows!
Henceforth, I'll rove where busy ploughs
    Are whistling thrang,
An' teach the lanely heights an' howes
    My rustic sang.

55 I'll wander on wi' tentless heed,
How never-halting moments speed,
Till fate shall snap the brittle thread;
    Then, all unknown,
I'll lay me with th' *inglorious dead*,
60   Forgot and gone!

But why o' Death begin a tale?
Just now we're living sound an' hale;
Then top and maintop croud the sail,
    Heave *Care* o'er-side!
65 And large, before Enjoyment's gale,
    Let's tak the tide.

This life, sae far's I understand,
Is a' enchanted fairy-land,
Where Pleasure is the magic-wand,
70   That wielded right,
Maks hours like minutes, hand in hand,
                     Dance by fu' light.

The *magic-wand* then let us wield;
For ance that five an' forty's speel'd,
75 See crazy, weary, joyless Eild,
                     Wi' wrinkl'd face,
Comes hostan, hirplan owre the field,
                     Wi' creeping pace.

When ance *life's day* draws near the gloamin,
80 Then fareweel vacant, careless roamin;
An' fareweel chearfu' tankards foamin,
                     An' social noise;
An' fareweel dear, deluding woman,
                     The joy of joys!

85 O *Life*! how pleasant in thy morning,
Young Fancy's rays the hills adorning!
Cold-pausing Caution's lesson scorning,
                     We frisk away,
Like school-boys, at th' expected warning,
90   To joy and play.

We wander there, we wander here,
We eye the *rose* upon the brier,
Unmindful that the *thorn* is near,
                     Among the leaves;
95 And tho' the puny wound appear,
                     Short while it grieves.

Some, lucky, find a flow'ry spot,
For which they never toil'd nor swat;
They drink the *sweet* and eat the *fat*,
100   But care or pain;
And haply eye the barren hut,
                    With high disdain.

With steady aim, some Fortune chase;
Keen hope does ev'ry sinew brace,
105 Thro' fair, thro' foul, they urge the race,
                    And sieze the prey:
Then canie, in some cozie place,
                    They close the *day*.

And others, like your humble servan',
110 *Poor wights*! nae rules or roads observin;
To right or left, eternal swervin,
                    They zig-zag on;
Till curst with age, obscure an' starvin,
                    They aften groan.

115 Alas! what bitter toil an' straining –
But truce wi' peevish, poor complaining!
Is Fortune's fickle *Luna* waning?
                    E'en let her gang!
Beneath what light she has remaining,
120   Let's sing our sang.

My pen I here fling to the door,
And kneel, 'Ye *Pow'rs*,' and warm implore,
'Tho' I should wander *Terra* o'er,
                    In all her climes,
125 Grant me but this, I ask no more,
                    Ay rowth o' rhymes.

'Gie dreeping roasts to *countra Lairds*,
Till icicles hing frae their beards;
Gie fine braw claes to fine *Life-guards*,
130   And *Maids of Honor*;
And yill and whisky gie to *Cairds*,
                    Until they sconner.

'A *Title*, Dempster merits it;
A *Garter* gie to Willie Pitt;
135 Gie Wealth to some be-ledger'd Cit,
          In cent per cent;
But give me real, sterling Wit,
          And I'm content.

'While ye are pleas'd to keep me hale,
140 I'll sit down o'er my scanty meal,
Be't *water-brose* or *muslin-kail*,
          Wi' chearfu' face,
As lang's the Muses dinna fail
          To say the grace.'

145 An anxious e'e I never throws
Behint my lug, or by my nose;
I jouk beneath Misfortune's blows
          As weel's I may;
Sworn foe to *sorrow*, *care*, and *prose*,
150   I rhyme away.

O ye, douse folk, that live by rule,
Grave, tideless-blooded, calm and cool,
Compar'd wi' you – O fool! fool! fool!
          How much unlike!
155 Your hearts are just a standing pool,
          Your lives, a dyke!

Nae hare-brain'd, sentimental traces,
In your unletter'd, nameless faces!
In *arioso* trills and graces,
160   Ye never stray,
But *gravissimo*, solemn basses
          Ye hum away.

Ye are sae *grave*, nae doubt ye're *wise*;
Nae ferly tho' ye do despise
165 The hairum-scairum, ram-stam boys,
          The rattling squad:
I see ye upward cast your eyes –
         – Ye ken the road –

Whilst I – but I shall haud me there –
170   Wi' you I'll scarce gang *ony where* –
Then *Jamie*, I shall say nae mair,
                    But quat my sang,
Content *with you* to mak a *pair*,
                    Whare'er I gang.

Scotch Drink

Gie him strong Drink *until he wink,*
    That's sinking in despair;
And liquor *guid to fire his bluid,*
    That's prest wi' grief an' care;
There let him bowse an' deep carouse,
    Wi' bumpers flowing o'er,
Till he forgets his loves *or* debts,
    An' minds his griefs no more.
        Solomon's Proverbs, xxxi. 6, 7

Let other Poets raise a fracas
'Bout vines, an' wines, an' druken *Bacchus*,
An' crabbed names an' stories wrack us,
                    An' grate our lug,
5   I sing the juice *Scotch bear* can mak us,
                    In glass or jug.

O thou, my Muse! guid, auld Scotch Drink!
Whether thro' wimplin worms thou jink,
Or richly brown, ream owre the brink,
                    In glorious faem,
10   Inspire me, till I *lisp* an' *wink*,
                    To sing thy name!

Let husky Wheat the haughs adorn,
And Aits set up their awnie horn,
15   An' Pease an' Beans, at e'en or morn,
                    Perfume the plain,
Leeze me on thee *John Barleycorn*,
                    Thou king o' grain!

On thee aft Scotland chows her cood,
20   In souple scones, the wale o' food!
Or tumbling in the boiling flood
          Wi' kail an' beef;
But when thou pours thy strong *heart's blood*,
          There thou shines chief.

25 Food fills the wame, an' keeps us livin;
Tho' life's a gift no worth receivin,
When heavy-dragg'd wi' pine an' grievin;
          But oil'd by thee,
The wheels o' life gae down-hill, scrievin,
30   Wi' rattlin glee.

Thou clears the head o' doited Lear,
Thou chears the heart o' drooping Care;
Thou strings the nerves o' Labor-sair,
          At's weary toil;
35 Thou even brightens dark Despair,
          Wi' gloomy smile.

Aft, clad in massy, siller weed,
Wi' Gentles thou erects thy head;
Yet humbly kind, in time o' need,
40   The *poor man's* wine;
His wee drap pirratch or his bread,
          Thou kitchens fine.

Thou art the life o' public haunts;
But thee, what were our fairs and rants?
45 Ev'n godly meetings o' the saunts,
          By thee inspir'd,
When gaping they besiege the *tents*,
          Are doubly fir'd.

That *merry night* we get the corn in,
50 O sweetly, then, thou reams the horn in!
Or reekan on a *New-year-mornin*
          In cog or bicker,
An' just a wee drap *sp'ritual burn* in,
          An' gusty sucker!

55   When Vulcan gies his bellys breath,
        An' Ploughmen gather wi' their graith,
        O rare! to see thee fizz an' freath
                    I' the lugget caup!
        Then *Burnewin* comes on like death
60   At ev'ry chap.

        Nae mercy, then, for airn or steel;
        The brawnie, banie, ploughman-chiel
        Brings hard owrehip, wi' sturdy wheel,
                    The strong forehammer,
65   Till block an' studdie ring an' reel
                    Wi' dinsome clamour.

        When skirling weanies see the light,
        Thou maks the gossips clatter bright,
        How fumbling coofs their dearies slight,
70   Wae worth them for't!
        While healths gae round to him wha, *tight*,
                    Gies famous sport.

        When neebors anger at a plea,
        An' just as wud as wud can be,
75   How easy can the *barley-brie*
                    Cement the quarrel!
        It's aye the cheapest lawyer's fee
                    To taste the barrel.

        Alake! that e'er my *Muse* has reason,
80   To wyte her countrymen wi' treason!
        But monie daily weet their weason
                    Wi' liquors nice,
        An' hardly, in a winter season,
                    E'er spier her price.

85   Wae worth that *Brandy*, burnan trash!
        Fell source o' monie a pain an' brash!
        Twins monie a poor, doylt, druken hash
                    O' half his days;
        An' sends, beside, auld *Scotland's* cash
90   To her warst faes.

Ye Scots wha wish auld Scotland well,
Ye chief, to you my tale I tell,
Poor, plackless devils like *mysel*,
        It sets you ill,
95 Wi' bitter, dearthfu' *wines* to mell,
        Or foreign gill.

May *gravels* round his blather wrench,
An' *gouts* torment him, inch by inch,
Wha twists his gruntle wi' a glunch
100   O' sour disdain,
Out owre a glass o' *Whisky-punch*
        Wi' honest men!

O *Whisky*! soul o' plays an' pranks!
Accept a *Bardie's* gratefu' thanks!
105 When wanting thee, what tuneless cranks
        Are my poor verses!
Thou comes – they rattle i' their ranks
        At ither's arses!

Thee, *Ferintosh*! O sadly lost!
110 Scotland lament frae coast to coast!
Now colic-grips, an' barkin hoast,
        May kill us a';
For loyal Forbes' *charter'd boast*
        Is ta'en awa!

115 Thae curst horse-leeches o' th' Excise,
Wha mak the *Whisky stells* their prize!
Haud up thy han' *Deil*! ance, twice, *thrice*!
        There, sieze the blinkers!
An' bake them up in brunstane pies
120   For poor damn'd *Drinkers*.

Fortune, if thou'll but gie me still
Hale breeks, a scone, an' *whisky gill*,
An' rowth o' *rhyme* to rave at will,
        Tak a' the rest,
125 An' deal't about as thy blind skill
        Directs thee best.

Address to the Deil

O Prince, O chief of many throned pow'rs,
That led th' embattl'd Seraphim to war –
                                              Milton

O Thou, whatever title suit thee!
Auld Hornie, Satan, Nick, or Clootie!
Wha in yon cavern grim an' sootie,
                    Clos'd under hatches,
5   Spairges about the brunstane cootie,
                    To scaud poor wretches!

Hear me, *auld Hangie*, for a wee,
An' let poor, *damned bodies* bee;
I'm sure sma' pleasure it can gie,
10   Ev'n to a *deil*,
To skelp an' scaud poor dogs like me,
                    An' hear us squeel!

Great is thy pow'r, an' great thy fame;
Far kend an' noted is thy name;
15   An' tho' yon *lowan heugh's* thy hame,
                    Thou travels far;
An' faith! thou's neither lag nor lame,
                    Nor blate nor scaur.

Whyles, ranging like a roaran lion,
20   For prey, a' holes an' corners tryin;
Whyles, on the strong-wing'd tempest flyin,
                    Tirlan the *kirks*;
Whyles, in the human bosom pryin,
                    Unseen thou lurks.

25   I've heard my rev'rend *Graunie* say,
In lanely glens ye like to stray;
Or where auld, ruin'd castles, gray,
                    Nod to the moon,
Ye fright the nightly wand'rer's way,
30   Wi' eldritch croon.

When twilight did my *Graunie* summon,
To say her prayers, douse, honest woman!
Aft 'yont the dyke she's heard you bumman,
    Wi' eerie drone;
35 Or, rustling, thro' the boortries coman,
    Wi' heavy groan.

Ae dreary, windy, winter night,
The stars shot down wi' sklentan light,
Wi' you, *myself*, I gat a fright,
40   Ayont the lough;
Ye, like a *rass-buss*, stood in sight,
    Wi' waving sugh.

The cudgel in my nieve did shake,
Each bristl'd hair stood like a stake,
45 When wi' an eldritch, stoor *quaick*, *quaick*,
    Amang the springs,
Awa ye squatter'd like a *drake*,
    On whistling wings.

Let *Warlocks* grim, an' wither'd *Hags*,
50 Tell how wi' you on ragweed nags,
They skim the muirs an' dizzy crags,
    Wi' wicked speed;
And in kirk-yards renew their leagues,
    Owre howcket dead.

55 Thence, countra wives, wi' toil an' pain,
May plunge an' plunge the *kirn* in vain;
For Oh! the yellow treasure's taen
    By witching skill;
An' dawtet, twal-pint *Hawkie's* gane
60   As yell's the bill.

Thence, mystic knots mak great abuse,
On *Young-Guidmen*, fond, keen an' croose;
When the best *wark-lume* i' the house,
    By cantraip wit,
65 Is instant made no worth a louse,
    Just at the bit.

When thowes dissolve the snawy hoord,
An' float the jinglan icy boord,
Then *water-kelpies* haunt the foord,
70   By your direction,
An' nighted trav'llers are allur'd
                    To their destruction.

An' aft your moss-traversing *spunkies*
Decoy the wight that late an' drunk is:
75 The bleezan, curst, mischievous monkies
                    Delude his eyes,
Till in some miry slough he sunk is,
                    Ne'er mair to rise.

When Mason's mystic *word* an' *grip*,
80 In storms an' tempests raise you up,
Some cock or cat, your rage maun stop,
                    Or, strange to tell!
The *youngest brother* ye wad whip
                    Aff straught to Hell.

85 Lang syne in Eden's bonie yard,
When youthfu' lovers first were pair'd,
An' all the Soul of Love they shar'd,
                    The raptur'd hour,
Sweet on the fragrant, flow'ry swaird,
90   In shady bow'r.

Then you, ye auld, snick-drawing dog!
Ye cam to Paradise incog,
An' play'd on man a cursed brogue,
                    (Black be your fa'!)
95 An' gied the infant warld a shog,
                    'Maist ruin'd a'.

D'ye mind that day, when in a bizz,
Wi' reeket duds, an' reestet gizz,
Ye did present your smoutie phiz,
100   'Mang better folk,
An' sklented on the *man of Uzz*,
                    Your spitefu' joke?

An how ye gat him i' your thrall,
An' brak him out o' house an' hal',
105 While scabs an' botches did him gall,
        Wi' bitter claw,
An' lows'd his ill-tongu'd, wicked *scrawl*
        Was warst ava?

But a' your doings to rehearse,
110 Your wily snares an' fechtin fierce,
Sin' that day *Michael did you pierce,
        Down to this time,
Wad ding a *Lallan* tongue, or *Erse*,
        In Prose or Rhyme.

115 An' now, auld *Cloots*, I ken ye're thinkan,
A certain *Bardie's* rantin, drinkin,
Some luckless hour will send him linkan,
        To your black pit;
But faith! he'll turn a corner jinkan,
120   An' cheat you yet.

But fare-you-weel, auld *Nickie-ben*!
O wad ye tak a thought an' men'!
Ye aiblens might – I dinna ken –
        Still hae a *stake* –
125 I'm wae to think upo' yon den,
        Ev'n for your sake!

Extempore to Gavin Hamilton. Stanzas on Naething

To you, Sir, this summons I've sent,
    Pray, whip till the pownie is fraething;
But if you demand what I want,
    I honestly answer you – naething. –

* Vide Milton, [*Paradise Lost*] Book 6th. [RB]

5   Ne'er scorn a poor Poet like me,
        For idly just living and breathing,
    While people of every degree
        Are busy employed about – naething. –

    Poor Centum per centum may fast,
10   And grumble his hurdies their claithing;
    He'll find, when the balance is cast,
        He's gane to the devil for – naething. –

    The Courtier cringes and bows,
        Ambition has likewise its plaything;
15 A Coronet beams on his brows,
        And what is a Coronet? – naething. –

    Some quarrel the Presbyter gown,
        Some quarrel Episcopal graithing,
    But every good fellow will own
20   Their quarrel is all about – naething. –

    The lover may sparkle and glow,
        Approaching his bonie bit gay thing;
    But marriage will soon let him know,
        He's gotten a buskit up naething. –

25 The Poet may jingle and rhyme,
        In hopes of a laureate wreathing,
    And when he has wasted his time,
        He's kindly rewarded with naething. –

    The thundering bully may rage,
30   And swagger and swear like a heathen;
    But collar him fast, I'll engage
        You'll find that his courage is naething. –

    Last night with a feminine Whig,
        A Poet she could na put faith in,
35 But soon we grew lovingly big,
        I taught her, her terrors were naething. –

    Her Whigship was wonderful pleased,
        But charmingly tickled wi' ae thing;
    Her fingers I lovingly squeezed,
40   And kiss'd her and promised her – naething. –

The priest anathemas may threat,
   Predicament, Sir, that we're baith in;
But when honor's reveille is beat,
   The holy artillery's naething. –

45 And now I must mount on the wave,
   My voyage perhaps there is death in;
But what of a watery grave!
   The drowning a Poet is naething. –

And now as grim death's in my thought,
50   To you, Sir, I make this bequeathing:
My service as long as ye've ought,
   And my friendship, by God, when ye've naething. –

To a Mountain Daisy
On Turning One Down with the Plough in April – 1786

Wee, modest, crimson-tipped flow'r,
Thou's met me in an evil hour;
For I maun crush amang the stoure
        Thy slender stem:
5 To spare thee now is past my pow'r,
        Thou bonie gem.

Alas! it's no thy neebor sweet,
The bonie *lark*, companion meet!
Bending thee 'mang the dewy weet!
10   Wi' speckl'd breast,
When upward-springing, blythe, to greet
        The purpling East.

Cauld blew the bitter-biting *North*
Upon thy early, humble birth;
15 Yet chearfully thou glinted forth
        Amid the storm,
Scarce rear'd above the *Parent-earth*
        Thy tender form.

The flaunting *flow'rs* our gardens yield,
20 High-shelt'ring woods and wa's maun shield,
But thou, beneath the random bield
                    O' clod or stane,
Adorns the histie *stibble-field*,
                        Unseen, alane.

25 There, in thy scanty mantle clad,
Thy snawy bosom sun-ward spread,
Thou lifts thy unassuming head
                        In humble guise;
But now the *share* uptears thy bed,
30   And low thou lies!

Such is the fate of artless Maid,
Sweet *flow'ret* of the rural shade!
By love's simplicity betray'd,
                        And guileless trust,
35 Till she, like thee, all soil'd, is laid
                        Low i' the dust.

Such is the fate of simple Bard,
On life's rough ocean luckless starr'd!
Unskilful he to note the card
40   Of *prudent lore*,
Till billows rage, and gales blow hard,
                        And whelm him o'er!

Such fate to *suff'ring worth* is giv'n,
Who long with wants and woes has striv'n,
45 By human pride or cunning driv'n
                        To mis'ry's brink,
Till wrench'd of every stay but Heav'n,
                        He, ruin'd, sink!

Ev'n thou who mourn'st the *Daisy's* fate;
50 *That fate is thine* – no distant date;
Stern Ruin's *plough-share* drives, elate,
                        Full on thy bloom,
Till crush'd beneath the *furrow's* weight,
                        Shall be thy doom!

Epistle to a Young Friend

May – 1786

I lang hae thought, my youthfu' friend,
    A something to have sent you,
Though it should serve nae other end
    Than just a kind memento;
5 But how the subject theme may gang,
    Let time and chance determine;
Perhaps it may turn out a sang;
    Perhaps turn out a sermon.

Ye'll try the world soon my lad,
10   And Andrew dear believe me,
Ye'll find mankind an unco squad,
    And muckle they may grieve ye:
For care and trouble set your thought,
    Ev'n when your end's attained;
15 And a' your views may come to nought,
    Where ev'ry nerve is strain'd.

I'll no say, men are villains a';
    The real, harden'd wicked,
Wha hae nae check but *human law*,
20   Are to a few restricked:
But Och, mankind are unco weak,
    An' little to be trusted;
If *Self* the wavering balance shake,
    It's rarely right adjusted!

25 Yet they wha fa' in Fortune's strife,
    Their fate we should na censure,
For still th' *important end* of life,
    They equally may answer:
A man may hae an *honest heart*,
30   Tho' poortith hourly stare him;
A man may tak a neebor's part,
    Yet hae nae *cash* to spare him.

Ay free, aff han', your story tell,
   When wi' a bosom crony;
35 But still keep something to yoursel
   Ye scarcely tell to ony.
Conceal yoursel as weel's you can
   Frae critical dissection;
But keek thro' ev'ry other man,
40   Wi' sharpen'd, sly inspection.

The *sacred lowe* o' weel plac'd love,
   Luxuriantly indulge it;
But never tempt th' *illicit rove*,
   Tho' naething should divulge it:
45 I wave the quantum o' the sin;
   The hazard of concealing;
But Och! it hardens *a' within*,
   And petrifies the feeling!

To catch Dame Fortune's golden smile,
50   Assiduous wait upon her;
And gather gear by ev'ry wile,
   That's justify'd by Honor:
Not for to *hide* it in a *hedge*,
   Nor for a *train-attendant*;
55 But for the glorious priviledge
   Of being *independant*.

The *fear o' Hell's* a hangman's whip,
   To haud the wretch in order;
But where ye feel your *Honor* grip,
60   Let that ay be your border:
Its slightest touches, instant pause –
   Debar a' side-pretences;
And resolutely keep its laws,
   Uncaring consequences.

65 The great Creator to revere,
     Must sure become the *Creature*;
But still the preaching cant forbear,
     And ev'n the rigid feature:
Yet ne'er with Wits prophane to range,
70   Be complaisance extended;
An *atheist-laugh's* a poor exchange
     For *Deity offended*!

When ranting round in Pleasure's ring,
     Religion may be blinded;
75 Or if she give a *random-fling*,
     It may be little minded;
But when on Life we're tempest-driven,
     A Conscience but a canker –
A correspondence fix'd wi' Heav'n,
80   Is sure a noble *anchor*!

Adieu, dear, amiable Youth!
     Your *heart* can ne'er be wanting!
May Prudence, Fortitude and Truth
     Erect your brow undaunting!
85 In *ploughman phrase* 'God send you speed,'
     Still daily to grow wiser;
And may ye better reck the *rede*,
     Than ever did th' *Adviser*!

Lines Written on a Bank-Note

Wae worth thy pow'r, thou cursed leaf!
Fell source of a' my woe and grief!
For lake o' thee I've lost my lass;
For lake o' thee I scrimp my glass;
5 I see the children of Affliction
Unaided, thro' thy curs'd restriction.
I've seen the Oppressor's cruel smile
Amid his hapless victim's spoil;

And for thy potence vainly wish'd
10 To crush the villain in the dust:
For lake o' thee I leave this much-loved shore,
Never perhaps to greet Old Scotland more!

R. B.
Kyle

Address of Beelzebub

To the Right Honorable the Earl of Breadalbane, President of the Right Honorable the Highland Society, which met on the 23rd of May last, at the Shakespeare, Covent Garden, *to concert ways and means to frustrate the designs of five hundred Highlanders who, as the Society were informed by Mr McKenzie of Applecross, were so audacious as to attempt an escape from their lawful lords and masters whose property they are, by emigrating from the lands of Mr Macdonald of Glengary to the wilds of Canada, in search of that fantastic thing – Liberty –*

Long life, my lord, an' health be yours,
Unskaith'd by hunger'd Highland boors!
Lord grant nae duddie, desperate beggar,
Wi' dirk, claymore, or rusty trigger,
5 May twin auld Scotland o' a life
She likes – as Butchers like a knife!

Faith, you and Applecross were right
To keep the Highlan' hounds in sight!
I doubt na! they wad bid nae better
10 Than let them ance out owre the water;
Then up amang thae lakes an' seas,
They'll mak what rules and laws they please:
Some daring Hancocke, or a Frankline,
May set their Highlan' bluid a-ranklin;
15 Some Washington again may head them,
Or some Montgomery, fearless, lead them;

Till God knows what may be effected,
When by such heads and hearts directed.
Poor, dunghill sons of dirt an' mire,
20 May to Patrician rights aspire;
Nae sage North now, nor sager Sackville,
To watch an' premier owre the pack vile!
An' whare will ye get Howes an' Clintons
To bring them to a right repentance,
25 To cowe the rebel generation,
An' save the honor o' the nation?
They, an' be damned! what right hae they
To meat or sleep or light o' day,
Far less to riches, pow'r or freedom,
30 But what your lordships please to gie them?

But hear, my lord! Glengary, hear!
Your hand's owre light on them, I fear:
Your factors, greives, trustees and bailies,
I canna say but they do gaylies:
35 They lay aside a' tender mercies,
An' tirl the hallions to the birsies;
Yet while they're only poin'd and herriet,
They'll keep their stubborn Highlan spirit.
But smash them! crush them a' to spails!
40 And rot the dyvors i' the jails!
The young dogs, swinge them to the labour,
Let wark an' hunger mak them sober!
The hizzies, if they're oughtlins fausont,
Let them in Drury Lane be lesson'd!
45 An' if the wives, an' dirty brats,
Come thiggin at your doors an' yetts,
Flaffan wi' duds, an' grey wi' beese,
Frightan awa your deucks an' geese,
Get out a horsewhip, or a jowler,
50 The langest thong, the fiercest growler,
And gar the tatter'd gipseys pack
Wi' a' their bastarts on their back!

Go on, my lord! I lang to meet you,
   An' in my 'house at hame' to greet you;
55 Wi' common lords ye shanna mingle:
   The benmost newk, beside the ingle
At my right hand, assign'd your seat
   'Tween Herod's hip, an' Polycrate,
Or (if you on your station tarrow)
60 Between Almagro and Pizarro;
A seat, I'm sure ye're weel deservin't;
An' till ye come – your humble servant,
                 Beelzebub.

Hell,
1st June, Anno Mundi 5790

A Dream

Thoughts, words and deeds, the Statute blames with reason;
But surely Dreams *were ne'er indicted Treason.*

On reading, in the public papers, the Laureate's Ode, with the other
parade of June 4th, 1786, the Author was no sooner dropt asleep,
than he imagined himself transported to the Birthday Levee; and, in
his dreaming fancy, made the following address.

Guid-mornin to your Majesty!
   May heaven augment your blisses,
On ev'ry new *Birth-day* ye see,
   A humble Bardie wishes!
5 My Bardship here, at your Levee,
   On sic a day as this is,
Is sure an uncouth sight to see,
   Amang the Birth-day dresses
          Sae fine this day.

10   I see ye're complimented thrang,
        By many a *lord* an' *lady*;
    'God save the King's a cukoo sang
        That's unco easy said ay:
    The *Poets* too, a venal gang,
15   Wi' rhymes weel–turn'd an' ready,
    Wad gar you trow ye ne'er do wrang,
        But ay unerring steady,
                On sic a day.

    For me! before a Monarch's face,
20   Ev'n *there* I winna flatter;
    For neither pension, post, nor place,
        Am I your humble debtor:
    So, nae reflection on Your Grace,
        Your Kingship to bespatter;
25   There's monie *waur* been o' the Race,
        And aiblens *ane* been better
                Than you this day.

    'Tis very true, my sovereign King,
        My skill may weel be doubted;
30   But *Facts* are cheels that winna ding,
        An' downa be disputed:
    Your *royal nest*, beneath *your* wing,
        Is e'en right reft an' clouted,
    And now the third part o' the string,
35   An' less, will gang about it
                Than did ae day.

    Far be't frae me that I aspire
        To blame your legislation,
    Or say, ye wisdom want, or fire,
40   To rule this mighty nation;
    But faith! I muckle doubt, my Sire,
        Ye've trusted 'Ministration,
    To chaps wha, in a *barn* or *byre*,
        Wad better fill'd their station
45   Than *courts* yon day.

And now ye've gien auld *Britain* peace,
    Her broken shins to plaister;
Your fair taxation does her fleece,
    Till she has scarce a tester:
50 For me, thank God, my life's a *lease*,
    Nae *bargain* wearing faster,
Or faith! I fear that, wi' the geese,
    I shortly boost to pasture
              I' the craft some day.

55 I'm no mistrusting *Willie Pitt*,
    When taxes he enlarges,
(An' *Will's* a true guid fallow's get,
    A name not Envy spairges)
That he intends to pay your *debt*,
60   An' lessen a' your *charges*;
But Godsake! let nae *saving-fit*
    Abridge your bonie *barges*
              An' *boats* this day.

Adieu, my Leige! may Freedom geck
65   Beneath your high protection;
An' may ye rax Corruption's neck,
    And gie her for dissection!
But since I'm here, I'll no neglect,
    In loyal, true affection,
70 To pay your Queen, with due respect,
    My fealty an' subjection
              This great Birth-day.

Hail, *Majesty most Excellent*!
    While Nobles strive to please ye,
75 Will ye accept a compliment,
    A simple Bardie gies ye?
Thae bonie bairntime, Heav'n has lent,
    Still higher may they heeze ye
In bliss, till Fate some day is sent,
80   For ever to release ye
              Frae care that day.

For you, young Potentate o' Wales
   I tell your *Highness* fairly,
Down Pleasure's stream, wi' swelling sails,
85   I'm tauld ye're driving rarely;
But some day ye may gnaw your nails,
   An' curse your folly sairly,
That e'er ye brak Diana's *pales*,
   Or rattled dice wi' *Charlie*
90   By night or day.

Yet aft a ragged *cowte's* been known,
   To mak a noble *aiver*;
So, ye may dousely fill a throne,
   For a' their clish-ma-claver:
95 There, him at *Agincourt* wha shone,
   Few better were or braver;
And yet, wi' funny, queer *Sir *John*
   He was an unco shaver
           For monie a day.

100 For you, right rev'rend Osnaburg,
   Nane sets the *lawn-sleeve* sweeter,
Altho' a ribban at your lug
   Wad been a dress compleater:
As ye disown yon paughty dog,
105   That *bears* the Keys of Peter,
Then swith! an' get a *wife* to hug,
   Or trouth! ye'll stain the *Mitre*
           Some luckless day.

Young royal Tarry-breeks, I learn,
110   Ye've lately come athwart her;
A glorious †*Galley*, stem and stern,
   Weel-rigg'd for *Venus barter*;
But first hang out that she'll discern
   Your *hymeneal Charter*,
115 Then heave aboard your *grapple airn*,
   An' large upon her *quarter*,
           Come full that day.

* Sir John Falstaff, Vide Shakespeare. [RB]
† Alluding to the Newspaper account of a certain royal Sailor's Amour. [RB]

Ye lastly, bonie blossoms a',
   Ye *royal Lasses* dainty,
120 Heav'n mak you guid as weel as braw,
   An' gie you *lads* a plenty:
But sneer na *British-boys* awa;
   For Kings are unco scant ay,
An' German-Gentles are but *sma'*,
125   They're better just than *want ay*
          On onie day.

God bless you a'! consider now,
   Ye're unco muckle dautet;
But ere the *course* o' life be through,
130   It may be bitter sautet:
An' I hae seen their *coggie* fou,
   That yet hae tarrow't at it,
But or the *day* was done, I trow,
   The laggan they hae clautet
135   Fu' clean that day.

Elegy on the Death of Robert Ruisseaux

Now Robin lies in his last lair,
He'll gabble rhyme, nor sing nae mair,
Cauld poverty, wi' hungry stare,
          Nae mair shall fear him;
5 Nor anxious fear, nor cankert care
          E'er mair come near him.

To tell the truth, they seldom fash't him,
Except the moment that they crush't him;
For sune as chance or fate had husht 'em
10   Tho' e'er sae short,
Then wi' a rhyme or song he lash't 'em,
          And thought it sport. –

Tho' he was bred to kintra wark,
And counted was baith wight and stark,
15   Yet that was never Robin's mark
          To mak a man;
But tell him, he was learn'd and clark,
          Ye roos'd him then!

A Bard's Epitaph

Is there a whim-inspir'd fool,
Owre fast for thought, owre hot for rule,
Owre blate to seek, owre proud to snool,
          Let him draw near;
5   And o'er this grassy heap sing dool,
          And drap a tear.

Is there a Bard of rustic song,
Who, noteless, steals the crouds among,
That weekly this area throng,
10   O, pass not by!
But with a frater-feeling strong,
          Here, heave a sigh.

Is there a man whose judgment clear,
Can others teach the course to steer,
15 Yet runs, himself, life's mad career,
          Wild as the wave,
Here pause – and thro' the starting tear,
          Survey this grave.

The poor Inhabitant below
20 Was quick to learn and wise to know,
And keenly felt the friendly glow,
          And *softer flame*;
But thoughtless follies laid him low,
          And stain'd his name!

25 Reader attend – whether thy soul
Soars fancy's flights beyond the pole,
Or darkling grubs this earthly hole,
                    In low pursuit,
Know, prudent, cautious, *self-controul*
30   Is Wisdom's root.

To a Haggis

Fair fa' your honest, sonsie face,
Great Chieftan o' the Puddin-race!
Aboon them a' ye tak your place,
                    Painch, tripe, or thairm:
5 Weel are ye wordy of a *grace*
                    As lang's my arm.

The groaning trencher there ye fill,
Your hurdies like a distant hill,
Your *pin* wad help to mend a mill
10   In time o' need,
While thro' your pores the dews distil
                    Like amber bead.

His knife see Rustic-labour dight,
An' cut you up wi' ready slight,
15 Trenching your gushing entrails bright
                    Like onie ditch;
And then, O what a glorious sight,
                    Warm-reekin, rich!

Then, horn for horn they stretch an' strive,
20 Deil tak the hindmost, on they drive,
Till a' their weel-swall'd kytes belyve
                    Are bent like drums;
Then auld Guidman, maist like to rive,
                    Bethankit hums.

25   Is there that owre his French *ragout*,
Or *olio* that wad staw a sow,
Or *fricassee* wad mak her spew
              Wi' perfect sconner,
Looks down wi' sneering, scornfu' view
30   On sic a dinner?

Poor devil! see him owre his trash,
As feckless as a wither'd rash,
His spindle-shank a guid whip-lash,
              His nieve a nit;
35   Thro' bluidy flood or field to dash,
              O how unfit!

But mark the Rustic, *haggis-fed*,
The trembling earth resounds his tread,
Clap in his walie nieve a blade,
40   He'll mak it whissle;
An' legs, an' arms, an' heads will sned,
              Like taps o' thrissle.

Ye Pow'rs wha mak mankind your care,
An' dish them out their bill o' fare,
45   Auld Scotland wants nae skinking ware
              That jaups in luggies;
But, if ye wish her gratefu' pray'r,
              Gie her a *Haggis*!

There Was a Lad

(TUNE: DAINTY DAVIE)

There was a lad was born in Kyle,
But what na day o' what na style
I doubt it's hardly worth the while
        To be sae nice wi' *Robin*.

5   *Robin was a rovin' Boy,*
            Rantin' rovin', rantin' rovin';
       Robin was a rovin' Boy,
            Rantin' rovin' Robin.

Our monarch's hindmost year but ane
10 Was five and twenty days begun,
   'Twas then a blast o' Janwar Win'
        Blew hansel in on *Robin.*

The gossip keekit in his loof,
Quo' scho wha lives will see the proof,
15 This waly boy will be nae coof,
        I think we'll ca' him *Robin.*

He'll hae misfortunes great and sma',
But ay a heart aboon them a';
He'll be a credit 'till us a',
20   We'll a' be proud o' *Robin.*

But sure as three times three mak nine,
I see by ilka score and line,
This chap will dearly like our kin',
        So leeze me on thee *Robin.*

25 Guid faith quo' scho I doubt you Stir,
   Ye'll gar the lasses lie aspar;
   But twenty fauts ye may hae waur
        So blessin's on thee, *Robin!*

       Robin was a rovin' Boy,
30   *Rantin' rovin', rantin' rovin';*
       Robin was a rovin' Boy,
            Rantin, rovin' Robin.

*Lines Written Under the Portrait of Robert Fergusson,
the Poet, in a Copy of That Author's Works Presented
to a Young Lady in Edinburgh, March 19th, 1787*

Curse on ungrateful man, that can be pleas'd,
And yet can starve the author of the pleasure.
O thou my elder brother in misfortune,
By far my elder brother in the muses,
With tears I pity thy unhappy fate!
Why is the bard unpitied by the world,
Yet has so keen a relish of its pleasures?

My Harry Was a Gallant Gay

(TUNE: HIGHLANDER'S LAMENT)

My Harry was a gallant gay,
Fu' stately strade he on the plain;
But now he's banish'd far awa,
I'll never see him back again.

5   O for him back again,
       O for him back again,
       I wad gie a' Knockhaspie's land
       For Highland Harry back again.

When a' the lave gae to their bed,
10 I wander dowie up the glen;
I set me down and greet my fill,
And ay I wish him back again.
       O for him &c.

And were some villains hangit high,
15 And ilka body had their ain!
Then I might see the joyfu' sight,
My Highlan Harry back again.
       O for him &c.

Here Stewarts Once in Triumph Reigned (*Lines on Stirling Window*)

Here Stewarts once in triumph reign'd,
And laws for Scotland's weal ordain'd;
But now unroof'd their palace stands,
Their sceptre's fall'n to other hands;
5   Fallen indeed, and to the earth,
Whence grovelling reptiles take their birth. –
The injur'd Stewart line are gone,
A race outlandish fill their throne:
An idiot race, to honor lost –
10 Who know them best despise them most. –

My Peggy's Face

My Peggy's face, my Peggy's form,
The frost of hermit age might warm;
My Peggy's worth, my Peggy's mind,
Might charm the first of humankind.
5   I love my Peggy's angel air,
Her face so truly heavn'ly fair,
Her native grace so void of art,
But I adore my Peggy's heart.

The lily's hue, the rose's die,
10 The kindling lustre of an eye;
Who but owns their magic sway,
Who but knows they will decay!
The tender thrill, the pitying tear,
The gen'rous purpose nobly dear,
15 The gentle look that Rage disarms,
These are all Immortal charms.

An Extemporaneous Effusion on Being Appointed to the Excise

Searching auld wives' barrels,
     Ochon, the day!
That clarty barm should stain my laurels;
     But – what'll ye say!
5   These muvin' things ca'd wives and weans
Wad muve the very hearts o' stanes!

To Daunton Me

The blude red rose at Yule may blaw,
The simmer lillies bloom in snaw,
The frost may freeze the deepest sea,
But an auld man shall never daunton me.

5   To daunton me, and me sae young,
        Wi' his fause heart and flatt'ring tongue,
        That is the thing you ne'er shall see
        For an auld man shall never daunton me.

For a' his meal and a' his maut,
10   For a' his fresh beef and his saut,
For a' his gold and white monie,
An auld man shall never daunton me.
        To daunton me, &c.

His gear may buy him kye and yowes,
15   His gear may buy him glens and knowes,
But me he shall not buy nor fee,
For an auld man shall never daunton me.
        To daunton me, &c.

He hirples twa-fauld as he dow,
20   Wi' his teethless gab and his auld beld pow,
And the rain rains down frae his red blear'd e'e,
That auld man shall never daunton me.
        To daunton me, &c.

O'er the Water to Charlie

(TUNE: SHAWNBOY)

Come boat me o'er, come row me o'er,
Come boat me o'er to Charlie;
I'll gie John Ross another bawbee,
To boat me o'er to Charlie.

5   We'll o'er the water, we'll o'er the sea,
       We'll o'er the water to Charlie;
       Come weal, come woe, we'll gather and go,
       And live or die wi' Charlie.

I lo'e weel my Charlie's name,
10 Tho' some there be abhor him:
But O, to see auld Nick gaun hame,
And Charlie's faes before him!
       We'll o'er &c.

I swear and vow by moon and stars,
15 And sun that shines so early!
If I had twenty thousand lives,
I'd die as aft for Charlie.
       We'll o'er &c.

Rattlin, Roarin Willie

O rattlin, roarin Willie,
   O he held to the fair,
An' for to sell his fiddle
   And buy some other ware;
5 But parting wi' his fiddle,
   The saut tear blin't his e'e;
And rattlin, roarin Willie
   Ye're welcome hame to me.

O Willie, come sell your fiddle,
10   O sell your fiddle sae fine;
O Willie, come sell your fiddle,
    And buy a pint o' wine;
If I should sell my fiddle,
    The warl would think I was mad,
15 For mony a rantin day
    My fiddle and I hae had.

As I cam by Crochallan
    I cannily keekit ben,
Rattlin, roarin Willie
20   Was sitting at yon boord-en',
Sitting at yon boord-en',
    And amang guid companie:
Rattlin, roarin Willie,
    You're welcome hame to me.

Epistle to Hugh Parker

In this strange land, this uncouth clime,
A land unknown to prose or rhyme;
Where words ne'er cros't the Muse's heckles,
Nor limpit in poetic shackles:
5 A land that Prose did never view it,
Except when drunk he stacher't thro' it:
Here, ambush'd by the chimla cheek,
Hid in an atmosphere of reek,
I hear a wheel thrum i' the neuk,
10 I hear it – for in vain I leuk. –
The red peat gleams, a fiery kernel
Enhusked by a fog infernal:
Here, for my wonted rhyming raptures,
I sit and count my sins by chapters;
15 For life and spunk like ither Christians,
I'm dwindled down to mere existence;

Wi' nae converse but Gallowa' bodies,
Wi' nae kend face but Jenny Geddes.
Jenny, my Pegasean pride,
20 Dowie she saunters down Nithside,
And ay a westlin leuk she throws,
While tears hap o'er her auld brown nose!
Was it for this wi' cannie care
Thou bure the Bard through many a shire?
25 At howes or hillocks never stumbled,
And late or early never grumbled? –
O, had I pow'r like inclination,
I'd heeze thee up a constellation,
To canter with the Sagitarre,
30 Or loup th' Ecliptic like a bar,
Or turn the Pole like any arrow;
Or, when auld Phoebus bids good-morrow,
Down the Zodiac urge the race,
And cast dirt on his godship's face:
35 For I could lay my bread and kail
He'd ne'er cast saut upo' thy tail! –
Wi' a' this care and a' this grief,
And sma', sma' prospect of relief,
And nought but peat reek i' my head,
40 How can I write what ye can read? –
Tarbolton, twenty-fourth o' June,
Ye'll find me in a better tune;
But till we meet and weet our whistle,
Tak this excuse for nae epistle.

– Robert Burns

I Love My Jean

(TUNE: MISS ADMIRAL GORDON'S STRATHSPEY)

Of a' the airts the wind can blaw,
    I dearly like the west,
For there the bonie lassie lives,
    The lassie I lo'e best:
5   There's wild-woods grow, and rivers row,
    And mony a hill between;
But day and night my fancy's flight
    Is ever wi' my Jean.

I see her in the dewy flowers,
10   I see her sweet and fair;
I hear her in the tunefu' birds,
    I hear her charm the air:
There's not a bony flower, that springs
    By fountain, shaw, or green,
15 There's not a bony bird that sings,
    But minds me o' my Jean.

Tam Glen

(TUNE: MERRY BEGGARS)

My heart is a breaking, dear Tittie,
    Some counsel unto me come len',
To anger them a' is a pity,
    But what will I do wi' Tam Glen?

5   I'm thinking, wi' sic a braw fellow,
    In poortith I might mak a fen':
What care I in riches to wallow,
    If I mauna marry Tam Glen.

There's Lowrie the laird o' Dumeller,
10 'Gude day to you brute' he comes ben:
He brags and he blaws o' his siller,
    But when will he dance like Tam Glen.

My Minnie does constantly deave me,
      And bids me beware o' young men;
15   They flatter, she says, to deceive me,
      But wha can think sae o' Tam Glen.

My Daddie says, gin I'll forsake him,
      He'll gie me gude hunder marks ten:
But if it's ordain'd I maun take him,
20   O wha will I get but Tam Glen?

Yestreen at the Valentines' dealing,
      My heart to my mou gied a sten;
For thrice I drew ane without failing,
      And thrice it was written, Tam Glen.

25   The last Halloween I was waukin
      My droukit sark-sleeve, as ye ken;
His likeness cam up the house staukin,
      And the very grey breeks o' Tam Glen!

Come counsel, dear Tittie, don't tarry;
30   I'll gie you my bonie black hen,
Gif ye will advise me to marry
      The lad I lo'e dearly, Tam Glen.

Auld Lang Syne

(TUNE: FOR OLD LONG SINE MY JO)

Should auld acquaintance be forgot
      And never brought to mind?
Should auld acquaintance be forgot,
      And auld lang syne!

5   For auld lang syne my jo,
            For auld lang syne,
         We'll tak a *cup o' kindness yet,
            For auld lang syne.

* Some Sing, Kiss in place of Cup. [RB]

And surely ye'll be your pint stowp!
10   And surely I'll be mine!
And we'll tak a cup o' kindness yet,
    For auld lang syne.
          For auld &c.

We twa hae run about the braes,
15   And pou'd the gowans fine;
But we've wander'd mony a weary fitt,
    Sin auld lang syne.
          For auld &c.

We twa hae paidl'd in the burn,
20   Frae morning sun till dine;
But seas between us braid hae roar'd,
    Sin auld lang syne.
          For auld &c.

And there's a hand, my trusty fiere!
25   And gie's a hand o' thine!
And we'll tak a right gude-willie-waught,
    For auld lang syne.
          For auld &c.

Louis What Reck I by Thee

Louis, what reck I by thee,
Or Geordie on his ocean:
Dyvor, beggar louns to me,
I reign in Jeanie's bosom.
5   Let her crown my love her law,
And in her breast enthrone me:
Kings and nations, swith awa!
Reif randies I disown ye!

Elegy on the Year 1788

For Lords or kings I dinna mourn,
E'en let them die – for that they're born!
But oh! prodigious to reflect,
A *Towmont*, Sirs, is gane to wreck!
5   O *Eighty-eight*, in thy sma' space
What dire events ha'e taken place!
Of what enjoyments thou hast reft us!
In what a pickle thou has left us!

The Spanish empire's tint a head,
10 An' my auld teethless Bawtie's dead;
The toolzie's teugh 'tween Pitt an' Fox,
An' our guidwife's wee birdy cocks;
The tane is game, a bluidy devil,
But to the *hen-birds* unco civil;
15 The tither's dour, has nae sic breedin',
But better stuff ne'er claw'd a midden!

Ye ministers, come mount the pulpit,
An' cry till ye be haerse an' rupit;
For *Eighty-eight* he wish'd you weel,
20 An' gied you a' baith gear an' meal;
E'en mony a plack, an' mony a peck,
Ye ken yoursels, for little feck!

Ye bonny lasses, dight your een,
For some o' you ha'e tint a frien';
25 In *Eighty-eight*, ye ken, was ta'en
What ye'll ne'er ha'e to gi'e again.

Observe the very nowt an' sheep,
How dowff an' dowie now they creep;
Nay, even the yirth itsel' does cry,
30 For Embro' wells are grutten dry.

O *Eighty-nine*, thou's but a bairn,
An' no owre auld, I hope, to learn!
Thou beardless boy, I pray tak' care,
Thou now has got thy Daddy's chair,

35 Nae hand-cuff'd, mizl'd, haff-shackl'd *Regent*,
But, like himsel', a full free agent.
Be sure ye follow out the plan
Nae war than he did, honest man!
As muckle better as you can.

January 1, 1789

Epistle to William Stewart

In honest Bacon's ingle-neuk,
    Here I maun sit and think,
Sick o' the warld and warld's folk,
    And sick, damn'd sick, o' drink!
5 I see, I see, there is nae help,
    But still doun I maun sink,
Till some day, laigh enough, I yelp: –
    'Wae worth that cursed drink!'
Yestreen, alas! I was sae fu'
10   I could but yisk and wink;
And now, this day, sair, sair I rue
    The weary, weary drink.
Satan, I fear thy sooty claws,
    I hate thy brunstane stink,
15 And ay I curse the luckless cause –
    The wicked soup o' drink.
In vain I would forget my woes
    In idle rhyming clink,
For past redemption damn'd in Prose,
20   I can do nought but drink.
To you my trusty, well-tried friend,
    May heaven still on you blink;
And may your life flow to the end,
    Sweet as a dry man's drink!

Afton Water

Flow gently, sweet Afton, among thy green braes,
Flow gently, I'll sing thee a song in thy praise;
My Mary's asleep by thy murmuring stream,
Flow gently, sweet Afton, disturb not her dream.

5   Thou stock dove whose echo resounds thro' the glen,
Ye wild whistling blackbirds in yon thorny den,
Thou green crested lapwing thy screaming forbear,
I charge you disturb not my slumbering Fair.

How lofty, sweet Afton, thy neighbouring hills,
10   Far mark'd with the courses of clear, winding rills;
There daily I wander as noon rises high,
My flocks and my Mary's sweet cot in my eye.

How pleasant thy banks and green vallies below,
Where wild in the woodlands the primroses blow;
15   There oft as mild ev'ning weeps over the lea,
The sweet scented birk shades my Mary and me.

Thy chrystal stream, Afton, how lovely it glides,
And winds by the cot where my Mary resides;
How wanton thy waters her snowy feet lave,
20   As gath'ring sweet flow'rets she stems thy clear wave.

Flow gently, sweet Afton, among thy green braes,
Flow gently, sweet river, the theme of my lays;
My Mary's asleep by thy murmuring stream,
Flow gently, sweet Afton, disturb not her dream.

To Alexander Findlater

Ellisland Saturday morning

Dear Sir,
       our Lucky humbly begs
Ye'll prie her caller, new-laid eggs:
Lord grant the cock may keep his legs,
       Aboon the chuckies;
5   An' wi' his kittle, forket clegs,
       Claw weel their dockies!

Had Fate that curst me in her ledger,
A Poet poor, and poorer Gager,
Created me that feather'd sodger,
10   A generous cock,
How I wad craw and strut and r-ger
       My kecklin flock!

Buskit wi' mony a bien, braw feather,
I wad defied the warst o' weather:
15 When corn or bear I could na gather
       To gie my burdies;
I'd treated them wi' caller heather,
       And weel-knooz'd hurdies.

Nae cursed Clerical Excise
20 On honest Nature's laws and ties;
Free as the vernal breeze that flies
       At early day,
We'd tasted Nature's richest joys,
       But stint or stay. —

25 But as this subject's something kittle,
Our wisest way's to say but little;
And while my Muse is at her mettle,
       I am, most fervent,
Or may I die upon a whittle!
30   Your Friend and Servant —
           Robt. Burns

To a Gentleman Who Had Sent Him a Newspaper and Offered to Continue It Free of Expense

Kind Sir, I've read your paper through,
And faith, to me, 'twas really new!
How guessed ye, Sir, what maist I wanted?
This mony a day I've grain'd and gaunted,
5   To ken what French mischief was brewin;
Or what the drumlie Dutch were doin;
That vile doup-skelper, Emperor Joseph,
If Venus yet had got his nose off;
Or how the collieshangie works
10   Atween the Russians and the Turks;
Or if the Swede, before he halt,
Would play anither Charles the twalt:
If Denmark, any body spak o't;
Or Poland, wha had now the tack o't;
15   How cut-throat Prussian blades were hingin;
How libbet Italy was singin;
If Spaniard, Portuguese or Swiss,
Were sayin or takin aught amiss:
Or how our merry lads at hame,
20   In Britain's court kept up the game:
How royal George, the Lord leuk o'er him!
Was managing St Stephen's quorum;
If sleekit Chatham Will was livin,
Or glaikit Charlie got his nieve in;
25   How daddie Burke the plea was cookin,
If Warren Hasting's neck was yeukin;
How cesses, stents, and fees were rax'd,
Or if bare arses yet were tax'd;
The news o' princes, dukes and earls,
30   Pimps, sharpers, bawds, and opera-girls;
If that daft buckie, Geordie Wales,
Was threshin still at hizzies' tails,
Or if he was grown oughtlins douser,
And no a perfect kintra cooser,

35   A' this and mair I never heard of;
      And but for you I might despair'd of.
      So gratefu', back your news I send you,
      And pray, a' gude things may attend you!

Ellisland, Monday-morning, 1790

Tibbie Dunbar

(TUNE: JOHNNY MCGILL)

O wilt thou go wi' me, sweet Tibbie Dunbar;
O wilt thou go wi' me, sweet Tibbie Dunbar;
Wilt thou ride on a horse, or be drawn in a car,
Or walk by my side, O sweet Tibbie Dunbar.

5   I care na thy daddie, his lands and his money,
     I care na thy kin, sae high and sae lordly:
     But say thou wilt hae me for better for waur,
     And come in thy coatie, sweet Tibbie Dunbar.

The Taylor Fell Thro' the Bed

(TUNE: BEWARE OF THE RIPPELS)

The Taylor fell thro' the bed, thimble an' a',
The Taylor fell thro' the bed, thimble an' a';
The blankets were thin and the sheets they were sma',
The Taylor fell thro' the bed, thimble an' a'.

5   The sleepy bit lassie she dreaded nae ill,
     The sleepy bit lassie she dreaded nae ill;
     The weather was cauld and the lassie lay still,
     She thought that a Taylor could do her nae ill.

Gie me the groat again, cany young man,
10 Gie me the groat again, cany young man;
The day it is short and the night it is lang,
The dearest siller that ever I wan.

There's somebody weary wi' lying her lane,
There's somebody weary wi' lying her lane,
15 There's some that are dowie, I trow wad be fain
To see the bit Taylor come skippin again.

Ay Waukin, O

Simmer's a pleasant time,
Flow'rs of ev'ry colour;
The water rins o'er the heugh,
And I long for my true lover!

5   Ay waukin, O,
Waukin still and weary:
Sleep I can get nane,
For thinking on my Dearie.

When I sleep I dream,
10   When I wauk I'm irie;
Sleep I can get nane
For thinking on my Dearie.
Ay waukin &c.

Lanely night comes on,
15   A' the lave are sleepin:
I think on my bony lad
And I bleer my een wi' greetin.
Ay waukin &c.

Lassie Lie Near Me

(TUNE: LADDIE LIE NEAR ME)

Lang hae we parted been,
Lassie my dearie;
Now we are met again,
Lassie lie near me.

5   Near me, near me,
Lassie lie near me
Lang hast thou lien thy lane,
Lassie lie near me.

A' that I hae endur'd,
10 Lassie, my dearie,
Here in thy arms is cur'd,
Lassie lie near me.
       Near me, &c.

My Love She's But a Lassie Yet

My love she's but a lassie yet,
My love she's but a lassie yet,
We'll let her stand a year or twa,
      She'll no be half sae saucy yet.

5 I rue the day I sought her O,
I rue the day I sought her O,
Wha gets her needs na say he's woo'd,
      But he may say he's bought her O.

Come draw a drap o' the best o't yet,
10 Come draw a drap o' the best o't yet:
Gae seek for pleasure where ye will,
      But here I never misst it yet.

We're a' dry wi' drinkin o't,
We're a' dry wi' drinkin o't:
15 The minister kisst the fidler's wife,
  He could na preach for thinkin o't.

Jamie Come Try Me

Jamie come try me,
Jamie come try me,
If thou would win my love
Jamie come try me.

5 If thou should ask my love,
Could I deny thee?
If thou would win my love
Jamie come try me.

If thou should kiss me, love,
Wha could espy thee?
10 If thou wad be my love,
Jamie come try me.
  Jamie come &c.

Farewell to the Highlands

(TUNE: *FAILTE NA MIOSG* – THE MUSKET SALUTE)

My heart's in the Highlands, my heart is not here;
My heart's in the Highlands a chasing the deer;
A chasing the wild deer, and following the roe,
My heart's in the Highlands, wherever I go.
5 Farewell to the Highlands, farewell to the north,
The birth place of Valour, the country of Worth,
Wherever I wander, wherever I rove,
The hills of the Highlands for ever I love.

Farewell to the mountains high cover'd with snow;
10   Farewell to the straths and green vallies below:
Farewell to the forests and wild hanging woods;
Farewell to the torrents and loud pouring floods.
My heart's in the Highlands, my heart is not here,
My heart's in the Highlands, a chasing the deer:
15   Chasing the wild deer, and following the roe,
My heart's in the Highlands, wherever I go.

John Anderson My Jo

John Anderson my jo, John,
When we were first acquent;
Your locks were like the raven,
Your bony brow was brent;
5   But now your brow is beld, John,
Your locks are like the snaw;
But blessings on your frosty pow,
John Anderson my jo.

John Anderson my jo, John,
10   We clamb the hill the gither;
And mony a canty day, John,
We've had wi' ane anither:
Now we maun totter down, John,
And hand in hand we'll go:
15   And sleep the gither at the foot,
John Anderson my jo.

The Battle of Sherra-moor

(TUNE: CAMERONIAN RANT)

O cam ye here the fight to shun,
    Or herd the sheep wi' me, man,
Or were ye at the Sherra-moor,
    Or did the battle see, man.
5 'I saw the battle sair and teugh,
And reekin-red ran mony a sheugh,
My heart for fear gae sough for sough,
To hear the thuds, and see the cluds
O' Clans frae woods, in tartan duds,
10 Wha glaum'd at kingdoms three, man.
        La, la, la, &c.

'The red-coat lads wi' black cockauds
    To meet them were na slaw, man,
They rush'd, and push'd and blude outgush'd,
15   And mony a bouk did fa', man:
The great Argyle led on his files,
I wat they glanc'd for twenty miles,
They hough'd the Clans like nine-pin kyles
They hack'd and hash'd while braidswords clash'd,
20 And thro' they dash'd, and hew'd and smash'd,
Till fey men di'd awa, man.
        La, la, la, &c.

'But had ye seen the philibegs
    And skyrin tartan trews, man,
25 When in the teeth they dar'd our Whigs,
    And covenant Trueblues, man;
In lines extended lang and large,
When baiginets o'erpower'd the targe,
And thousands hasten'd to the charge;
30 Wi' Highland wrath they frae the sheath
Drew blades o' death, till out o' breath
They fled like frighted dows, man.'
        La, la, la, &c.

'O how deil Tam can that be true,
35   The chace gaed frae the north, man;
I saw myself, they did pursue
    The horse-men back to Forth, man;
And at Dunblane in my ain sight
They took the brig wi' a their might,
40 And straught to Stirling wing'd their flight,
But, cursed lot! the gates were shut
And mony a huntit, poor Red-coat
For fear amaist did swarf, man.
           La, la, la, &c.

45 'My sister Kate cam up the gate
    Wi' crowdie unto me, man;
She swoor she saw some rebels run
    To Perth and to Dundee, man:
Their left-hand General had nae skill;
50 The Angus lads had nae gude will,
That day their neebour's blude to spill;
For fear by foes that they should lose
Their cogs o' brose, they scar'd at blows
And hameward fast did flee, man.'
55   La, la, la, &c.

They've lost some gallant gentlemen
    Amang the Highland clans, man;
I fear my Lord Panmuir is slain,
    Or in his en'mies hands, man:
60 Now wad ye sing this double flight,
Some fell for wrang and some for right,
And mony bad the warld gudenight;
Say pell and mell, wi' muskets knell
How Tories fell and Whigs to hell
65 Flew off in frighted bands, man.
           La, la, la, &c.

Sandy and Jockie

(TUNE: JENNY'S LAMENTATION)

Twa bony lads were Sandy and Jockie;
Jockie was lov'd but Sandy unlucky,
Jockie was laird baith of hills and of vallies,
But Sandy was nought but the king o' gude fellows.
5 Jockie lov'd Madgie, for Madgie had money;
And Sandie lov'd Mary, for Mary was bony:
      Ane wedded for love,
      Ane wedded for treasure,
      So Jockie had siller,
10   And Sandy had pleasure.

Tam o' Shanter. A Tale

Of Brownyis and of Bogillis full is this buke.
Gawin Douglas

When chapman billies leave the street,
And drouthy neebors, neebors meet,
As market–days are wearing late,
An' folk begin to tak the gate;
5 While we sit bousing at the nappy,
An' getting fou and unco happy,
We think na on the lang Scots miles,
The mosses, waters, slaps and styles,
That lie between us and our hame,
10 Whare sits our sulky sullen dame,
Gathering her brows like gathering storm,
Nursing her wrath to keep it warm.

    This truth fand honest *Tam o' Shanter*,
As he frae Ayr ae night did canter,
15 (Auld Ayr wham ne'er a town surpasses,
For honest men and bonny lasses.)

O *Tam*! hadst thou but been sae wise,
As ta'en thy ain wife *Kate's* advice!
She tauld thee weel thou was a skellum,
20 A blethering, blustering, drunken blellum;
That frae November till October,
Ae market day thou was nae sober;
That ilka melder, wi' the miller,
Thou sat as lang as thou had siller;
25 That ev'ry naig was ca'd a shoe on,
The smith and thee gat roaring fou on;
That at the Lord's house, ev'n on Sunday,
Thou drank wi' Kirkton Jean till Monday.
She prophesy'd that late or soon,
30 Thou would be found deep drown'd in Doon;
Or catch'd wi' warlocks in the mirk,
By *Alloway's* auld haunted kirk.

Ah, gentle dames! it gars me greet,
To think how mony counsels sweet,
35 How mony lengthen'd, sage advices,
The husband frae the wife despises!

But to our tale: Ae market night,
Tam had got planted unco right;
Fast by an ingle, bleezing finely,
40 Wi' reaming swats, that drank divinely;
And at his elbow, Souter *Johnny*,
His ancient, trusty, drouthy crony;
Tam lo'ed him like a vera brither;
They had been fou for weeks thegither.
45 The night drave on wi' sangs and clatter;
And ay the ale was growing better:
The landlady and *Tam* grew gracious,
Wi' favours, secret, sweet, and precious:
The Souter tauld his queerest stories;
50 The landlord's laugh was ready chorus:
The storm without might rair and rustle,
Tam did na mind the storm a whistle.

Care, mad to see a man sae happy,
E'en drown'd himself amang the nappy,
55 As bees flee hame wi' lades o' treasure,
The minutes wing'd their way wi' pleasure:
Kings may be blest, but *Tam* was glorious,
O'er a' the ills o' life victorious!

But pleasures are like poppies spread,
60 You seize the flow'r, its bloom is shed:
Or like the snow falls in the river,
A moment white – then melts forever;
Or like the borealis race,
That flit ere you can point their place;
65 Or like the rainbow's lovely form
Evanishing amid the storm. –
Nae man can tether time nor tide;
The hour approaches Tam maun ride;
That hour, o' night's black arch the key-stane,
70 That dreary hour he mounts his beast in;
And sic a night he taks the road in,
As ne'er poor sinner was abroad in.

The wind blew as 'twad blawn its last;
The rattling show'rs rose on the blast;
75 The speedy gleams the darkness swallow'd;
Loud, deep, and lang, the thunder bellow'd:
That night, a child might understand,
The Deil had business on his hand.

Weel mounted on his gray mare, *Meg*,
80 A better never lifted leg,
Tam skelpit on thro' dub and mire,
Despising wind, and rain, and fire;
Whiles holding fast his gude blue bonnet;
Whiles crooning o'er some auld Scots sonnet;
85 Whiles glow'ring round wi' prudent cares,
Lest bogles catch him unawares:
Kirk-Alloway was drawing nigh,
Whare ghaists and houlets nightly cry. –

By this time he was cross the ford,
90 Where in the snaw, the chapman smoor'd;
And past the birks and meikle stane,
Whare drunken *Charlie* brak's neck-bane;
And thro' the whins, and by the cairn,
Whare hunters fand the murder'd bairn;
95 And near the thorn, aboon the well,
Whare *Mungo's* mither hang'd hersel. –
Before him *Doon* pours all his floods:
The doubling storm roars thro' the woods:
The lightnings flash from pole to pole;
100 Near and more near the thunders roll:
When, glimmering thro' the groaning trees,
Kirk Alloway seem'd in a bleeze;
Thro' ilka bore the beams were glancing;
And loud resounded mirth and dancing. –

105 Inspiring bold *John Barleycorn*!
What dangers thou canst make us scorn!
Wi' tipenny, we fear nae evil;
Wi' usquebae we'll face the devil! –
The swats sae ream'd in *Tammie's* noddle,
110 Fair play, he car'd na deils a boddle.
But *Maggie* stood right sair astonish'd,
Till, by the heel and hand admonish'd,
She ventur'd forward on the light;
And, vow! *Tam* saw an unco sight!
115 Warlocks and witches in a dance;
Nae cotillion brent new frae *France*,
But hornpipes, jigs, strathspeys, and reels,
Put life and mettle in their heels,
A winnock-bunker in the east,
120 There sat auld Nick, in shape o' beast;
A towzie tyke, black, grim, and large,
To gie them music was his charge:
He screw'd the pipes and gart them skirl,
Till roof and rafters a' did dirl. –
125 Coffins stood round, like open presses,
That shaw'd the dead in their last dresses;

And by some devilish cantraip slight
Each in its cauld hand held a light. –
By which heroic *Tam* was able
130 To note upon the haly table,
A murderer's banes in gibbet airns;
Twa span-lang, wee, unchristen'd bairns;
A thief, new-cutted frae a rape,
Wi' his last gasp his gab did gape;
135 Five tomahawks, wi' blude red-rusted;
Five scymitars, wi' murder crusted;
A garter, which a babe had strangled;
A knife, a father's throat had mangled,
Whom his ain son o' life bereft,
140 The grey hairs yet stack to the heft;
Wi' mair o' horrible an' awefu',
Which ev'n to name wad be unlawfu'.

　　As *Tammie* glowr'd, amaz'd, and curious,
The mirth and fun grew fast and furious;
145 The piper loud and louder blew;
The dancers quick and quicker flew;
They reel'd, they set, they cross'd, they cleekit,
Till ilka carlin swat and reekit,
And coost her duddies to the wark,
150 And linket at it in her sark!

　　Now *Tam*, O *Tam*! had thae been queans,
A' plump and strapping in their teens,
Their sarks, instead o' creeshie flannen,
Been snaw-white seventeen hunder linnen!
155 Thir breeks o' mine, my only pair,
That ance were plush, o' gude blue hair,
I wad hae gi'en them off my hurdies,
For ae blink o' the bonie burdies!

　　But wither'd beldams, auld and droll,
160 Rigwoodie hags wad spean a foal,
Lowping and flinging on a crummock,
I wonder didna turn thy stomach.

But *Tam* kend what was what fu' brawlie,
There was ae winsome wench and wawlie,
165   That night enlisted in the core,
(Lang after kend on *Carrick* shore;
For mony a beast to dead she shot,
And perish'd mony a bony boat,
And shook baith meikle corn and bear,
170   And kept the countryside in fear)
Her cutty sark, o' Paisley harn,
That while a lassie she had worn,
In longitude tho' sorely scanty,
It was her best, and she was vauntie. –
175   Ah! little kend thy reverend grannie,
That sark she coft for her wee Nannie,
Wi' twa pund Scots ('twas a' her riches)
Wad ever grac'd a dance o' witches!

But here my Muse her wing maun cour;
180   Sic flights are far beyond her pow'r;
To sing how Nannie lap and flang,
(A souple jade she was, and strang),
And how *Tam* stood, like ane bewitch'd,
And thought his very een enrich'd;
185   Ev'n Satan glowr'd, and fidg'd fu' fain,
And hotch'd and blew wi' might and main:
Till first ae caper, syne anither,
Tam tint his reason a' thegither,
And roars out, 'Weel done, Cutty-sark!'
190   And in an instant all was dark:
And scarcely had he Maggie rallied,
When out the hellish legion sallied.

As bees bizz out wi' angry fyke,
When plundering herds assail their byke,
195   As open pussie's mortal foes,
When pop! she starts before their nose;
As eager runs the market-crowd,
When 'Catch the thief!' resounds aloud;
So Maggie runs, the witches follow,
200   Wi' mony an eldritch skreech and hollow.

Ah, *Tam*! Ah, *Tam*! thou'll get thy fairin!
In hell they'll roast thee like a herrin!
In vain thy *Kate* awaits thy comin!
Kate soon will be a woefu' woman!
205   Now, do thy speedy utmost, Meg,
And win the key-stane* of the brig;
There at them thou thy tail may toss,
A running stream they dare na cross.
But ere the key-stane she could make,
210   The fient a tale she had to shake!
For Nannie, far before the rest,
Hard upon noble Maggie prest,
And flew at Tam wi' furious ettle;
But little wist she Maggie's mettle –
215   Ae spring brought off her master hale,
But left behind her ain gray tail:
The carlin claught her by the rump,
And left poor Maggie scarce a stump.

Now, wha this tale o' truth shall read,
220   Ilk man and mother's son, take heed:
Whene'er to drink you are inclin'd,
Or cutty sarks run in your mind,
Think, ye may buy the joys o'er dear,
Remember Tam o' Shanter's mare.

---

* It is a well known fact that witches, or any evil spirits, have no power to follow a poor wight any farther than the middle of the next running stream. – It may be proper likewise to mention to the benighted traveller, that when he falls in with *bogles*, whatever danger there may be in his going forward, there is much more hazard in turning back. [RB]

The Banks o' Doon

(TUNE: CALEDONIAN HUNT'S DELIGHT)

Ye banks and braes o' bonie Doon,
    How can ye bloom sae fresh and fair;
How can ye chant, ye little birds,
    And I sae weary fu' o' care!
5 Thou'll break my heart, thou warbling bird,
    That wantons thro' the flowering thorn:
Thou minds me o' departed joys,
    Departed never to return.

Oft hae I rov'd by bonie Doon,
10   To see the rose and woodbine twine
And ilka bird sang o' its luve,
    And fondly sae did I o' mine.
Wi' lightsome heart I pu'd a rose,
    Fu' sweet upon its thorny tree;
15 And my fause luver staw my rose,
    But ah! he left the thorn wi' me.

To Robert Graham of Fintry, Esq.

Late crippl'd of an arm, and now a leg,
About to beg a *pass* for leave to beg;
Dull, listless, teas'd, dejected, and deprest,
(Nature is adverse to a cripple's rest);
5 Will generous Graham list to his Poet's wail?
(It soothes poor Misery, hearkning to her tale),
And hear him curse the light he first survey'd
And doubly curse the luckless rhyming trade.

Thou, Nature, partial Nature, I arraign;
10 Of thy caprice maternal I complain.
The lion and the bull thy care have found,
One shakes the forests, and one spurns the ground:

Thou giv'st the ass his hide, the snail his shell,
Th' envenom'd wasp, victorious, guards his cell. –
15   Thy minions, kings, defend, controul, devour,
In all th' omnipotence of rule and power. –
Foxes and statesmen, subtile wiles ensure;
The cit and polecat stink, and are secure.
Toads with their poison, doctors with their drug,
20   The priest and hedgehog in their robes, are snug.
Ev'n silly woman has her warlike arts,
Her tongue and eyes, her dreaded spear and darts.

But Oh! thou bitter step-mother and hard,
To thy poor, fenceless, naked child – the Bard!
25   A thing unteachable in world's skill,
And half an idiot too, more helpless still.
No heels to bear him from the op'ning dun;
No claws to dig, his hated sight to shun;
No horns, but those by luckless Hymen worn,
30   And those, alas! not Amalthea's horn:
No nerves olfact'ry, Mammon's trusty cur,
Clad in rich Dulness' comfortable fur.
In naked feeling, and in aching pride,
He bears th' unbroken blast from ev'ry side:
35   Vampyre booksellers drain him to the heart,
And scorpion Critics cureless venom dart.

Critics – appall'd, I venture on the name,
Those cut-throat bandits in the paths of fame:
Bloody dissectors, worse than ten Monroes;
40   He hacks to teach, they mangle to expose.

His heart by causeless wanton malice wrung,
By blockheads' daring into madness stung;
His well-won bays, than life itself more dear,
By miscreants torn, who ne'er one sprig must wear:
45   Foil'd, bleeding, tortur'd, in th' unequal strife,
The hapless Poet flounders on thro' life.
Till fled each hope that once his bosom fir'd,
And fled each Muse that glorious once inspir'd,

Low-sunk in squalid, unprotected age,
50 Dead, even resentment, for his injur'd page,
He heeds or feels no more the ruthless Critic's rage!

So, by some hedge, the gen'rous steed deceas'd,
For half-starv'd snarling curs a dainty feast;
By toil and famine worn to skin and bone,
55 Lies, senseless of each tugging bitch's son.

O Dulness! portion of the truly blest!
Calm shelter'd haven of eternal rest!
Thy sons ne'er madden in the fierce extremes
Of Fortune's polar frost, or torrid beams.
60 If mantling high she fills the golden cup,
With sober selfish ease they sip it up:
Conscious the bounteous meed they well deserve,
They only wonder 'some folks' do not starve.
The grave sage hern thus easy picks his frog,
65 And thinks the mallard a sad worthless dog.
When disappointment snaps the clue of hope,
And thro' disastrous night they darkling grope,
With deaf endurance sluggishly they bear,
And just conclude that 'fools are fortune's care.'
70 So, heavy, passive to the tempest's shocks,
Strong on the sign-post stands the stupid ox.

Not so the idle Muses' mad-cap train,
Nor such the workings of their moon-struck brain;
In equanimity they never dwell,
75 By turns in soaring heav'n, or vaulted hell.

I dread thee, Fate, relentless and severe,
With all a poet's, husband's, father's fear!
Already one strong hold of hope is lost,
Glencairn, the truly noble, lies in dust;
80 (Fled, like the sun eclips'd as noon appears,
And left us darkling in a world of tears:)
O! hear my ardent, grateful, selfish prayer!
Fintry, my other stay, long bless and spare!
Thro' a long life his hopes and wishes crown;
85 And bright in cloudless skies his sun go down!

May *bliss domestic* smooth his private path;
Give energy to life; and soothe his latest breath,
With many a filial tear circling the bed of death!

Ae Fond Kiss

(TUNE: RORY DALL'S PORT)

Ae fond kiss, and then we sever;
Ae farewell and then forever!
Deep in heart-wrung tears I'll pledge thee,
Warring sighs and groans I'll wage thee.

5 Who shall say that fortune grieves him
While the star of hope she leaves him?
Me, nae chearfu' twinkle lights me;
Dark despair around benights me.

I'll ne'er blame my partial fancy,
10 Naething could resist my Nancy:
But to see her, was to love her;
Love but her, and love for ever.

Had we never lov'd sae kindly,
Had we never lov'd sae blindly,
15 Never met – or never parted,
We had ne'er been broken-hearted.

Fare thee weel, thou first and fairest!
Fare thee weel, thou best and dearest!
Thine be ilka joy and treasure,
20 Peace, Enjoyment, Love and Pleasure!

Ae fond kiss, and then we sever;
Ae fareweel, Alas! for ever!
Deep in heart-wrung tears I'll pledge thee,
Warring sighs and groans I'll wage thee.

The Bonie Wee Thing

Bonie wee thing, canie wee thing,
Lovely wee thing was thou mine;
I wad wear thee in my bosom,
Least my Jewel I should tine.

5 Wishfully I look and languish
In that bonie face of thine;
And my heart it stounds wi' anguish
Least my wee thing be na mine.
Bonie wee &c.

10 Wit, and Grace, and Love, and Beauty,
In ae constellation shine;
To adore thee is my duty,
Goddess o' this soul o' mine!
Bonie wee &c.

I Hae a Wife o' My Ain

I hae a wife o' my ain,
I'll partake wi' naebody;
I'll tak Cuckold frae nane,
I'll gie Cuckold to naebody.

5 I hae a penny to spend,
There, thanks to naebody;
I hae naething to lend,
I'll borrow frae naebody.

I am naebody's lord,
10 I'll be slave to naebody;
I hae a gude braid sword,
I'll tak dunts frae naebody.

I'll be merry and free,
I'll be sad for naebody;
15 Naebody cares for me,
I care for naebody.

O for Ane and Twenty Tam!

(TUNE: THE MOUDIEWORT)

An O, for ane and twenty Tam!
  An hey, sweet ane and twenty, Tam!
I'll learn my kin a rattlin sang,
  An I saw ane and twenty Tam.

5 They snool me sair, and haud me down,
    And gar me look like bluntie, Tam;
  But three short years will soon wheel roun',
    And then comes ane and twenty Tam.
      An O, for &c.

10 A gleib o' lan', a claut o' gear,
     Was left me by my Auntie, Tam;
   At kith or kin I need na spier,
     An I saw ane and twenty, Tam.
       An O, for &c.

15 They'll hae me wed a wealthy coof,
     Tho' I mysel hae plenty, Tam;
   But hearst thou, laddie, there's my loof,
     I'm thine at ane and twenty, Tam!
       An O, for &c.

Lady Mary Ann

O Lady Mary Ann looks o'er the castle wa',
She saw three bonie boys playing at the ba',
The youngest he was the flower amang them a',
My bonie laddie's young but he's growin yet.

5   O Father, O Father, an ye think it fit,
We'll send him a year to the College yet,
We'll sew a green ribban round about his hat,
And that will let them ken he's to marry yet.

Lady Mary Ann was a flower in the dew,
10 Sweet was its smell and bonie was its hue,
And the langer it blossom'd, the sweeter it grew,
For the lily in the bud will be bonier yet.

Young Charlie Cochran was the sprout of an aik,
Bonie, and bloomin and straught was its make,
15 The sun took delight to shine for its sake,
And it will be the brag o' the forest yet.

The simmer is gane when the leaves they were green,
And the days are awa that we hae seen;
But far better days I trust will come again,
20 For my bonie laddie's young but he's growin yet.

The Gallant Weaver

(TUNE: WEAVER'S MARCH)

Where Cart rins rowin to the sea,
By mony a flow'r and spreading tree,
There lives a lad, the lad for me,
    He is a gallant Weaver.
5 Oh I had wooers aught or nine,
They gied me rings and ribbons fine;
And I was fear'd my heart would tine,
    And I gied it to the Weaver.

My daddie sign'd my tocher-band
10 To gie the lad that has the land,
But to my heart I'll add my hand,
    And give it to the Weaver.

While birds rejoice in leafy bowers;
While bees delight in opening flowers;
15 While corn grows green in simmer showers,
    I love my gallant Weaver.

Hey Ca' Thro'

Up wi' the carls of Dysart,
And the lads o' Buckhiven,
And the kimmers o' Largo,
And the lasses o' Leven.

5   Hey ca' thro' ca' thro'
      For we hae mickle a do,
      Hey ca' thro' ca' thro'
      For we hae mickle a do.

We hae tales to tell,
10 And we hae sangs to sing;
We hae pennies to spend,
And we hae pints to bring.
      Hey ca' thro' &c.

We'll live a' our days,
15 And them that comes behin',
Let them do the like,
And spend the gear they win.
      Hey ca' thro' &c.

When Princes and Prelates

When Princes and Prelates and het-headed zealots
All Europe hae set in a lowe,
The poor man lies down, nor envies a crown,
And comforts himsel with a mowe. –

5 And why shouldna poor folk mowe, mowe, mowe,
And why shouldna poor folk mowe:
The great folk hae siller, and houses and lands,
Poor bodies hae naething but mowe. –

When Brunswick's great Prince cam a cruising to France
10 Republican billies to cowe,
Bauld Brunswick's great Prince wad hae shawn
  better sense,
At hame with his Princess to mowe. –
  And why shouldna &c.

Out over the Rhine proud Prussia wad shine,
15 To *spend* his best blood he did vow;
But Frederic had better ne'er forded the water,
But *spent* as he docht in a mowe. –
  And why &c. –

By sea and by shore! the Emperor swore,
20 In Paris he'd kick up a row;
But Paris sae ready just leugh at the laddie
And bad him gae tak him a mowe. –
  And why &c. –

Auld Kate laid her claws on poor Stanislaus,
25 And Poland has bent like a bow:
May the deil in her a–se ram a huge pr–ck o' brass!
And damn her in h–ll with a mowe!
  And why &c. –

But truce with commotions and new-fangled notions,
30 A bumper I trust you'll allow:
Here's George our gude king and Charlotte his queen,
And lang may they tak a gude mowe!

Logan Water

O Logan, sweetly didst thou glide,
The day I was my Willie's bride;
And years sinsyne hae o'er us run,
Like Logan to the simmer sun.
5 But now thy flow'ry banks appear
Like drumlie winter, dark and drear,
While my dear lad maun face his faes,
Far, far frae me and Logan braes.

Again the merry month o' May
10 Has made our hills and vallies gay;
The birds rejoice in leafy bow'rs,
The bees hum round the breathing flow'rs:
Blythe morning lifts his rosy eye,
And ev'ning's tears are tears o' joy:
15 My soul, delightless, a' surveys,
While Willie's far frae Logan braes.

Within yon milk-white hawthorn bush,
Amang her nestlings sits the thrush;
Her faithfu' mate will share her toil,
20 Or wi' his song her cares beguile: –
But I, wi' my sweet nurslings here,
Nae mate to help, nae mate to cheer,
Pass widow'd nights, and joyless days,
While Willie's far frae Logan braes.

25 O wae upon you, men o' state,
That brethren rouse in deadly hate!
As ye make mony a fond heart mourn,
Sae may it on your heads return!
Ye mind na, mid your cruel joys,
30 The widow's tears, the orphan's cries!
But soon may peace bring happy days,
And Willie hame to Logan braes!

O, Whistle an' I'll Come to Ye, My Lad

O, whistle an' I'll come to ye, my lad!
O, whistle an' I'll come to ye, my lad!
Tho' father an' mother an' a' should gae mad,
O, whistle an' I'll come to ye, my lad!

5   But warily tent when ye come to court me,
And come nae unless the back-yett be a-jee;
Syne up the back-style, and let naebody see,
And come as ye were na comin to me.
And come as ye were na comin to me.

10   At kirk, or at market, whene'er ye meet me,
Gang by me as tho' that ye car'd na a flie;
But steal me a blink o' your bonie black e'e,
Yet look as ye were na looking to me.
Yet look as ye were na looking to me.

15   Ay vow and protest that ye care na for me,
And whiles ye may lightly my beauty awee;
But court na anither, tho' jokin ye be,
For fear that she wile your fancy frae me.
For fear that she wile your fancy frae me.

Scots Wha Hae

(TUNE: HEY, TUTTI TAITIE)

Scots, wha hae wi' Wallace bled,
Scots, wham Bruce has aften led,
Welcome to your gory bed
        Or to victorie!

5   Now's the day, and now's the hour:
See the front o' battle lour,
See approach proud Edward's power –
        Chains and slaverie!

Wha will be a traitor knave?
10 Wha can fill a coward's grave?
Wha sae base as be a slave? –
            Let him turn, and flee!

Wha for Scotland's king and law
Freedom's sword will strongly draw,
15 Freeman stand or freeman fa',
            Let him follow me!

By Oppression's woes and pains,
By your sons in servile chains,
We will drain our dearest veins
20   But they shall be free!

Lay the proud usurpers low!
Tyrants fall in every foe!
Liberty's in every blow! –
            Let us do, or die!

A Red, Red Rose

(TUNE: MAJOR GRAHAM)

My luve is like a red, red rose,
    That's newly sprung in June:
My luve is like the melodie,
    That's sweetly play'd in tune.
5 As fair art thou, my bonie lass,
    So deep in luve am I,
And I will luve thee still, my dear,
    Till a' the seas gang dry.

} [twice]

Till a' the seas gang dry, my dear,
10   And the rocks melt wi' the sun!
And I will luve thee still, my dear,
    While the sands o' life shall run.
And fare-thee-weel, my only luve,
    And fare-thee-weel a while!
15 And I will come again, my luve,
    Tho' it were ten-thousand mile.

} [twice]

Sae Flaxen Were Her Ringlets

(TUNE: OONAGH'S WATERFALL)

Sae flaxen were her ringlets,
 Her eyebrows of a darker hue,
Bewitchingly o'erarching
 Twa laughing een o' bonie blue;
5 Her smiling, sae wyling,
  Wad make a wretch forget his woe;
What pleasure, what treasure,
  Unto these rosy lips to grow:
Such was my Chloris' bonie face,
10 When first her bonie face I saw;
And ay my Chloris' dearest charm,
 She says, she lo'es me best of a'.

Like harmony her motion;
 Her pretty ancle is a spy,
15 Betraying fair proportion,
  Wad make a saint forget the sky.
Sae warming, sae charming,
  Her fauteless form and gracefu' air;
Ilk feature – auld Nature
20 Declar'd that she could do nae mair:
Hers are the willing chains o' love,
  By conquering Beauty's sovereign law;
And ay my Chloris' dearest charm,
 She says, she lo'es me best of a'.

25 Let others love the city,
  And gaudy shew at sunny noon;
Gie me the lonely valley,
  The dewy eve, and rising moon.
Fair beaming, and streaming
30 Her silver light the boughs amang;
While falling, recalling,
  The amorous thrush concludes his sang;

There, dearest Chloris, wilt thou rove
    By wimpling burn and leafy shaw,
35 And hear my vows o' truth and love,
    And say, thou lo'es me best of a'.

Ode to Spring

(TUNE: THE TITHER MORN)

When maukin bucks, at early f—s,
    In dewy glens are seen, Sir;
And birds, on boughs, take off their m—s,
    Amang the leaves sae green, Sir;
5 Latona's sun looks liquorish on
    Dame Nature's grand impètus,
Till his p—go rise, then westward flies
    To r—ger Madame Thetis.

Yon wandering rill that marks the hill,
10   And glances o'er the brae, Sir,
Slides by a bower where many a flower
    Sheds fragrance on the day, Sir;
There Damon lay with Sylvia gay,
    To love they thought no crime, Sir;
15 The wild-birds sang, the echoes rang,
    While Damon's a—se beat time, Sir.

First, wi' the thrush, his thrust and push
    Had compass large and long, Sir;
The blackbird next, his tuneful text,
20   Was bolder, clear and strong, Sir:
The linnet's lay came then in play,
    And the lark that soar'd aboon, Sir;
Till Damon, fierce, mistim'd his a—,
    And f—'d quite out o' tune, Sir.

Is There for Honest Poverty

(TUNE: FOR A' THAT)

Is there for honest poverty
    That hings his head, an' a' that?
The coward slave, we pass him by –
    We dare be poor for a' that!
5   For a' that, an a' that,
            Our toils obscure, an' a' that,
        The rank is but the guinea's stamp,
        The man's the gowd for a' that.

What tho' on hamely fare we dine,
10   Wear hodden grey, an' a' that?
Gie fools their silks, and knaves their wine –
    A man's a man for a' that!
        For a' that, an' a' that,
            Their tinsel show, an' a' that,
15   The honest man, tho' e'er sae poor,
        Is king o' men for a' that.

Ye see yon birkie ca'd a lord,
    Wha struts, and stares, an' a' that;
Tho' hundreds worship at his word,
20   He's but a coof for a' that.
        For a' that, an' a' that,
            His ribband, star, an' a' that,
        The man o' independent mind,
        He looks an' laughs at a' that.

25 A prince can mak a belted knight,
    A marquis, duke, an' a' that,
But an honest man's aboon his might –
    Gude faith, he mauna fa' that!
        For a' that, an' a' that,
30   Their dignities, an a' that,
        The pith o' sense an' pride o' worth
        Are higher rank than a' that.

Then let us pray that come it may –
    As come it will, for a' that –
35 That sense and worth, o'er a' the earth
    Shall bear the gree, an' a' that;
        For a' that, an' a' that,
           It's comin yet for a' that,
        That man to man the world o'er,
40   Shall brothers be for a' that.

Lines Written on Windows of the Globe Inn, Dumfries

(A)

The greybeard, old wisdom, may boast of his treasures,
    Give me with gay folly to live;
I grant him his calm-blooded, time-settled pleasures,
    But folly has raptures to give.

(B)

My bottle is a holy pool,
That heals the wounds o' care an' dool;
And pleasure is a wanton trout,
An' ye drink it, ye'll find him out.

(C)

In politics if thou would'st mix,
    And mean thy fortunes be;
Bear this in mind, be deaf and blind,
    Let great folks hear and see.

I Murder Hate

I murder hate by field or flood,
   Tho' glory's name may screen us;
In wars at hame I'll spend my blood –
   Life-giving wars of Venus.
5 The deities that I adore
   Are social Peace and Plenty;
I'm better pleas'd *to make one more*,
   Than be the death of twenty.

I would not die like Socrates,
10   For all the fuss of Plato;
Nor would I with Leonidas,
   Nor yet would I with Cato:
The zealots of the Church and State
   Shall ne'er my mortal foes be;
15 But let me have bold *Zimri's fate
   Within the arms of Cosbi.

Kirkcudbright Grace

Some have meat and cannot eat,
   Some cannot eat that want it:
But we have meat and we can eat,
   Sae let the Lord be thankit.

* Vide, Numbers Chap. 25th Verse 8th–15th – [RB]

Last May a Braw Wooer

(TUNE: LOTHIAN LASSIE)

Last May a braw wooer cam down the lang glen,
    And sair wi' his love he did deave me;
I said there was naething I hated like men,
    The deuce gae wi'm, to believe me, believe me,
5   The deuce gae wi'm, to believe me.

He spak o' the darts in my bonie black e'en,
    And vow'd for my love he was dying;
I said he might die when he liked, for Jean,
    The Lord forgie me for lying, for lying,
10   The Lord forgie me for lying!

A weel-stocket mailen, himsel for the laird,
    And marriage aff-hand, were his proffers:
I never loot on that I kend it, or car'd,
    But thought I might hae waur offers, waur offers,
15   But thought I might hae waur offers.

But what wad ye think? in a fortnight or less,
    The deil tak his taste to gae near her!
He up the Gateslack to my black cousin Bess,
    Guess ye how, the jad! I could bear her, could bear her,
20   Guess ye how, the jad! I could bear her.

But a' the niest week as I fretted wi' care,
    I gaed to the tryste o' Dalgarnock,
And wha but my fine fickle lover was there,
    I glower'd as I'd seen a warlock, a warlock,
25   I glower'd as I'd seen a warlock.

But owre my left shouther I gae him a blink,
    Least neebors might say I was saucy;
My wooer he caper'd as he'd been in drink,
    And vow'd I was his dear lassie, dear lassie,
30   And vow'd I was his dear lassie.

I spier'd for my cousin fu' couthy and sweet,
    Gin she had recover'd her hearin,
And how her new shoon fit her auld shackl'd feet,
    But heavens! how he fell a swearin, a swearin,
35   But heavens! how he fell a swearin.

He begged, for Gudesake! I wad be his wife,
    Or else I wad kill him wi' sorrow:
So e'en to preserve the poor body in life
    I think I maun wed him to-morrow, to-morrow,
40   I think I maun wed him to-morrow.

Wantonness

Wantonness for ever mair,
Wantonness has been my ruin;
Yet for a' my dool and care,
It's wantonness for ever!

5 I hae lov'd the Black, the Brown,
I hae lov'd the Fair, the Gowden:
A' the colours in the town
I hae won their wanton favour.

Charlie He's My Darling

'Twas on a Monday morning,
    Right early in the year,
That Charlie cam to our town,
    The young Chevalier.
5   An' Charlie he's my darling,
        My darling, my darling,
        Charlie he's my darling, the young Chevalier.

As he was walking up the street,
   The city for to view,
10 O there he spied a bonie lass
   The window looking thro'. – An' Charlie &c.

Sae light's he jimped up the stair,
   And tirled at the pin;
And wha sae ready as hersel,
15   To let the laddie in. – An' Charlie &c.

He set his Jenny on his knee,
   All in his Highland dress;
For brawlie weel he ken'd the way
   To please a bonie lass. – An' Charlie &c.

20 It's up yon hethery mountain,
   And down yon scroggy glen,
We daur na gang a milking,
   For Charlie and his men. – An' Charlie &c.

It Was a' for Our Rightfu' King

(TUNE: MALLY STEWART)

It was a' for our rightfu' king
   We left fair Scotland's strand;
It was a' for our rightfu' king,
   We e'er saw Irish land, my dear,
5   We e'er saw Irish land.

Now a' is done that men can do,
   And a' is done in vain:
My Love and Native Land fareweel,
   For I maun cross the main, my dear,
10   For I maun cross the main.

He turn'd him right and round about,
    Upon the Irish shore,
And gae his bridle reins a shake,
    With adieu for evermore, my dear,
15   With adieu for evermore.

The soger frae the wars returns,
    The sailor frae the main,
But I hae parted frae my Love,
    Never to meet again, my dear,
20   Never to meet again.

When day is gane, and night is come,
    And a' folk bound to sleep;
I think on him that's far awa,
    The lee-lang night and weep, my dear,
25   The lee-lang night and weep.

Oh Wert Thou in the Cauld Blast

(TUNE: LENOX LOVE TO BLANTYRE)

Oh, wert thou in the cauld blast,
    On yonder lea, on yonder lea;
My plaidie to the angry airt,
    I'd shelter thee, I'd shelter thee:
5 Or did misfortune's bitter storms
    Around thee blaw, around thee blaw,
Thy bield should be my bosom,
    To share it a', to share it a'.

Or were I in the wildest waste,
10   Sae black and bare, sae black and bare,
The desart were a paradise,
    If thou wert there, if thou wert there.
Or were I monarch o' the globe,
    Wi' thee to reign, wi' thee to reign;
15 The brightest jewel in my crown,
    Wad be my queen, wad be my queen.

Notes

The following abbreviations are used in the notes:

1CPB	J. C. Ewing and Davidson Cook, eds., *Robert Burns's Commonplace Book 1783–85* (facsimile), Glasgow: Gowans and Gray, 1938.
2CPB	W. Jack, ed., *The Edinburgh (Second) Commonplace Book*, reprinted in *Macmillan's Magazine*, Vols. 39 and 40 (1879–80).
Ashmead and Davison	John Ashmead and John Davison, *The Songs of Robert Burns*, New York: Garland, 1988.
BE	Maurice Lindsay, ed., *The Burns Encyclopedia*, London: Hutchinson, 1970.
Chambers and Wallace	*The Life and Works of Robert Burns*, edited by Robert Chambers, revised by William Wallace, 4 vols., Edinburgh: W. and R. Chambers, 1896.
Crawford	Thomas Crawford, *Burns: A Study of the Poems and Songs*, Edinburgh: Oliver and Boyd, 1960.
Cromek	Robert Hartley Cromek, ed., *Reliques of Robert Burns, Consisting Chiefly of Original Letters, Poems and Critical Observations on Scottish Songs*, London: Cadell and Davies, 1808.
Currie	James Currie, ed., *The Works of Robert Burns*, 4 vols., London: Cadell and Davies, 1801. (This is the second edition.)
Dick	J. C. Dick, ed., *The Songs of Robert Burns, Now First Printed with the Melodies for Which They Were Written; A Study in Tone-Poetry*, London, 1903; reprinted New York: AMS, 1973.
Egerer	J. W. Egerer, *A Bibliography of Robert Burns*, Edinburgh: Oliver and Boyd, 1964.

Glenriddell	Desmond Donaldson, ed., *The Glenriddell Manuscripts of Robert Burns* (facsimile), Hamden, Conn.: Archon, 1973.
HH	W. E. Henley and T. F. Henderson, eds., *The Poetry of Robert Burns*. 4 vols., London: Caxton (Boston: Houghton Mifflin), 1896–7.
JK	James Kinsley, ed., *The Poems and Songs of Robert Burns*, 3 vols., Oxford: Clarendon, 1968.
Letters	G. Ross Roy and J. DeLancey Fergusson, eds., *The Letters of Robert Burns*, 2 vols., Oxford: Clarendon, 1985.
Mackay	James Mackay, *A Biography of Robert Burns*, Edinburgh: Mainstream, 1992.
MMC	Legman, G., *The Merry Muses of Caledonia*, New Hyde Park, N.Y.: University Books, 1965.
Notes	J. C. Dick, ed., *Notes on Scottish Song by Robert Burns; Written in an Interleaved Copy of the 'Scots Musical Museum'*, 1908; reprinted New York: AMS, 1973.
Poems	Burns, Robert, *Poems, Chiefly in the Scottish Dialect*, Kilmarnock: J. Wilson, 1786. Later editions are specified by cities and dates: Edinburgh 1787, 1793–4, etc.
SC	George Thomson, ed., *A Select Collection of Original Scotish Airs*, Edinburgh: G. Thomson, 1793–1818.
SMM	James Johnson and Robert Burns, eds., *Scots Musical Museum*. Edinburgh: J. Johnson, 1787–1803.
Stewart	Thomas Stewart, ed., *Poems Ascribed to Robert Burns*, Glasgow: Stewart, 1801; or Thomas Stewart, ed., *Stewart's Edition of Burns's Poems*. Glasgow: Stewart, 1802. (The date is always given to distinguish the two.)

O Once I Lov'd (Tune: I am a man unmarried)

Text: *1CPB*. Transcribed in August 1783; written in autumn 1774. The manuscript source best retains the boyish touches – the erratic spelling, the flourish of 'Finis' at the end. First printed in *SMM* (1803).

In 1787, Burns looked back on the song and the girl who inspired it: 'In my fifteenth autumn, my partner [in the harvest] was a bewitching creature who just counted an autumn less ... Among her other love-inspiring qualifications, she sung sweetly; and 'twas her favorite reel to which I attempted giving an embodied vehicle in rhyme' (*Letters* 1, 137–8). That Burns's first composition should be a love song inspired by personal experience – and that the girl's name (unveiled by classical allusion or pseudonym) should be emphasized – suggest that the young poet saw clearly some features of his future path.

Nellie Kilpatrick, a farm servant who was daughter of a blacksmith (Dick), farmer (JK), or miller (*BE*), married William Bone, the laird of Newark's coachman; she may have died in 1820 (*BE*; see also JK 3, 1003). James MacKay's biography has revived an old tradition, however, that the song's heroine was another harvest helper, Nellie Blair, later a farmer's wife. Whatever her name, the tune that the poet's partner sang at harvest was composed (according to Burns) by the son of a neighbouring laird; it has never been traced.

Behind Yon Hills Where Lugar Flows (Tune: My Nanie, O)

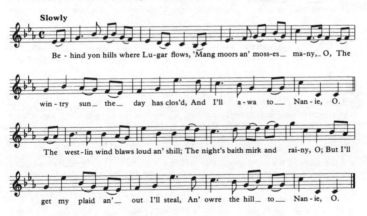

Text: *Poems* 1787 (Edinburgh). Transcribed in *1CPB* in April 1784; probably written before 1780. Music from Dick.

Burns described this as 'very early' (Stair MS, 1786); the poet's youngest sister Isabella told the early Victorian scholar-editor Robert Chambers that it had been much admired by Burns's father (d. February 1784). Allan Cunningham reported that Agnes Fleming, a farmer's daughter who lived near Lochlea, was convinced the song was written for her – 'Aye, atweel he made a great wark about me' – but this may be apocryphal (*BE*). In stanza 5, the lyric departs from its conventional catalogue of Nanie's charms (reminiscent of the inventory of Nellie's in the previous poem) to a self-portrait of the young farmer as a man of feeling. The expressive air (Burns once called it 'the most beautiful' he knew) was first transcribed in the Graham MS (1694).

'Stinchar', the river named in the copy-text (l.1), was changed by Burns in 1792: 'In the printed copy ... the name of the river is horridly prosaic – I will alter it ... "Girvan" is the river that suits the idea of the stanza best, but "Lugar" is the most agreable modulation of syllables' (*Letters* 2, 154).

Mary Morison (*Tune: Duncan Davison*)

Text: Currie (1801). Not in *1CPB*; probably written in 1781. Music from Dick.

Currie wrongly identifies 'Bide Ye Yet' as the musical setting; Burns's choice was a jocular song that may have struck Currie (or his song-adviser, the officious George Thomson) as unseemly. Even when slowed, the air Burns chose is not well matched to these tender and pensive stanzas, which Hugh MacDiarmid singled out as Burns's 'most powerful'.

Like many of the early songs, this is difficult to date. The surviving manuscript was transcribed in March 1793 and sent to George Thomson: the poet unenthusiastically describes it as 'one of my juvenile works ... I do not think it very remarkable, either for its merits or demerits' (*Letters* 2, 186). JK argues for 1784 as the date of composition, which would make the Mary Morison residing in Mauchline (d. 1791 aged twenty) a possible, if at fourteen somewhat precocious, recipient. I place the song in 1781, however, when Mauchline's Mary Morison was ten years old: too young to have lent the poet more than a name exactly fitted to his air ('Duncan Davison'). Though Burns did not reside near Mauchline until 1783, three strong arguments favour 1781. It is unlikely that Burns would refer to a song from 1784 (his annus mirabilis as well as his twenty-sixth year) as 'juvenile'. Furthermore, the poet's brother Gilbert (as a rule dourly accurate in his record of Burns's romances) said that it was 'Ellison' (Alison) Begbie who inspired the song; and the biographers' consensus is that Burns proposed to and was rejected by Ellison in 1781. (Mackay has argued that tradition has garbled the name, and the girl in question was Eliza Gebbie.) In any case, the song's sentiment – its extreme rhetorical delicacy – is reminiscent of letters to 'dear E' written in 1781: 'It would be weak and unmanly to say that without you I can never be happy; but sure I am, that sharing life with you would have given it a relish, that wanting you I can never taste . . . I had formed the most delightful images . . . but now I am wretched for the loss of what I really had no right to expect' (*Letters* 1, 13). Perhaps, as with other songs, the earlier drafts were built round a different proper name, later replaced by Mary Morison as a better match for the tune.

In l. 12, 'nor' is 'or' in the copy-text; emended as in Dalhousie MS.

It Was Upon a Lammas Night (*Tune: Corn rigs are bonie*)

Text: *Poems* 1786 (Kilmarnock). Not in *1CPB*; written before 1782 (*Letters* 1, 142). One of four early songs published in *Poems* 1786 (Kilmarnock). Music from Dick.

The graceful crafting of the song – nature's harvest used as a lyric setting for the lovers' reaping of mutual pleasure – is best seen by contrast with the wooden model from which the poet worked, Allan Ramsay's concluding song in *The Gentle Shepherd* (1725):

Let maidens of a silly mind
Refuse what maist they're wanting;
Since we for yielding are design'd,
We chastely should be granting;
Then I'll comply, and marry Pate,
And syne my cockernony,
He's free to touzle, air or late,
Where corn-riggs are bonny.

The exuberant tune perfectly matches Burns's lyrics. Anne Rankine Merry (d. 1843), who grew up at Adamhill farm near Lochlea (she was daughter of the poet's friend John Rankine), fascinated early bardolaters with her insistence that she was this song's 'Annie' – although some suspected she was only seeking publicity for her husband's inn at Cumnock.

In l. 22 'hour' is given as 'night' in the copy-text; emended here as in subsequent editions of *Poems*. Burns made the change to eliminate awkward repetition of 'that night', used again in l. 23.

Song Composed in August (Original tune: I had a horse, I had nae mair)

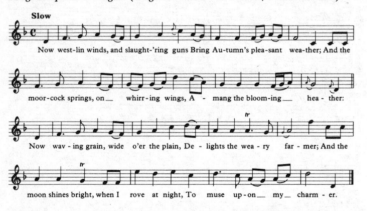

Now west-lin winds, and slaught-'ring guns Bring Au-tumn's plea-sant wea-ther; And the moor-cock springs, on__ whirr-ing wings, A - mang the bloom-ing__ hea - ther: Now wav-ing grain, wide o'er the plain, De - lights the wea - ry far - mer; And the moon shines bright, when I rove at night, To muse up-on__ my__ charm - er.

Text: *Poems* 1786 (Kilmarnock). Music from Dick. First printed with music in 1792 (*SMM* 351), but set to the wrong air. A fragment adapted to Jean Armour's name was transcribed in *1CPB* in August 1785. This song was begun in 1775 and completed in or before 1782 (cf. *Letters* 1, 142). Despite the tune given in the copy-text, the tune above is a setting later suggested by Burns, 'Port Gordon'. It is better matched to these stanzas and is Dick's musical setting. (For the original tune, see music for 'When First I Came to Stewart Kyle', p. 204.)

Like 'Corn Rigs', this was evidently a favourite work – one of just four songs chosen for publication in *Poems* 1786 (Kilmarnock). Margaret Thomson ('a charming Fillette') lived next door to the school in Kirkoswald where Burns was sent to study surveying in summer of 1775 (*Letters* 1, 140); JK dates the song accordingly. The poet's youngest sister told Robert Chambers, however, that Burns and Peggy met and courted again when he was twenty-five, so that the date of composition might be as late as 1784 (JK 3, 1004). John Neilson of Monnyfee married Margaret Thomson in 1784 (Glenriddell 21, where Burns spells her name 'Thompson'); the couple were among the friends of whom Burns took formal leave when he planned to emigrate to Jamaica in 1786: 'When I was . . . intending to go to the West Indies, when I took farewell of her, neither she nor I could speak a syllable. – Her husband escorted me three miles on my road, and we both parted with tears' (*BE*). Burns sent Peggy Neilson a copy of the Kilmarnock edition inscribed 'Once fondly lov'd, and still remember'd dear'.

John Barleycorn. A Ballad (Original tune: Cold and raw)

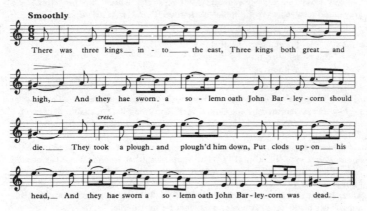

Text: *Poems* 1787 (Edinburgh). Transcribed in *1CPB* in June 1785, but written before 1782 (see below). The tune suggested in the copy-text (also called 'Up in the morning early') is not as well matched as 'Lull me beyond thee', later suggested by Burns. The latter setting is given here, following Dick.

This was copied twice in 1785 but was identified in Burns's autobiographical letter to Dr John Moore as among 'my eldest pieces' completed 'before my twenty third year' (*Letters* 1, 141–2). 'I once heard the old song . . . sung; and being very fond of it . . . [I] remember . . . two or three verses of it viz. the 1st, 2d & 3d, with some scraps which I have interwoven here' (*1CPB* 22). Kinsley could find no precedent for stanza 1, with its audacious reverse epiphany – three kings coming out of the east intent on mayhem. Otherwise this ballad's imagery was already traditional in 1568, when 'Allan-a-Maut' was transcribed in the Bannantyne MS. Burns breaks up the folk-allegory into more stages, as the grain (personified as victim/redeemer John Barleycorn) is processed through harvest, soaking, threshing, roasting, and milling. Transubstantiated as whisky, John Barleycorn's 'heart's blood' lives on, raising courage and soothing care.

The Death and Dying Words of Poor Mailie

Text: *Poems* 1786 (Kilmarnock). Transcribed in *1CPB* (June 1785); written at Lochlea and completed by 1782 (*Letters*, 1, 141–2).

The incident occurred at Lochlea farm, where (in contrast to her poetic fate) Mailie was rescued. Gilbert Burns recalled that his brother was 'much tickled by the herdsman Huoc's appearance and postures on the occasion' when Robert's tethered pet ewe fell into a ditch; 'when we returned from the plough in the evening, he repeated to me her *Death and dying words* pretty much in the way they now stand' (JK 3, 1018).

This is Burns's first vernacular narrative poem, possibly inspired by the poet's first reading of Robert Fergusson's *Poems* (which occurred some time between 1782 and 1785). The genre representing the 'dying words' of low-life characters or emblematic animals was taken up first among the Scots vernacular revivalists by William Hamilton of Gilbertfield (*c.* 1665–1751), whose 'Bonnie Heck' – a greyhound resolved on dying well – burlesques Blind Harry's *Wallace*:

> I was a dog much in respect
> For doughty deed:
> But now I must hing by the neck
> Without remead.

(Watson's Choice Collection, 1706)

Mailie's lament also recalls Robert Fergusson's Miltonic burlesque 'The Sow of Feeling' (1773; narrated by the Sow herself, lamenting her inevitable slaughter), a sardonic commentary on Henry Mackenzie's best-selling and lachrymose novel *The Man of Feeling* (1771).

In the copy-text, l. 47 reads 'An' warn him ay at ridin time'. Burns changed the line in *Poems* 1787 (Edinburgh) to 'An' warn him, what I winna name', as printed here. Though JK criticizes the syntax of the emended line, it better conveys Mailie's comic prudery. A final stroke of comic characterization occurs in l. 64, where (canny and cautious to the end) Mailie wills her least valuable or delectable organ – her bladder – to Hughoc to pay him for his trouble.

William Clark, Burns's servant in 1790, listed pet sheep among the favoured livestock at Burns's last farm, Ellisland: 'Burns kept nine or ten milch cows, some young cattle, four horses, and several pet sheep: of the latter he was very fond' (W. L. Renwick, *Burns As Others Saw Him*, Edinburgh: Saltire Society, 1959, p. 27).

Poor Mailie's Elegy

Poems 1786 (Kilmarnock). Placed out of chronological order because designed to follow Mailie's 'Death and Dying Words'; written shortly before publication. The 'standart Habbie' stanza Burns uses here – named by Allan Ramsay in honour of 'The Life and Death of Habbie Simpson' by Robert Semphill (*c.* 1595–*c.* 1668) – was conventional in Scottish vernacular poetry for comic elegies such as this, as well as for familiar epistles. 'The Ewie wi' the Crookit Horn', by John Skinner (1721–1807) – an Episcopalian minister and song-writer much admired by Burns – may also have influenced this elegy for Mailie:

> I'm really fleyt that our guidwife
> Will never win aboon't ava.
> Oh! a ye bards benorth Kinghorn,
> Call your muses up and mourn,
> Our ewie wi' the crookit horn,
>   Stown frae's, and fell'd, an a'.

(John Murdoch, *Familiar Links With Burns*, Ayr: Stephen and Pollock, 1933: 25;

published – unsigned and in a slightly variant text – in *SMM*, vol. 3, 1790; but probably written by Skinner two decades earlier, in imitation of a similar poem by James Beattie.)

My Father Was a Farmer (*Tune: The weaver and his shuttle, O*)

Text: Cromek 1808. Transcribed in *1CPB* (April 1784). Tentatively dated 1782 by JK (3, 1015), the song is not among those Burns describes in *1CPB* or *Letters* as 'early'. A date of 1783 is more probable, given the anxiety and defiance reflected in the final stanzas: throughout 1783 the poet's father was fighting bankruptcy proceedings brought against him by his landlord. Music from Dick's setting for 'Again Rejoicing Nature Sees', with the third and fourth bars corrected as in Low, Songs of Robert Burns (London: Routledge, 1993), p. 74.

The poet called this 'a wild rhapsody, miserably deficient in versification, but as the sentiments are the genuine feelings of my heart, for that reason I have a particular pleasure in conning it over' (*1CPB*, April 1784; JK 1, 26). In the later vernacular epistles, Burns also praises an honest heart and high spirits as proof against misfortune – a motif he may be adapting from contemporary song-writers. The sentiments resemble John Skinner's stanzas for 'John o' Badenyond':

> When first I came to be a man of twenty years or so,
> I thought myself a handsome youth, and fain the world would know;
> In best attire I stept abroad, with spirits brisk and gay,
> And here, and there, and every where, was like a morn in May.
> No care had I, nor fear of want, but rambled up and down;
> And for a beau I might have pass'd in country or in town [.]
> I still was pleas'd where'er I went, and when I was alone,
> I tun'd my pipe and pleas'd myself with John of Badenyond.
>
> . . .
>
> When love had thus my heart beguiled, with foolish hopes and vain,
> To friendship's port I steer'd my course, and laugh'd at lovers' pain;

A friend I got by lucky chance, 'twas something like divine,
An honest friend's a precious gift, and such a gift was mine.
And now whatever might betide a happy man was I,
In any strait I knew to whom I freely could apply:
A strait soon came, my friend I try'd, he laugh'd and spurn'd my moan[.]
I hy'd me home, and pleased myself with John of Badenyond.

I thought I should be wiser next, and would a patriot turn,
Began to doat on Johnny Wilkes, and cry up Parson Horne,
Their noble spirit I admir'd and prais'd their manly zeal,
Who had with flaming tongue and pen maintained the public weal:
But e'er a month or two was past, I found myself betray'd;
Twas Self and Party after all, for all the stir they made;
At last I saw those factious knaves insult the very throne,
I curs'd them a', and tun'd my pipe, to John of Badenyond.

(*SMM* 1790; first printed, with 'Tullochgorum', in 1776)

The difference (typical even of his early revisions of popular material) is in the self-dramatization and narrative economy of Burns's stanzas.

The tune (also known under the title 'Jockie's Grey Breeks') may be northern Irish: its rolling, busy rhythm (which suggests a weaver's thrumming shuttle) is not a good match for narrative stanzas, though the lilting chorus well illustrates a merry defiance.

The copy-text gives 'broil' for 'moil' in l. 18; emended as in *1CPB*.

Epitaph on William Muir of Tarbolton Mill

Text: HH, 2; but title and punctuation from *1CPB*. Transcribed in *1CPB* and probably written in April 1784.

Muir was alive when this subdued tribute was composed, but his old friend William Burnes, the poet's father, had recently died. William Muir (1745–93) was miller at Tarbolton: he and his wife gave Jean Armour shelter in 1786–7 when her parents disowned her during her second pregnancy. The final couplet belies the old charge – originated by Henry Mackenzie in his obituary of the poet – that Burns was conventional in his religious beliefs until 'spoiled' by his two seasons of celebrity in Edinburgh.

In the Centenary edition Henley and Henderson capitalize the personal pronoun referring to the deity ('His'), a practice not usual for Burns: l. 2 is given here as in *1CPB*. 'Miln' (copy-text) has been modernized to 'mill' (title).

Green Grow the Rashes. A Fragment (Tune: Green grows the rashes)

Text: *Poems* 1787 (Edinburgh); transcribed in *1CPB* and probably written in August 1784. Music from Dick.

Unlike traditional Scottish bawdry (immersed, like the ballads, in the dark ironies of rape and incest), Burns's genial revisions typically emphasize consensual sex, mutual pleasure-giving. Following this song in *1CPB* is a characteristic defence of sexual pleasure (and probable misreading of a favourite treatise, Adam Smith's *Theory of Moral Sentiments*, 1759). As sex is a means to good feelings, the poet argues, it may also be seen as a means to goodness itself: 'I do not see that the ... pursuits of such a one as the above verses describe ... are in the least more inimical to the sacred interests of piety and virtue than the ... lawful bustling and straining after the world's riches and honors: and I do not see but he may gain Heaven as well' (JK 3, 1034).

As Raymond Bentman has pointed out, 'grow the rashes' in the copy-text is grammatical English, while 'grows the rashes' (*SMM*) is grammatical Scots ('Robert Burns's Use of Scottish Diction' in *From Sensibility to Romanticism*, ed. Hilles and Bloom, London: Oxford, 1965, p. 240).

GREEN GROW THE RASHES

Epistle to Davie, a Brother Poet

Text: *Poems* 1786 (Kilmarnock). Transcribed in *1CPB* (January 1785); begun in 1784.

Though dated January 1785, the 'principal part' of this poem (probably ll. 43–98) was repeated to Gilbert Burns by the poet in summer 1784 (JK 3, 1039). David Sillar (1760–1830) joined the Tarbolton Bachelor's Club in 1781. A collection of his poems (unsuccessful in every sense) was published in 1789; but Sillar was a good fiddler who composed the tune for 'The Rosebud', a Burns song not printed here. Sillar was briefly schoolmaster at Tarbolton and then a grocer at Irvine, going bankrupt but later in life inheriting wealth from his uncle, a Liverpool merchant. Sillar's vivid account of Burns as a young man first appeared in Peterkin's edition of Burns's *Works* (1811). In 1827, David Sillar was a founding member of the Irvine Burns Club.

In 1585 King James VI referred to the traditional Scots stanza used here as 'all kyndis of cuttit and broken verse': it was the stanza-form of 'The Cherry and the Slae' by Alexander Montgomerie (c. 1545–c. 1611), a poem known to Burns through Ramsay's *Ever Green* (1724) or possibly Watson's *Choice Collection* (1706).

David Sillar's 'Meg' (l. 107) was Margaret Orr (d. 1837), a servant in Stair House and an admirer of Burns's songs. She became engaged to Sillar but (perhaps daunted by the financial difficulties mentioned in this poem) married instead John Paton, an Edinburgh shoemaker. The poet's 'Jean' (l. 108) was Jean Armour, later his wife. In l. 55 'we'll time' is correct; 'well' in copy-text.

Holy Willie's Prayer

Text: Stewart 1801; stanzas 7–10 (missing from the copy-text) from HH. Probably written in February 1785.

Following eighteenth-century custom in presenting dramatic monologues and other 'portrait' poems (Pope's 'Eloisa to Abelard'; Ramsay's 'Elegy on John Cowper, Kirk-Treasurer's Man'), the Glenriddell text is prefaced by a florid prose 'Argument':

> Holy Willie was a rather oldish batchelor Elder in the parish of Mauchline, and much and justly famed for that polemical chattering which ends in tippling Orthodoxy, and for that Spiritualized Bawdry which refines to Liquorish Devotion. – In a Sessional process with a gentleman in Mauchline, a Mr Gavin Hamilton, Holy Willie, and his priest, father Auld, after full hearing in the Presbytry of Ayr, came off but second best; owing partly to the oratorical powers of Mr Robt. Aiken, Mr Hamilton's Counsel; but chiefly to Mr Hamilton's being one of the most irreproachable and truly respectable characters in the country. – On losing this Process, the Muse overheard him at his devotions as follows.

Gavin Hamilton (1751–1805) was Burns's landlord; he subleased Mossgiel farm to Robert and Gilbert to protect the family from their father's bankruptcy. *Poems* 1786 (Kilmarnock) is dedicated to Hamilton and, according to the Train MS, it was at Hamilton's office in spring 1788 that Burns finally solemnized his marriage to Jean Armour. William Auld (1709–91) was the conservative ('Auld Licht') minister of Mauchline parish; Burns usually prefixes his surname with the sarcastic epithets 'Father' or 'Daddy'. It was Auld who presided over Burns's three Sundays of public penance as a fornicator in 1786 – a punishment imposed (the poet always insisted) in retaliation for such satires as 'Holy Willie's Prayer'. Robert Aiken (1739–1807) was an early patron of the poet and a popular local lawyer retained by Hamilton in his battles with the parish. Aiken was dedicatee of 'The Cotter's Saturday Night' and father of Andrew Aiken, the youth addressed in 'Epistle to a Young Friend' (p. 125). Holy Willie himself was William Fisher (1737–1809), an elder of Mauchline parish. Although Burns calls him a 'batchelor', Fisher was married and a father. In 1790, he was rebuked by William Auld for public drunkenness; in February 1809, he froze to death in a ditch. He is buried near Mary Morison in Mauchline churchyard.

The quarrel between Hamilton and the parish dated at least to 1778, when William Auld brought charges that Hamilton (collector of poor-taxes for Mauchline) fell more than six pounds short. Hamilton (a lawyer) counter-charged that the shortage was caused by parishioners unable to pay the stent. The quarrel continued and in August 1784, Hamilton faced new charges: absence from church for five sabbaths, sabbath travel, and failure to hold family worship (*BE*). Censured at the local level, Hamilton was exonerated on appeal.

The poem was considered too libellous to print, but manuscripts circulated briskly in the parish. In 1787, Burns recalled that the satire 'alarmed the kirk-Session so much that they held three several meetings to look over their holy artillery, if any of it was pointed against profane Rhymers' (*Letters* 1, 144). Burns later transcribed the poem in several manuscript compilations, including Glenriddell (1791; JK's copy-text). Stewart's is the first publication in book-form and was

probably printed from an early manuscript now lost. Stewart's text is preferable –
sounding more like transcribed speech – but I have used Glenriddell for the
epigraph and for ll. 17, 64, and 83–4 (see final paragraph below).

JK notes that Willie's prayer is conventional in form, moving from 'invocation
and praise' through 'confession' and 'repentance' to 'intercession and petition' (3,
1048–9). The satire proceeds from the incongruity between pious form and
malicious content, for Willie has mastered only the style, not the spirit of
Scripture. The insidious suppleness of language itself – its capacity for twisting
and bending the facts – is emphasized, for Willie's unctuous words serve mainly
to provide a flattering dress for acts of vanity, envy, lust, drunkenness, and greed.
Even Willie's confessed sins of the flesh – rather numerous if this prayer records a
typical week – stimulate no remorse but are instead used as further evidence of
Willie's conspicuous 'giftedness': for have not other notable saints been tormented
by the thorn in the flesh? Willie's closing petitions, too, serve his own interests
whether he is begging blessings for 'me and mine' or calling for God's destruction
of Gavin Hamilton and Robert Aiken – men who (readers should remember,
though Willie has forgotten) did not begin this quarrel and acted only in
Hamilton's defence. So Willie's prayer, for all its scriptural allusion, is notable
mainly for its perverse projection of Willie's own spitefulness onto the deity.
When are the words of God the words of a vindictive, petty-minded bully? When
they are in Holy Willie's mouth.

Willie sees himself as marked by God for 'gifts an' grace'; readers experience
him differently, however – as marked by Burns for ridicule. Yet this is not one of
Burns's bitter or angry satires. Willie's spite comes to so little, after all. And he is
so fluent in his self-love, so creative in his relationship with words. The linguistic
world that Willie inhabits is so full, fair, and false that it almost could be that of a
poet; the difference lies only in his comic blindness to his own artifice. On the
matter of rich men entering the kingdom of Heaven, for instance, the Bible is
quite clear; but Willie's final request in his prayer is for continued 'gear' – wealth
– and grace (l. 93), an unconscious lapse into syllepsis. This figure of speech –
dissonant or incongruous items slipped into a pairing or series as if innocently
coordinate – is frequent among Scottish vernacular poets, especially Robert
Fergusson; but Burns was also familiar with the trope – sometimes called zeugma
– from his favourite English mock-epic:

> Whether the Nymph shall break Diana's Law,
> Or some frail China jar receive a flaw.
> Or stain her Honour, or her new Brocade,
> Forget her Pray'rs, or miss a Masquerade,
> Or lose her Heart, or Necklace, at a Ball . . .
>
> (Pope, *The Rape of the Lock*, Canto 2, ll. 105–9)

Horatian Pope uses syllepsis to teach the confusion of values in Belinda's world;
Burns uses it somewhat differently – to dramatize the confusion of values in
Willie's mind.

JK recognized in Willie's request that God blight Hamilton down to his 'kail
an' potatoes' (l. 72) a trivialization of Deuteronomy's majestic 'Cursed shall be thy
basket and thy store'; but Willie is also echoing the comic anathema on Obadiah
pronounced by the fanatical Roman Catholic Dr Slop in *Tristram Shandy*, a novel
the poet counted among his 'bosom favourites'. Sterne's Dr Slop probably

inspired Burns's frequent equation of Auld Licht Calvinism with Catholicism, as in the poet's mocking references to William Auld as 'Father' (i.e., authoritarian purveyor of superstitious fears).

The major literary influence on this poem is Scottish, however, for self-damning dramatic monologues such as Willie's were a well-established vernacular genre by Burns's day. In 'Lucky Spence's Last Advice', for instance, Allan Ramsay records the dying speech of an Edinburgh bawd, dramatizing bad values and providing a psychological portrait rich in grotesque touches:

> My bennison come on good doers,
> Who spend their cash on bawds and whores;
> May they ne'er want the wale of cures
>   For a sair snout:
> Foul fa' the quacks wha that fire smoors,
>   And puts nae out.

> My malison light ilka day
> On them that drink, and dinna pay,
> But tak a snack and rin away;
>   May't be their hap
> Never to want a gonorrhoea,
>   Or rotten clap.
>
>   (c. 1718)

Robert Burns was reared to his scepticism about the Auld Licht: his father wrote with John Murdoch a short manuscript entitled 'A Manual of Religious Belief' to counter the teachings of local ministers and to emphasize the importance of charity, good works, and independence of mind. (In the manual, the child questions the parent, not – as in traditional catechisms – vice versa.) Some biographers have speculated that Burnes's hiring of Murdoch as a private schoolmaster to instruct Robert and Gilbert during the 1760s was in itself a provocative anti-Auld Licht gesture reflecting Burnes's disdain for the values being disseminated in the parish school. William Burnes taught all his children to reject the exclusive focus on divine election – salvation through grace alone – that has corrupted Willie. So Burns mocks Willie as any son of his father would. He also wrote as a grateful friend of Hamilton, who had generously provided shelter for the Burnes family in its worst crisis – a kindness fresh in the poet's mind, as the bankruptcy trial and subsequent death of Burns's father had occurred only a year before 'Holy Willie's Prayer' was written.

Even though it does not appear in the printed text, the epigraph (from Alexander Pope) probably was included in the copy Stewart worked from: Stewart (who invented the title 'The Jolly Beggars' for Burns's cantata 'Love and Liberty') typically deletes Burns's allusions to English poetic tradition. Lines 17 and 64 of the Glenriddell text offer slight improvements upon the earlier text ("'fore my creation' is changed to 'ere my creation' and 'grit an' sma'' to 'great an' sma''). The most significant change is in ll. 83–4: 'While Auld wi' hingin lip gaed sneakin',/And hid his head' (Glenriddell) is more lucid (if less dramatic) than the earlier version in Stewart: 'While he wi' hingin' lips and shakin',/Held up his head'.

Death and Dr Hornbook. A True Story

Text: *Poems* 1787 (Edinburgh); written 'early' in 1785, according to Gilbert Burns.

This comedy darkened by its grotesque setting – Death intercepted on his nightly stroll through the parish – portrays Nature's Death as a skinny, disgruntled, oddly likable working man armed only with a scythe and a dart. By contrast stands the poem's mock-hero Hornbook, whose infernal prescience, arcane potions, and lethal skill are emphasized (ll. 109–25). The peerless quackery of the 'bauld *Apothecary*' – who is really just a schoolmaster supplementing his income – has vanquished and pre-empted mere Death.

In its emphasis on narrative 'truth' and 'lies', its drunken protagonist, its ironic treatment of folkloric motifs, and its essentially comic presentation of the supernatural, the poem could be seen as an early sketch for 1790's 'Tam o' Shanter'. Like that later mock-epic, 'Hornbook' is rich in contrasts – not only between the competitors of the title but between the reader, who presumably is sober, and the bosky narrator of this 'true story' that is so plainly a drunken yarn. 'Death' speaks, surprisingly enough, in particularly animated Scots, and this is among Burns's most linguistically agile poems. Yet though the energy is sustained, the structure is unbalanced. The two final stanzas (stressing interruption, not closure) are mismatched to the rest of the poem.

The model for 'Dr Hornbook' was John Wilson (*c.* 1751–1839), who became Tarbolton's schoolmaster in 1781. Wilson also ran a shop in the parish, selling groceries and dispensing drugs and medical advice. Burns's impecunious friend David Sillar had temporarily been Tarbolton's schoolmaster prior to Wilson's appointment – one possible reason for the poet's animus. Gilbert Burns reported that the poem was inspired by a Masonic meeting in which Wilson (secretary of the Tarbolton Lodge from 1782 to 1787) boasted of his medical prowess (JK 3, 1053; *Letters* 2, 487). None the less, even after the circulation of this satire the poet and John Wilson were never enemies: Burns in 1790 supplied him with a letter of introduction. Wilson quarrelled with his minister and eventually was dismissed as schoolmaster for neglect of his duties. In 1792, he moved from Tarbolton, eventually returning to Glasgow (where he had studied at the university). He held several teaching posts and for years served as Session Clerk of Gorbals parish, where he is buried.

Hornbooks were still in use for elementary instruction in Burns's day; they were pieces of parchment printed with numbers and the alphabet, placed between a wooden backing and a cover of transparent horn. Burns's name for his hero falls – like so many of his figures – somewhere between classical metonymy and folkloric emblem. 'Great lies and nonsense' (l. 5) is given in JK as 'A rousing whid, at times, to vend'. Kinsley is following the poet's autograph addition to Bishop Geddes' copy of *Poems* 1787 (Edinburgh), now at the Huntington Library. In the line as printed, the repetition of 'lie' for the third time in one stanza may be seen as redundant – or emphatic. In l. 26, 'Willie's mill' refers to the Tarbolton mill of William Muir, also addressed in Burns's early elegy 'On My Friend, and My Father's Friend'. Taking their hint from ll. 39–42 and Death's 'queerest shape', nineteenth-century illustrators (among whom this poem was a favourite) invariably depict Death as a skeleton. The reference in l. 20 to 'ABC' slyly reminds us of 'Hornbook's' real area of expertise. In the catalogue of quackish *materia medica* offered in ll. 121–32, 'calces o' fossils . . . true sal-marinum . . . farina of beans . . .

aqua-fontis ... urinus spiritus ... sal-alkali' are pretentious aliases for (respectively) bone meal, salt-water, vegetable meal, fresh water, urine, and salt. Finally, in ll. 153–7 – 'to mend her head,/When it was sair', etc. – the imagery is similar to that in the supernatural ballad 'Clerk Colven' (first printed in 1769), in which an unfaithful husband dies of a headache inflicted by his mermaid lover: 'Ochon, alas! cried Clerk Colvin/And aye sae sair it's in my head/Then merrily leuked the mermaid up/Twill aye be waur till ye be dead' (Child 42).

When First I Came to Stewart Kyle (*Tune: I had a horse, I had nae mair*)

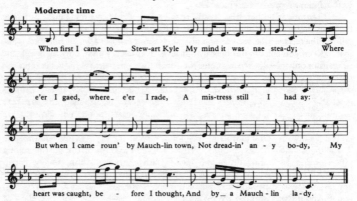

Moderate time

When first I came to___ Stew-art Kyle My mind it was nae stea-dy; Where

e'er I gaed, where_ e'er I rade, A mis-tress still I had ay:

But when I came roun' by Mauch-lin town, Not dread-in' an - y bo-dy, My

heart was caught, be - fore I thought, And by_ a Mauch - lin la - dy.

Text: *1CPB* (transcribed August 1785); probably written in spring 1785. Musical setting is taken from Dick. Probably written for Jean Armour, whom Burns met some time between November 1784 and January 1785. She was town-bred: her father was a mason and builder in Mauchline.

Epistle to John Lapraik, an Old Scotch Bard. April 1st, 1785

Text: *Poems* 1786 (Kilmarnock); transcribed in *1CPB* on 1 April 1785.

The major impetus of the eighteenth-century Scots vernacular revival was the interchange of verse-epistles between William Hamilton of Gilbertfield and Allan Ramsay beginning around 1718; like Burns's, these used the 'standart Habbie' stanza. Defined by Ramsay/Gilbertfield as a means of interchange between patriotic Scots poets, the genre also incorporated Horatian themes: country pleasures, disdain of 'greatness', praise of friendship, discussion of current issues, and (especially) the state of Scottish poetry.

John Lapraik (1727–1807) was known as the bard of Muirkirk: Burns encouraged him to publish his poems – marginally better than David Sillar's – in 1788. Lapraik, ruined by the failure of the Ayr Bank and forced to sell his freehold farm, could not make a profit as a tenant farmer and in 1785 was imprisoned for debt in Ayr. Some of his poems were written in prison. It is probable that Burns knew of these difficulties: Lapraik's first wife Margaret was the sister of Burns's friend and former neighbour John Rankine, who may well have hosted the 'rockin' – evening social gathering – at which Burns heard Lapraik's song. Compassion and identification stimulated this genial and consoling address to a stranger: the humiliation of bankruptcy, only narrowly averted by Burns's own father in 1784, had become the fate the poet himself most feared. Burns's admiration for Lapraik's song (l. 13) is a tactful pretext, then, designed to emphasize Lapraik's reasons for pride rather than shame. The song itself (even with Burns's later help in revising it for publication in *SMM*) is, while warm and affectionate in tone, undistinguished in style:

> When I upon thy bosom lean,
> And fondly clasp thee a' my ain,
> I glory in the sacred ties
> That made us ane, wha ance were twain:
> A mutual flame inspires us baith,
> The tender look, the melting kiss:
> Even years shall ne'er destroy our love,
> But only gie us change o' bliss.
>
> Hae I a wish? it's a' for thee;
> I ken thy wish is me to please;
> Our moments pass sae smooth away
> That numbers look on us and gaze,
> Weel pleas'd they see our happy days,
> Nor envy's sel finds aught to blame;
> And ay when weary cares arise,
> Thy bosom still shall be my hame.
>
> I'll lay me there, and take my rest;
> And if that aught disturb my dear,
> I'll bid her laugh her cares away,
> And beg her not to drap a tear:
> Hae I a joy? it's a' her ain;
> United still her heart and mine;
> They're like the woodbine round the tree,
> That's twin'd till death shall them disjoin.

As the stanzas also appeared in *Weekly Magazine* (1773), Lapraik has been accused of plagiarizing them. Lapraik's collected *Poems* (1788) do contain lines lifted from such English poets as John Byrom, yet as JK points out, Lapraik – two generations older than Burns – might well have published the *Weekly Magazine* verses himself in 1773. Plagiarism is perhaps not the exact term in any case. The idea of copyright or ownership of words is esoteric in an orally transmitted tradition. Burns himself made a distinction between his narrative poems, epistles, and satires (which he signed and for which he accepted payment) and his songs (whose authorship he often concealed and for which, on principle, he declined payment).

The famous prayer of l. 73 – 'Gie me ae spark o' Nature's fire' – recalls, as JK notes, two of Burns's favourite writers, Laurence Sterne and Alexander Pope: 'Great Apollo! If thou art in a giving humour – give me – I ask no more, but one stroke of native humour, with a single spark of thy own fire among it' (*Tristram Shandy* 3, xii); 'Nature! informer of the poet's art,/Whose force alone can raise or melt the heart' ('Prologue' to *Sophonisba*, which also influenced the 'anonymous' epigraph Burns provided for the Kilmarnock edition). Another echo of Pope occurs in ll. 43–4, whose images recall 'Epistle to Dr Arbuthnot': 'I lisp'd in numbers, for the numbers came' (l. 128). There are Scottish references, too: most charmingly, the climax of ll. 79–81: 'Allan', 'Fergusson', 'Lapraik', where Burns compliments his prospective friend by linking him with two great Scots vernacular predecessors, Ramsay and Fergusson. And Lapraik was charmed: he responded to Burns's epistle promptly, though not in kind. As JK notes, Lapraik's answers (not extant) were all in prose (3, 1057). Between 1784 and 1785 Burns sought out several candidates for true Gilbertfield/Ramsay exchanges in verse, but never found a peer.

To the Same. April 21st, 1785

Text: *Poems* 1786 (Kilmarnock); transcribed in *1CPB* (June 1785).

At the end of a day's labour late in April, the poem begins over the objections of a fretful Muse, who complains of how much the poet/speaker has been writing lately. More tired than the speaker, the cows who have just calved, or the farm ponies, still sweating after long hours pulling the harrow and plough, the poet's Muse pleads a headache. The conversational 'blether' of this introduction (ll. 1–42) modulates to flattering portraiture of Lapraik and Burns and hostile caricature of worshippers of the false values of wealth and title (ll. 43–102). The justification of honest men and poets increases in intensity (and hyperbole) until apotheosis occurs in the final stanza: penniless as ever but finally 'justified', Lapraik and Burns ascend into the skies in the manner of Belinda's stolen curl in Pope's *The Rape of the Lock*.

The second letter to Lapraik irritated adherents of the Auld Licht, whose fire-and-brimstone sermons are parodied in the lines redefining the 'charter of our state' (79–96), where Burns boldly substitutes 'Nature's law' for scripture. In *Animadversions on Some Poets and Poetasters of the Present Day, Especially Robert Burns and John Lapraik* (Paisley 1789), James Maxwell can take comfort only in the thought that 'The time will soon come when they'll howl in despair' (7). On the other hand, this was among William Wordsworth's favourite poems – he relished the rich dialect of the first four stanzas and once declaimed them for Allan Cunningham (JK 3, 1060).

Pope's *An Essay on Man* probably suggested the allusion to 'great Nature's plan' in l. 89. As many critics have noted, Burns's emphasis on sociability and benevolence is characteristic of eighteenth-century writing on ethics and morality. Burns often quoted from Adam Smith's *Theory of Moral Sentiments* (1759); Smith was a student of Francis Hutcheson, who was the third Earl of Shaftesbury's most influential disciple. Through the university lectures of Hutcheson and Smith, benevolism and the cult of sensibility had a strong influence on Scottish writers and intellectuals from the mid eighteenth century.

To William Simson, Ochiltree. May – 1785

Text: *Poems* 1786 (Kilmarnock); transcribed in *1CPB* (and probably written) in May 1785.

William Simson (1758–1815) – Burns spelled it 'Simpson' – had studied at Glasgow University and was schoolmaster at Ochiltree; he later taught at Cumnock. The poem replies to a verse-epistle from Simson (not extant) praising Burns's early satire 'The Holy Tulzie'. Ridicule of the Auld Licht is deferred to a postscript, however: the body of the poem focuses on the beauty of Ayrshire, which no poet had yet immortalized. The major subjects – poets' sensitivity to landscape and the relation between solitary musing and poetic inspiration – recur throughout Burns's poems, but were dismissed by many contemporaries as merely conventional. John Logan wrote in 1787 to Henry Mackenzie: 'Mr Burns is a clever fellow, a Man of Observation, and a Country Libertine, but I am much mistaken if he has anything of the Penseroso in his character' (Low, *Robert Burns: The Critical Heritage*, p. 79).

Such earlier poets as John Milton, Anne Finch, John Dyer, William Collins, and James Thomson had established the link between topography and poetic inspiration, but Burns is observing a Lowland landscape that had (as he says in this poem) never yet been seen through poetic eyes. The poet describes the contours of the low hills, with their streams, wild flowers, bounding hares, and calling doves – a pastoral setting despite the fierceness of winter storms. Although born almost within sight and sound of the Atlantic, Burns seldom followed the Ossianic fashion for sublime imagery of oceans, torrents, and mountains (the major exception is the next poem, 'The Vision'). More like Anne Finch in 'A Nocturnal Reverie', Burns seeks solace as well as inspiration from landscape on an intimate (not, as in Ossian or Thomson, panoramic) scale.

As in so many of his early poems, Burns invokes the names of his Scots precedessors: 'Allan' Ramsay and William Hamilton of 'Gilbertfield' – whose genial exchange of vernacular epistles initiated the eighteenth-century Scots vernacular revival – and also Robert 'Fergusson' (ll. 15–17), a poet born at mid-century who far surpassed either. Fergusson (1750–74) – Burns's spelling of the name with one 's' has been corrected – excelled in narrative poetry and cutting satire, not song and gentle humour; he never achieved the wide popularity of either Ramsay or Burns. Burns was among the first to praise him justly; on arrival in Edinburgh, he ordered a memorial stone to mark the grave of his 'elder brother in misfortune'. (The ensuing debt for £5.10 was not paid until 1792, when Burns wrote regarding the delay, 'He was two years in erecting it . . . I have been two years paying him . . . He had the hardiesse [*sic*] to ask me interest on the sum; but considering the money was due by one Poet, for putting a tombstone over another, he may, with grateful surprise, thank Heaven that ever he saw a farthing' (*Letters* 2, 133).) Consensus now judges Fergusson – barely twenty-four when he died in the Edinburgh madhouse – second only to Burns among the eighteenth-century vernacular poets: some (including Hugh MacDiarmid) have rated Fergusson the higher. Fergusson's premature death is especially tragic when the influence the two poets could have had on each other is considered. At the very least, Fergusson – only nine years older than Burns – would have been capable of full reciprocation had he lived to be addressed in one of Burns's vernacular epistles.

Ochiltree must have been partly moorland, as Burns emphasizes moorland customs. Or perhaps the word 'braxies' (sheep dead by bowel disease yet deemed edible by shepherds, l. 104) makes its only appearance in British poetry as a consequence of the puzzle Burns has set himself: finding, three times in four lines, two-syllable words rhyming with 'taxes'.

Imagery of sheep and the 'herds' who direct them is continued in the Postscript. The Bible speaks tenderly of the Lord's flock and the Good Shepherd, but Burns also alludes to the Lowland sport of affray, the contention of flocks at fairs and festivals. The 'herds' of the Postscript are ministers whose quarrel – sublimely irrelevant to real life – concerns the phases of the moon. In ll. 139–56, Burns compares Auld Licht ministers to Catholic clergy during the Reformation; they likewise preferred the old ways, dictated to their 'flocks', and punished dissent. In the absurd conclusion, the Auld Licht reveals its plan to use one of the new balloons to fly to the moon for a long inspection, taking a piece back with them. Burns is calling the Auld Licht's resistance to new ideas 'moonshine' or lunacy.

The tract *The Scripture Doctrine of Original Sin Proposed to Free and Candid Examination*, published in 1740 by 'Dr Taylor of Norwich' (l. 112n), was widely credited with (or blamed for) initiating the New Licht movement.

The Vision

Text: *Poems* 1786 (Kilmarnock); the copy-text is some fifty lines shorter than the version printed in later editions of *Poems*. Probably begun at Lochlea in 1784 and completed (as printed here) in late spring 1785.

In this experimental poem that most critics agree is successful only in part, a digressive form (cf. the poet's note to the title) does only partial justice to a highly dramatic setting: a vision of (and conversation with) the muse of Lowland poets. As in 'Epistle to Simson', written concurrently with this poem, Burns praises the rivers and towns of his own district. In the expanded text of later editions, descriptions of Scottish history are added to the diorama of scenes projected on Coila's mantle: after l. 90 seven further stanzas depict historical scenes; and after l. 120, later editions of *Poems* add a stanza on Lowland bards and sages. While appropriate enough in a 'digressive' poem, the additional stanzas defer the conversation between Coila and the speaker, retarding the dramatic pacing.

The text printed here, the earliest published version, attempts no such synthesis between Burns's personal history and Scottish national experience. Here, the focus remains entirely on the personal; the division into Duans emphasizes two contradictory views of a poet's place in the world. The exhausted speaker of Duan One is ready to believe that he belongs nowhere; he has achieved nothing 'stringing blethers up in rhyme/For fools to sing'. Half-mad, half-clothed, half-starved, he resolves to pursue some profitable profession. Providentially, Coila appears, and in Duan Two she offers her aesthetic theodicy. Contradicting the bard's despondent assessment of his own life, she shows it to him again from birth through adolescence (ll. 158–80), arguing that in her own eyes and those of her employer (the 'Genius of this land') a bard's contribution is both necessary and valued. So Duan One's bitter retrospective is countered by a comforting alternative 'vision' that assigns the rustic bard a place in the natural order and explains his suffering and his poverty. His lonely struggle has always had a meaning; he has never been alone. His tangible reward is only a bard's crown of holly (not wealth or even the bay or laurel wreath of classical poets). Yet Coila has reminded the bard of the intangible he seeks: fame for himself (l. 195) and for his native place.

Burns's faintly archaic Scots in the opening stanzas emulates Allan Ramsay's diction in a forgery also titled 'The Vision', presented by Ramsay as translated into Scots in 1524 from a fourteenth-century Latin text. Like Burns's poem, Ramsay's opens with a speaker depressed and plaintive, in this case over John Balliol's appeasement of England's King Edward. As in Burns, a vision (of a warrior/'sanct') suddenly appears to interrupt the speaker's complaints and to comfort him:

> Quhilk held a thistle in his paw,
> And round his collar graift I saw
>   This poesie pat and plain,
> Nemo me impune lacess-
> -et: – In Scots Nane sall oppress
>   Me, unpunist with pain.
> Still schaking, I durst naithing say,
>   Till he with kynd accent
> Sayd, 'Fere let nocht thy hairt affray,
>   I cum to hier thy plaint;
>   Thy graining and maining
>   Hath laitlie reikd myne eir,
>   Debar then affar then
>   All eiryness or feir.'
>
> (*Ever Green*, 1724; reprinted in *Longer Scottish Poems*, Vol. 2, ed.
> Crawford, Hewitt, and Law, Edinburgh: Scottish Academic Press,
> 1987, p.33)

Ramsay's 'sanct' bears a thistle and a prophecy of Scottish history; 'Coila' bears holly and a prophecy of Burns's poetic destiny.

With the exception of William Fullarton (1754–1808) and the Whig MP George Dempster (1732–1818) – local agricultural 'improvers' who are praised in ll. 121–2 – all the heroes in this version of the poem are men of letters. James Beattie (1735–1803) in 1770 published a treatise attacking Hume's scepticism (cf. ll. 123–6): Beattie's popular Spenserian poem *The Minstrel; or The Progress of Genius* (1771–4) strongly influenced Burns in its emphasis on poetry as the noblest calling (though one likely to result in poverty). Beattie's English diction, by turns insipid and pompous, was usually a bad influence, although Burns's memorable 'light from heaven' stanza (ll. 187–92) emulates – and surpasses – Beattie's bardic sublime. James Thomson (1700–1748) was born in Scotland but emigrated to London in 1725, soon publishing 'Winter' and the subsequent poems (all written in English blank verse) of *The Seasons*. As Burns hints in l. 200, Thomson's scale was broad and his diction neo-Miltonic and grandiloquent: extravagant images reminiscent of Thomson, especially such fancy periphrastic constructions as 'embryo-tuneful' (l. 155) or 'army shade' (l. 208), are contradictory in a poem that defines Burns's role as that of a modest, simple bard. None the less, Thomson was (like Beattie) important to Burns as a Scot who had achieved literary fame outside Scotland and who – in emphasizing the idealism and altruism of poetry – encouraged the high ambition and confident self-assertion that marks so much of Burns's early work. William Shenstone (1714–63) – mentioned in l. 202 – was an English poet much admired by the young Burns: the phrase 'the genial bowl' in Burns's first letter to Lapraik, for instance, comes from Shenstone's elegies, a group of poems Burns quarried for English iambs. What Burns admired in Shenstone, especially his elegies, was his effort at an unadorned 'middle' English style and his echo of the Horatian values with which Burns was also familiar from the work of Allan Ramsay. Possibly Burns also perceived in Shenstone an impractical kindred spirit, for it was widely known that Shenstone had died in debt after spending his patrimony on the improvement of the gardens at 'Leasowes', his family's farm. Thomas Gray (1716–71), mentioned in l. 203, was another English poet important to Burns: the epigraph of 'The Cotter's Saturday

Night' is taken from 'Elegy in a Country Churchyard'. The reference in l. 221 to the 'Universal Plan' probably echoes both Beattie and Pope, referring not only to *An Essay on Man* but also (in emphasizing Nature's care of true poets) Beattie's *Minstrel*. Also drawn from Pope is Burns's 'machinery'. The 'light, aerial band' (l. 104) who act as unseen guardians to Ayrshire's statesmen, patriots, and poets are highly reminiscent of the Rosicrucian machinery of sylphs, salamanders, nymphs, and gnomes in *The Rape of the Lock*.

The poem's opening stanzas are among Burns's most effective in setting the scene and dramatizing the speaker's mood. In ll. 7–20 (as in the second letter to Lapraik), the speaker declares himself exhausted by the hard labour of the day. As in 'Epistle to Hugh Parker', he is quite alone, staring glumly into the small fire that warms his house and coughing from the smoke. Burns is probably describing not only his own late-afternoon fatigue but his family's house at Lochlea, where squeaking 'rattons' (l. 17) were to be expected: the roof of a 'clay biggin' (made of branches and wattle) attracted vermin. The speaker's solitude is an invention designed to emphasize his emotional isolation, however; the ingleside at Lochlea itself could seldom have been deserted – not in Scotland's cold April, with nine people sharing one room and one fire.

In l. 63, the copy-text's 'my Bess, I ween' was changed to 'my bonie Jean' in later editions of *Poems*, reflecting the poet's shift of affection from Elizabeth Paton to Jean Armour. The earlier reference is worth retaining as a reminder of the differences in the imagery the two women inspired. Jean Armour is most often praised for her gentle, loving temperament: for looking up to Burns. By contrast, Betsey Paton is praised – as in this line – for her handsome figure, especially (in other early poems as well as here) her 'tapered white leg', her 'limbs so clean'. In l. 86, the phrase 'an ancient Borough' refers to the city of Ayr, about two miles from Burns's birthplace at Alloway. In l. 55 ('sentimental trace') Burns is quoting himself. Apparently he inserted the quotation marks because the 'Epistle to James Smith', in which the phrase also occurs, was (though written later) printed before 'The Vision' in *Poems* 1786 (Kilmarnock).

A Poet's Welcome to His Love-Begotten Daughter; The First Instance that Entitled Him to the Venerable Appellation of Father

Text: Stewart (1801); stanzas 3 and 6 from HH; five lines from Glenriddell. Probably written soon after 22 May 1785. The three manuscripts differ in the sequence of stanzas, and Stewart's (the earliest printed text) does not include two stanzas. So the version given here is a composite text. I see Stewart's racier text as preferable (in all but five lines) to Glenriddell (1791), JK's copy-text; but using Stewart requires the addition of the two excellent stanzas which Burns added between 1785 and 1791. JK acknowledged that Stewart's text was earliest but speculated (on the basis of contradictions in ll. 26–7) that it was 'perhaps not derived from holograph but a careless copy' (3, 1068). Yet the perceived contradiction – in Stewart the father's toil is now (not 'no') all 'tint' (lost), which introduces regret into the poem – could be a typographical error or (more probably, as the tone of regret continues into l. 27) a faithful record of Burns's earliest text and an honest reflection of his earliest (mixed) reaction to paternity. (The birth of their child did terminate the poet's intimacy with Elizabeth Paton, who returned to her parents' home after the birth.) The warmer line (more congruent with the overall tone) could have been introduced later to pull together the mood of the poem.

The differences between the 1785 and 1791 versions of this poem reveal – as does 'Holy Willie's Prayer', also preserved both in Stewart's (mid–1780s) text and Glenriddell (1791) – that Burns continued to work on his unpublished texts over a period of years and that when he did so on his own – independent of self-appointed mentors such as Frances Dunlop or Hugh Blair – his revisions show a consistent pattern: earlier versions are more 'realistic' and energetically expressive, while the late text in Glenriddell is more 'poetic'; the lines from Glenriddell are both more condensed and more inverted; two of the five lines introduce tropes. For more detailed discussion of textual variants between Glenriddell and Stewart, see the final paragraphs below.

The poet greets Elizabeth, his illegitimate first-born – she arrived on 22 May 1785 – with a characteristic mixture of warm affection (directed towards infant and mother) and defiance (directed towards parish gossips). The baby's mother, Elizabeth Paton, was a servant at Lochlea farm, hired during the crisis of William Burnes's last illness. According to reminiscences collected by Robert Chambers, she was well liked by the poet's mother, who urged the couple to marry when Betsey's pregnancy became matter for local scandal. Gilbert Burns and the poet's sisters, however, disliked her: 'very plain-looking . . . the faults of her character would soon have disgusted [Burns]. She was rude and uncultivated to a great degree; a strong masculine understanding, with a thorough (tho' unwomanly) contempt for every sort of refinement' (JK 3, 1068). The baby Elizabeth – first grandchild of the poet's mother – was reared by her grandmother at Mossgiel farm (Betsey Paton returning home to Lairgieside), though the poet offered to take the child when he settled down with Jean Armour in 1788. In 1786, Burns paid the elder Elizabeth £20 for the child's support out of the profits of the Kilmarnock edition (though at this time Betsey was not raising her). Ten years later – by then married to a farm servant – Elizabeth Paton did reclaim their daughter when the poet died. Young Elizabeth received £200 of the profits from Currie's posthumous edition of her father's *Works* on her twenty-first birthday in 1806. She married John Bishop, land steward of the Baillie of Polkemmet; tradition reports that she died giving birth to her seventh child on 8 December 1816. Among her descendants is Viscount Weir of Cathcart, whose estate is near Mauchline.

The title is given in Stewart as 'Address to an Illegitimate Child'; here titled as in Glenriddell. The forthright title in the Rosenbach MS ('A Poet's Welcome to His Bastart Wean') is often preferred, but Glenriddell's title sets up a more dynamic pattern for the opening, with its stuffy, orotund formality ('venerable appellation', etc.) simply melting into tenderness in l. 1, with its intimate 'thou' and the homely, affectionate term 'wean'. Line 2 – 'If thoughts o' thee' – is from Glenriddell; the line in Stewart is vaguer: 'If ought of thee, or of thy mammy'. In l. 26, 'My funny toil is now a' tint' is the reading given in Stewart; here given as in Glenriddell – 'no [not] a' tint'. Stewart's version is, as mentioned, a careless transcription, a typographical error, or an early contradiction that was later written out. In l. 27, 'Tho' ye came to the warl asklent' is Glenriddell's reading; 'Sin' thou came' in the copy-text. In l. 38, 'Thy mither's looks, and gracefu' merit' is from Glenriddell; the line is less poetic in Stewart ('Thy mither's person, grace and merit'), though the original emphasis on 'person' (figure) bears out the testimony of a niece of the poet's that Elizabeth Paton's 'defects of character' and plainness of face were redeemed in the poet's eyes by her 'exceedingly handsome figure' (JK 3, 1068). The fifth line taken from Glenriddell is l. 41 – 'see thee heir it' – which reads 'hear and see't' in Stewart. Anthimeria – the noun 'heir' used as if a verb – is a figure of speech used often by Burns.

In resolving the final – and major – discrepancy between Glenriddell and Stewart, the concluding four lines, I have followed Stewart's version. Glenriddell has:

> I'll never rue my trouble wi' thee,
> > The cost or shame o't,
> But be a loving Father to thee,
> > And brag the name o't. –
> > > (JK 1, 100)

The copy-text, by contrast, dwells on the probability that Elizabeth will not survive infancy: 'If thou be spar'd'. Infant mortality was very high, and only six of Burns's own thirteen children – including, however, this first-born daughter – survived to adulthood. The touch of uncertainty about the infant's survival is another factor suggesting that this version was written very soon after her birth. Glenriddell's text – transcribed after the mother's successful claim on part of the profits of *Poems* 1786 (Kilmarnock) – emphasizes instead the 'trouble' and 'cost' of child-rearing.

The Fornicator. A New Song (Tune: Clout the Caldron)

Text: JK from a transcript by Robert Dewar – MS not traced (1, 101). *MMC* text lacks sixteen lines. Probably written between April and June 1785. Music taken from Dick's setting for 'Clout the Caldron'.

When Elizabeth Paton's pregnancy became obvious, Burns was chastised in church and made to pay a fine. This song defiantly emphasizes the shameful title the kirk has imposed on him but changes the definition: fornication (moved from the realm of church censure to high comedy) becomes a hero's strength, not a sinner's weakness. Libertines pay for their pleasures: the speaker denies them the rank of 'fornicator'. Hypocrites such as Holy Willie pray that the 'bonie lass' will not 'discover' – sustain the pregnancy long enough to cause a scandal – and scoundrels deny paternity: as in his poem 'The Court of Equity', Burns excludes all such ignoble men 'from the quorum'. True fornicators, as this song defines them, share what they have with the partner in their pleasure: the scandal and the joy in the birth of a child – a 'roguish boy' in this song addressed to 'jovial boys'. (The mention of a male child, though congruent with the imagery in the song, might mean that the song was written before the baby was born; if so, it was written before 'A Poet's Welcome'. Neither the exact date of the censure nor the parish in which it occurred – whether Mauchline, Tarbolton, or Lairgieside – is known.)

The free love of fornicators is contrasted with the kirk's guinea fine for fornication, disdainfully equated with prostitution by the term used: 'buttock-hire'. The ecclesiastical term 'fornicator' is opposed by Latin rhymes and classical references – 'frater', 'pater', 'esse mater', 'quorum', 'Cèsar', 'conquering Alexanders' – that suggest an alternative world more pagan and more heroic than Auld Licht Mauchline, with its perverse substitution of money for pleasure. The mock-heroic bluster of the military imagery ('pass the muster', 'convoy', 'warlike kings and heroes bold') recalls the *double entendre* of one of Burns's favourite novels, Sterne's *Tristram Shandy*.

To the first collected edition of the poet's *Works* (1800), James Currie added a long essay on the 'character and condition' of the Scottish peasantry, attempting to provide a social context for Burns's views, especially on sexuality. Currie noted that the peasants of south-western Scotland were highly literate compared to their English and European counterparts, but also (Currie thought) reprehensibly lax. Scots peasants, defying the surveillance of the kirk – which despite the Reformation had retained the Catholic 'stool of repentance' and the medieval practice of public humiliation of sinners – were, wrote Currie, far too tolerant of sexual activity before (and outside) marriage. Mortality was high, the need for youthful helpers on the farms was great, and conjugal arrangements in the Lowlands often remained informal unless there was property to bestow (seldom the case for tenant farmers). Spoken agreement eventually to wed was one form of legal marriage in Burns's community.

The tune, 'Clout the Caldron', was old and had long been associated with bawdry. It is also the tune of the Tinker's Song in 'Love and Liberty'. Appropriately, its tempo is quickstep, or military march.

The Rantin Dog the Daddie O't (Tune: Whare wad bonie Annie lie)

Text: *SMM* 1792 (words only); Dick (music). *SMM* wrongly sets the stanzas to 'East Nook of Fife'. The date of composition is unknown; perhaps May or June 1785.

Burns's interleaved copy of *SMM* states only that this was written 'pretty early in life and sent ... to a young girl, a very particular acquaintance of mine, who was at that time under a cloud'. JK follows long tradition in assuming that Burns is referring to Jean Armour, whose pregnancy became a Mauchline scandal in the summer of 1786: she gave birth to twins in September. The speaker, however, sounds more like forthright Betsey Paton than timid, dutiful Jean Armour. (In addition, Burns – infuriated by Jean's retreat from their betrothal – refused to sit beside her (cf. l. 10) during their public penance.) If the song was written in May or June 1785, it is a companion piece to 'The Fornicator': defiance of local scandal is expressed from an unrepentant woman's point of view. The speaker, briefly but boldly sketched, simply assumes she has a right to sexual pleasure. Without a trace of the penitential spirit the parish would wish to see in a woman in her condition, she anticipates future kisses. Her courage and practicality – her anxieties about her first lying-in are limited to wondering who will pay for the childbed ale and linens – are as striking as her confidence in her lover.

THE RANTIN DOG THE DADDIE O'T

Lively

O— wha my ba - bie - clouts will buy; Wha will tent me— when I cry;

Wha will kiss— me— where I lie; The ran - tin— dog the— dad - die o't.

Wha— will— own he did the faut, Wha— will— buy the groan - in maut,

Wha— will— tell me how to ca't, The ran - tin— dog— the— dad - die o't.

Address to the Unco Guid, or the Rigidly Righteous

Text: *Poems* 1787 (Edinburgh) – not printed in 1786. The date of composition is unknown; perhaps June 1785.

JK uses similar thoughts set down in prose in *1CPB* to conjecture a date of March 1784: 'Let any of the strictest character for regularity . . . examine how many of his virtues are owing to constitution and education . . . [and] scan the failings . . . around him, with a brother's eye.' More probably, however, the poem responds to local scandal either over Elizabeth Paton's pregnancy (spring 1785) or Jean Armour's (mid-1786) – which would explain the sympathetic emphasis (not expressed in *1CPB*) on women who transgress. While the legal format – the speaker 'proponing defences' for transgressors – supports a date of 1786 (when the similarly legalistic 'Court of Equity' was written), in style, language, and length the poem is more reminiscent of the vernacular epistles of 1785.

JK notes allusions to *Hamlet*, *Paradise Lost*, Gray's 'Elegy in a Country Churchyard', Pope's *Essay on Man*, Hume's *Treatise on Human Nature*, Smith's *Theory of Moral Sentiments* and Addison and Steele's *Spectator* (3, 1030–31). Scripture, however, supplies the main outline of this defence of human frailty – not only the Book of Ecclesiastes, from which the epigraph is taken, but John 8: 3–7, in which Jesus dissuades a crowd led by Scribes and Pharisees from stoning the woman taken in adultery.

Man Was Made to Mourn. A Dirge (Tune: Peggy Bawn)

When chill No-vem-ber's sur-ly blast Made fields and_ for-ests bare, One ev'n-ing,_ as I wan-der'd forth, A-long the_ banks of Ayr, I_ spy'd a man whose a-gèd step Seem'd wea-ry, worn with care; His face was_ fur-row'd o'er with years, And_ hoa-ry_ was his hair.

Text: *Poems* 1786 (Kilmarnock). Transcribed in *1 CPB* (August 1785). Music from Dick.

The song, with its emphasis on human ills both physical and emotional, draws on eighteenth-century English didactic poetry (Young's *Night Thoughts*; Blair's *The Grave*; Shenstone's *Elegies*) as well as an old song Burns's mother often sang to her blind uncle. The song's refrain was 'Man was made to moan' and sobbing aloud while hearing it sung was the 'most voluptuous enjoyment' of the 'good old man' (*Letters* 1, 306–7).

The song's famous phrase – 'man's inhumanity to man' – draws on lines from Thomson's 'Winter':

> Ah little think the gay licentious Proud,
> Whom Pleasure, Power, and Affluence surround;
> They, who their thoughtless Hours in giddy Mirth,
> And wanton, often cruel, Riot waste;
> Ah little think they, while they dance along
> How many feel, this very Moment, Death
> And all the sad Variety of Pain.
>   . . . How many bleed,
> By shameful Variance betwixt Man and Man[.]
>   (1746 version, ll. 322–31)

Burns's simpler rendering is further simplified by Wordsworth in 'Lines in Early Spring':

> If this belief from heaven be sent,
> If such be Nature's holy plan,
> Have I not reason to lament
> What man has made of man?
>   (1798, ll. 21–4)

Though several of Burns's stanzas have passion and power, the song suffers from a failure fully to dramatize its encounter between youth and age. The consummate rendition of these traditional images is probably Wordsworth's in 'Resolution and Independence' (1802), where complex contrasts are developed – not only between youth and age, but between hope and despair, anxiety and security. 'Resolution and Independence' is also the work in which Wordsworth memorializes Burns as one of fortune's victims.

The Holy Fair

Text: *Poems* 1786 (Kilmarnock); begun soon after the second Sunday in August 1785.

A pamphlet of 1759 describes, much in Burns's terms, Scotland's crowded, convivial open-air communion services, which originated in Covenanting times: 'At first, you find a great number of men and women lying together upon the grass; here they are sleeping and snoring ... there you find a knot of young fellows and girls making assignations to go home together in the evening, or to meet in some ale-house; in another place, you see a pious circle sitting round an ale-barrel ... This sacred assembly ... is an odd mixture of religion, sleep, drinking, courtship, and a confusion of sexes, ages and characters' (Crawford, *Burns: A Study of the Poems and Songs*, p. 69).

At the holy fair (less flippantly called 'Occasion') held in Mauchline in August 1785, some 1,200 people took communion after listening to sermons. Many in the crowd (which numbered about 2,000, or four times the ordinary population of the little parish of Mauchline) attended only to hear the preaching or to socialize. Yet though a historical event is described in the poem, Burns's ironic frame – his speaker's encounter with 'Fun' and their shared laughter at the 'Hypocrisy' and 'Superstition' also convening in Mauchline – derives from Robert Fergusson's 'Leith Races', which itself is adapting Milton's 'L'Allegro':

'An' wha are ye, my winsome dear,
    That takes the gate sae early?
Whare do ye win, gin ane may spier,
    For I right meikle ferly,
That sic braw buskit laughing lass
    Thir bonny blinks shou'd gi'e,
An' loup like Hebe o'er the grass,
    As wanton and as free
        Frae dule this day.'

'I dwall amang the caller springs
    That weet the Land o' Cakes,
And aften tune my canty strings
    At bridals and late-wakes.
They ca' me Mirth; I ne'er was kend
    To grumble or look sour,
But blyth wad be a lift to lend,
    Gif ye wad sey my pow'r
        An' pith this day.'

'A bargain be't, and, by my feggs,
　　Gif ye will be my mate,
Wi' you I'll screw the cheery pegs,
　　Ye shanna find me blate;
We'll reel an' ramble thro' the sands,
　　And jeer wi' a' we meet;
Nor hip the daft and gleesome bands
　　That fill Edina's street
　　　　Sae thrang this day.'
　　　　　　(1773; reprinted in *Longer Scottish Poems*, Vol. 2, ed. Crawford,
　　　　　　Hewitt, and Law, Edinburgh: Scottish Academic Press, 1987,
　　　　　　　　　　　　　　　　　　　　　　　　　　　pp. 164-5)

The nine-line stanza of 'The Holy Fair', adapted by Burns from Fergusson, is also that of such Scots classics as 'Chrystis Kirk on the Green' and 'Peblis to the Play'; it was a measure traditional for 'brawl' poems. Irreverently, Burns casts New and Auld Licht ministers as his brawlers. The first is Alexander Moodie (ll. 100–109), familiarly addressed as 'Sawney'. Also satirized in 'The Holy Tulyie' (an early work not in the present selection – it is similar to but surpassed by 'The Holy Fair'), Moodie (1728–99) was minister at Riccarton, near Kilmarnock. His style was evangelical, and his dramatic, violent Auld Licht sermons (which Burns suggests by the verb 'speels', which has acrobatic connotations) often focused on the devil as the father of human nature.

Moodie is followed by George Smith (d. 1823), New Licht minister of Galston, whose dull lecture on morals falls on hostile ears (ll. 122–35). Critical consensus is correct in noting that Burns is ridiculing Smith's cautious and barren English sermon as far inferior in style to fiery Moodie's histrionics; but consensus errs in reading these lines literally, as an attack on the New Licht. Burns here slyly adopts the evangelical point of view of the majority of the listening communicants – folk convinced that faith alone (not kindness or moral living) is the mark of the saints; his point is that the 'angry' rejection of charity and ethics by these 'saints' is hardly to their credit. Furious at Smith, the congregation all get up and leave to have a drink.

William Peebles of Newton-upon-Ayr (1753–1826) next 'ascends' the pulpit (ll. 136–44). His message is more to the taste of the congregation, because he attacks the 'poisonous' common-sense positions of Smith: again, in these brawl stanzas the poem takes on the evangelicals' point of view. 'Common Sense' (l. 142) is usually said to be a personification of Burns's friend Dr John Mackenzie (cf. JK 3, 1102), but that reading is unlikely given this poem's delight in naming names. A similar stanza in 'The Holy Tulyie' (which also assumes, for satiric purposes, an Auld Licht point of view) illuminates Burns's characteristic positioning of common sense (which he champions) against orthodox faith as evangelicals define it:

Then Orthodoxy yet may prance,
And Learning in a woody dance;
And that curst cur ca'd Common Sense
　　Wha bites sae sair,
Be banish'd o'er the seas to France –
　　Let him bark there!
　　　　(HH 2, 25; their title is 'The Twa Herds; or, the Holy Tulyie')

In these lines, more explicitly than in 'The Holy Fair', the 'saints' exile common sense (like the Jacobite cause) to enlightened France. The poet is suggesting that the wrong force – faith (narrowly defined) rather than charity – rules in Scotland.

Alexander Miller (d. 1804) was in 1785 assistant minister at St Michael's; he later was appointed minister of Kilmaurs over the objections of parishioners who, Miller claimed, had been turned against him by ll. 145–54, where Burns hints that 'Wee Miller' preaches to evangelical interests – though he knows better – solely to speed his promotion to a parish. (The Scottish manse is the house provided by the parish for its incumbent minister.) Lines 181–9 describe John Russel (c. 1740–1817), minister at Kilmarnock in 1785. A fiery, saturnine Auld Licht preacher whose sermons (as in this poem) emphasized the tortures of the damned, Russel literally awakens these dozing sinners with his shouted harangue.

The epigraph was taken from Tom Brown's *The Stage Beaux Toss'd in a Blanket; or, Hypocrisie Alamode*, 1704; cf. JK 3, 1096. Lines 59–60 ('barefit . . . In silks and scarlets') offer a stroke of comic realism: although wearing their best silks and scarlet cloaks, the country girls walk to town barefoot to save their shoes. The 'sweet-milk cheese' that will provide lunch for the farmers' families (l. 61) was an unusual indulgence: cheese and butter were produced for sale, not for consumption by such families. (In fact, cheese production was quite limited on small farms because – in order to secure the needed rennet - it required the slaughter or accidental death of a calf.) In ll. 64–7, Burns's amused gaze focuses on the collection-plate: the congregation, requested to give two pennies, have been slipping in a halfpenny instead. (Tuppence was one quarter of a day's wages according to JK (3, 1098); Burns's speakers, however, often mention much less – a penny – as a day's wage for a ploughman.) 'Black-bonnet' (l. 66) – a reference to the preferred headgear of Covenanters – is the man entrusted with taking up the collection. As JK notes, parishioners supplied their own seating for eighteenth-century worship (l. 70): chairs, stools, and planks, brought to church weekly or 'set aside in the church . . . were handy missiles in congregational brawls' (3, 1099).

In l. 75, 'racer Jess' is Janet Gibson (d. 1813), retarded daughter of 'Poosie Nansie', hostess of the disreputable Mauchline alehouse described in 'Love and Liberty' (see pp. 220–21). The prostitutes are loitering outside the gentry's sheltered enclave. Other non-pious folk in attendance include the 'Wabster lads' of l. 79: town-dwelling weavers had a reputation as dangerous free-thinkers, and this group of 'blackguarding' young men from Kilmarnock have not come for the sermons.

As in 'Holy Willie's Prayer', syllepsis or zeugma concentrates the confusion of motives and values at the fair: 'some are thinkan on their sins . . . some upo' their claes [clothes]' (ll. 82–3). A mixture of the sacred and profane similarly marks l. 91's impudent echo of the metrical Psalm 146 ('happy is that man, an' blest' who succeeds in reposing his hand on a compliant mistress's bosom); and l. 116, where the inflammatory preaching of Moodie is said to raise the passions of the elder congregation just as courting has inflamed the young ('cantharidian plaisters' are poultices containing the aphrodisiac spanish fly). In l. 103, the mocking reference to 'salvation' so shocked Hugh Blair that he insisted the word be changed: 'The line . . . gives just offence. The Author may easily contrive some other rhyme in place of the word Salv——n' (JK 3, 1100). The poet complied by changing the word to 'damnation' in later editions of *Poems*.

Burns's contribution to the brawl tradition in 'The Holy Fair' lies precisely in his readiness to be bold, to 'give offence', to see drunken, bawdy comedy in what the (self-proclaimed) pious saw as a day of pure and holy striving. The energy of the poem largely proceeds from its deft counterpoint: the ripening harvest of the opening stanzas and the equally ripe young lovers; the passion of the preachers and the passion of courting couples; the melting of the hard hearts of sinners and of lasses.

To the Rev. John M'Math, Inclosing a Copy of Holy Willie's Prayer

Text: Cromek 1808; typographical errors silently corrected. Dated 17 September 1785.

Correctly sensing a kindred spirit in M'Math (a friend of Gavin Hamilton's and at that time an assistant minister at Tarbolton), the poet directly addresses views on the Auld Light more obliquely presented in 'Holy Willie's Prayer'. The epistle's strongest stanzas (like 'Holy Willie's Prayer') attack the Auld Licht's vindictive prosecution of Hamilton and its self-admiring hypocrisy. The praise of Alexander Pope (ll. 37-42) reminds us that the English satirist and author of moral epistles was as important an influence as Robert Fergusson. The final stanzas, with their praise of true religion as 'maid divine', are more perfunctory and may reflect Burns's consideration of the probable values of his addressee, whose Master of Arts in theology was from Glasgow University.

Born in Galston, John M'Math (1755-1825) became chief minister at Tarbolton. Because he was (as the parish charge read) 'too fond of convivial society', however, he was asked to resign in 1791, whereupon he enlisted in the army; he died on Mull (*Letters* 2, 466).

To a Mouse

Text: *Poems* 1786 (Kilmarnock). Written, according to Gilbert Burns, on the day of the incident described in the poem and 'composed . . . while the author was holding the plough' (JK 3, 1092).

Burns emphasizes the vulnerability common to his dual subject: mice and men. The terrified mouse has been torn from her shelter by the violent crash of the ploughshare. Like the tenant farmer who addresses her, she is hardy and needs little to survive (ll. 13-18); but, also like a tenant, the mouse has few resources to counter sudden disaster: leaves for a new nest are scarce in November, and she will be hard pressed to last out the winter. Like the poet's father, who died fighting bankruptcy, the field-mouse has been denied by unmerited misfortune the cosy security that should have resulted from her prudent, 'weary' work. Mossgiel farm itself, the setting of the poem, had been sub-leased from Gavin Hamilton as emergency housing for the Burnes family.

That all creatures are bound together in natural and mutual benevolence (l. 8) was the foundation of Smith's *Theory of Moral Sentiments* (1759; quoted by Burns in *1CPB*), a work that echoes, through Smith's teacher Francis Hutcheson, the philosophy of the third Earl of Shaftesbury. Burns synthesizes eighteenth-century moral philosophy with the Scottish tradition of didactic poems appropriating the 'voices' or experiences of beasts. Burns's refusal of burlesque, however – his view of the mouse as object of compassion, not occasion for satire – is unusual.

Love and Liberty. A Cantata

Text: Stewart 1801. Probably written in November 1785; the two surviving manuscripts were most likely transcribed in 1786 (Woodburn) and 1787 (Don). Printed as a pamphlet ('The Jolly Beggars; or, Tatterdemallions') by Stewart & Meikle in 1799; reset for book publication in 1801. Music from Dick.

Stewart used Woodburn but changed the title (see below). Variants in the more anglicized Don MS, as HH have noted, indicate the poet's deference to its aristocratic recipient, Lady Don, sister of the Earl of Glencairn. John Richmond told Stewart (his nephew) that both surviving manuscripts were missing songs by a sailor, a sootyman, and 'Racer Jess' Gibson (see below). Richmond himself gave Stewart the manuscript of a song by a simpleton ('Merry Andrew'), which Stewart duly added in 1802. J. C. Weston has established, however, that Merry Andrew's song was part of a rejected early draft (JK 3, 1148). As rendered in both surviving manuscripts, the cantata seems complete: symmetrically arranged round the central triangle of tinker–carlin–fiddler. John Richmond was probably remembering songs included in the first drafts but later deleted: Richmond left Mauchline for Edinburgh some time in November 1785, carrying in his pocket the same copy of Merry Andrew's song he later gave his nephew.

The cantata was written during the same winter as 'The Cotter's Saturday Night', and both poems describe characters at the bottom of the economic and class system. The deserving poor (the cotter's family) choose pious submission – hard work, sobriety, thrift. The beggars – the undeserving poor and proud to say so – choose rebellion: vagrancy, thievery, drunkenness, extravagance (cotters mend their clothes; beggars pawn theirs). Unlike the Bible-reading cotters, on Saturday night the beggars roar up sentimental ballads in the company of tavern cronies. The cotters' hope of heaven is incomprehensible to the beggars: how could there be a better place than here, another time than now? Both groups are heroic, for in both poems heroism is a matter of making the best of a bad lot. Yet though clearly admiring the self-respect of his cotters, the vitality and courage-in-adversity of his beggars, Burns distances himself (the clues are the extreme sentimentality of 'The Cotter's Saturday Night', the extreme irony of 'Love and Liberty') from both groups' unthinking acceptance of their lot. Cotters may have each other and God, but their children (some of them already servants on richer farms) have no chance for a better life. Beggars have each other and the pleasurable now – and even less chance of escaping the cycle of hereditary poverty. Burns was pondering his community and his own life, past and future, in the year following the near-bankruptcy and then the death of his father; and these poems define his sense of the poles of possibility for poor folk in eighteenth-century Scotland: unrewarded yet unremitting labour – or beggary. Seeing his world as he did, it is no wonder that in January 1786 he booked a passage for Jamaica.

Both poems also owe much to Burns's friendships. If 'Orator Bob' Aiken is named as the recipient of 'The Cotter's Saturday Night', Burns's rakish friends John Richmond and James Smith are addressed almost as directly in this cantata. Richmond – possibly Smith as well – accompanied Burns on the autumn night described in the poem: together, they watched the beggars and thieves gathered at Agnes Gibson's ('Poosie Nansie's') tavern in Mauchline.

Agnes Gibson herself had been rebuked by William Auld in 1773 for habitual drunkenness but had defied him and been stricken from the parish rolls. An outcast in Mauchline's tight-knit community – respectable citizens did not drink at her tavern – she also provided rooms for Mauchline's prostitutes, who may have included her retarded daughter Racer Jess (cf. 'The Holy Fair', l. 75). Pussy Gibson is a fitting 'hostess' for this group intent on insisting that a 'life of pleasure', pursued through strong punch and casual sex, is the best antidote to a universe of pain: the soldier's amputations, the Highland woman's hanged lover, the peace-treaty that ruins the camp-follower, the dwarf fiddler's crooked body. The beggars sing their own stories: fate has not silenced them. All share the euphoria of the moment. Like the field-mouse also addressed by Burns in November 1785, however, all will face the worst of winter without shelter – or even the rags and blankets they have pawned for drink.

Although Burns probably never read Gay's *The Beggar's Opera* (1728), its portrait-in-ballads of 'gentlemen of the sword' and their wanton doxies strongly influenced British popular song. Among the selections beholden to John Gay in Allan Ramsay's *Tea Table Miscellany* (1724–37) – a popular songbook whose contents Burns had evidently memorized – are 'Scots Cantata', 'Merry Beggars', and 'Jolly Beggars'. The pastoral view of vagabonds dates back in Scottish lyric tradition at least as far as 'The Gaberlunzie Man' (*c.* 1520). What eighteenth-century British popular song appropriated was Gay's addition of social commentary to the pastoral idealization of beggars. Like Gay, Burns moves his lovers' scenario indoors (into town and the underclass). Gay aimed his satire chiefly at Walpole and the court, but Burns is using the terms of chivalry and honour (his characters are burlesque 'soldiers', 'poets', 'musicians', 'lovers') to force these high ideals into contact with the harsh facts of real beggars' lives.

In its view of both 'love' and 'liberty', the cantata is darker than is usually acknowledged. What can 'mutual love' – the contract called 'Nature's social union' in 'To a Mouse' – possibly mean to people in this antithesis of a sentimental setting? The poet's implied answer: mere words in a high-sounding song. As the bard-character says – and the behaviour of the other characters illustrates – 'inclination' is a more compelling motive than altruism or faithfulness, however those nobler qualities might be privileged by the conventions governing love-lyrics. The gap between the songs' conventional lyric statements and the beggars' actual conduct is emphasized throughout. The inconsolable 'carlin' who sings of her lost 'John Highlandman', for instance, selects a replacement lover from two candidates that very evening. And the tender pastoral of the fiddler's song to her – 'Let me rike up to dight that tear/An' go wi' me an' be my Dear' – contrasts with his later sexual encounter with one of the Bard's doxies behind the chicken-coop: he 'rakes' her 'fore and aft', subjecting her to his will just as the threats of the tinker earlier forced submission on him. Burns shows that his beggars are indeed governed by 'Nature's law': love in this feral setting is momentary 'inclination', and brutal force wins all arguments. So the sentiments of the beggars' Bible – the popular songs they live by – are merely wistful lies. The distance between lyric or pastoral idealism and 'natural' human behaviour is conveyed even in Burns's diction: the narrative of action ('recitativo') is written mostly in graphic vernacular Scots, while the songs are written mostly in neoclassical English. Burns's favourite couplet, and the cantata's most defiant – 'Courts for cowards were erected,/Churches built to please the priest' – sees law and conscience, socialization and religion, as feeble forces compared to the deep hungers of the heart.

Burns considered including 'Love and Liberty' in the 1787 edition of *Poems*

(Edinburgh) but Hugh Blair was horrified: 'The Whole of What is called the Cantata, the Songs of the Beggars and their Doxies, with the Grace at the end of them, is in my opinion altogether unfit for publication. They are by much too licentious; and fall below the dignity which Mr Burns possesses in the rest of his poems and would rather degrade them.' Years later, the song-editor George Thomson (who had evidently heard – or heard of – the 'carlin's' toast to 'John Highlandman') requested that Burns send the whole cantata, but the poet replied: 'I kept no copy, & indeed did not know that [any was still] ... in existence; however, I remember that none of the songs pleased myself, except the last – something about, 'Courts for cowards were erected,/Churches built to please the priest' (*Letters* 2, 244). The concluding song that Burns remembered best is, though eloquent on the page, mismatched to its air; the cantata is seldom performed because of this failed final chorus. In addition, as often happens with dance tunes originally improvised by fiddlers but transposed by Burns for voice, several of the songs are multi-octave in range or so fast-moving that they are almost unsingable.

The title in the copy-text is 'The Jolly Beggars' – probably Stewart's invention. The manuscripts are titled 'Love and Liberty' and echo Pope's 'Eloisa to Abelard' (with *An Essay on Man* and *The Rape of the Lock*, among the poems most often quoted by Burns):

> If there be yet another name more free,
> More fond than mistress, make me that to thee!
> O happy state! when souls each other draw,
> When love is liberty, and nature law: (ll. 89–92)

Stewart's misleading title promises light comedy in the vein of similarly titled beggar-songs in Ramsay's *Tea Table Miscellany*. The modified 'Chrystis Kirk on the Green' stanza-form of the recitativo (ll. 1–28) was traditional for poems commemorating brawls (cf. 'The Holy Fair'). Allan Ramsay, writing two genera-tions before Burns, called it 'a Stanza of Verse the most difficult to keep the Sense complete ... without being forced to bring in words for Crambo's sake, where they return so frequently' (JK 3, 1095).

In l. 16, 'mealy bags' refers to the Scottish practice of distributing alms in the form of oatmeal; the beggars are reclining upon their sacks of meal, but will later (l. 51) trade them for drink. In l. 19 – 'wi' usquebae and blankets warm' – Burns employs syllepsis (see notes to 'The Holy Fair', p. 218, and 'Holy Willie's Prayer', p. 201), a trope that provides further opportunities for the poet to introduce reality into the the the haze of sentimental idealism that hangs over the songs. In ll. 204–5, it is both love – and drunkenness – from which the 'carlin' swoons.

In his song (ll. 29–53), the soldier cheerfully discloses that he was discharged from the army into a life of begging after more than twenty years of active service. Disabled and homeless for at least two years, he still loyally wears his red regimentals – now in tatters, as the song of his mistress emphasizes. (Her song ignores everything but the romance of the soldier's situation: those bright rags of his 'flutter'd so gaudy' (l. 84) that he stole her heart at first sight.) His first foreign battle was the storming of the 'heights of Abram' at the battle of Quebec (September 1759) under General Wolfe, who died of his wounds (l. 34); the soldier then took part in the siege of 'the Moro', the fort guarding Santiago, Cuba (1762). The soldier's final campaign (l. 39) was at Gibraltar, where Admiral Curtis broke the French and Spanish siege (1779–83); forces on Gibraltar itself were commanded by General George Eliot (l. 41). Regret for his amputations is expressed only in terms of regret for loss of his 'hero's' role, though fortunately he has found a mistress to toast him as her hero (l. 90). The song of the 'raucle carlin', like that of the soldier, describes an idealized (and probably somewhat falsified) past that in any case no longer obtains (ll. 100-132): however deeply she loved and grieved as a girl, John Highlandman's weeping 'widow' is now a tough, efficient old pickpocket with an eye for the laddies. Her ready selection of a lusty new lover immediately upon concluding her song suggests, in fact, an unspoken motive – perfectly human, if not at all 'noble' – for her song's eloquent insistence on her loneliness. Standing in contrast to the carlin is the professional prostitute or camp-follower, the 'martial chuck' (l. 60), who – declaring her fidelity to her soldier – passes as the ingénue in this poem. The word 'chuck' – unlike 'callet' or 'carlin' – is a term of endearment and not negative in connotation.

The legend of Dainty Davie (l. 218) is given in Burns's notes on Scottish song: he was a minister, David Williamson, who married seven times. Williamson 'begot the Lady Cherrytrees with child, while a party of dragoon were searching her house to apprehend him for being an adherent to the Solemn League and Covenant. – The pious woman had put a lady's night-cap on him ... and passed him to the soldiery as ... her daughter's bedfellow.' The daughter became Williamson's third wife (J K 3, 1159).

Textual variants: in l. 85, 'a sodger' reads 'my sodger' in the copy-text; in l. 96, 'Her love' reads 'Her dove'; in l. 139, 'hand on hainch' reads 'on haunch'; in l. 146, 'an' be my' reads 'to be my'; in l. 188, 'and been' reads 'I've been'; finally, in l. 236, 'wife eneugh' reads 'wife enough'. All are given here as corrected by Dick.

'Merry Andrew's' song (printed in Dick) has been omitted (see second paragraph on p. 220). Dick's musical texts for 'For a' that' and 'Soldier's Joy' – taken from Bremner's *Scots Reels* (1759) and McGlashan's *Scots Measures* (1781) – differ markedly from today's settings of those songs.

To a Louse

Text: *Poems* 1786 (Kilmarnock). Probably written in December 1785.

Jenny is comically blind to the real source of the attention she is receiving: not her costly new bonnet, but the louse plainly visible (to all but herself) as it marches up her 'Lunardi's' faddish balloon. Like its companion-poem 'To a Mouse', this is genial Horatian satire, linking an *exemplum* or observed experience with a final *sententia* or maxim. Set during a church service, the poem preaches an alternative text for the week: as in Luke's gospel (and Pope's *The Rape of the Lock*), she who exalts herself shall be humbled. The *sententia*, however, becomes broader when it prays for the power 'to see oursels as others see us', acknowledging that young women such as Jenny have no monopoly on vanities of 'dress' and 'gait'.

'To a Louse', even more than its companion-poem, satirizes Augustan decorum by addressing itself to a creature not only unpoetic but downright unhygienic. (The louse is 'plump' with Jenny's blood.) In addition to being a more difficult subject to manage poetically, the louse differs from the field-mouse in being no victim of fate but rather a jaunty mock-hero who 'boldly' sets his 'feet' on Jenny's body, thereby achieving a contact with this inaccessible local goddess that the poem's rustic narrator would never 'dare'. A sardonic edge is also visible in the narrator's naïve suggestion that many in the congregation would be more suitable hosts for the louse: any of the farm wives or little boys, or (not of the congregation but best of all from a louse's viewpoint) any of the countryside's numerous beggars, whose unwashed bodies and layers of rags would furnish much more reliable room-and-board than Jenny's bloodless 'gauze and lace' confection.

In l. 17, the phrase 'horn nor bane' is metonymic: combs were made of horn or bone. As beggars never comb their hair, their parasites – fleas ('ither . . . jumping cattle') as well as lice – enjoy utopian conditions of peace and plenty. '[R]ozet' and 'smeddum' (ll. 27–8) are insecticides: the louse is being threatened appropriately; but 'dress your droddum' (kick your backside) addresses the louse as an impudent male aggressor whose assault on Jenny's person (and the consequent damage to her reputation) must in honour be avenged.

A 'flainen toy' (l. 32) is a close-fitting home-made cap of woollen flannel with two long flaps falling down to the shoulders. Comfortable, warm, and wholly unfashionable, the flannel toy is the antithesis of Jenny's 'towering' bonnet, store-bought and overtrimmed. As the narrator points out, however, the toy would seem (to a louse) a much cosier residence. In l. 41, the phrase 'winks and finger-ends' refers to the congregation, who are winking and pointing as they 'take notice' of Jenny's louse. 'Lunardi' (l. 35) refers to the balloonist Vincenzo Lunardi (1759–1806), who created a sensation on 15 September 1784, when – accompanied by a cat and a pigeon – he flew a hydrogen balloon from Moorfields in London to Ware in Hertfordshire, covering twenty-four miles in just over two hours. In 1785 Lunardi was in Scotland and made several balloon ascents. Like the aeronautics pioneer Lunardi, the mock-heroic louse aspires to 'the tapmost, towering heights'. The contemporary account of Lunardi in *The Scots Magazine* praised 'the cool, intrepid manner in which the adventurer conducted himself' (*BE*): Burns, quite interested in ballooning (cf. the Postscript to 'Epistle to Simson'), may be deliberately imposing Lunardi's *sang froid* on this louse. As for Jenny, the poem suggests that she is, like her balloon-shaped bonnet, fashionable and showy but laughably puffed-up.

The Author's Earnest Cry and Prayer

Text: *Poems* 1786 (Kilmarnock). Probably written in December 1785 or January 1786; at any rate, before the passage of the Distillery Act of 1786, which amended the Wash Act of 1784 – the unpopular law that inspired this satire.

Despite the poem's exaggerated claim, the Wash Act did not ban whisky from Scotland; but it did greatly increase the excise tax on liquor exported to England, which reduced the Scots distilleries' already narrow profit-margin: legitimate distillers in Scotland competed with illegal distillers (and brandy-smugglers) who paid no excise or duties. The Wash Act, which brought Scottish distilleries to the brink of bankruptcy, had been urged by English distillers, who had successfully argued that the Scots had been receiving preferential treatment under the excise laws. The notion that Parliament, at any point in its history, had enacted legislation favourable to Scotland strikes the poet as richly humorous; but an underlying anger at Parliament's indifference to Scottish welfare deepens the significance of his comic hyperbole. Scotland, as is usual in Burns, is personified as female; here he argues that whisky is all the comfort the poor old lady can hope for, now that her forty-five representatives in the House of Commons have sold out her best interests in order to keep their sinecures and cabinet posts.

The epigraph burlesques *Paradise Lost* (Book IX, 896–901), the scene in which Adam, as yet unfallen, grieves for Eve's lost innocence:

O fairest of Creation, last and best
Of all God's Works, Creature in whom excell'd
Whatever can to sight or thought be form'd,
Holy, divine, good, amiable, or sweet!
How art thou lost, how on a sudden lost,
Defac'd, deflow'r'd, and now to Death devote?

Burns begins the body of the poem by emphasizing policies that unfairly single out the Scots: 'Irish lords' (l. 1) were allowed to represent Scotland in Parliament, but elder sons of Scottish peers were not eligible (cf. JK 3, 1140). Subsequent passages describe leading Scotsmen and MPs.

The 'Premier Youth' of l. 19 is William Pitt the Younger (1759-1806), who had become Prime Minister in 1783 at the age of twenty-four. The 'Montgomeries' (l. 57) refer to the warlike Earls of Eglinton. The eloquence of James Boswell (1740-95) is mentioned in l. 58: *Journal of a Tour to the Hebrides with Dr Johnson* (1785) had just appeared, but the biography of Johnson would not be published until 1791. Boswell was active in local politics and a neighbour of Burns's in Ayrshire: the Boswell home was at Auchinleck. The poet once sent Boswell a letter – respectfully docketed and saved by Boswell but never answered. Boswell's eldest son, Alexander (1775-1822), became an admirer of the poet, however, publishing his own volume of vernacular poems and laying the foundation stone of the Doon Burns Memorial in 1820, two years before his death in a duel.

George Dempster (1732-1818), Whig MP for Forfar Burghs from 1761-1790, is praised in l. 73. Burns also includes friendly references to him in 'The Vision' and 'Epistle to James Smith'. Dempster was popular among tenant farmers because of his advocacy of tenants' rights and his enlightened management of his own estate and fishery. In l. 74, 'aith-detesting Kilkerran' refers to Sir Adam Fergusson (1733-1813), third Baronet of Kilkerran, a close friend of Dempster's known for his dislike of cursing. Kilkerran served as MP for Ayrshire from 1774 to 1780 and from 1790 to 1796, and so was not in office when this poem was written – either a slip by the poet or a sacrifice of fact to rhyme, for Burns needs a match for 'warran', 'Baron', 'Graham', and 'auldfarran'. The 'Laird o' Graham' (l. 76) was James Graham (1755-1836), frequent office-holder in Pitt's government (Postmaster General, President of the Board of Trade, Paymaster of the Forces): as an elder son of a Scottish peer, Graham could not represent Scotland but served for Richmond (1780) and Wiltshire (1784). It was Graham who persuaded Parliament to lift the ban on the wearing of the tartan; he became third Duke of Montrose in 1790. 'Dundas' (l. 78) was Henry Dundas (1742-1811), MP for Midlothian (1774-90). One of Pitt's most valued political operatives, Dundas held successive posts as Treasurer of the Navy and Home Secretary; he also used his power as government election agent for Scotland to control election results. 'Erskine' (l. 79) was Thomas Erskine (1750-1823), third son of the tenth Earl of Buchan, MP for Portsmouth in 1785 and later (1806) Lord Chancellor: he supported Thomas Paine against accusations of treason in 1792, and was famous for his oratorical skill and wit. 'Frederick an' Ilay' (l. 80) refers to kinsmen: Lord Frederick Campbell (1736-1816), third son of the fourth Duke of Argyll and MP for the Glasgow and Ayr boroughs (1761-80), later Argyll (1780-99); and Sir Ilay Campbell (1734-1823), MP for the Glasgow boroughs. 'Liviston' (l. 81) was Sir William Augustus Cunninghame, laird of Milncraig and Livingston and MP for Linlithgow from 1774 to 1790.

The reference to 'Demosthenes or Tully' (l. 83) compares the preceding list of partisans and pragmatists to the highest-minded orators of Greece and Rome; negative comparison is produced by such hyperbole. In l. 87, the speaker wagers his new plough-cleaning tool that Mother Scotland will become violent if Parliament does not change the law. She is already in a cranky mood over the defeat in 1782 of the militia bill, and is prepared to commit acts of violence if the Wash Act is not repealed (ll. 91–108). Though comic in context, echoes of the Jacobite rebellions are pronounced: Scotland tucks up her once-proscribed tartan petticoat and pulls out her Highland dirk.

'Charlie Fox' (1749–1806), addressed in l. 109, was Pitt's strongest adversary within the Whig party: he spent nearly all of his Parliamentary career in opposition. Fox advocated radical Parliamentary reform, extension of the franchise, abolition of the slave-trade, and elimination of all test acts: a century ahead of his time as a legislator, he was in his personal life a throwback to the dissipated era of Charles II – a combination Burns found appealing. Fox's Tory adversary, Pitt the Younger, reappears in l. 115 as 'yon guid bluid o' auld Boconnock's', an epithet referring to the estate of Pitt's grandfather at Boconnoc in Cornwall. Burns then produces three near-rhymes for this difficult sound: 'bonnock' (bannock), 'winnock', and 'Tinnock'. (Nanse Tinnock, a tavern landlady in Mauchline, who evidently was insensitive to rhyme-scheme, later complained that she did not know why she was named in the poem, as Burns seldom drank at her establishment.) Lines 119–21 ('tea ... winnocks ... commutation') refer to Pitt's ingenious Commutation Act (1784), which repressed the smuggling trade in tea by sharply reducing the import duty and making it cheaper to buy from legitimate importers. Windows (winnocks) were taxed at a higher rate to offset the reduced revenue.

The concluding Postscript, a dark gem of a peroration, is built round an extended comparison between whisky and wine, Scotland and Europe. The speaker argues in closing (for this is a burlesque maiden-speech, the poet's first address to Parliament) that providing incentives for increased production of Scottish whisky will improve national security. A whisky-sodden British soldier recruited from among the starving Highlanders, he 'earnestly' argues, will fight much more fiercely than a merely wine-sodden French or Spanish soldier recruited from the starving peasantry of Europe. Wine drinkers run away, but whisky drinkers will slaughter everything in their path without a second thought: they make fine soldiers for 'Royal George'. Through burlesque, the poet makes a point also touched on in the earlier reference to the 'lost militia': Parliament has made an insufficient return to Scotland on her two major exports since the Union of Parliaments – defined in this poem as whisky and cannon-fodder.

The concluding four lines (ll. 183–6) are in later editions of *Poems* changed to:

> Till when ye speak, ye aiblens blether;
> > Yet deil-mak-matter!
> Freedom and Whisky gang thegither,
> > Tak aff your whitter. (JK 1, 191)

The copy-text's image of an elderly woman drunk to the point of incontinence brings out the darker tones in this satiric portrait of whisky's centrality in the Scottish culture and economy.

The Twa Dogs. A Tale

Text: *Poems* 1786 (Kilmarnock); begun in 1784 but completed by February 1786 (*Letters* 1, 28).

Burns chose this work – a beast fable of a more traditional sort than 'To a Mouse' – to open all editions of his *Poems*, and it well introduces many of his central concerns, emphasizing the ties of mutual regard and assistance that connect all living beings, and yet also expressing dismay and some anger at the enormous gulf between the busy and the idle, the needy and the privileged.

Seen from the perspective of two dogs, any inflated idea of mankind as 'Lords o' the creation' is reduced to sensible proportions. Caesar, the rich man's purebred, is (being a dog) down-to-earth and sociable in his own tastes (ll. 15–22); he defends simple pleasures and criticizes decadence (ll. 159–70). Caesar's description of wealthy ladies afflicted with spleen and addicted to gambling (ll. 219–28), a matter outside Burns's own realm of experience, is translated from Augustan convention, especially Pope's *Moral Epistles*. Robert Fergusson's 'Hame Content', which satirizes the Grand Tour, also influences Caesar's share in the dialogue. Luath, the ploughman's collie, evokes the joys and sorrows of cotters and tenants with more consistent success than 'The Cotter's Saturday Night', for no self-conscious sentiment debilitates his dog's-eye-view:

> The cantie auld folks, cracking crouse,
> The young anes rantan thro' the house –
> My heart has been sae fain to see them,
> That I for joy hae barket wi' them. (ll. 135–8)

In dialogue format and octosyllabic metre, the poem resembles Fergusson's 'The Mutual Complaint of Plainstanes and Causey, in their Mother-Tongue'. ('Plainstanes' was the pavement or sidewalk in Edinburgh; 'causey' was the causeway or street: their midnight quarrel is over which sees harder use.)

'Luath' was the name of the poet's border collie, 'killed by the wanton cruelty of some person the night before my father's death', wrote Gilbert Burns in Currie (1801). The poem was originally planned as a tribute to Luath. Newfoundland dogs – Caesar's breed – had been newly introduced to Britain: a generation later, Lord Byron made them even more fashionable. According to Gilbert Burns, Caesar was 'merely the creature of the poet's imagination'.

JK uses Burns's autograph notations to a copy of the Kilmarnock edition (now held by the Huntington Library) for ll. 43–4:

> Untill wi' daffin weary grown,
> Upon a knowe they sat them down,
>   (JK 1, 139)

Burns probably experimented with the new lines in response to criticism of his use of the word 'arse', but he never had them printed.

The reference to 'racked rents' (l. 51) touches on a matter close to Burns. On rack-rented estates, tenants paid annually rent that 'equalled (or nearly equalled)' (*OED*) the market value or purchase price – had the land been for sale – of their acreage. Improvement in agricultural methods greatly increased the yield of farms in the eighteenth century, but not enough to cover this inflation. 'Cotters' (l. 72) were the poorest of tenants, sub-leasing a few acres (in Scotland usually less than two) from tenant farmers, with rent – as their crops went to feed their families –

to be paid in the cotters' labour. (The term 'cottar' itself goes back to the Domesday Book, where it signified 'a villein occupying a cot or cottage with an attached piece of land (usually 5 acres) held by service or labour (with or without payment in produce or money)' (*OED*).) William Burnes's first holding at Alloway was (at about seven acres) larger than that of a cotter, and he had prepaid his long leasehold, obviating any need for quarterly rent or for labouring in exchange for his land; Burnes had also emphasized his independence by building his own house. His subsequent farm at Mount Oliphant was (though hopelessly infertile) ten times larger than his first holding. The poet's own first farm at Mossgiel – sub-leased from Gavin Hamilton, who was factor to the Earl of Loudon and had leased the land from his employer – was fairly large: 118 acres. So the poet was neither a cotter nor from a cotter's family. As l. 80 and Luath's reference to 'want o' masters' makes clear, the problem with being a cotter was almost more a matter of dependency than of limited economic prospects: cotters, like dogs, could only hope for kindly 'masters', as they were wholly dependent upon them. The following fifteen lines, with ll. 101–36, are a sketch for 'The Cotter's Saturday Night', which Burns began while still working on this poem.

In l. 96 – 'thole a factor's snash' – Burns is drawing on painful memories of his family's last years at Lochlea farm: after their kindly 'Master' (landlord) died, his estate was managed by a 'factor' (steward) who dunned the family without mercy: 'my indignation yet boils at the recollection of the scoundrel tyrant's insolent, threatening epistles, which used to set us all in tears' (*Letters* 1, 137). The lines following l. 157 – 'make a tour' – describe fashionable destinations on the Grand Tour. Like Swift in 'A Modest Proposal', Burns emphasizes the decadent pleasure-seeking of absentee landlords.

In l. 2, 'auld king Coil' was in legend an ancient king of Kyle (Burns's region). In l. 28 – 'lord knows how lang' – the speaker slyly refers to the debate over the authenticity of 'Ossian', reserving judgement on the exact date of the composition of *Fingal*. A condensed self-portrait of the poet as a 'rhyming, ranting, raving billie' is provided in l. 24. Fittingly, as he is cast as the poem's mongrel, Luath's ring tail – cf. 'wi' a swirl' (l. 36) – does not conform to today's standard for his breed. The reference in l. 204 – 'her dizzen's done' – is to a day's quota for a spinster: 3,720 yards of yarn, or twelve 'cuts' of 310 yards each.

The Cotter's Saturday Night

Text: *Poems* 1786 (Kilmarnock). Completed before 16 February 1786 (*Letters* 1, 27–8).

The Spenserian stanza-form and the subject – the evening meal of a peasant family – were inspired by Fergusson's 'The Farmer's Ingle'. The generalizing impulse and often elevated English diction, however, show the influence of Gray's 'Elegy Written in a Country Churchyard', from which the epigraph is taken. As a sketch of Scottish peasants, Fergusson's poem is often preferred to Burns's:

> . . . the guidman, new come hame, is blyth to find,
>   Whan he out o'er the halland flings his een,
> That ilka turn is handled to his mind,
>   That a' his housie looks sae cosh and clean:
>   For cleanly house looes he, tho' e'er sae mean.

Weel kens the gudewife that the pleughs require
    A heartsome meltith, and refreshing synd
O' nappy liquor, o'er a bleezing fire:
    Sair wark and poortith douna weel be join'd.
Wi' butter'd bannocks now the girdle reeks,
    I' the far nook the bowie briskly reams;
The readied kail stand by the chimley cheeks,
    And had the riggin het wi' welcome steams,
Whilk than the daintiest kitchen nicer seems.
(*Longer Scottish Poems*, Vol. 2; ed. Crawford, Hewitt, and Law, Edinburgh:
Scottish Academic Press, 1987, p. 156)

The difference in scope should be considered, however. Fergusson confines himself to what peasants see and eat: a house, a fireside, a rustic menu. Burns, in an occasionally awkward mixture of high English and vernacular Scots, captures what peasants feel: their mutual affection and their religious faith. Fergusson's is a didactic poem, while Burns's more fully dramatizes its characters.

The poem moves between generalizations (mediated by Gray) about the noble poor to sharper, more particular images – the thinning grey hair of the father; the watchful care of the 'garrulous' mother – descriptive of Burns's own family. The portrait of the patriarch leading family worship (ll. 100–144) is certainly a tribute to Burns's own father (d. 1784). The poem is not completely autobiographical, however: Burns describes a family several degrees poorer than his own. Unlike the Burnes children, who worked on their father's farm, the cotter's older children – 'woman-grown' Jenny is perhaps sixteen – go out to neighbouring farms as day-labourers or servants, each 'penny-fee' (a day's wage for a young worker) being needed.

The unevenness of the poem, which is often blamed on linguistic or cultural confusion between English and Scots, may result from Burns's ambivalence about the values he is praising. Clearly the poet sees his cotters as morally and spiritually superior to the wealthy. As clearly, however, he sees that their virtues – their thrift, for instance, and their humility – have been conditioned by an unremitting poverty that enforces their economic dependency on a series of 'masters'. The father admonishes his working children to submit to authority – 'to obey' and never to joke or play (ll. 47–9): the patriarch's advice does not match the poet's values. Emphasizing (as Gray did) the peasants' human value, and successfully capturing their affectionate family life, Burns also sees their vulnerability and fears for their future (as in the much criticized lines that imagine a seducer capable of betraying Jenny).

In writing of his own youth to Dr John Moore in 1787, Burns confessed that he had had to distance himself from his family's constant struggle: 'I saw my father's situation entailed on me perpetual labor' (*Letters* 1, 139). Where the poem rings false – as in opening lines insisting that prosperous Ayr lawyer Robert Aiken would have been far happier as a cotter; or l. 177, with its prayer that cotters who can scarcely feed and clothe themselves be spared the unlikely curse of 'luxury' – Burns is following, too blindly, nostalgic eighteenth-century literary convention. It is only when he draws his images from earliest childhood (as in ll. 19–27) that he fully reanimates Gray's fiction (and Fergusson's) that peasants, secured from temptation and sheltered from the world, lead the lucky lives.

The inscription is to Robert Aiken, the poet's 'chief Patron' during this highly productive winter (*Letters* 1, 28); see also notes to 'Holy Willie's Prayer' (p. 200) and 'Epistle to a Young Friend' (p. 237). In l. 75, the phrase 'weary, mortal round' recalls Shenstone's 'Written at an Inn.' 'The Schoolmistress', a Spenserian poem by Shenstone, also was an influence, especially on Burns's lines describing family worship. In l. 93, 'The soupe' for the family's oatmeal is cow's milk. The family's treasured 'hawkie' is nearby: the byre is separated only by a low partition (the 'hallan') from the family's living-area. 'Dundee', 'Martyrs', and 'Elgin' (ll. 111–13) refer to musical settings of the Psalms. In l. 122, the 'royal Bard' is King David, traditionally considered the author of the Psalms. line 166: 'An honest man's the noble work' in copy-text; emended as in the Egerton MS.

The Auld Farmer's New-Year-Morning Salutation to His Auld Mare, Maggie

Text: *Poems* 1786 (Kilmarnock). Probably written in January 1786.

Maggie, sometimes entered during her youth in long-distance races, may be one of the new Clydesdales; at any rate, she is massive and has more stamina than the sleek hunters of the gentry (ll. 55–60). The farmer's affectionate New Year's address to the plough-horse who has served him at work and play for twenty-nine years – she arrived as chief part of his wife Jenny's dowry – pays tribute, like 'The Twa Dogs' and 'The Cotter's Saturday Night', to a laborious farming life that the poet, newly resolved on emigration to the West Indies, has decided he must reject. A backward glance at his late father's world of long-term and faithful mutual support between horse and rider, servant and master, this may be the most successful of the poet's attempts in the year following William Burnes's death to capture something of his upright father's voice and values. Maggie – said by Maurice Lindsay to be the name of an old horse belonging to Burns in 1786 (*BE*) – is also the name of Tam o' Shanter's mare.

The title's 'hansel' is the traditional New Year's gift, given to close friends on the first Monday of the year.

To James Smith

Text: *Poems* 1786 (Kilmarnock). Probably written in January or February 1786.

Smith's humanity (ll. 15–18) compensates for his short stature (l. 14), as Burns's wit (l. 36) compensates for his poverty (l. 31). The epistle's emphasis on uncharted wanderings suggests that Smith was also desperate enough to be considering emigration in 1786. Apart from their shared interest in escaping to the new world, Smith and Burns shared with John Richmond a reputation as Mauchline's wildest 'ramstam boys'. Smith, born in 1765 and raised after the age of ten by a devout but austere stepfather, had much in common with the poet, despite six years' difference in their ages; he served as intermediary in the stormy early years (1786–8) of the poet's relationship with Jean Armour. Following a venture in calico-printing – begun in 1787 and failed by 1788 – Smith did emigrate, landing either in Jamaica (J K 3, 1137) or St Lucia (*Letters* 2, 480). According to Cromek (1808), Smith died young in the tropics.

The epigraph is from Robert Blair's *The Grave* (1743): an implied reference to death opens this convivial epistle, and suggests that Smith already was consumptive or otherwise fragile in health when Burns knew him. In l. 19, the expression 'fit o' rhyme' sees poetry as a 'fit' or mild disability, like the weakly and 'scrimpet' stature of Smith. Burns may also have in mind the ancient division of poetry into cantos or 'fits' (*OED* records uses from AD 888); or perhaps he is recalling Ben Jonson's pun in 'A Fit of Rhyme Against Rhyme'. (Though not among the poets Burns mentions, Jonson was generally well known among Scots poets, who remembered the story of Jonson's 400-mile walk to visit Drummond of Hawthornden in 1618.)

Burns transcribed a variant stanza for ll. 25–30 in an undated notebook now at the Kilmarnock Monument Museum:

> Some rhyme because they like to clash,
> And gie a neebor's name a lash;
> And some (vain thought) for needfu' cash;
>   And some for fame;
> For me, I string my dogg'rel trash
>   For fun at hame.   (J K 1, 179)

In l. 32, 'the russet coat' is metonymic: country folk used dull-coloured natural dyes. Only the affluent could afford brilliant silks or velvets. On the poet's 'luckless lot' as a disguised blessing uniting him with nature, see also Beattie's *Minstrel*:

> Ah! who can tell how many a soul sublime
> Hath felt the influence of malignant star,
> And waged with Fortune an eternal war!
> Checked by the scoff of Pride, by Envy's frown,
> And Poverty's unconquerable bar,
> In life's low vale remote hath pined alone,
> Then dropped into the grave, unpitied and unknown!
>
> . . .
>
> Though richest hues the peacock's plumes adorn,
> Yet horror screams from his discordant throat.
> Rise, sons of harmony, and hail the morn,
> While warbling larks on russet pinions float;
> Or seek at noon the woodland scene remote,
> Where the grey linnets carol from the hill.
> Oh, let them ne'er with artificial note,
> To please a tyrant, strain the little bill,
> But sing what Heaven inspires, and wander where they will!
>   (Canto 1, ll. 3–9; 7–40)

In Beattie's poem it is nature's singers, the lark and linnet, who wear the peasant's grey and russet colours.

In l. 38 – 'guid, black prent' – Burns refers for the first time to publication, my reason for dating this poem in January or February 1786 rather than (as J K does) the autumn or early winter of 1785. (*Letters* concurs, placing the epistle after Burns's letter of 17 February to John Richmond (1, 30).) On 3 April Burns wrote that he had resolved to publish 'about the latter end of 1785' (*Letters* 1, 30). He evidently acted on two decisions just after the New Year – to emigrate (it was probably in January that he booked passage for Jamaica) and to publish before he left: proposals were sent to the press early in April. Printing his poems was a farewell gesture and also a way of arranging for the continuing support of his infant daughter Elizabeth, to whom he at first planned to assign the copyright. (Both the plans to emigrate and the assignment of copyright were disrupted by Jean Armour's pregnancy, which started in January or February 1786 and greatly complicated Burns's responsibilities. But Burns continued to see publication of his poems not so much as a way to escape financial difficulty – emigration was his solution to that problem – as a way to 'compensate my little ones, for the stigma I have brought on their names' (*Letters* 1, 121).)

The allusion to Atropos, third of the fatal sisters (cf. 'snap the brittle thread', l. 56), is ironic in a poem that emphasizes the poet's ignorance of classical culture. In l. 59 'inglorious dead' is an echo both of 'mute inglorious Milton' and 'unhonoured dead' in Gray's 'Elegy' (ll. 59; 93), while 'high disdain' (l. 102) recalls 'Nor Grandeur hear with a disdainful smile,/The short and simple annals of the poor' ('Elegy', ll. 31–2). Lines 85–114 revisit another poem by Gray, 'On a Distant Prospect of Eton College' – a text, like Burns's, built upon contrasts: youth versus age, joy versus sober prudence.

The reference in l. 74 to the sorrows of 'five an' forty' reminds us of the early onset of old age in the eighteenth century; the poet and Smith were at any rate spared those ills, for both died before the age of forty. Line 98 contains an echo of Genesis in 'toil'd nor swat': a fortunate few escape Adam's fate, remaining in a 'flow'ry' yet somehow unnatural Eden of plentiful resources. Line 99 – 'drink the sweet and eat the fat' – describes the diet of the rich, later (l. 141) contrasted with the bard's scanty peasant diet of water-brose (oatmeal prepared without milk, salt, or butter) and muslin-kail (barley and cabbage broth prepared without meat stock or bones). Line 122 – 'wander Terra over' – suggests, as mentioned, that Smith and the poet had been discussing emigration. Finally, l. 149 – 'sorrow, care, and prose' – shows the use of syllepsis so characteristic of Burns's early style: see also notes to 'Holy Willie's Prayer', (p. 201), 'The Holy Fair', (p. 218), and 'Love and Liberty' (p. 222).

In l. 166 'rattling squad' is 'rambling squad' in the copy-text; as emended in *Poems* 1787 (Edinburgh) and subsequent editions.

Scotch Drink

Text: *Poems* 1786 (Kilmarnock). Written before 17 February 1786, when it is mentioned in a letter to John Richmond. A copy was sent on 20 March to Robert Muir of Kilmarnock.

A stanza of Fergusson's 'Caller [Fresh] Water' celebrates the same subject and shares a tipsy-sounding exuberance in rhymes. (Burns's opening flourish rhymes 'Bacchus' and 'fracas'; Fergusson matches 'Anacreontic' and 'Pontic'.) Burns praises whisky as democratic, smoothing over the difficulties of life for rich and poor alike. This high-spirited comic poem is deepened by an underlying melancholy sentiment: 'life's a gift no' worth receivin'' without the illusion of well-being fostered by whisky – an illusion and a lie (however heart-easing and pleasant) with which poetry is in collusion, as whisky is the Muse of poetry.

In l. 7 ('my Muse') the speaker, like the Bard in 'Love and Liberty', salutes whisky as his source of inspiration. The reference in l. 8 ('wimplin worms') is to the network of tubes at the top of a still. 'John Barleycorn' (l. 17) was hero of Burns's early ballad and here stands as the personified source not only of the Scots' preferred drink but also, in the form of barley scones and soup, much of their diet. The 'souple scones' of l. 20 link whisky with butter – both were precious (though rare) elements in a peasant's diet. Dry scones become more 'supple' – go down more easily – with a generous application of butter, just as sober reality becomes palatable or at least endurable when moistened and 'oiled' by whisky. In l. 21 – 'tumbling in the boiling flood' – the grandiose diction of James Thomson (*c.* 1740) is burlesqued in Burns's solemn description of cabbage-and-beef broth on the boil. The 'burn' and 'sucker' of ll. 53–4 are the water and sugar added to New Year's punch.

Whisky's contributions to the work-place are described in ll. 55–66. Vulcan, the hard-luck god (lamed by Jove, betrayed by Venus, frequently drunken), relies on whisky for strength to operate his bellows, just as weary ploughmen gather round the lugget cup to recruit their strength before repairing their equipment ('graith') with anvil ('studdie') and sledge-hammer ('forehammer'). 'Burnewin' (l. 59) is burn-the-wind, an epithet (reminiscent of an old Norse 'kenning') for the blacksmith/artisan Vulcan. If whisky helps men through their most strenuous work, it also eases a woman's different species of labour: the centrality of drink in Scottish childbirth customs is presented in ll. 67–72. The 'gossips' (women friends assembled to help) partake enough of the groaning-malt (ale served at a childbirth; also given the mother to ease labour pains) to 'clatter bright' (become noisy), while the anxious father progresses to such an advanced stage of 'fumbling' drunkenness that he forgets to tip the midwives or take notice either of his 'dearie' or the 'skirling weanie' (wailing infant) itself (l. 67).

Brandy is personified as a villain in the poem, and Burns was not the first Scotsman to disparage this foreign-made liquor, so often preferred to whisky by wealthy Scots: as JK notes, Whisky and Brandy engage in pastoral dialogue in Fergusson's bizarre poem 'A Drink Eclogue' (3, 1134). Burns suggests (ll. 89–90) that brandy drinkers were selfishly depriving Scottish distillers of needed profits. The plural in 'warst faes' (l. 90) is interesting: France and perhaps Spain, brandy producers and traditional foes of the British, could be intended; but so also could England, traditional 'foe' of Scotland; for in Burns's view England received an undue share of excise and other revenues (see note to 'The Author's Earnest Cry and Prayer', p. 224). 'Ferintosh' (l. 109) was a peaty single-malt whisky that had enjoyed exemption from duty between 1695 and 1785 because of the loyalty of the distiller, Forbes of Culloden, during the Jacobite wars. Burns calls it 'lost' because its price had risen after its tax exemption was removed. (The distiller eventually sued for damages and was awarded £21,580.)

Address to the Deil

Text: *Poems* 1786 (Kilmarnock). Like 'Scotch Drink', mentioned as freshly completed in a letter to John Richmond dated 17 February 1786. Gilbert Burns, no doubt recalling an early version, dated the poem in 1784: like several of Burns's major poems, this was probably begun at Lochlea but completed at Mossgiel.

A ringing blow in Burns's quarrel with the Auld Licht, this satire caused a major local scandal. Several of the anonymous contributors to *Animadversions*, James Maxwell's compilation of evangelical attacks on Burns (Paisley, 1788), saw this poem as final proof of Burns's evil values. Alexander ('Saunders') Tait of Tarbolton, a mantua-maker and tailor who considered himself Burns's equal as a satirist, also seized upon this as Burns's most shocking poem, publishing his attack in 1790.

Burns intended it to shock, and so structures the poem round what any Auld

Licht partisan would see as a heretical statement of Arminianism: the deil's long-ago invasion of Eden only 'almost' 'ruined all' for Adam and Eve (l. 96): the stain of sin is not ineradicable and even Satan (if he wished) could 'tak a thought' and mend – change and receive forgiveness. Burns's 'deil' is neither the sadistic demon of Auld Licht sermons nor the tragic hero Milton's Satan considered himself to be. A rather forlorn and unsuccessful mischief-maker, his smudged ('smoutie') face ashy from brimstone and his plots against humanity invariably thwarted, the deil is addressed more or less as just another 'poor, damned body'. The poet is dramatizing his rejection of predestination. The Arminians had challenged Calvinist 'election' (salvation through grace alone, not human effort) but Burns focuses on its corollary – repudiation, a doctrine that insisted that the reprobated are eternally cast away from grace, whatever their benighted individual efforts to be (and do) good. Burns, by contrast, announces that he considers himself salvageable (ll. 119–20) – and if 'a certain Bardie' can be saved, then there must be hope for a mere devil. The poet is paying a backhanded compliment to his own sinfulness as he mocks the Auld Licht. No one – not even the deil – is all bad and forever incapable of change, the poem argues with a cheerful perversity that enraged the Auld Licht. A more orthodox point is also made: hope of heaven is more likely to convert sinners than fear of damnation.

Like 'The Holy Fair', which admires the power of evangelical sermons even as it mocks their theology, this address to the devil almost envies the credulous their heightened imaginative engagement with the world. The dim-witted rustic who narrates up to l. 84 has been convinced by his illiterate grandmother that he has repeatedly 'seen' and 'heard' the deil – for she has taught him to penetrate the deceptively prosaic guises Satan assumes: an owl at twilight (l. 30), a quacking duck (l. 47), floating ragweed (l. 50). Even while mocking superstition, the poem captures the world as it must have appeared to the pious and unlettered of Burns's parish: as magically saturated with symbolic significance. Common bullrushes by the riverbank might part to reveal (as in the Bible) a floating baby, God's future champion – or (as in l. 47) God's adversary himself, 'squattering' away. Wallace Stevens wrote that the death of Satan is a tragedy for the imagination: Burns's use up to l. 84 of a speaker more naïve than himself averts that tragedy, allowing him to see 'the deil' in contradictory ways: he satirizes credulity, but he also captures the imaginative (even if in this poem also imaginary) richness that belief in things invisible confers on ordinary human experience.

The epigraph is from *Paradise Lost* (Book 1, l. 129). Beelzebub is speaking – first of the rebel angels to address Satan after their incarceration in Hell. This anticipates the poet's final audacious statement of himself and Satan as fellow reprobates, differing only (like Beelzebub and Satan) in degree. In l. 2, the terms 'Hornie' and 'Clootie' are synecdochal, referring to the deil's horned head and cloven hoof. The lines parody Pope's address to Swift in 'The Dunciad': 'O Thou! whatever title please thine ear,/Dean, Drapier, Bickerstaff or Gulliver!' (Book 1, ll. 19–20).

In l. 11 ('poor dogs like me'), the speaker identifies with the 'damned bodies' of sinners in the 'lowan heugh' (flaming pit) of hell, reproaching Satan; later he sees Satan himself as just another condemned wretch. The reference to 'boortries' (l. 35) is to the practice of planting elder bushes in farmyards as protection against witchcraft. Line 44 – 'each bristl'd hair' – parodies the speech of the Ghost in *Hamlet* (I, v, 18–20). 'As yell's the bill' (l. 60) is a proverb: milkless (barren) as the bull. Satan and his minions – local witches and warlocks – have charms enabling them to steal butter from the farm wives' churns and dry up the milk even in the most productive cows ('dawtet' – treasured – twelve-pint 'hawkies'). To the rustic speaker, this mischief is much more serious than Satan's temptation of Adam and Eve, which after all happened 'lang syne' (l. 85).

In ll. 63–6, Burns's narrator solemnly asserts that Satan causes many local cases of impotence, casting his spell on the vigorous young Guidman's 'wark-lume' and rendering it useless ('no worth a louse') right at the point of crisis: 'just at the bit'. Hugh Blair tried but failed to convince the poet to delete the stanza. Lines 85–96 offer a twelve-line précis and burlesque of Milton's *Paradise Lost*; having disposed of the greatest English epic, Burns then takes on the Old Testament, retelling the story of Job (ll. 97–108).

Extempore to Gavin Hamilton. Stanzas on Naething

Text: HH 2, with silent correction of punctuation. Transcribed twice, in *2CPB* (Edinburgh 1787) and the Glenriddell MS (1791), but never published by Burns. Probably composed in February or March 1786: the poet was then absorbed in plans for emigration (ll. 45–9) and courting Jean Armour (ll. 33–40); he quarrelled with her parents in April.

The short, choppy stanzas and English rhymes suggest by contrast Burns's greater skill with longer, more intricate schemes and metres. The song is reminiscent of 'Song LXVI' in Ramsay's *Tea Table Miscellany*:

> A parson's a trifle at sea,
> A widow's a trifle in sorrow,
> A peace is a trifle today,
> To break it a trifle tomorrow.
>
> . . .
>
> But with people's malice to trifle,
> And to set us all on a foot,
> The author of this is a trifle,
> And his song is a trifle to boot.
>
> (2: 70–71)

The 'Merry Andrew' song added to Burns's folk-cantata on testimony from John Richmond (see note to 'Love and Liberty', p. 220) shows similar variations on 'fool':

> Sir Wisdom's a fool when he's fou;
>   Sir Knave is a fool in a Session,
> He's there but a prentice I trow,
>   But I am a fool by profession.
>
> (JK 1, 199)

On Gavin Hamilton's quarrel with the Auld Licht and his friendship with Burns, see notes to 'Holy Willie's Prayer' (p. 200). In l. 33, the comparison is to the poet/narrator as a king: the 'feminine Whig' questions his absolute authority, being inclined to assert her autonomy. Despite this poem's attack on marriage (ll. 21–4) and the boast of l. 40 that the 'feminine Whig', for all her manoeuvring, has been promised 'naething' (l. 40), Jean Armour and the poet were legally betrothed by April. The hostility of these lines may well reflect the poet's resentment of the commitment Jean was exacting. (Elizabeth Paton had not expected courtship or commitment.)

To a Mountain Daisy

Text: *Poems* 1786 (Kilmarnock). Sent to John Kennedy on 20 April as 'the very latest of my productions' (*Letters* 1, 32). Kennedy's copy bears a variant title: 'The gowan – A Scotch Poem – on turning down a mountain daisie with the plough'. In James Currie's edition (1800), Gilbert Burns noted that, like 'To a Mouse', this was inspired by an incident that occurred at Mossgiel farm and written while 'the author was holding the plough'.

In a letter dated 16 December 1787, the adolescent Dorothy Wordsworth singled out her favourite poem in the Kilmarnock edition: 'there is one, to a mountain daisy, which is very pretty' (Low, ed., *Robert Burns: The Critical Heritage*, p. 92). This was also Henry Mackenzie's favourite poem by Burns – not surprisingly, as (in its intense pity for suffering, even that of a plant) it shows the influence of Mackenzie's sentimental novel *The Man of Feeling* (1771), a copy of which the young poet always carried in the pocket nearest his heart. (Mackenzie's doomed hero Harley cannot get on with his own life because he is so moved by the sufferings of others; he can never act in self-interest, being a man of feeling as opposed to a competent, heartless 'man of the world'. Harley was, with *Tristram Shandy*'s sweet but equally impotent trio of heroes – Uncle Toby, Yorick, and the narrator – among a very few novel-heroes ever to engage the poet's imagination.)

The daisy, like the field-mouse addressed in November 1785, is a hardy, self-sufficient, humble, 'chearful' reminder that few resources are absolutely needed for survival. Yet like the mouse, the daisy – needing little – fails to receive even the small share of protection from catastrophe that she requires. Like 'The Cotter's Saturday Night', this poem has been dismissed by most critics as excessively sentimental, yet it has always been among Burns's most popular works. Stanzas 2 and 4 are rather blandly post-Miltonic and conventional – though ll. 21-4 bore fruit in one of Wordsworth's Lucy poems. (The lines recall Gray's flower 'born to blush unseen/And waste its sweetness on the desert air' (Elegy', ll. 55-6) and anticipate Wordsworth's description of lost Lucy as 'a violet by a mossy stone/Half hidden from the eye!' ('She dwelt among the untrodden ways').) The opening stanza, however, is among Burns's most effective, and the last four, built on analogies close to home, are (if read in the context of Burns's life at that time) affecting. The 'artless Maid' of ll. 31-6 is undoubtedly Jean Armour (once the petted favourite of her father, now pregnant by Burns and in disgrace with her lover as well as her family: fearful of Burns's poverty, she had agreed to her father's destruction of their betrothal contract and broken their engagement). To save 'ruin'd' Jean now was indeed 'past' the poet's 'pow'r', as she was being sent away to live with an uncle in Paisley and pressured to marry a richer suitor there. The 'simple Bard' of ll. 37-42 is the poet himself, daily more anxious about his recent decision to submit himself to the 'billows' and 'gales' of a hazardous ocean crossing, and fearful of continued misfortune even in the New World. The stanza on 'suff'ring worth' (ll. 43-8) refers to the poet's late father, whose exemplary piety remained wholly unrewarded in this world and whose life ended in February 1784 on a note of barely averted bankruptcy. Bad sentimental writing is based on exaggerated or invented strong emotions. The urgency of this poem – expressed even in an unusually high number of elided, compressed words (showing a 'crushing' action even at the level of language) – is at any rate utterly sincere.

Apart from Gray's 'Elegy', the poem echoes (ll. 7–12) the image of the lark in Milton's 'L'Allegro' (ll. 41–6) and also (ll. 49–54) the penultimate couplets of Pope's 'Elegy to the Memory of an Unfortunate Lady':

> Poets themselves must fall, like those they sung;
> Deaf the prais'd ear, and mute the tuneful tongue.
> Ev'n he, whose soul now melts in mournful lays,
> Shall shortly want the gen'rous tear he pays.

Epistle to a Young Friend. May – 1786

Text: *Poems* 1786 (Kilmarnock). Dated 15 May 1786 in the manuscript copy now owned by the city of Kilmarnock (probably the text actually sent to Andrew Aiken).

Like 'The Cotter's Saturday Night' (dedicated to Robert Aiken, father of the boy addressed here), this epistle is directly and self-consciously didactic. The Aikens must have exuded an aura of high seriousness. The poet cannot impersonate Polonius with entire conviction – his gravity collapses in the final couplet. But ll. 41–8 and 73–6 sketch convincingly the boundary between harmless high spirits and libertinism. As so often in Burns, this borderline is set not by actions but by motives – especially by sensitivity to the needs of others. Love seeketh not itself to please, and systematic selfishness, even in the pursuit of fun, is a dangerous habit of mind because it 'harden's a'', 'petrifying' instead of nourishing 'the feelings'.

Andrew Hunter Aiken (d. 1832) became wealthy as a Liverpool merchant and served for many years as British consul at Riga.

BE notes (with scepticism) the claim of William Niven (1759–1844) – a schoolmate of Burns's in Kirkoswald and recipient of several of the poet's earliest prose letters – that, although he had no manuscript to show as proof, he remembered receiving this epistle years before it was ever sent to Andrew Aiken. As Burns did rework much of his juvenilia for inclusion in *Poems* 1786 (Kilmarnock), it is possible that Niven was recalling lines, sentiments, or whole stanzas originally addressed to himself but later used in the epistle to Andrew Aiken. A schoolboy version sent to Niven would explain this poem's atypical metre. The only other major verse-epistle not composed in 'standart Habbie' was 'Epistle to Davie', itself very early – and composed, according to Gilbert Burns, in two stages: general moral reflections first and, many months later, introductory and concluding stanzas tailored to the recipient. There is, then, evidence that this epistle, like that written to David Sillar, was begun much earlier than the other great epistles completed in 1785–6 – and so (unlike them) was not extemporaneous in composition.

Lines Written on a Bank-Note

Text: HH; punctuation silently corrected. The original was transcribed on a Bank of Scotland guinea note. The lines must have been written in late spring, 1786, as they address Burns's concerns of that period – his rejection by Jean Armour because of his poverty and his second thoughts about emigration. Lines 3, 4, and

11 are anglicized to 'lack' in the copy-text; emended as in Kinsley. In l. 8 'victim's' is 'victims' in the copy-text; emended as in Kinsley.

Address of Beelzebub

Text: HH; punctuation silently corrected. The copy in the Watson MS at the National Library of Scotland (the copy-text both for HH and JK) is dated 1 June 1786. Not printed until February 1818, when it appeared in *The Scots Magazine*. The manuscript had been provided by 'R. W. of Ayr', who said he had received it from John Rankine (d. 1810). Rankine was a farmer near Tarbolton and a favourite neighbour of the poet's.

Assuming the voice of Beelzebub (who also speaks in the epigraph of 'Address to the Deil'), the poet sarcastically applauds the recent resolution of London's Highland Society to raise a subscription to prevent the emigration to Canada of 500 tenants of Macdonald of Glengary. Some scholars have found Burns's anger baffling, as the Society had resolved merely to send the impoverished clansmen enough financial aid to enable them to stay in their own country. Yet the emotion is in keeping with Burns's politics. As may be seen also in 'The Author's Earnest Cry', Burns viewed with scepticism any schemes drawn up by rich folk in London to produce so-called benefits for poor folk in Scotland. Emigration, too, was a thorny subject, especially as the date of his own planned departure drew near. Leaving for the new world was a poor Scotsman's only hope of eventual independence, and Scottish aristocrats (Burns reasoned) were being oppressive in tempting their countrymen away from this wise course of action. The poem argues that as they are now, where they are now, the clansmen are no better than beggars (ll. 44–52) – and who are the Highland Society to resolve to keep them so in perpetuity? What right have absentee landlords to deny freedom to their dependants at home? Besides, this gesture of assistance is too little and too late: the Highland clearances had been under way for two generations. Burns's own father had had to leave north-eastern Scotland after the battle of Culloden because – even though the family had played no part in the war – the unrest in the area had severely disrupted farming and eventually bankrupted Robert Burnes, the poet's grandfather.

This may be Burns's most underrated dramatic monologue. The strategy of the poem – recording Beelzebub's speech as he addresses his peers, the evil-doers of the Highland Society – allows Burns to dramatize, with grotesque intensity (cf. especially ll. 35–52), the scorn and contempt with which, in Burns's judgement, the powerful habitually view (and exploit) the powerless.

In l. 1, 'my lord' – as in the sarcastic repetition of 'Right Honorable' in the epigraph – emphasizes the Highland Society's aristocratic status. In l. 6, 'Butchers' reads 'lambkins' in the copy-text – pure editorial invention. Burns's metaphor of the butcher's knife is logical if it is seen that the poem defines two groups representative of Scotland – both reluctant to stay in their homeland. One 'Scotland' is the ruling aristocrats of the Highland Society – who are, as the poem emphasizes, managing their estates from their London town houses. Another 'Scotland' is the oppressed tenantry of those landowners, forced by rack-renting (a practice in favour among such absentee landlords) to seek a freer life in exile. It is that first 'Scotland', absentee and arrogant, that 'likes' Breadalbane, her powerful tool of oppression – just as a butcher likes a sharp, efficient knife.

In ll. 13–15, three leaders of the American revolution are praised: John

NOTES TO PAGES 130–34   239

Hancock (1737–93), Benjamin Franklin (1706–90), and George Washington (1732–99). '[S]ome Montgomery' (l. 16) refers to Richard Montgomery (b. 1738), Brigadier General in the Continental army, who was killed in the battle of Quebec, 30 December 1775. Burns uses him here as an example of a freedom-loving Scottish emigrant, but Montgomery was actually born and educated in Dublin. Line 21 refers to Frederick, Lord North (1732–92), Britain's Prime Minister during the American Revolution; also to Lord George Sackville (1716–85), who had fought with Cumberland at the battle of Culloden and was Lord North's chief adviser (Secretary of State) on the American colonies. The additional sarcasm of 'sager' might be explained by Sackville's court-martial (for unfitness for military duty) in 1759. Sir William Howe (d. 1814) commanded British forces at the battle of Bunker Hill (l. 23); Sir Henry Clinton (1738–95) also commanded British forces during the Revolutionary War (l. 23). The reference in l. 33 to 'factors, greives, trustees and bailies' is to their frequent employment as collection agents for absentee landlords. In l. 44, 'Drury Lane' refers to its reputation as the haunt of London prostitutes.

Lines 58–60 search human history for villains comparable to the bad landlords of the Highland Society. Herod Antipas figures in the Bible as the executioner of John the Baptist and judge of Jesus; as tetrarch of Galilee he was a minor functionary of the Roman empire. Polycrates, tyrant of Samos (d. *c.* 515 BC), used his fleets to establish an empire throughout the Aegean basin. Diego D'Almagro (1475–1538) was put to death by his commander, Francisco Pizarro (*c.* 1478–1541), when they quarrelled during their conquest of Peru. All of these historical figures were empire-boosters who oppressed the colonized, enriching themselves in the process – activities for which the poet consigns them to a warm seat in Hell.

A Dream

Text: *Poems* 1786 (Kilmarnock). Written soon after Burns had read (and been irritated by) Thomas Warton's customary ode celebrating George III's birthday (4 June 1786).

Burns, a penniless 'Bardie' rather than a pensioned Laureate, refuses to flatter. The poem's stanza-form is similar to that of the didactic 'Epistle to a Young Friend', completed a few weeks before this was begun; but the metre (also used in 'The Holy Fair' and parts of 'Love and Liberty') was also traditional for Scottish 'brawl' poems. Here the poet begins by sketching the crush of brightly apparelled courtiers at the birthday levée, but the 'brawl' or festive element is soon subsumed by moralizing commentary. If the Auld Light considered 'Address to the Deil' Burns's most shocking poem, this satire was his most offensive (of the poems printed in the Kilmarnock volume) to the wealthy and landed. Burns would have inspired no controversy if he had kept to parody of Warton, but his satire 'spairges' (bespatters; disparages) the King himself – a turn of attack even more likely to give offence in Scotland than in England. The Scots were obsessed with their country's Jacobite past, and in Burns's day criticism of the Hanoverians was assumed to signify loyalty to the Stuarts. Jacobitism was worse than treasonous in Edinburgh – it was unfashionable, lower-class, an obstacle to patronage. (Hugh Blair, writing of Burns's Jacobitism after the poet's death, was contemptuous: 'His politics always smelt of the smith's shop.') Edinburgh's aristocrats and cultured literati could see the joke when Burns mocked rustics in Mauchline or fanatical Auld Licht preachers, but they could only deplore his 'faulty' taste when the poet turned his formidable sarcasm on something they held sacred: not so much King George himself as the historical outcome the Hanoverians represented, which upper- and middle-class Scottish consensus now saw as providential. It would have been in Burns's interest either not to have written such a poem at all – or (as his kindly if conservative friend Frances Dunlop expostulated in 1787) at least to have the common sense not to keep on publishing it (the satire appeared in all editions of *Poems*). The fact is that Burns was stimulated by prohibitions, driven to defy them. So, not content with the implied Jacobitism of his 'spairging' of George, he gaily announces (ll. 26–7) that 'aiblens' (perhaps) 'ane' other person – Charles Edward Stuart (1720–88) – would have made a 'better' king.

Lines 32–6 refer to the recent loss of the American colonies, often blamed on George because of his preference for weak, easily bullied ministers such as Lord North. Lines 66–7 mention the practice of giving the bodies of the hanged (raxed = stretched) to medical schools. George and Charlotte's very large family of children (l. 77) consisted of seven sons and six daughters still living – truly a 'bairntime' or brood. 'Charlie' (l. 89) is Charles Fox, a brilliant, dissolute Whig statesman who advised (and often gambled with) the Prince of Wales: see also the note to 'The Author's Earnest Cry and Prayer' (p. 226). The Duke of York (1763–1827) – cf. l. 100 and the 'lawn-sleeve' of l. 101 – had been made bishop of Osnaburg in Westphalia during his infancy, an absurdity that Burns was not the first to point out. The youngest royal brother addressed (l. 109) – for the Dukes of Kent, Cumberland, Sussex, and Cambridge are not mentioned in the poem – is Prince William (1765–1837), who was created Duke of Clarence in 1789 and ruled as William IV from 1830 to his death. William had entered the Navy in 1779; 'Tarry-breeks' is Burns's jovial expansion of 'tar'. The lines that follow refer (in nautical *double entendre*) to Prince William's widely reported flirtation with Sarah Martin, daughter of the Portsmouth dockyard's Commissioner. The 'royal Lasses' of l. 119 were the Princesses Charlotte, Augusta, Elizabeth, Mary, Sophia, and Amelia. The poet warns that there are simply not enough kings – perhaps not enough even of that more plentiful last resort, German royal dukes – to supply them all with husbands. (One wonders what Queen Victoria – as yet unborn daughter of the Duke of Kent and future wife of a German prince – thought of these lines, if she ever read them.) Because of the shortage of eligible European bachelors, the Princesses are gravely advised not to think that British suitors are beneath them. In fact, Mary (1776–1857), the only sister who married, chose an Englishman, the Duke of Gloucester.

Elegy on the Death of Robert Ruisseaux

Text: Cromek 1808. Though JK conjectures a date of 1787, the nineteenth-century editor Scott Douglas makes a stronger case for 1786, arguing that this was originally the concluding poem for the Kilmarnock edition but was rejected after the composition of 'A Bard's Epitaph' (a broader conclusion for the volume). Yet this elegy is the more revealing poem, memorializing the youthful self Burns was leaving behind as he made his plans for publication, emigration, and provision for his children. While mock-elegy is a favourite Scottish vernacular form, the poem also recalls *Tristram Shandy*'s elegiac treatment of Yorick, similarly merry in the face of misfortune until the moment he is crushed by his fate. The title alludes to Jean-Jacques Rousseau (1712–78), whose writings would soon help to spark the

French Revolution. Burns's misspelling is deliberate and punning: French 'ruis-seaux' are English 'streams' which in Scotland are known as 'burns'.

In line 13, 'wight and stark' (stout and strong) refers to Burns's unusual physical strength, not captured in Alexander Nasmyth's ubiquitous but idealized portrait (which no one considered a good likeness) but often mentioned by contemporaries. A certain burliness of shoulder was, with the 'glow' in the poet's eyes, what Sir Walter Scott chiefly remembered of his one boyhood encounter with Burns.

A Bard's Epitaph

Text: *Poems* 1786 (Kilmarnock). The final poem in Burns's first collection provides a last didactic word for the volume – and a retreat from the vernacular epistles and satires, in which pleasure sweetens life, prudence is unpoetic, and caution is cowardly. The poem is Burns's attempt to bury or put to rest that part of poetic identity that, he thought, bridled against all 'controul' (even self-control) – an acknowledgement of the wilfulness that had, by June of 1786, 'stain'd' Burns's name in Mauchline.

Wordsworth's 'A Poet's Epitaph' (written in 1799; published in 1800) evidently remembers this poem, partly agreeing with its despondent assessment of the poetic temperament but rejecting mere 'prudent, cautious self-controul' as 'wisdom's root'. Wordsworth's poet 'clad in homely russet brown' is very likely a sketch of Burns himself:

> . . . But who is He, with modest looks,
> And clad in homely russet brown?
> He murmurs near the rustic brooks
> A music sweeter than their own.
>
> . . . The outward shews of sky and earth,
> Of hill and valley he has viewed;
> And impulses of deeper birth
> Have come to him in solitude.
>
> In common things that round us lie
> Some random truths he can impart
> The harvest of a quiet eye
> That broods and sleeps on his own heart.
>
> But he is weak; both man and boy,
> Hath been an idler in the land;
> Contented if he might enjoy
> The things which others understand.   (*Lyrical Ballads*)

In l. 9, 'area' is often editorially emended to 'arena', which scans correctly. Yet it is unlikely that an inadvertent error would – as 'area' did – survive all three editions of *Poems* published in Burns's lifetime. More probably, the poet intended readers to stress the second syllable – 'aréa' – as with his pronunciation of 'idéa'. (This is not necessarily a Scotticism; cf. Pope's Eloisa and her reference to the 'déar idéãs' of Abelard.)

To a Haggis

Text: *Poems* 1787 (Edinburgh). Written before 19 December 1786, when it appeared in the *Caledonian Mercury* (Burns's first publication in a periodical).

The Victorian editor Robert Chambers collected evidence that this exuberant mock-epic was composed extempore, during a dinner-party at the house of John Morrison in Mauchline. James Hogg's edition of Burns, however, identifies the host as Andrew Bruce, a merchant in Edinburgh (where Burns arrived on 29 November 1786). It is possible that the poet performed the poem (as if extemporaneous) at both.

As JK says, haggis was a delicacy for Scottish country folk: its main ingredients are highly perishable and the cook needs several different kinds of fresh meat – easy in a city, but not on a small farm. (Ingredients varied, but a haggis recipe contemporary with Burns calls for hard-boiled liver and beef grated and blended with suet, onions and spiced oatmeal, sewed into a parboiled sheep's stomach and slowly steamed.) According to the testimony of Jean Armour late in her life, the poet usually 'hated' fatty sausages and puddings: he once wrote extempore lines (to a tavern landlady named Mrs Bacon) objecting strongly even to bacon. So Burns's praise of haggis is a deflected tribute to an enjoyable evening, a salute to an unusually tasty version, or perhaps – as in other early poems – simply an inspired comic metaphor by which a homely element in Scottish diet is linked to the homely virtues of the people it sustains. (Burns may have begun the poem at an Edinburgh dinner-party, but the gorging peasants within the text are rustics.)

Because of this poem, the dish is now seen as strictly – one might say peculiarly – Scottish, but in Burns's day haggis was eaten (under varying names) in all European and British countries. Food was one of Robert Fergusson's favourite topics, and several of his poems influenced Burns – not only 'Caller Oysters' and 'The Farmer's Ingle' but also the Miltonic burlesque 'Good Eating', whose mock-hero is a 'smoking sirloin':

> Behold, at thy approach what smiles serene,
> Beam from the ravish'd guests. – Still are their tongues,
> While they with whetted instruments prepare
> For deep incision. – Now the abscess bleeds,
> And the devouring band, with stomachs keen
> And glutting rage, thy beauteous form destroy,
> Leave you a marrowless skeleton and bare . . .
>
> *(Poems of Robert Fergusson*, ed. Matthew McDiarmid,
> Edinburgh: Scottish Text Society, 1954-6, 2, p. 100)

'Painch, tripe, or thairm' (l. 4) are almost interchangeable words meaning belly, entrails, intestines. These were difficult to make palatable but were sometimes served slow-cooked and heavily spiced, or (more often) used as pudding casings. The 'pin' or skewer of l. 9 can also (in jocular Scottish usage) mean penis – not a far-fetched possibility here, as the haggis's swelling 'hurdies' (buttocks) have just been personified (l. 8). In ll. 13–42, the contrast between strapping 'haggis-fed' rustics (ham-fisted and energetic) and European ragout and fricassee eaters (bloodless and skinny) recalls the contrast between whisky drinkers and wine bibbers in the Postscript to 'The Author's Earnest Cry'; both poems attribute the Scots' warlike propensities to diet. Spoons were made of horn, so 'horn for horn' (l. 19) is metonymic. As the haggis vanishes into the 'kytes' (bellies) of the farmers (ll. 21–3), its swelling and glistening properties are transferred to them: the distended stomach of the patriarch ('auld Guidman') is 'maist like to rive', or ready to burst.

Poems 1787 (Edinburgh) was set twice in about half the gatherings. According to Egerer, the two printings occurred because the size of the subscription list continued to increase after the book had gone to press. Only after the gatherings A-Ii and Ll-Mm had been printed and the type disassembled was it decided to increase the size of the printing. Sufficient copies of the final gatherings were run and then the earlier gatherings were reset and run again. Of the 300 variations that resulted from the separate settings, the most important occurs in l. 45 of 'To a Haggis', where the correct word, 'skinking', probably marks the first printing; hasty resetting accounts for the misprint 'stinking' in the second. (Burns either did not proof-read the reprinted gatherings at all or did not work as carefully as he had with the first printing.) The printing of l. 45 is still how the two are distinguished, as in Egerer's concluding remarks on *Poems* 1787 (Edinburgh): 'Copies of either (a) the "skinking" or (b) the "stinking" edition in original boards are very rare.'

There Was a Lad (*Tune: Dainty Davie*)

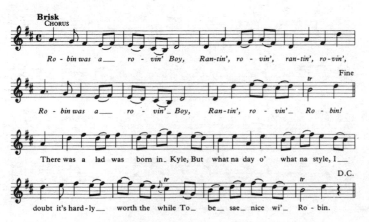

Text: Cromek 1808. Music from Dick. Transcribed in *2CPB* after the first entry (dated 9 April 1787), but probably written earlier as a birthday poem: the poet turned twenty-eight on 25 January 1787. Today the song is usually set to the tune 'O an ye were dead Gudeman' (the setting of 'John Highlandman' in 'Love and Liberty'). Burns's choice, whose oldest traditional stanzas were graphic and bawdy, is equally well matched and may have been rejected by nineteenth-century editors because of its jocular associations.

The reference in l. 9 is to George III, who began his reign in 1760; a year before ('hindmost year but ane'), Burns had been born. The 'Janwar Win' of l. 11 alludes to the storm that, soon after the poet's birth on 25 January, damaged the roof of the cottage at Alloway; infant and mother were temporarily lodged with neighbours until repairs could be made. Burns sees this as an omen of later storms in life. In l. 25, 'Stir' is 'Sir' in the copy-text – a typographical error or polite evasion, for in l. 26, 'lie aspar' is rendered only as four asterisks in the copy-text; as emended in *2CPB*.

Lines Written Under the Portrait of Robert Fergusson

Text: Cromek 1808.

The 'young Lady' of the title was Rebeccah Carmichael, an aspiring poet. Burns does not exaggerate: Fergusson had been 'unpitied by the world'. He died at twenty-four in the Edinburgh madhouse, never having received – unlike Ramsay or Burns – much popular or critical acclaim. A drunken fall only hastened his end, for Fergusson was (according to early biographers) both syphilitic and severely alcoholic: Runciman once painted him as the Prodigal Son. When Burns arrived in Edinburgh one of his first actions was to order a memorial stone for Fergusson's unmarked grave.

My Harry Was a Gallant Gay (Tune: Highlander's Lament)

Text and music: *SMM* 1790 (unsigned); the air is probably mid eighteenth century in origin. Burns's notes in his interleaved copy of *SMM* say the chorus was transcribed from the singing of an old woman during the poet's visit to Dunblane (August 1787): 'the rest of the song is mine'. A more specifically Jacobite version ('He left me and his native plain/And rush'd his sair wrang'd prince to join') was transcribed in the Hastie MS, a collection of materials concerning *SMM* now in the British Library; but the variant text is not in Burns's hand or even much in his style; it was most likely the work of one of Johnson's other contributors.

Cunningham's note to l. 7 explains that 'part of the farm of Mossgiel' was known as Knockhaspie's land (JK 3, 1241); the singer herself, then, has been displaced to a Lowland setting.

Here Stewarts Once in Triumph Reigned (*Lines on Stirling Window*)

Text: HH; punctuation silently corrected. Probably written 27 or 26 August 1787; the latter date was given when 'R. B., Ayrshire' indiscreetly published the extempore lines in the *Edinburgh Courant* (5 October).

The earliest transcription was by diamond-tipped pen, on the window of the bedroom in the inn at Stirling where the poet lodged on 26–28 August; stung by criticism, however, Burns returned in October and broke the window-pane. The lines almost cost Burns the position with the Excise for which he was being considered, as he angrily wrote to Agnes M'Lehose: 'I have almost given up the excise idea ... Why will Great people ... be so very dictatorially wise? I have been question'd like a child about my matters, and blamed and schooled for my Inscription on Stirling window' (*Letters* 1, 220). Allan Cunningham's edition of Burns (1834) makes it clear that the lines were still considered seditious some fifty years later, for Cunningham printed only the first six lines: 'The concluding couplet [*sic*], forming the epigrammatic sting, is cut out. What was improper in the days of Burns is not proper now' (3, 294). HH follow Cunningham's 1834 printing of 'glory' instead of 'triumph' in l. 1; emended as in the Glenriddell MS (1791).

My Peggy's Face (*Original tune: Ha a' chaillich; SMM setting: My Peggy's Face*)

Text and music: *SMM* 1803; signed ('Written for this work by Robert Burns'). Probably composed in October 1787, when it was sent to Margaret Chalmers (1763–1843), a relative of Gavin Hamilton's stepmother and a friend of kindly Dr Thomas Blacklock (1721–91), the blind poet who first urged Burns to visit Edinburgh. In her later years, Peggy Chalmers (who married the banker Lewis Hay in 1788 and was widowed in 1800) disclosed that in 1787 she rejected Burns's proposal of marriage. She also opposed publication of this song, for which, in a letter of 21 November, Burns scolds her: 'Now none of your polite hints about flattery: I leave that to your lovers, if you have or shall have any ... Charlotte

[Hamilton, Gavin's half-sister] and you are just two favorite resting places for my soul in her wanderings through the weary, thorny wilderness of this world' (*Letters* 1, 174). As Margaret Chalmers remained reluctant to be complimented in print, the song did not appear until seven years after the poet's death; it was set to a neoclassical air rather than the 'old Highland' air (now lost) that Burns had requested.

An Extemporaneous Effusion on Being Appointed to the Excise

Text: Cromek 1808. Probably written in autumn 1787 or winter 1788, the time of Burns's early instruction in his duties; he was not actually commissioned until 14 July 1788. The Excise regulated and taxed a variety of commodities, including (according to Burns's Excise commission) 'Beer, Ale, Spirits . . . Candles, Hops, Soap, Paper . . . Silks, Calicoes, Linens and Stuffs . . . Starch, Gilt and Silver Wire . . . Hides and Skins . . . Vellum and Parchment . . . Coffee, Tea and Chocolate . . . Malt . . . Mum, Cyder and Perry [and] . . . every Coach, Berlin, Landau, Chariot' (*BE* 386). Excisemen kept accounts of the quantities of these goods held and shipped within their jurisdiction, collecting any taxes; they also were authorized to seize any contraband (smuggled 'Brandy, Arrack, Rum, Spirits, Strong Waters, Coffee, Tea, Chocolate . . . Cocoa Nuts'). DeLancey Ferguson's excellent biography, *Pride and Passion* (Oxford, 1939), confirms Burns's own assertion that his appointment (considered part-time) involved some 200 miles of horseback travel a week.

'Ochon' (l. 2) is 'Och, ho!' in the copy-text; evidently Cromek's effort to make this Gaelic word (of expostulation and lamentation) more accessible. As emended in Kinsley, following Burns's customary spelling of the word. Many Gaelic words entered Burns's vocabulary as a result of his Highland tours; he no doubt also learned some Gaelic from his father, who had grown up in the north-east.

To Daunton Me (*Tune: To daunton me*)

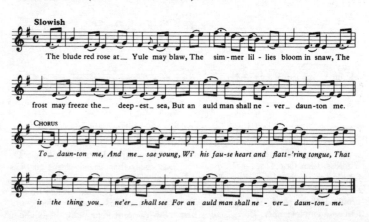

Slowish

The blude red rose at_ Yule may blaw, The sim-mer lil-lies bloom in snaw, The frost may freeze the_ deep-est_ sea, But an auld man shall ne-ver_ daun-ton me.

CHORUS

To_ daun-ton me, And me_ sae young, Wi' his fau-se heart and flatt-'ring tongue, That is the thing you_ ne'er_ shall see For an auld man shall ne-ver_ daun-ton_ me.

Text: *SMM* 1788; unsigned. Sent to Johnson in October or November 1787 (*Letters* 1, 169). The air is seventeenth century and had been printed in several songbooks known to Burns; the most popular stanzas before Burns's had combined Jacobitism with the May/December theme, but Burns simplifies the conflict. He often uses female speakers in songs expressive of rebellion or defiance.

O'er the Water to Charlie (Tune: Shawnboy)

Come boat me o'er, come row me o'er, Come boat me o'er to Char-lie; I'll gie— John Ross— a-no-ther baw-bee, To boat— me o'er— to Char-lie.

CHORUS

We'll o'er— the wa-ter, we'll o'er— the sea, We'll o'er— the wa-ter to Char-lie; Come weal, come woe,— we'll ga-ther and go, And live— or die— wi' Char-lie.

Text and music: *SMM* 1788. Unsigned, but there is a holograph copy in the Hastie MS (British Library). Written late in 1787 or early in 1788: the volume was available for sale on 14 February 1788 (Egerer 20). The tune, now known under Burns's title, dated from 1745; the hero is Charles Edward Stuart (Bonnie Prince Charlie), who died in exile on 31 January 1788. The air was printed in *The True Loyalist* (1779) with similar verses in Gaelic: '*O falbhmaid thairis gu Tearlach*' – 'O let us cross over to Charlie' (JK 3, 1270).

Rattlin, Roarin Willie (Tune: Rattlin, roarin Willie)

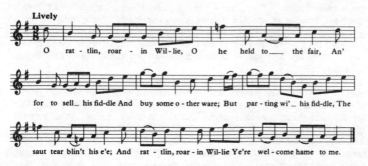

O rat-tlin, roar-in Wil-lie, O he held to— the fair, An' for to sell— his fid-dle And buy some o-ther ware; But par-ting wi'— his fid-dle, The saut tear blin't his e'e; And rat-tlin, roar-in Wil-lie Ye're wel-come hame to me.

Text and music: *SMM* 1788; unsigned. Composed in 1787, either before or (more probably) after Burns's tours of the Border (May) and Highlands (June, August–September, October). Sir Walter Scott's notes to *Lay of the Last Minstrel* say that an ancient Border minstrel bore this name because of his legendary brawling; but Burns's song (like *Tristram Shandy*) also exploits the jocular possibilities of the term 'fiddle': this hint of bawdy innuendo is Burns's contribution to Willie's legend. Burns's notes to *SMM* call the final stanza a tribute to a favourite drinking crony, William Dunbar (d. 1807), a fellow-Mason in Edinburgh's Canongate lodge who also (like Burns) belonged to 'The Crochallan Fencibles' (cf. l. 17), an Edinburgh men's club which met in Dawnie Douglas's tavern in Anchor Close.

Epistle to Hugh Parker

Text: H H; punctuation silently corrected. Written in June 1788 soon after Burns's arrival at Ellisland, his newly leased farm in Dumfriesshire. A house had to be built before he could send for Jean (with whom he had been reconciled in March); Burns was uncomfortably lodged in a hut warmed by a smoky peat-fire. Dreading the prospect of a solitary summer, Burns projects his own depression onto Jenny Geddes, his faithful old horse and only companion in Nithside. If he had 'power' to match his 'inclination', they would both just ride away into the clear night sky, escaping this strange new place and leaving the earth and its unpleasant realities altogether.

Burns named his high-mettled mare – she had carried the poet through his recent tours of the Border and the Highlands (ll. 23–4) – after the defiant old presbyterian who in 1637 threw her stool at the newly appointed bishop of Edinburgh during a service at St Giles.

Hugh Parker was a banker in Kilmarnock.

I Love My Jean (*Tune: Miss Admiral Gordon's Strathspey*)

Text and music: *SMM* 1790; signed R. Written for Jean Armour during the summer of 1788 and perhaps included among the 'cargo of songs' which Burns mailed to James Johnson in July (*Letters* 1, 299). In a letter to Alexander Cunningham dated 27 July, the poet discusses his newly acknowledged wife: 'I have been a Farmer since Whitsunday, & am just now building a house . . . I am, too, a married man . . . On my return to Ayr-shire, I found a much-lov'd Female's positive happiness, or absolute Misery among my hands; and I could not trifle with such a sacred Deposite . . . I am really more & more pleased with my Choice. – When I tell you that Mrs Burns was once, *my Jean*, you will know the rest. – Of four children she bore me, in seventeen months, my eldest boy is only living' (*Letters* 1, 298–9).

Yet no touch of the poet's unconscious reservation (she was 'once' his Jean) marks these affectionate stanzas. The air was adapted by William Marshall, butler of the Duke of Gordon, from an appropriately titled traditional tune ('Alace I lie my alon'): the couple were separated that first summer of their settled married life. There is no repetition in the melody, which extends over both stanzas. Ashmead and Davison note its musical complexity: 'The Ionian tune has a wide range – an octave and a sixth; an unusual second half has lower tessitura [range], with a pentatonic structure on which eighteenth-century major scale passages have been superimposed' (194).

I LOVE MY JEAN

Of a' the airts the wind can blaw, I dear-ly like the west, For

there the bo-ny Las-sie lives, The Las-sie I lo'e best: There's

wild-woods grow, and ri-vers row, And mony a hill_ bet-ween; But_

day and night my fan-cy's flight Is ev-er wi' my Jean.

I_ see her in the de-wy flowers, I see her sweet and fair; I_

hear her in the tune-fu' birds, I hear her charm the_ air: There's

not a bo-ny flower, that springs By foun-tain, shaw, or_ green, There's

not a bo-ny bird that sings, But minds me o' my Jean.

Tam Glen (*Tune: Merry Beggars*)

Text and music: *SMM* 1790; unsigned. Sent to Johnson on 15 November 1788 (*Letters* 2, 339). First published (also anonymously) in 1789 in the *Edinburgh Magazine* (x, 357). The English tune's 9/8 'slip-jig' signature is perfectly matched to the talkative and Tam-obsessed adolescent speaker, who names her lover eight times in thirty-two lines, in the concluding phrase of every stanza. Performers must deliver her rapid-fire monologue almost without drawing a breath. JK notes that 'like all Burns's dramatic lyrics, the song is a challenge to the singer, who is tempted either to an over-simple interpretation or to ... operatic comedy which the air will not support' (3, 1285). Jean Redpath's richly nuanced performance in *Songs of Robert Burns*, Vol. IV, avoids those extremes.

A disdain for wealth as a factor in successful courtship marks Burns's songs in the years following his initial rejection by Jean Armour and her family because of his poverty. Jean's parents had bribed and scolded her – as this girl's 'Daddie' and 'Minnie' do – to stay away from the poet and marry a richer man. The speaker, however, in her turn bribes her sister (l. 30), offering her a favourite hen if she will only 'give her the ... advice she wants to hear' (Crawford, p. 307). The speaker reveals her childlike naïvety in ll. 19–26, where she summons as proof that Tam is her destined husband not only the results of the 'Valentines' dealing' – an annual drawing of lots to predict future lovers – but the Halloween custom of the 'droukit' sleeve. (A sark with one wet sleeve was left in front of the fire: the lass's future lover would come during the night to turn it.) Sure enough, the speaker says triumphantly, she did see Tam (or his ghost-'likeness') 'stalking' up to her house that night, though he was never pulled there by a dripping sleeve: the boy here is clearly as lovesick (and insomniac) as the girl.

Predestination is grouped with the speaker's other superstitions in l. 19, when she points out that it is no good struggling and protesting if God has already 'ordain'd' she 'maun take' Tam. Her many articles of blind faith, though gently mocked, none the less also are shown to underlie this speaker's generous capacity for unconditional love – her similarly blind faith in a young man without land or wealth to help them build a life together. For Burns here, as for Dickens in *David Copperfield*, 'a loving heart is better than wisdom'.

JK suggests that the puzzling reference to 'brute' in l. 10 is the speaker's sarcastic mental addition to Lowrie's greeting.

TAM GLEN

My heart is a break-ing, dear Tit-tie, Some coun-sel un-to me come len', To

an-ger them a' is a pi-ty, But what will I do wi' Tam Glen?

Auld Lang Syne (Tunes: For old long Sine my jo; The Miller's Daughter)

Text and music: *SMM* 1796; signed Z. (Burns instructed Johnson to code songs that he contributed but did not wish fully to sign. Songs marked R, B, and X were his own, while Z was their code for traditional material slightly altered. Johnson, however, used the system erratically.)

Completed before 7 December 1788, when it was sent to Frances Dunlop (that version substitutes 'Let's hae a waught o' Malaga' for 'We'll tak a cup o' kindness yet'). In the letter accompanying this first version, Burns (as in his code with Johnson) says that he collected rather than composed the stanzas: 'Light be the turf on the breast of the heaven-inspired Poet who composed this glorious Fragment!' (*Letters* 2, 345). Burns, as in his elegy and epitaph of 1786, is addressing himself; for the work is his own. Similar nostalgic sentiments may be traced through Scottish literary culture as far back as the sixteenth-century Bannantyne Manuscript's 'Auld Kyndnes foryett'; both the Union of Parliaments and the Jacobite wars stimulated many songs about happier days 'lang syne'. Yet Burns's version is unique in not didactically stating but rather subtly dramatizing the theme of affection enduring despite time and loss. Resemblances to earlier lyrics are merely superficial; moreover, use of a source does not preclude authorship of a text. One earlier eighteenth-century dramatic lyric by Allan Ramsay uses the phrase 'auld lang syne' and opens with the same first line as Burns's; it may serve to show how misleading it can be to speak of Burns's 'debt' to 'folk-sources':

> Should auld Acquaintance be forgot,
> Tho they return with scars?
> These are the noble Heroe's Lot,
> Obtain'd in glorious Wars:
> Welcome my *Varo* to my Breast,
> Thy Arms about me twine,
> And make me once again as blest,
> As I was lang syne.   ('The Kind Reception', 1721)

When Burns wished a lyric to be taken seriously he often divorced himself from its authorship, calling it collected rather than composed. After 1787, Burns signed songs of personal compliment. Otherwise, he often masked his own voice, projecting it outward as the general voice of Scottish history and tradition. By the date of the composition of the first version of 'Auld Lang Syne' in 1788, then, the poet had made the transition from prominent satirist and local colourist (author of the *Poems* and hero/victim of a personality-cult that had already begun in Edinburgh) to anonymous and impersonal national bard. Robert Burns was only a farmer, tax-collector, and co-editor of the *Scots Musical Museum*: a harmless drudge. Like Chatterton and James Macpherson, Burns went underground.

In 1968, JK reached the opposite conclusion; he called the work almost completely traditional and accused editors who think otherwise (including Cromek, Thomson, Douglas, and Dick) of 'wilful *naïveté*' (3, 1290–91). Yet of the texts Kinsley cites as sources, none (as with Allan Ramsay's lyric) sounds much like Burns's. But perhaps the strongest evidence against JK lies in the song's imagery. In ll. 14–22, the speaker shows that he has been separated from his childhood playmate not only by time but by protracted exile: 'braid' seas and 'weary' wanderings. This song of displacement is framing itself round images deriving specifically from the Jacobite wars and the ensuing late-century Highland clearances. The double loss it expresses – nostalgia for places as well as for times irretrievably past – is rooted in Burns's own immediate past: this would have been his own story if he had emigrated to Jamaica, and it was his father's story. (The poet's brother Gilbert once wrote to Frances Dunlop: 'I have often heard my father describe the anguish of mind he felt when he parted with his elder brother Robert on the top of a hill, on the confines of their native place [Kincardineshire], each going off his several way ... and scarcely knowing whither he went' (*BE* 387).) If there were a mid- to late-century analogue for Burns's stanzas that might have suggested these images to the poet, we would know about such a text: there were many Jacobite songbooks. No such source has ever been found, which was why in 1903 J. C. Dick, the most knowledgeable editor who has ever worked with Burns's songs, declared 'Auld Lang Syne' a composed (rather than a lightly revised) work.

The sad and stately air Burns first suggested to Johnson ('For old long Sine my jo') is not the setting used today. George Thomson, with whom Burns collaborated after 1793, printed (in *SC* 1799) the alternative air ('The Miller's Daughter') that had been suggested by Burns in a letter of 19 November 1794 (*Letters* 2, 329); it is now universally preferred.

Auld Lang Syne

Should auld ac-quain-tance be for-got And ne - ver brought to mind? Should

auld ac-quain-tance be for-got, And auld lang syne! *For auld lang_ syne my jo, For*

auld_ lang_ syne, We'll tak a cup o' kind-ness yet for auld lang_ syne.

Louis What Reck I by Thee (Tune: Louis what reck I by thee)

Lou - is, what reck I by_ thee, Or Geor-die on_ his_ o - cean:

Dy - vor,_ beg-gar louns to_ me, I reign in Jean - ie's_ bo - som.

Text and music: *SMM* 1796; signed R. Probably written in December 1788, when Jean Armour and their two-year-old son Robert rejoined the poet at Ellisland. Louis XVI would soon face the beginning of the French Revolution: the states-general convened on 4 May 1789. George III (the 'Geordie' of l. 2) was being treated for insanity between October 1788 and March 1789: the newspapers were full of scandal concerning Pitt's controversial Regency Bill. So it is true that neither king was much to be envied. In *Illustrations of the Lyric Music and Poetry of Scotland* (1839), William Stenhouse speculates that Burns himself collected this air (similar to 'The British Grenadiers'); no other stanzas to the tune are known.

Elegy on the Year 1788

Text: Stewart 1801. Written on New Year's Day 1789 and sent to the *Edinburgh Courant*, which published it on 10 January. During the year Burns memorializes, the King of Spain had died (13 December) and George III had been declared insane; the Prince of Wales and his mentor Fox were squabbling openly with the Prime Minister (Pitt) over the Regency Bill, which established an interim government.

Fox, who led the opposition to the Regency Bill, is the pleasure-loving cock (ll. 13–14). William Pitt is his dour and straitlaced opponent (ll. 15–16). The Bill, which restricted the power of the Prince of Wales, was supported by Pitt because of the Prince's close alliance with Pitt's enemy Fox. Beyond partisanship, Pitt, a shrewd politician determined to avoid an English revolution, knew that the Prince was less popular than the unfortunate King (he openly ridiculed his father, displaying what most observers felt to be an unseemly impatience to rule). The battle continued until the Bill itself was dropped in March 1789 following the King's unexpected recovery.

Burns emphasizes what is natural about the passing of power from the older to the younger generation; what is positive about the experience of change, whether social or personal. The bad omen of dry wells in Edinburgh (l. 30) – during December 1788, cold weather had caused a water shortage in the capital when the wells were frozen – is countered by the good omen of new fertility: in ll. 24-7, the poet addresses the young women introduced to sexual experience during 1788, an event that – like the Prince of Wales's accession to power – in Burns's view marks an accession to adult privileges. As for those who represent entrenched, impenetrable power – Auld Licht ministers (ll. 17-22), the old Spanish King, the infirm British King – 'e'en let them die'. The poet will miss his aged, toothless hound (l. 10), but he can easily spare the King of Spain (l. 9): the passing of both old dogs was in any case inevitable.

In the final stanza, commentary on the Regency Bill resumes: the poem concludes with the hope that the New Year, a free agent rather than a half-shackled Regent, will do no worse than his parent.

Epistle to William Stewart

Text: HH; punctuation silently corrected. Letters (1, 364) places this undated epistle 'early' in 1789, before a letter dated 24 January. There is a manuscript (JK's copy-text) in the National Library of Scotland; but, curiously, the first printing was in *Notes and Queries* (30 July 1881).

Burns wrote many drinking poems, but this is his only poetic record of a rueful morning after. William Stewart (1748?-1812) was the son of a tavern-owner and the brother of Mrs Bacon, landlady at Brownhill inn, where (l. 1) this epistle was written. When Burns knew him, Stewart was factor of an estate near Ellisland – a warm friend with a raffish side (he shared Burns's love of satire and bawdry) that made the poet like him all the more.

Afton Water (*Tune: Afton Water*)

Text and music: *SMM* 1792; signed B. Completed before 5 February 1789, when Burns sent a copy to Frances Dunlop. The Afton flowed into the Nith near Burns's new home. Though JK is sceptical, it is often assumed that the song remembers Margaret Campbell ('Highland Mary' – 1763-86), whom Burns courted when first estranged from Jean Armour: she had died in the autumn of 1786. While Burns had never known Mary in a Dumfriesshire setting, this song does exhibit the febrile tenderness characteristic of his other songs to her; moreover, except for stanza five (where, like doomed Ophelia, Mary gathers wild flowers by the riverbank), the song presents her as asleep, oddly inert – an unconscious (and therefore unreceptive) female subject. Perhaps Mary's slumberous absence is the source of the song's melancholy charm, for otherwise the imagery is conventional.

The air (unknown except by this name) is either Burns's discovery or that of James Johnson's song-advisers, Stephen Clarke or his son William.

AFTON WATER

To Alexander Findlater

Text: JK 1, 502, from a transcript by Robert Dewar; the MS is in private hands and the text in the Chambers and Wallace edition (1896) is incomplete. The undated epistle is conjecturally assigned to 1789 in *Letters* (1, 466). Sent from Ellisland and written in the 'standart Habbie' form traditional for vernacular epistles, the poem accompanied a basket of fresh-laid eggs from Jean's prized hens – a circumstance that inspired a bawdy train of thought. Findlater (1754–1839) was Burns's Excise supervisor and (in several crises) a loyal friend.

To a Gentleman Who Had Sent Him a Newspaper

Text: Currie 1801. JK follows Currie's date of January 1790, acknowledging, however, that the epistle's references to public affairs would have been current at any time between the King's recovery in March 1789 and Emperor Joseph's death in February 1790. Like some other editors, I place the poem in April or early May 1789, when Burns wrote to Peter Stuart (fl. 1788–1805), editor of the London *Morning Star*, enclosing the vituperative 'Ode Sacred to the Memory of the late Mrs Oswald of Auchencruive'. (Members of her funeral cortège, travelling up from London, had insisted on his eviction from their reserved accommodation at an inn, forcing the poet out into a bitter storm.) Stuart, grateful for Burns's interest in his struggling paper (this was the poet's third letter to Stuart; two had enclosed poems), evidently began a gift subscription, which Burns immediately terminated, writing a further letter enclosing (I believe) this satiric verse-epistle. The ode to Mrs Oswald (appropriately signed Tom Nettle) was duly published in the *Morning Star* on 7 May along with two prose letters. Stuart did not print this epistle but probably could not: it speaks libel against powerful people who (unlike Mrs Oswald) were still alive to complain; and Stuart was already under fire for his severe critiques of Pitt's Regency Bill.

The lively topical satire makes one wish that Burns had continued to receive some newspaper on a regular basis (the *Star* itself ceased publication in June). But the gift savoured too much of charity. There is a hint of peremptory dismissal in the final couplet of the poem, reflected also in the poet's final letter in the exchange: 'the paper . . . is more than I can in decency accept of, as I can do little or nothing on my part to requite the obligation. For this reason, I am at liberty to resign your favour at pleasure, without any imputation of pride or pettish humour' (*Letters* 1, 408). No MS copies exist (of the Ode, of the frequent letters to Stuart written that spring, or of this satire itself), so dating and sequence must remain conjectural; but the resemblances of tone between this poem and the poet's letter refusing the subscription are striking.

'Emperor Joseph' (l. 7) was Joseph II, who led the Holy Roman (Austro-Hungarian) Empire. Born in 1741, he died in February 1790. The epithet 'doup-skelper' (bottom-stroker) refers to Joseph's reputed lechery. Gustavus III ('the Swede' of l. 11) was in 1789 at war with Russia, concluded in a stalemate in August 1790; Gustavus (reigned 1771–92) was assassinated in 1792. His ancestor Charles XII (1682–1718) had also waged war (more decisively) against Russia. Maintaining his imagery of Europe as decadent, degenerate, and incapacitated, Burns dismisses politically unstable Italy as 'libbet' (l. 16) – castrated, like some of its opera singers. Turning to English leadership (ll. 23–4), the poet mocks 'Chatham Will' – Pitt the Younger, the Tory Prime Minister – and his perpetual feud with 'glaikit Charlie' Fox. Warren Hastings' impeachment trial (ll. 25–6) was similarly long-running and inconclusive until 1795, when despite the enmity of Burke and the House of Commons, Hastings (first Governor General of India) was finally cleared of charges by the House of Lords.

The poem's disrespectful survey of misconduct (political, colonial, and sexual) among the powers-that-be concludes sarcastically with the hope that power-to-be 'Geordie Wales', the King's son, has begun to develop habits of prudent circum-spection and has stopped behaving like a perfect 'kintra cooser' – country stallion.

Tibbie Dunbar (Tune: Johnny McGill)

Text and music: *SMM* 1790; signed ('Written for this work by Robert Burns'). This, like the next nine songs, was probably sent to Johnson on 24 April 1789. Burns wrote again on 19 June: 'what is the reason you have sent me no proof-sheet to correct? . . . Let me hear from you first post' (*Letters* 1, 417). Despite the occasional difficulties of collaborating with a printer and musical consultant located in Edinburgh, the poet increasingly used *SMM* as his incentive to keep writing (at shorter lengths) despite increasing professional and family obligations. As he wrote on 5 August to David Sillar: 'I hear you have commenced Married Man; so much the better, though perhaps your Muse may not fare the better for it. – I know not whether the NINE GIPSEYS are jealous of my Lucky, but they are a good deal shyer since I could boast the important relation of Husband' (*Letters* 1, 433).

Johnny McGill, composer of this air, was a fiddler in Girvan. Though Burns's stanzas seem rather slight on the page, they are beautifully matched to the tune, a slowed-down jig. From 1789 to 1792, many of Burns's courtship songs focus on the same conflict – financial prudence versus unconditional love – that had plagued the poet's courtship of Jean Armour; as if he felt compelled to rewrite the painful early chapters of their relationship.

TIBBIE DUNBAR

The Taylor Fell Thro' the Bed (Tune: Beware of the rippels)

Text and music: *SMM* 1790; unsigned. Probably sent to Johnson in April 1789 (see note to 'Tibbie Dunbar', above). Traditional bawdy fragments are turned to ambiguous purposes, for convention dictates (even in bawdry) that the lassie bewail the tricks of her seducer, who has 'cost' her probable social disgrace as well as the loss of her maidenhead. (Male power, not sexual pleasure, is the main subject of traditional bawdry, which was kept in currency through performance and recitation at the male clubs – such as the Crochallan Fencibles – so popular in eighteenth-century Scotland.) Burns enjoyed and collected bawdry, but in composing it he revises tradition; for Burns's speakers, male and female, tend to experience their sexuality as 'pleasure' rather than as 'power'. In stanza three of this song, for instance, the speaker (who should be expressing the straightforward reproach of the seduced maiden) is not sure whether her status is that of a victim: it all depends on whether the tailor returns. Loss of her virginity is costly – 'dearest siller', a paradoxical phrase, for the meaning of 'dear' is emotional as well as economic. The long night has cost her dear; but it has also brought her something dear: for she has awakened to passion in the bare furnishings of that cold and comically inadequate bed.

Burns's stanzas are well matched to an air lightened by skipping eighth-notes and sixteenths: as Ashmead and Davison say, 'the rhythmic pattern sometimes called the "Scotch snap" . . . is almost an emblem of Scots music' (29). JK notes that Burns 'takes full advantage of the emphatic lift in the second part of the air' (3, 1329).

Ay Waukin, O (Tune: Ay waukin, O)

Text and music: *SMM* 1790; unsigned. Probably sent to Johnson in April 1789 (see note to 'Tibbie Dunbar', p. 255). JK cites a similar old fragment from David Herd's manuscripts:

> O wat, wat – O wat and weary!
> Sleep I can get nane
> For thinking on my deary.
> A' the night I wak,
> A' the day I weary,
> Sleep I can get nane
> For thinking on my dearie. (3, 1330)

As in several songs by Burns, the speaker lies alone in her bed. Equally characteristic is the opening stanza, which extends into nature the echoes of his speaker's sadness. Here, paradox is created by the disparity between the 'pleasant', fertile season and the speaker's unfruitful passion. The 3/2 time signature and 'slow' pace suit a haunting tune that is 'one of that large class of Scots tunes that we generally regard as major, ending unstably on the fifth note of the scale . . . Or are they Mixolydian, ending on an unstable tonic? Actually, [the air] . . . leaves out the fourth degree of the major scale and is therefore technically hexatonic (Lydian/Ionian ending on its fifth, or Ionian/Mixolydian ending on its tonic)' (Ashmead and Davison, 230–32, using terminology from Bertrand Bronson's scholarship on the musical modes of the Child ballads). In non-technical terms, Burns's air captures the unfulfilled, apparently unrequited longings of its speaker in the failing, falling cadence and pattern of its tune. A livelier alternative air which Burns suggested later (*SMM* 1792) has become more popular but is not quite as well matched; this second setting is also often begun (following Johnson's careless printing in 1792) with its chorus, which spoils the dramatic effect of l. 4 and diminishes the opening stanza.

Lassie Lie Near Me (*Tune: Laddie lie near me*)

Text: *SMM* 1790; unsigned and marked 'Old Words'. But in his interleaved *SMM* Burns writes that 'the title of the song only is old, the rest is mine' (quoted in JK 3, 1331). Probably sent to Johnson in April 1789 (see note to 'Tibbie Dunbar', p. 255). Spare and expressive on the page, the stanzas are not well matched to the rather pompous air, 'a typical Baroque dance-melody, almost minuet-like' (Ashmead and Davison, 155). Music is from Dick; *SMM* does not set the words.

My Love She's But a Lassie Yet (*Tune: My love she's but a lassie yet*)

Text: *SMM* 1790; unsigned. Probably sent to Johnson in April 1789 (see note to 'Tibbie Dunbar', p. 255). Burns's speaker, bewitched yet exasperated by his 'saucy', immature, mercenary lassie, seeks alternative and more reliable comfort in whisky. The final stanza is traditional and was popular in Burns's day, appearing in at least two songbooks predating Burns's text (cf. JK 3, 1331). The air, a Scots reel, has the infectious gaiety of good dance music, but vocalists must inhale deeply before starting: the phrasing of the tune does not allow for breathing except at the stanza breaks.

MY LOVE SHE'S BUT A LASSIE YET

Jamie Come Try Me (*Tune: Jamie come try me*)

Text and music: *SMM* 1790; unsigned. Probably sent to Johnson in April 1789 (see note to 'Tibbie Dunbar', p. 255). These understated stanzas are matched to haunting music. In the traditional bawdy fragment Burns is revising ('Jenny come tye me,/Jenny come tye me,/ Jenny come tye my bonny cravat') the word 'cravat' has, as HH delicately note, 'an equivocal sense': the male speaker is in a jovial mood. Burns's song transforms the fragment by making the speaker female and taking her desire quite seriously. The slow-moving, heavily ornamented air explores a demanding range of an octave and a fourth.

Farewell to the Highlands (Tune: Failte na miosg (The Musket Salute))

My heart's in __ the High-lands, my heart is not __ here; My heart's in the High-lands a__ chas-ing the __ deer; A __ chas - ing the __ wild deer, and fol - low-ing the roe, __ My __ heart's in the High - lands, wher - ev - er I __ go.

Fare - well to the __ High-lands, fare - well to the north, The birth place of __ Val-our, the coun-try of __ Worth, Wher - ev - er__ I wan - der, wher - ev - er__ I rove, __ The __ hills of the __ High - lands __ for__ ev - er I __ love.

Text and music: *SMM* 1790; signed Z (see note to 'Auld Lang Syne', p. 250). Probably sent to Johnson in April 1789 (see note to 'Tibbie Dunbar', p. 255). In his interleaved copy of *SMM* Burns writes, 'The first half stanza of this song is old; the rest is mine.' As with 'Auld Lang Syne', the text draws its images from painful and recent Scottish historical experience: Jacobite defeat and exile, followed by the clearance of the Highlands. Ashmead and Davison praise this as one of Burns's most inspired (as well as most popular) syntheses of music, words, and feelings: 'The tune Burns chose is nobly ornate, with a magnificent Celtic sweep ... It has a pentatonic substructure, but has been ornamented and filled out into a major mode tune which is not a cheerful major but a nostalgic, even melancholy outpouring. Its slow ornaments are, in fact, reminiscent of a bagpipe lament' (242).

John Anderson My Jo (Tune: John Anderson my jo)

Text and music: *SMM* 1790; signed B. Probably sent to Johnson in April 1789 (see note to 'Tibbie Dunbar', p. 255). The traditional stanzas (included in *MMC*) are graphically bawdy and to this day remain (in Scotland) more popular than Burns's. In the old stanzas, the speaker is a young woman frustrated by her elderly husband's impotence and repelled by his ageing body. In Burns's idealized revision, the speaker (still female) is as old as John. This couple have everything in common: mutual love, mutual decline, approaching death. Now, at the end of their long love story, the same grave is waiting for them both. So the movement of the stanzas is from tenderness to pathos. This could be seen as another of the poet's honeymoon songs to Jean Armour; it is for Burns, at any rate, an uncharacteristically tender and non-ironic portrait of a marriage. Ashmead and Davison, calling the tune English or Continental, analyse it as 'Minor ... the common eighteenth-century harmonic-melodic minor. The range is an octave and a minor third' (141).

JOHN ANDERSON MY JO

The Battle of Sherra-moor (Tune: Cameronian Rant)

Text and music: SMM 1790; signed ('Written for this Work by Robt. Burns'). Probably sent to Johnson in April 1789 (see note to 'Tibbie Dunbar', p. 255). The song re-creates the drawn battle (13 September 1715) that, with the battle of Preston in England one day later, ended the Jacobite war of 1715. The battle of Sheriffmuir (near Dunblane in Perthshire) pitted 12,000 Highlanders under the command of John Erskine, Earl of Mar, against 4,000 Hanoverians led by John Campbell, second Duke of Argyll. Burns's civilian witnesses (a shepherd, his friend Tam, and the shepherd's sister Kate) offer conflicting accounts of the battle, parts of which each has seen while going about their daily routines. (There is still debate in Scotland over which side won that costly battle, which ended in about 500 deaths on each side.) Dick explains that there were topographical reasons for the confusion: 'The two armies approached each other on the broad muir between the Ochils and the Grampians. It is an undulating platform of gentle hummocky hills, and neither army saw very clearly the position and movements of the other ... The rebels outnumbered the Government army, but lost the advantage by rushing the attack' (462).

The song exemplifies Burns's complex view of authorship, for notwithstanding his full signature in SMM, two passages in this text (ll. 1–4 and 34–54) closely follow earlier stanzas ('Dialogue between Will Lick-ladle and Tom Clean-Cogue ... to the tune of the "Cameron's" March"') written by Rev. John Barclay (1734–98). Burns changes the original tone of playful burlesque (cf. Barclay's speakers' names), concentrating instead on dramatizing multiple conflicts – the confusion of the pitched battle, but also the confusion of completely contradictory eyewitness accounts. And unlike Barclay, as JK says, the poet fully exploits 'the hard alliterative diction of traditional battle poetry' (3, 1338). JK and Dick both emphasize the neutrality of viewpoint in Burns's version, saying that the conflicting partisan accounts of the 'double flight' cancel each other out. Yet the penultimate line dispatching the Whigs to hell gives the Jacobites the final word.

The air, a strathspey, has a limited vocal range but a punishing tempo that offers a melodic pause once in fifteen syllables for the first four lines of each stanza – but then no pause for six lines. For that reason the song is seldom performed successfully: opera singers who have the necessary breath tend to over-dramatize, spoiling the folk simplicity. Jean Redpath has, however, recorded a vivid interpretation in *Songs of Robert Burns*, Vol. 5.

In the copy-text, l. 28 ends with the word 'charge' – repeated in the next line, and a typographical error; here corrected to 'targe' (a kind of shield), as in JK.

THE BATTLE OF SHERRA-MOOR

Sandy and Jockie (Tune: *Jenny's Lamentation*)

Twa bo-ny lads were San-dy— and— Jock - ie;— Jock-ie was
lov-'d but— San-dy un - luc-ky, Jock-ie— was laird baith of
hills and of val-lies, But— San-dy was nought but the— king o' gude fel-lows.
Jock-ie lov'd Mad-gie, for Mad-gie had mo-ney, And San-die lov'd
Ma-ry, for Ma-ry was— bo-ny: Ane wed-ded for— Love,— Ane—
wed-ded for— trea-sure, So— Jock-ie had sil-ler, And San-dy had plea-sure.

Text and music: *SMM* 1790; unsigned. Probably sent to Johnson in April 1789 (see note to 'Tibbie Dunbar', p. 255). These simple stanzas are neatly fitted to a complex English tune that extends over both stanzas. The first two lines are from Thomas D'Urfey's 'Unfortunate Jockey' in *The Royalist* (1682); the rest are by Burns, who (characteristically) defines his lovers' dilemma as a choice between love or land, beauty or riches. In Burns's terms, wealthy Jockie remains the unlucky one.

Tam o' Shanter. A Tale

Text: *Poems* 1793 (Edinburgh). Written in the autumn of 1790. A draft was sent to Mrs Dunlop in November, and the full text was sent on 1 December to Captain Francis Grose, the antiquary who had requested that Burns write him a witch-story about Alloway kirk. First printed in the *Edinburgh Herald* (18 March 1791) and the *Edinburgh Magazine* (March 1791). Burns must have been disappointed at the printing format Grose chose for what the poet immediately recognized as his most 'finished' work: 'Tam o' Shanter' appeared as a double-column, reduced-type footnote in Vol. 2 of *Antiquities of Scotland* (pp. 199–201), which was published on 11 April.

Alloway was Burns's birthplace; his family's house had been located less than a mile from the roofless ruin of Alloway kirk – abandoned since 1690 when the parish had been absorbed by the town of Ayr (some two miles distant). The tiny church had become by Burns's boyhood the focal point of local ghost and witch stories, three of which Burns sent (in prose as genially sceptical as 'Tam o' Shanter's' verse) to Captain Grose, perhaps in June 1790 (*Letters* 2, 29–31). As a boy, Burns had watched his father and several neighbours rebuild the crumbling stone wall of the kirk's untended cemetery to keep out the grazing sheep. According to Gilbert Burns, because of his work tending the ruin and protecting its ancient dead, William Burnes 'came to consider' Alloway kirkyard 'as his burial-place, and we learned that reverence for it people generally have for the burial-place of their ancestors' (HH 2, 437–8). The family followed William Burnes's wishes: he was buried in the ruined kirkyard in February 1784. The brig of Doon, located about 200 yards south of Alloway kirk on today's road, was in the eighteenth century the only means of crossing the small but high-banked river Doon between Kyle and Carrick.

Tam and his wife Kate also were drawn from life. Douglas Graham (1739–1811) was tenant of the farm 'Shanter' in Carrick and sailed a boat named 'Tam o' Shanter'; his superstitious wife Helen McTaggart (1742–98) was a notorious scold. 'Graham was noted for his convivial habits, which his wife's ratings tended rather to confirm than eradicate. Tradition relates that once, when his long-tailed grey mare had waited even longer than usual for her master at the tavern door, certain humorists plucked her tail to such an extent as to leave it little better than a stump, and that Graham, on his attention being called to its state next morning, swore it had been depilated by the witches at Alloway kirk' (HH 2, 437).

As with 'The Holy Fair', Burns's ironic frame stylizes and transforms the realistic elements in the story. From its epigraph (taken from Gavin Douglas's middle-Scots translation of the *Aeneid*) to the mock-adventures of its game but drunken mock-hero, 'Tam o' Shanter' is a neoclassically refurbished folk-tale, the narrative equivalent of what Burns was doing in his work with folk-song. Folk-derived but neoclassically balanced – Burns had learned from Milton and Pope how to counterpoint antithetical symbols throughout long poems – 'Tam o' Shanter' was Burns's favourite among his works, the poem he regarded as having the brightest 'polish'. Thomas Carlyle was disappointed in the 'sparkling rhetoric' of 'Tam o' Shanter', for Carlyle expected a witch-story to convey a mood of horror alien to this poem, which – for all its stormy setting and burlesque encounter with the devil – may be Burns's least Romantic work.

Like mock-heroic Tam, too fuddled to know his danger, the poem itself refuses to be intimidated by darkness, stormy weather, natural or supernatural atrocities. The poem's refusal to take fear seriously, along with its refusal to pass judgement (either on drunken Tam or on the dancing witches), seems obliquely addressed to the austere, beloved, disapproving father who lay buried in Alloway kirkyard. The cautious voice of William Burnes ('think!'; 'remember!') – which also haunts 'The Cotter's Saturday Night' – is displaced into Tam's bad-tempered wife and thereby effectively discredited. Tam, who refuses to behave like a responsible adult (and has plenty of local company), successfully escapes the consequences of his imprudent behaviour and his taste for brazen females. He does not get what he deserves and is never punished for what the poem insists on seeing as his innocent (perhaps even heroic) pursuit of pleasure. Kate's ill-natured (if not unlikely) epic prophecy – that one day he will be found drowned in the Doon – goes unfulfilled. Tam has a hostile wife but a faithful mare Meg, who brings him safely home at nominal cost to herself. A 'female' who loves Tam – not his wife – saves him. Burns has, moreover, arranged matters in such a way that readers rejoice at his escape.

This poem's alternating homophones, its counterpointed 'tales' (lying narratives shared with an audience) and 'tails' (exposed posteriors, also shared with an audience), are a dynamic feature of the poem's language and also mark its chief contrast. Itself subtitled a 'tale', 'Tam o' Shanter' includes sub-narratives: Kate's prophecy, the allusion to Souter Johnny's 'queerest stories', the omniscient narrator's account of Nannie's future mischief. All these are tall tales: wildly improbable lies solemnly presented as facts. The alternative homophone substitutes the naked truth for the fictional lie: the tail Maggie ultimately loses is balanced by description of the tail being so energetically exhibited in the abandoned kirkyard. The coarse sense of the word as Burns knew it meant the female sexual organs, but both warlocks and witches have cast aside most of their clothing in the heat of their dancing; and even the narrator, getting into the spirit of things, offers up his breeches, his 'only pair'. There is a general atmosphere of comic self-exposure that counterpoints the equally prevalent atmosphere of face-saving lying: perhaps the message is that words often lie, but bodies never. Nannie the witch is only revealing what Maggie the mare will soon be unable to conceal: the fact that her body marks her as a sexual being.

The poem is a comedy darkened by its anti-sentimental, anti-heroic reading of human character (as essentially infantile, narcissistic, pleasure-obsessed) and also by glints of sardonic social criticism. Nannie exposes her nakedness because she dances with such youthful abandon, but also because she is still wearing her best 'sark' from her childhood, now 'cutty' – too short to cover her newly adult body. Nanny wears her cutty-sark because she is too poor to 'coft' (buy) a new one: in fact she is so poor that she is 'vauntie' (proud) of the ill-fitting old one, for which the cloth, though only sackcloth or 'harn', was purchased for her, not homespun from even coarser fabrics. The poem implies that it is no wonder if Nannie seeks power and pleasure through witchcraft: dutifulness has not even provided her with adequate clothing. More broadly, the poem is implying that the witches' commitment to general mischief is as understandable as Tam's habitual drunkenness, given the dull and thankless routine of ordinary adult life, not to mention the meagre return on effort for Scottish farmers, spinsters, and small tradesmen. A flash of lightning any given midnight might well reveal the shadowy forms of those in Burns's community who have finally abandoned the struggle to maintain decency amid the unrelenting poverty that chains them to a grey and powerless existence.

One need not be a Freudian to see that this poem uses images such as Nannie's cutty-sark to suggest the utter insufficiency of civilization to clothe human desire in some semblance of decent restraint. It is not that the Auld Licht is correct and that human nature is degenerate and evil: far from it. Burns clearly feels affectionate sympathy for these human foibles. None the less, he does see Tam and Nannie as possessing major foibles; and he did take from Calvinism a sense that the combined forces of civilization (duty, law, conscience, and scolding Kate) are unlikely to have much effect on strong individual 'inclination', natural propensity. The responsibilities of adult life, the poem suggests, too insistently demand the restraint of desire: people need and want so much more pleasure and power than they are likely to get if they are well behaved. The sark that links renegade Nannie to her innocent past – it was the gift of her pious granny – is still very important to her ('It was her best'). But it simply fails to fit her after she has reached puberty.

The elusive meaning of 'Tam o' Shanter' resides somewhere within its contrasts: somewhere between men and women, lies and truth, horror and pleasure. Yet 'Tam o' Shanter' refuses to total its sum, offering only a mocking parody in its final maxim: 'Think . . . Remember.' The poem has already shown us that the very people addressed by this prudent advice – hedonists such as Tam and Nannie – are constitutionally incapable of hearing (let alone heeding) it.

Robert Cromek recorded Jean Armour's memories of the early autumn day the poem was begun. She had arrived with their sons Robert and Frank to meet the poet by the banks of the Nith, where he had been writing all morning. A family outing had been planned for the afternoon, but as they approached Jean saw that the poet 'was busily engaged *crooning to himself*; and Mrs Burns, perceiving that her presence was an interruption, loitered behind with her little ones among the broom. Her attention was presently attracted by the strange and wild gesticulations of the bard, who now, at some distance, was agonised with an ungovernable access of joy. He was reciting very loud, and with the tears running down his cheeks' (Lockhart, quoting Cromek, in *Life of Robert Burns*, 1828; reprinted London: Everyman, 1959, p. 149). As Burns once wrote to Mrs Dunlop, however, 'All my poetry is the effect of easy composition, but of laborious correction': he spent at least two months revising his early draft (HH 2, 438).

In l. 1, 'chapman billies' (brother pedlars) opens the poem on a fraternal note: poets, like their brothers the chapbook salesmen, are pedlars of pleasant lies. The sustained contrast between the 'brotherhood' of men-drinkers and 'sisterhood' of women-dancers in the poem is discussed in my book *Robert Burns and the Sentimental Era* (Athens: University of Georgia Press, 1985), pp. 149–61. In l. 23 'melder' is meal ground to order for a customer: Kate is accusing Tam of drinking the profits of the miller as well as the blacksmith. 'Lord's house' in l. 27 was 'L—s's' in the earliest holograph: Jean Kennedy kept 'The Leddie's House', the Kirkoswald tavern Kate is referring to here. A 'kirkton' is a village (such as Alloway before 1690) in which a parish church is located (JK 3, 1355). Lines 43–4 offer a particularly sardonic non-sequitur. 'As bees' (l. 55) is an epic simile; it is followed (ll. 59–72) by an epic digression. (Another epic trait is seen in l. 188: like an epic hero, Tam loses his wits, though not from grief or romantic betrayal but sheer childish pleasure.) The word 'nightly' (l. 88) reminds us that the witches' dance is as routine and predictable a local event as Tam's drunkenness.

In ll. 89–96, natural horrors – accidental death, suicide, infanticide – precede description of Alloway's supernatural horrors. The numerous drunken falls commemorated by the passing landmarks should serve Tam as a warning. Yet whether real or imagined, horror has no hold over 'heroic Tam', insulated by his pleasant evening at the tavern. The final graveyard prop described (ll. 138–42) is a knife used in a parricide, a detail that has puzzled critics attempting to assess William Burnes's role in this poem. Burns's bloodied knife is, I think, an acknowledgement of how deeply he felt his father's disapproval – but also of how completely he rejected William Burnes's self-righteous authority and sobriety. Their worst quarrel occurred when the poet (as an adolescent) went out one night to a dancing class 'in absolute defiance' of his father's 'commands'. 'My father was the sport of strong passions: from that instance of rebellion he took a kind of dislike to me, which I believe was one cause of that dissipation which marked my future years. – I only say, Dissipation, comparative with the strictness and sobriety of Presbyterian country life' (*Letters* 1, 139). So the witches are not the only folk who have ever defied a prohibition on nocturnal dancing, nor is Nannie the only young person who, turning from the piety of her elders, has ever brought a scandalous celebrity to her family name. The 'seventeen hunder linnen' of l. 154 is a 'manufacturer's term for a fine linen, woven on a reed of 1700 divisions' (Cromek).

In l. 18, 'thy ain wife' is 'they' in the copy-text, a typographical error.

The Banks o' Doon (*Tune: Caledonian Hunt's Delight*)

Slow and tender

Ye banks and braes o' bo - nie Doon, How can_ ye bloom sae fresh and fair; How can ye chant, ye lit - tle birds, And I____ sae wea - ry fu'_ o' care! Thou-'ll break my heart thou warb- ling bird, That wan-tons thro' the flower-ing thorn: Thou minds me o' de - par - ted joys,_ De - par - ted ne - ver to_ re-turn.

Text and music: *SMM* 1792; signed B. Burns's two songs bearing this title – similar in wording but set to very different tunes – are distinguished as versions A and B. The version given here, much more effectively matched to its music, is B; it was among Byron's favourite songs. The date of B is unknown; but the A stanzas were sent in a letter of 11 March 1791 to Alexander Cunningham (*Letters* 2, 81); editors have assumed that B was composed soon after. The legendary fiddler Neil Gow (1727–1807) named this air 'Caledonian Hunt's Delight' in a book of reels published in 1788. That title also heads the transcript of B in the Hastie MS (British Library) but has been crossed out.

The song's emotional power lies in its contrast between festive nature and the desolate speaker; also (as in 'Auld Lang Syne') in its contrast between past and present. In earlier days, the female speaker was united with nature; its 'twining' rose and woodbine mirrored her own loving dependency on her suitor. Now that she has been abandoned, her song has become a lonely counterpoint to the heartless 'chanting' of happily mated birds.

Burns praised the air as among his favourites, though his account of its origin is apocryphal: 'Many years ago, a Mr Jas. Miller ... expressed an ardent ambition to compose a Scots air. – Mr Clarke [musical consultant for *SMM*], partly by way of a joke, told him, to keep to the black keys of the harpsichord ... [and] in a few days, Mr Miller produced the rudiments of an air, which Mr Clarke ... fashioned into the tune in question ... Now to shew you how difficult it is to trace the origin of our airs, I have heard it repeatedly asserted, that it was an Irish air; ... while ... a Lady of fashion ... informed me, that the first person who introduced the air into this country was a Baronet's Lady ... who took down the notes from an itinerant Piper on the Isle of Man' (*Letters* 2, 325–6). Neil Gow almost certainly composed the air; but the pentatonic tune is indeed most easily played using only the black keys.

To Robert Graham of Fintry, Esq.

Text: *Poems* 1793 (Edinburgh); dated 5 October 1791 in several transcripts. Earlier versions exist: one to Mrs Dunlop dated 29 October 1788 (titled 'The poet's Progress, an embryotic Poem in the womb of Futurity') includes ll. 9-55; another also sent to Dunlop on New Year's Day 1789 (titled 'Apostrophe to Dulness') includes ll. 56-75. On 6 October, Burns enclosed this version in a prose letter to Fintry: 'I inclose you a sheetful of groans, wrung from me in my elbow-chair, with one unlucky leg on a stool before me' (*Letters* 2, 117). But Burns's petulance in this revealing epistle is not due wholly to his injured leg; it stems from financial anxieties that had become all-consuming by the autumn of 1791. The poet badly needed an increase in his Excise income (which varied between £40 and £70 per year; the fluctuation was caused by his inability to ride his circuit during frequent, sometimes protracted illnesses). Robert Graham of Fintry (1749-1814) was a Commissioner on the Board of Excise; in 1791 he was working behind the scenes to ensure a promotion for Burns, but there were difficulties because of the poet's politics, widely (and probably correctly) perceived to be both Jacobite and Jacobin.

The financial crisis was in part the result of growing family obligations: in 1791 Burns's illegitimate daughter Elizabeth and his son William Nichol had both been born; while continuing to assist his brother Gilbert with the support of his mother, unmarried sisters, and his little girl by Betsey Paton, he was now also providing for Jean and four small children. (Helen Anne Park, his new daughter's mother, had either died in childbirth or – more likely, given Burns's unbroken friendship with Helen's relatives – had left the infant in Burns's care so that she could make a new beginning elsewhere; a course of action Burns had earlier followed with Betsey Paton and attempted – unsuccessfully – with Jenny Clow. Accustomed to twins and apparently resigned to her husband's infidelity, Jean was nursing both infants.) The approximately £400 that had been cleared from subscriptions to *Poems* 1787 (Edinburgh) and sale of the copyright (a substantial amount for an eighteenth-century poet) was none the less entirely gone by 1791. Half had been lent to Burns's brother Gilbert (who still farmed Mossgiel and housed their mother and sisters); the loan was not repaid until 1820, when Gilbert reimbursed the poet's estate. Most of the rest had been spent stocking the unlucky farm at Ellisland, an experiment Burns had abandoned in near-despair just two weeks before sending this verse-letter. (Incidentally, Burns received no income from *SMM*, refusing payment except in books. But Johnson, a poor man, could not have paid him much in any case. Despite the cost-cutting resulting from Johnson's innovative use of cheap pewter plates for his engraving, *SMM* – today regarded as the most important collection of Scottish folk-song ever published – was never a financial, critical, or popular success. Johnson's widow died in 1819 in the Edinburgh workhouse.)

The epistle shows that Burns's continuing financial dependency caused him periods of agonized humiliation. The one noble patron he had liked personally – James Cunningham, fourteenth Earl of Glencairn, who had arranged the support of the Caledonian Hunt for *Poems* 1787 (Edinburgh) – had died in January 1791. Only Fintry was left, a train of thought Burns tactlessly reveals in the letter that accompanied this epistle: 'I will make no apology for addressing [the enclosed epistle] to *you*: I have no longer a *choice* of Patrons: the truly noble Glencairn is no more!' (*Letters* 2, 17). The poet had reason to fear that he was friendless and unprotected, as he had some reason to blame his poetry for his current crisis. The enemies he had made through his satires and Jacobite songs were now blocking his advancement in the Excise; indeed (by late 1792) they were demanding his summary dismissal on the grounds of political disaffection.

In l. 7, 'curse the light' echoes the Book of Job. Line 22 read 'Her dreaded spear and nameless other parts' before 1793 – a better (or at least more characteristic) line, but too lighthearted for the context. 'Amalthea's horn' (l. 30) was the horn of Zeus's nurse-goat, which became a cornucopia. In l. 39, 'ten Monroes' is truly a reference to multiple Monroes. In his second Horatian epistle, Pope declares his imminent need for the services of 'ten Monroes' (James Monro was a physician at Bedlam). And Alexander Monro (1733–1817) was professor of anatomy at Edinburgh University, as his father had been before him and as his son was in training to become: they were the most eminent medical family in the city. Among the sources for ll. 56–71, with their imagery of blissful folly and triumphant Dulness, are Pope's *Dunciad* and Swift's 'Digression Concerning Madness' from *Tale of a Tub*.

Ae Fond Kiss (*Tune: Rory Dall's Port*)

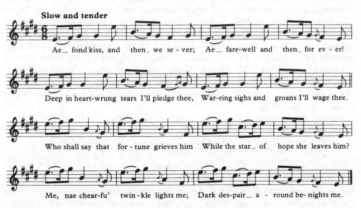

Text and music: *SMM* 1792, signed X. Sent to Agnes M'Lehose, the 'Nancy' of these stanzas, on 27 December 1791. This is the last and best of the ten songs she inspired. The couple had met in December 1787 and had parted in February 1788, just before Burns's reconciliation with Jean Armour. The romance between the celebrity-poet and the woman he usually addressed as 'Clarinda' (the title was borrowed from Allan Ramsay's pastoral alias for the Duchess of Queensberry) had been complicated by her marriage. When the poet met her, Agnes M'Lehose (1759–1841) was the mother of three children; married at seventeen against the wishes of her father, an Edinburgh surgeon, she had left her (by all accounts) dissolute husband by the age of twenty-one. They had been separated for years when she met Burns. Biographers and critics have been unduly harsh in discussing

Agnes M'Lehose. She and the poet understood each other very well. They were drawn together by their shared consciousness of being on the fringes of polite society – 'Sylvander' (Burns's alias) because of his social class and 'Clarinda' because of her marital status. It is no wonder that their intimacy began with an assumption of artificial names: they both needed this fresh start in a pastoral world.

An impetuous, flirtatious style marks her letters to the poet: 'I believe I have a tolerably just idea of your character. No wonder; for had I been a man, I should have been you ... I am formed with a liveliness of fancy, and a strength of passion little inferiour ... I have thought that Nature threw me off in the same mould, just after you. We were born, I believe, in a year. Madame Nature has some merit by her work that year. Don't you think so?' (New Year's Day 1788). In a later note, she wrote with even more warmth: 'Say, my lover, poet, and my friend, what day next month will Eternity end? ... Farewell, Sylvander. I may sign, for I am already sealed your friend' (from *Sylvander and Clarinda*, ed. Amelia Barr, New York: Doran, 1917).

Like so many of Burns's best works, 'Ae Fond Kiss' was inspired by a prospective emigration. The couple had met again briefly in Edinburgh on 6 December 1791, when Clarinda had told Burns of her plans to reconcile with her husband, now an overseer on a plantation in Jamaica. Three weeks later, Burns mailed her the text of this song, and by January Clarinda had sailed on the *Roselle*. (Unfortunately, James M'Lehose refused to meet her, preferring the company of his mistress and their child; Agnes M'Lehose went back to Edinburgh on the *Roselle*'s return sailing. 'The heat was so excessive and the mosquitoes so annoying,' was her response when asked in 1829 by a prying bardolater why she did not stay.) In 1831, Agnes M'Lehose, who lived into her eighties, wrote in her journal: 'This day [6 December] I can never forget. Parted with Burns, in the year 1791, never more to meet in this world. Oh, may we meet in Heaven!' (*BE*).

Stanzas similar in sentiment (if not in lyric power) had been written by Robert Dodsley (1703–64):

> One fond kiss before we part,
> Drop a Tear and bid adieu;
> Tho' we sever, my fond Heart
> Till we meet shall pant for you.   (HH 3, 379)

Rory Dall was the family name of 'a succession of harpers attached to the family of Macleod of Skye. *Port* is the generic name for the national Celtic airs of the Highlands of Scotland' (Dick 379). Ashmead and Davison note the air's 'repetition ... an insistent, almost wailing monotony' (209).

The Bonie Wee Thing (Tune: Bonie wee thing)

Text and music: *SMM* 1792; signed R. Sent to Deborah Duff Davies (d. 1794?), the fragile and consumptive girl who inspired it, on 6 April 1793; oddly enough, the song had already appeared in *SMM* (published August 1792). The MS poem and accompanying letter, now in private hands, once were owned by Lord Byron.

Deborah Davies was related to Burns's friends the Riddells. In a letter sent in June 1793 to Mrs Dunlop, the poet describes Deborah in contrast to a rangier (now mercifully unidentifiable) woman of their acquaintance: 'Miss D—— you must know, is positively the least creature ever I saw, to be at the same time unexceptionably, & indeed uncommonly handsome & beautiful; & besides has the felicity to be a peculiar favorite toast of mine. – On the contrary, Mrs S—— is a huge, bony, masculine, cowp-carl horse-godmother, he-termagant of a six-feet figure, who might have been bride to Og, king of Bashan; or Golia of Gath' (*Letters* 2, 215).

The song likewise addresses Davies as the most cherished of 'least creatures', her frailty and smallness of stature forming the basis of her claim to tender, almost maternal protection (cf. l. 3). And if the speaker is almost motherly, his 'goddess' is nearly neuter: a thing, a jewel, a constellation, finally a divinity. That womanly, fleshly images are not used is sometimes given as proof of excessive rhetoric and poetic inhibition caused by Burns's sense of the disparity between his and Deborah Davies's social classes. Yet this reticence of imagery, which creates much of the song's loving pathos, also reflects the poet's instinctive response to the girl's youth and her physical fragility. Deborah Davies had been sent to France to recruit her health in 1792, the year these stanzas were written; and though the date of her death is unknown, she is known to have died very young.

Quoted fragments from this song figure in Mr Rochester's eccentric courtship of the similarly slight and child-like Jane Eyre: Burns had been (with Byron) among the literary heroes included in the fantasy worlds the Brontës shared as children. The best analysis of the tune, with its repeated 'Scotch snaps' echoing the frequent repetition of 'wee thing', is by Caterina Ericson-Roos in *The Songs of Robert Burns*, a University of Uppsala dissertation (1977), No. 30 in their British Studies series (pp. 56–8).

In l. 8 'Least' is given as 'Lest' in the copy-text; probably a typographical error, as 'least' is the spelling in l. 4.

THE BONNIE WEE THING

I Hae a Wife o' My Ain (*Tune: I hae a wife o' my ain*)

I hae a wife o' my ain, I'll par-take wi' nae-bo-dy;
I'll tak Cuck-old frae nane, I'll gie Cuck-old to nae-bo-dy.
I hae a pen-ny to spend, There, thanks to nae-bo-dy;
I hae nae-thing to lend, I'll bor-row frae nae-bo-dy.

Text and music: *SMM* 1792; signed B. The song is often assumed to be one of the honeymoon songs for Jean Armour written in 1788. As JK notes, however, no proof exists to date this poem before its publication in 1792. Nor, despite the first line, is the speaker's tone that of a delighted newly wed: this implacable-sounding air is fitted to implacable stanzas. The flawed consensus that sees this as a lighthearted comic song ('Burns at his . . . airiest': JK 3, 1395) might be corrected if the late Ewan McColl's memorably truculent performance in *Songs of Robert Burns* (Folkways, recorded 1959) were more widely known.

O for Ane and Twenty Tam! (*Tune: The Moudiewort*)

Text and music: *SMM* 1792; signed B. The well-known air was traditionally matched to erotic stanzas in which the blind moudiewort (mole) slyly builds a mole-hill under the apron of the speaker. Burns's genial revision transforms the context from unwanted pregnancy to courtship. His speaker is a plucky eighteen-year-old willing to delay her marriage for the three years that must pass before she can claim the well-stocked farm left her by her aunt and marry penniless Tam, the man of her choice. Until then she will resist her family's pressure to marry a wealthy 'coof' (clown).

The stanzas parody Richardson's *Clarissa*, which Burns had read some time between 1789 and 1791. Clarissa Harlowe will not claim the estate her grandfather has left her or go to law against her mercenary family, who have arranged her marriage to rich but sexually repulsive Mr Solmes: Clarissa's own wish is to remain single. By contrast, Burns's heroine is willing to marry and downright eager to fight: she will 'learn [teach] her kin a rattlin sang' if they continue to stand in her way. Clarissa blushes and faints during romantic interviews; Burns's bluff heroine extends her hand ('there's my loof') for a comradely handshake in sealing her betrothal to Tam. Burns criticizes Richardson in a letter to the novelist Dr John Moore dated 28 February 1791: 'unhappily, his Dramatis personae are beings of some other world; & however they may captivate the unexperienced, romantic fancy of a boy or a girl, they will ever, in proportion as we have made human nature our study, disgust our riper minds' (*Letters* 2, 74).

Dick speculates that the 'moudiewort' entered Scottish folklore as a friendly trickster in 1702, after King William was killed when his horse stumbled on a mole-hill – an accident that delighted the Jacobites. As J K says, however, the bawdy stanzas probably pre-date the eighteenth century. Genteel nineteenth-century editors usually followed George Thomson's *SC* in setting Burns's stanzas to the air 'Up in the morning early', probably judging that the old erotic stanzas somehow disgraced the tune. Burns's choice – a lilting yet emphatic air – is a much better match for his stanzas.

O FOR ANE AND TWENTY TAM!

Lady Mary Ann (*Tune: Lady Mary Ann*)

Text and music: *SMM* 1792; unsigned. Several ballads and popular songs contributed to the archaic-sounding diction and imagery. Burns did not tamper with already eloquent fragments, however; most of the sources are trivial:

> And he'll be daily growing,
> Growing, deary, growing, growing.
> Growing, said the bonny maid,
> Slowly my bonie love's growing.

The fragment closest to Burns's in literary quality was among David Herd's ballad manuscripts, which Burns had probably seen while in Edinburgh:

> She look'd o'er the castle wa',
> She saw three lads play at the ba',
> O the youngest is the flower of a'!
>   But my love is lang o' growing.
>
> 'O father, gin ye think it fit,
> We'll send him to the college yet;
> And tye a Ribban round his hat,
>   And, father, I'll gang wi' him!'
>   (both texts from H H 3, 389-90)

There was an original for this 'College Boy', although his name was not transmitted in the folk-tradition. He was the grandson and heir of John Urquhart of Craigston (d. November 1634). The heir, a boy when he came into the property, was persuaded to marry Elizabeth Innes, his guardian's eldest (in the folk accounts, elderly) daughter; the boy then died, probably not of natural causes, when away at school:

> In his twelfth year he was a married man,
> In his thirteenth year then he got a son;
> In his fourteenth year his grave grew green,
>   And that was the end of his growing. (Dick 488)

Burns's stanzas contradict his folk-sources. His version refuses the viewpoint either of the tragic ballads or the burlesque songs (which emphasize the ridiculous passion of a middle-aged woman for a husband still a boy). The poet's stanzas are emotionally complex, blending hope for the future with regret for the vanished past. Burns's stanzas are also characteristic in giving proper names to the 'college boy' and the loving older lass. In this art-song crafted from popular fragments, Charlie Cochran, no victim, is still 'to marry yet'; and Lady Mary Ann, in her distant, watchful tenderness, might be his mother. The song, so folk-like in its alternation of viewpoint between different implied speakers, none the less exemplifies the poet's typically bold revision of tradition. Perhaps it was Scottish history that taught Scots poets to locate happiness only in the remotest past; but Burns's stanzas dare to hope for 'far better days' in a future whose promise is symbolized by a healthy, growing child. Time fulfils and does not destroy: Lady Mary Ann herself, looking down at young Charlie as he plays outside the 'castle-wall' of her maturer vantage-point, has only grown 'sweeter' and 'bonier' with age.

The haunting, well-matched air was first published in *SMM* to Burns's stanzas; it is thought to have been collected on one of his Highland tours.

LADY MARY ANN

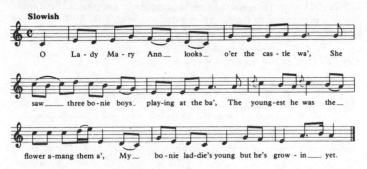

The Gallant Weaver (Tune: Weaver's March)

Text and music: *SMM* 1792; signed R. The female speaker's conquering hero is not a military man but a gallant weaver from Paisley. (The river Cart runs through the town; in the 1790s Paisley was already on its way to becoming a world centre for weaving.) In rejecting her father's favourite, 'the lad who has the land', for a town-dwelling artisan, the speaker has chosen the path of the future. Weavers and other skilled workers were in the nineteenth century among the most vociferous agitators for Parliamentary reform; in Burns's day many supported the French Revolution. The weaver's 'gallantry' in the eyes of the speaker no doubt lies in his style of courtship; yet the poet is also obliquely conveying his approval of the weavers' political activism.

George Thomson, editor of *SC*, re-published this song posthumously in 1799 but (with characteristic officiousness and political timidity) eliminated Burns's implied social comment by changing the hero into a sailor. The air is a military-sounding march known under several names (including 'Weaver's March' and

'Frisky Jenny'). A similar march is identified as Swedish in a songbook published in 1715 (Dick 395). JK prints the song in quatrains (2, 649), but *SMM*'s octave format is more suited to the air, which extends through eight lines and is then repeated.

Hey Ca' Thro' (*Tune: Hey ca' thro'*)

With spirit

Up wi' the carls___ of Dy - sart, And the lads o' Buck-hiven,

And the Kim - mers o' Lar - go, And the las - ses o' Leven.

CHORUS

Hey   ca'   thro'   ca'   thro'   For   we   hae   mic - kle   a   do,

Hey   ca'   thro'   ca'   thro'   For   we   hae   mic - kle   a   do.

Text and music: *SMM* 1792; unsigned. No holograph copy exists, but no folk-source has ever been found for this traditional-sounding work-song, which summons the men and women of four villages to their daily labour. The stanzas may have been written several years before publication, for, as Dick notes, in September 1787 Burns had passed near or through Dysart, Buckhaven, Largo, and Leven, the fishing villages – all located on the south coast of Fife – named in these stanzas. The song's speakers, who have work to do and 'pennies to spend', reject prudence. These folk 'spend' their lives in work and their money on pleasure (their 'pints'). The rhythmic, repetitive air echoes the stanzas' pattern: an alternate production and consumption of the fruits of labour. The final stanza cheerfully enjoins future generations – 'Them that comes behin'' – to 'do the like' and 'spend the gear' (wealth) they 'win' (earn).

Dick calls the air 'a characteristic small pipe tune, in compound triple time, common to the Border'. The music, which Burns is said to have communicated when he sent the verses, is not in any collection prior to the copy in the *Museum* (443).

When Princes and Prelates (*Tune unknown*)

Text: JK 3, 668–9; the *MMC* text (the earliest printed source) contains several stanzas not by Burns. JK's copy-text was a letter dated 12 December 1792, enclosing 'a song, just finished this minute' (*Letters* 2, 168). The recipient was Robert Cleghorn (d. 1798), a farmer at Saughton Mills and fellow collector of bawdry: like Burns, Cleghorn belonged to the Crochallan Fencibles, a roisterous Edinburgh men's club.

Editions of Burns's writings that exclude his bawdry are obscuring an important element in his personality and also in Scottish folk-tradition. As the poet wrote in mock-contrition to like-minded Cleghorn on 25 October 1793: 'There is, there must be, some truth in original sin. – My violent propensity to B—dy convinces me of it. – Lack a day, if that species of Composition be the sin against "the Haly Ghaist", "I am the most offending soul alive" ... Forgive this *wicked* scrawl' (*Letters* 2, 255). This song expresses scorn for the impotent or perverse power-plays of wealthy sovereigns. In this deflected way, focusing on the 'Princes'' power-drives as misdirected sex-drives, Burns achieves a comic, curiously weight-less overview of the rapid revolutionary changes transforming Europe during the early 1790s. As in Swift's 'Digression Concerning Madness', these titled invaders and hostile penetrators into alien soil are really victims in the grip of some mad sublimation. 'Poor bodies', by contrast, turn to a 'gude mowe' for comfort in a bleak world; because they can have what they desire, they are more truly powerful than their titled 'princes and prelates'. Burns also suggests that the object of the poor man's desire is more wholesome than the aggression and violence of princely warfare. (Incidentally, George and Charlotte, who were known for their mutual affection and their quiet, domestic tastes, are for once viewed favourably by Burns, standing in contrast to their decadent and warlike relatives in Europe.)

The song was written during the same month that Burns was charged with political disaffection, prompting an inquiry by the Board of Excise. In a letter of 31 December asking Graham of Fintry's help in fighting the charges, Burns uses the rhetoric of this song. Yet in this inhibiting context – a begging letter to a patron in a real-life crisis, not a scatological lyric sent to a fellow farmer and trusted friend – the position of the classes is tellingly reversed: 'Fortune, Sir, has made you powerful & me impotent; has given you patronage & me dependance' (*Letters* 2, 169).

If Burns thought himself to be under surveillance and near-powerless after 1792, he was by and large correct – and he was not alone. The violence in France and growing unrest in Britain caused Parliament to suspend habeas corpus in 1793 and 1795. Anti-sedition laws and prohibitions on public assembly were enacted and strictly enforced. In 1803, William Blake faced prosecution in England under these repressive laws, accused (by a vindictive soldier Blake had evicted from his garden) of shouting obscenities against King George. Though cleared on inquiry, Blake was shaken; he wrote from Felpham to his friend Thomas Butts in London: 'Every Man is now afraid of speaking to or looking at a Soldier' (Erdman and Bloom, ed., *Complete Poetry and Prose of William Blake*, New York: Doubleday, 1988, p. 733). Unlike Blake, Burns was an employee of the government. When his penchant for political commentary imperilled his Excise position, his satire sought refuge underground in his bawdry. Yet *MMC*, the volume of bawdry that has come down to us as partly the work of Burns, is suspiciously slender: though new evidence has now suggested that Burns wrote many more of the songs in *MMC* than the twenty or so existing in Burns's holograph, a 'violent propensity' would probably have generated even more songs than the whole of *MMC*. Some other works of 'political bawdry' such as this song may well have been destroyed after the poet's death, most probably by the humanitarian but prudish James Currie, Burns's first posthumous editor, who is known to have burned some letters (on request by Burns's correspondents) and who had received Gilbert Burns's permission to do as he wished with the poet's unpublished papers. G. Ross Roy's revised edition of Burns's *Letters*, too, has established that Currie –

who was the first to publish any of Burns's letters – added the disclaimer 'a very few are my own' to a letter of Burns's discussing the songs in *MMC* – a misguided effort to 'protect' the bard's reputation that suggests that Currie might in other ways have concealed (or obliterated) evidence of Burns's authorship of bawdy songs.

Lines 9–10 refer to the Duke of Brunswick (1735–1806), brother of Britain's Queen Charlotte; he led a Prussian and Austrian invasion of France in September 1792 but was defeated at the battle of Valmy (20 September). In l. 16, 'Fredric' is Frederick William II, King of Prussia (1744–97), who conducted campaigns in 1792 and 1793 against republican France. He had a reputation for promiscuity. Catherine II of Russia (1729–96) spent most of her reign attempting to subdue Poland (ll. 24–5): in 1763 she placed Stanislaus Poniatowski (her lover) on its throne; and in 1772 and 1793 she participated with Prussia in its partition. Like Frederick William II, Catherine was reputed to be sexually promiscuous.

In *MMC* (first publication 1799–1800, possibly under the auspices of the Crochallan Fencibles) Burns's stanzas are unsuitably set to 'The Campbells are Comin'.

Logan Water (*Tune: Logan Water*)

Text and music: *SC* (1803), checked against Currie (1800; words without music). Sent in an undated letter to George Thomson, editor of *SC*, perhaps in June 1793.

The letter transmitting these stanzas opens: 'Have you ever felt your bosom ready to burst with indignation, on reading of, or seeing, how these mighty villains . . . divide kingdom against kingdom, desolate provinces & lay Nations waste out of the wantonness of Ambition, or often from still more ignoble passions? – In a mood of this kind today, I recollected the air of Logan Water & it occurred to me that its querulous melody probably had its origin from the plaintive indignation of some swelling, suffering heart, fired at the Tyrannic strides of some Public Destroyer; & overwhelmed with private distresses . . . If I have done anything like justice to my feelings, the following song, composed in three-quarters of an hour's lucubrations in my elbow-chair, ought to have some merit' (*Letters* 2, 217). Burns's speaker is a young woman struggling with loneliness and the responsibilities of child-rearing during her husband's absence as a soldier in a foreign war. In dramatizing this speaker's grief and anxiety, the song also implicitly criticizes the post-1745 British policy of recruiting the ever-diminishing number of remaining male Highlanders into the Scottish regiments of the regular army. Though Burns wrote two further letters urging Thomson to publish this song, the editor evidently feared to because of its social criticism. Words and music were not printed in *SC* until 1803, three years after Currie's publication of the words alone. The air 'Logan Water' was popular from the mid seventeenth century; one set of stanzas in *MMC* is jocular. Burns is accurate, however, in defining its melody as 'querulous' and 'plaintive'. The air is beautifully matched to his stanzas.

In l. 29, 'cruel joys' is oxymoronic in its emphasis on sadistic pleasure taken from inflicting pain. The poet later substituted a weaker line ('How can your flinty hearts enjoy,' printed in *SC*), but his change may be disregarded because Burns proposed it only after Thomson gave his dislike of the original line as his reason for rejecting the song.

O, Whistle an' I'll Come to Ye, My Lad (*Tune: Whistle an' I'll come to ye, my lad*)

Text and music: Dick. The stanzas as printed were sent to George Thomson in a letter probably written on 25 August 1793. A simpler set (not as effectively matched to the air) had appeared in *SMM* 1788:

O whistle, an' I'll come to you, my lad;
O whistle, an' I'll come to you, my lad;
Though father and mither should baith gae mad,
O whistle, an' I'll come to you, my lad.

Come down the back stairs when ye come to court me,
Come down the back stairs when ye come to court me,
Come down the back stairs, and let naebody see;
And come as ye were na' coming to me.

On 3 August 1795, Burns (also in a letter to Thomson) transmitted his final version, which changes the chorus, substituting 'Thy JEANIE will venture wi' ye, my lad' for line four. This personalization of the stanzas, a compliment to Jean Lorimer (see note to 'Sae Flaxen Were Her Ringlets', p. 284), weakens them by introducing an extraneous element. This speaker is too intent on making arrangements to see her lover to be dwelling lovingly on her own name in every chorus.

I have followed Dick (also Ashmead and Davison (217)) in printing the intermediate setting of 1793, which is best matched both to the speaker (a typical Burns heroine in her independence of mind and her air of practical supervision) and the beautiful, vocally challenging air, which was one of Burns's favourite Scots tunes. Its wide range (one note short of two octaves) and heavy ornamentation of trills and Scotch snaps indicate its probable origin as a fiddle-tune; or, despite its irregular and therefore folk-collected sound, the air might have been composed specifically as an operatic song, for stanzas to it appear in the ballad-opera *The Poor Soldier* (1783), the earliest printed record.

The stanzas, neglected today, pleased the Victorians. Anthony Trollope muses on them in *Dr Thorne* (1858), quoting Burns's chorus in full and regretting that the eager acquiescence of Burns's lassies would be a strategic error for his own heroines: 'To love thoroughly, truly, heartily, with her whole body, soul, heart, and strength; should not that be counted for a merit in a woman? And yet we are wont to make a disgrace of it . . . [In our day] it becomes a young lady to be icy-hearted as a river-god in winter' (Chapter 23).

Scots Wha Hae (*Tune: Hey, tutti taitie*)

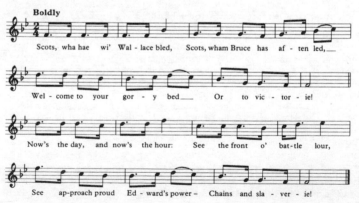

Text: Dick (text and music). Unsigned on its first appearance in the *Morning Chronicle* (8 May 1794); signed under the title 'Robert Bruce's March to Bannockburn' in *SC* 1799; but *SC* printed an inferior set of stanzas altered by Burns to fit 'Lewie Gordon', the air George Thomson preferred. In the volume of *SC* issued in 1803, Thomson finally printed Burns's original words and tune (they had already become popular); but he still tried to draw the lyric's revolutionary sting: 'By changing *wha* into *who*, *hae* into *have*, *wham* into *whom*, *aften* into *often*, and *sae* into *so*, the following Song will be English; and by substituting GALLIA for EDWARD and BRITAIN for SCOTLAND it will be adapted to the present time.'

But the song, as Thomson well knew, was already adapted to the present time. It is a cry for national liberation, lyrically displaced to 1314 and Bannockburn (the mid-summer battle that re-established Scotland as a sovereign nation). The song was written in July or August 1793; possibly it was begun at the earlier date (given by Alexander Cunningham, the poet's companion on that summer's tour of Galloway) but completed by 30 August, the probable date of the letter to George Thomson that first transcribed the stanzas. Burns's letter to Thomson transmitting the song demonstrates with unusual clarity the sequence he followed in setting new stanzas to folk-collected tunes. Most emphatically, the tunes came first:

I am delighted with many little melodies, which the learned Musician despises as silly & insipid. – I do not know whether the old Air, 'Hey tutti taitie', may rank among this number; but well I know that . . . it has often filled my eyes with tears. – There is a tradition, which I have met with in many parts of Scotland, that it was Robert Bruce's March at the battle of Bannock-burn. – This thought, in my yesternight's evening walk, warmed me into a pitch of enthusiasm on the theme of Liberty and Independance, which I threw into a kind of Scots Ode, fitted to the Air . . . P.S. I shewed the air to [Pietro] Urbani [a song-editor Burns knew from Edinburgh and had met again in Galloway]. [He] . . . begged me to make soft verses for it; but I had no idea of giving myself any trouble on the Subject, till the accidental recollection of that glorious struggle for Freedom, associated with some glowing ideas of some other struggles of the same nature, *not quite so ancient*, roused my rhyming Mania'. (*Letters* 2, 235)

Burns's response to Scots music is at its most creative in this song, for 'Hey, tutti taitie' was a typically jovial drinking song. Though the air is undoubtedly very old, Burns's assertion that he took his hint from an oral tradition associating it with Robert Bruce's fourteenth-century campaign for Scottish independence sounds somehow suspect, even though Burns in 1788 had instructed Johnson to insert the same statement after 'Hey, tutti taitie' in *SMM*'s Table of Contents (Vol. 2). The poet knew George Thomson would resist printing an air with 'low' associations, and it would be like Burns to improvise an antiquarian pedigree to disarm his pretentious and mulish editor. (If this was the case, the poet accurately predicted Thomson's resistance; for the editor, who loved the new 'Scots Ode', none the less insisted it be altered to fit a different tune – written by Burns's friend Bishop Geddes – that he thought had more 'grandeur'.)

The main inspiration for 'Scots Wha Hae' may well have been Urbani's ludicrous suggestion that 'soft verses' would suit the tune: Burns appears immediately to have begun a set of 'hard' stanzas. His stanzas fully exploit the energy and defiance inherent in the air, which sounds somehow intransigent: Ashmead and Davison speak of its unusually 'narrow compass' as being 'appropriate for the bagpipe' (246).

Another telling feature of Burns's letter to Thomson is its disclosure that the song's double frame of temporal reference – 1314 and 'not quite so ancient' 1793 – is conscious and intentional. Enjoying the song does not require knowledge of the political upheavals of the 1790s, but understanding Burns's poetic achievement may well require such knowledge – as well as familiarity with the musical, cultural, and literary contexts also addressed in his writings. Burns's habitual multiplicity of reference is easier to see in his satires, but is equally central to his critically neglected later lyrics. It was the critic most attuned to the complexity of Burns's songs, J. C. Dick, who first noted in 1903 that the *Marseillaise*, written in 1792, also takes as its pretext the commemoration of 'an event more than five hundred years old' (449): like Burns's national anthem written some seventeen months later, it addresses the crisis of the present through re-enactment of a glorious past.

A Red, Red Rose (Tune: Major Graham)

Text and music: Dick. Printed in *SMM* 1796; signed R and also headed 'Written for this Work by Robert Burns'. Sent to Alexander Cunningham in November 1793 (JK gives 1794; *Letters* the earlier date).

The song was first printed by Pietro Urbani, a competitor of George Thomson. Burns protested to Thomson that he had never given Urbani permission to publish, but the poet's rather defensive letter to Cunningham enclosing the stanzas suggests otherwise. Burns knew his taste differed from his editor's: 'I would ... most gladly have seen it in our Friend's [Thomson's] publication; but though I am charmed with it, it is a kind of song on which ... I know ... we would think very differently ... – What to me, appears the simple & the wild, to him ... will be looked on as the ludicrous & the absurd' (*Letters* 2, 258–9). 'A

Red, Red Rose' is simpler in diction, more traditional in imagery, than the songs written for Thomson. JK even suggests (despite the double signature in *SMM*) that these stanzas were entirely folk-collected and unrevised (3, 1454–5); and HH concur, saying the posthumous song should not have been signed but instead coded 'Z' – i.e., collected, not revised: 'every single stanza . . . is borrowed' (3, 402).

As Yeats wrote in commenting on this song, however, Burns's stanzas offer more than the sum of their collected folk-parts: Yeats especially admired the repetition of 'red' in Burns's title and opening line, so effective in symbolically expressing both the passion of the speaker and the beauty of his 'luve'. J. C. Dick, who also sees Burns as author of this song, writes: 'like nearly everything he touched, Burns . . . transformed dead or commonplace verses into living, emotional song' (403–4). Ashmead and Davison agree: 'No surviving source . . . – and there are a surprising number – comes anywhere near the mastery of Burns's text' (161).

The debate itself is somewhat falsely grounded, for Burns's authorship does not reside in the originality of his images *per se* but rather in the use he puts them to. His procedure is never a tame, George Thomson-like snipping and tailoring of words to music. As in this song, his first step is evidently the creative projection of a character, a speaker. In this particular song, the speaker adopts the tautological language of ballads: roses are red; water is wet; ten thousand miles is far. But Burns's speaker does so in order to convey as equally rooted in the fundamental nature of things his equally tautological statement that his 'luve' is well beloved. That a single speaker almost always focuses and filters the folk-imagery in this way (to serve his or her own purpose) is the major difference between Burns's songs and traditional folk-songs. There are exceptions (such as 'Tam Lin' or 'Lady Mary Ann', for instance, with their half-submerged balladic characterizations), yet their very rarity among Burns's more than 300 songs serves to prove the rule.

In this song, the redness of the rose is no floating symbol; it is firmly anchored in, the property of, the speaker's mistress; the deepness of the ocean is likewise a property of the speaker's depth of love. By contrast, traditional folk-song works by accretion, not by appropriation: it is not only hospitable to but dependent upon extraneous 'voices', and its often multiple submerged speakers are evocative in part because they remain unidentified. Channelling traditional imagery through (often) highly self-conscious and identified speakers is a practice Burns probably learned from his early vernacular monologues, and also from British contemporary popular song, which had been strongly influenced by ballad-operas following Gay. Popular songs of Burns's day often characterize in something like Burns's fashion; but they do not use folk-collected imagery, aiming (like *The Beggar's Opera*) for a topical rather than an antiquarian effect.

Folklorists (such as Joseph Ritson in Burns's time) usually have disliked the purposiveness imposed by Burns on old and folk-collected material; but whether for good or ill, Burns's intentions are typically incarnated in a character of his own construction. In a traditional folk-song, by contrast, any stanza may initiate a new 'voice' reflecting a different author: a multiplicity of implied viewpoints is how its collectivity expresses itself. Folk-songs also invite auditors to add something new, while Burns's songs – including 'A Red, Red Rose' – seem decidedly 'finished'. Completing a song, Burns once wrote to Thomson, was a matter of 'threshing out the loose sentiments'.

The tradition that this song was addressed to Jean Armour may derive from its musical resemblance to 'Of a' the airts', which was certainly written for her (Dick 404). Neil Gow published 'Major Graham' in 1784: its wide range, which reflects its origin as a fiddle-tune, requires a voice either very well trained or naturally agile. Jean's strong, clear mezzo-soprano was just such a natural voice, and the poet might well have set the tune for her. Ashmead and Davison describe 'Major Graham' (and the similar tune 'Down in the Broom', to which the song is often performed today) as 'leaping, wide-ranging melodies in strathspey rhythm'; they also note that both melodies require 30 per cent more words than Burns provides: 'both are twelve-phrase tunes into which Burns's sixteen line (four quatrain) poem does not fit neatly' (158). Dick's setting has been chosen for the copy-text because of his sensible instruction to repeat the last four lines of both stanzas, which fully 'sets' the words to the music Burns chose. (*SMM* 'puts the first three quatrains under the music, leaving the fourth dangling' (Ashmead and Davison, 158); JK shortens the melody.)

Sae Flaxen Were Her Ringlets (*Tune: Oonagh's Waterfall*)

Text: *SMM* 1796; signed R. Punctuation silently corrected. Sent to George Thomson in September 1794. This is one of twenty-four songs inspired by Jean Lorimer (1775–1831), whom Burns describes in a letter to Thomson (19 October) as 'one of the finest women in Scotland; & in fact (entre nous) is in a manner to me what Sterne's Eliza was to him – a Mistress or Friend, or what you will, in the guileless simplicity of Platonic love' (*Letters* 2, 315). Many of the songs to 'Chloris' were written on behalf of Burns's friend and Excise colleague John Gillespie, who courted her unsuccessfully. Jean Lorimer was, in fact, the toast of the Dumfries Excise: the officers saw a good deal of her because of her parents' persistent efforts to supplement their farming income by smuggling.

She had been married, having eloped at eighteen to Gretna Green with a man named Whelpdale who had abandoned her three weeks later (he was fleeing his creditors). Chloris then returned to her parents shortly before their bankruptcy. Burns's poetic celebration of blonde beauties such as Jean Lorimer (also Helen Park and 'Highland Mary' Campbell) was unusual in his day, when fashion favoured brunettes. George Thomson changed Anna's 'gowden' locks to 'raven' when he printed 'Banks o' Banna' (not in this edition; it was written for Helen Anne Park); the editor also criticized the 'lintwhite locks' of Chloris. Burns would not change the colour of her hair, but did write in 1796 that the pastoral alias had been a mistake: blonde song-heroines, Burns said, should always be given a folk-name: 'on [second thoughts] it is a high incongruity to have a Greek a[ppellation] to a Scotch Pastoral ballad ... [what] you once mentioned of "flaxen" locks is just: th[ey cannot] enter into an *elegant* description of beauty' (*Letters* 2, 376).

This song, often attacked for its artificial diction, has suffered from the general failure to consider Burns's words in conjunction with his music. These stanzas are perfectly matched to an exquisite (and equally elaborate) Irish air. The tune was very popular in Burns's day, but remained unprinted until the poet provided this (in his word) 'decent' set of stanzas. The air's title explains the lack of printed sources: 'Oonagh's Waterfall, or The lock that scattered Oonagh's piss'. The repetition and insistent ardour in the printed stanzas replicate the yearning cadences of this tune. The melody, like the metre, emphasizes 'says' in the final line of each stanza, generating pathos. Does 'Chloris' mean what she says? Does she love him best? This capricious, beautiful adolescent is, like Jean Lorimer herself, much courted by many men; the speaker concludes every stanza of praise with an ambiguous insistence on her faithfulness.

Ode to Spring (*Tune: The Tither Morn*)

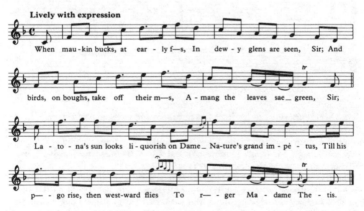

Text: JK 2, 762. Sent to George Thomson in January 1795 in the same letter that transmitted 'Is There for Honest Poverty', which follows this poem.

The poet explains his newest ode: 'For these three thousand years, we poetic folks have been describing the Spring ... & as the Spring continues the same, there must soon be a sameness in the imagery' (*Letters* 2, 335–6). Resolved to 'bring in the verdant fields, – the budding flowers, – the chrystal streams, – the melody of the groves, – & a love-story into the bargain & yet be original', the poet gravely offers Thomson this giddy, good-natured scatological parody of the typical magazine 'Ode to Spring'. The spice of graphic language considerably enlivens the sugar-coated diction of pastoral, which is probably the point Burns was trying to convey to Thomson. For this burlesque seems obliquely aimed at George Thomson's own execrable taste for just such cloyingly anglicized and cliché-ridden lyrics.

The stanzas are perfectly matched to a lively air collected by Burns on one of his Highland tours. 'The Tither Morn' is sometimes wrongly said to be Burns's own musical discovery, but it had appeared in at least three songbooks before its publication (to other stanzas) in *SMM*. Burns's stanzas appeared neither in *SMM* nor in *SC*; they first were printed in 1799–1800 in *MMC*, wrongly set to 'Push about the Jorum'.

Is There for Honest Poverty (*Tune: For a' that*)

Text: Dick, reprinting stanzas from Currie (1800) and air from *SMM* (1790). Sent to *SC* in a letter dated January 1795, though Thomson, fearful of controversy, did not print it until 1805, after it had become popular. It did appear in *The Glasgow Magazine* (1795), *The Oracle* (June 1796), and *The Scots Magazine* (August 1797), and was issued as a chapbook in Paisley (1796).

The stanzas are set to an old tune traditionally matched to bawdy or Jacobite lyrics; Burns draws on these subversive associations. He also draws on Thomas Paine's *The Rights of Man* (1791–2), the work that led to Paine's indictment for treason and his flight to republican France. The poet slights his stanzas in transmitting them to Thomson. 'A great critic, Aikin on songs, says, that Love & Wine are the exclusive themes for song-writing. – The following is on neither subject, & consequently is no Song; but will be allowed, I think, to be two or three pretty good *prose* thoughts, inverted into rhyme' (*Letters* 2, 336). This deprecation might well stem from the poet's fear, well grounded in Burns's foreknowledge of his editor's foibles, that George Thomson would find his new republican anthem just as unpublishable as 'Ode to Spring', the parody that accompanied it. Ashmead and Davison note the superb fit of the tune to the sentiments: 'Whenever a melody centers on . . . one clear-cut pitch as its tonic (the usual eighteenth century procedure) we might perhaps label that a hierarchical tonic. But [this] . . . tune . . . with [its] competing and ambiguous tonics – not uncommon in the Scots repertory – could perhaps be called anti-hierarchical, and seems somehow appropriate to its . . . words' (264).

Lines Written on Windows of the Globe Inn, Dumfries

Text: Stewart 1802. The dates of composition and transcription are not known. The Globe, still operating as an inn today, was Burns's favourite 'howff' throughout his years at Dumfries; these versicles might have been scratched on its window-panes at any time between 1790 and 1796. The poet's diamond-tipped pen had been a gift from the Earl of Glencairn (d. 1791).

I Murder Hate

Text: Stewart 1802 (first eight lines); final stanza (omitted by Stewart) from Dick. Lines 1–8 were inscribed on a window of the Globe inn, Dumfries, and might have been transcribed at any time between 1790 and 1796. The date of composition of the final stanza is not known.

With the exception of battle-songs set early in Scottish history (particularly songs about Wallace, who always inspired a fiery rhetoric), Burns refuses to romanticize the violence of warfare (or even of blood sports). He invariably deletes or makes ironic all references to the glories of battle, even when revising popular songs whose speakers or heroes are soldiers. 'Glory's name may screen us', but foreign wars (fought, in Burns's view, by poor men acting as proxies for the rich) bring only destruction and sorrow. True heroes seek the antithesis of war: the creation of new life at home. The poet was not a pacifist: he believed in national defence and served in the Dumfries militia during the 1790s. Still, his military service may have been intended in part to disarm local hostility to his politics; and one of his last requests (ignored) was that he not be given a military funeral. In fact, Burns was probably buried in the same Dumfries Volunteers uniform for which a 'rascal of a Haberdasher' was dunning him as he lay dying.

Socrates drank hemlock, Leonidas died attempting to hold the pass at Thermopylae for Sparta, and Cato committed suicide to protest Caesar's destruction of the Roman republic: all were martyrs of the classical world. The alternative heroic martyrdom Burns proposes is Scriptural: the Lord approved Phineas's slaying (and genital mutilation) of Zimri, a prince of the tribe of Simeon, and Cosbi, a Madianite princess, during the act of fornication.

Kirkcudbright Grace

Text: JK; first printed in Chambers and Wallace (1896). Collected early in the nineteenth century by James Grierson of Dalgoner; exact date of composition is not known. This is the most famous of the extempore graces that have come down to us. There were probably more, as the poet was often asked to improvise a blessing when he dined out. All of Burns's graces are simple and brief, reflecting his dislike of the 'hauf-mile' graces of the Auld Licht.

Last May a Braw Wooer (Tune: *The Lothian Lassie*)

Text: Currie 1801 (words only); his title ('Scottish Ballad') has been changed. Music from *SMM* 1803; numerous errors in the *SMM* stanzas suggest that Johnson was working from a faulty transcript. Sent to George Thomson in a letter dated 3 July 1795; first printed in *Scottish Airs* (1799).

Like the heroine of 'Tam Glen', this young speaker is formidably voluble, rapidly relating the unfolding drama of her courtship. The unusual five-line stanza – quatrains or octaves are the rule – matches a tune that imposes a lilting repetition in the extra line, used by Burns to convey the speaker's excitement (and relief) at catching her suitor after all, despite his mock-flirtation with her cousin. The lovers' exultant exchange of vows is comically counterpointed by their mutual tendency to mild swearing and oath-making: 'For Gudesake!'; 'deil tak his taste'; 'the deuce gae w'm'. This speaker is jealous, teasing, saucy, transparently prevaricating ('I said there was naething I hated like men') and thoroughly engaging. In Burns's songs, love-sickness is usually demonstrated by a speaker's obsessive dwelling on the name of the beloved. This song's bright-eyed lassie, absorbed in the tactics and strategy of the hunt itself, never names her lover – except as her rightful possession ('my wooer'). We do learn that he is 'braw' and sufficiently well-to-do; that he has the good sense to admire the speaker and the wit to trick her into admitting that she likes him.

Earlier stanzas to the tune ('The Lothian Lassie') had told a similar story, but with less dramatic verve:

> The Queen o' the Lothians cam cruisin to Fife
> > Fal de ral, lal de ral, lairo,
> To see gin a wooer wad tak her for life,
> > Sing hey fal de ral &c. (Dick 419)

The vehement energy of the speaker and the lively, easily singable tune make this song among Burns's most frequently performed.

In l. 18 'up the Gateslack' is 'up the lang loan' in the copy-text, a change made to accommodate George Thomson. 'Gateslack ... is positively the name of a particular place, a kind of passage up among the Lawther hills, on the confines of this County,' wrote the poet, responding to Thomson's criticism that the reference was obscure (*Letters* 2, 363; 3 August 1795). The same letter explains the reference in l. 22 to the 'tryste [assembly] o' Dalgarnock': 'a romantic spot, near the Nith, where are still a ruined Church, & a burial place'.

Wantonness (Tune: Wantonness)

Text and music: *SMM* 1796; unsigned. The date of composition is unknown, but probably 1795 or 1796. JK rejects this text, calling it collected rather than composed by Burns. Stenhouse, Dick, and HH argue for the poet's authorship. As in 'A Red, Red Rose', the imagery is clearly folk-collected; and that the stanzas and the air have identical titles also suggests that Burns worked with existing fragments, though none has come down to us. My reasons for thinking this Burns's own work are twofold: the use of first-person dramatization (third person is much more frequent in old folk-songs), and the elegance with which the words and sentiments are matched to the haunting music.

Charlie He's My Darling (Tune: Charlie he's my darling)

Text and music: *SMM* 1796; unsigned. Punctuation silently corrected. The date of composition is unknown, but probably 1795 or 1796. The holograph MS is in the British Library (Hastie MS). The song is not quite the 'pure original' Dick called it; in 1903, the same year Dick published his work on Burns's songs, Otto Ritter reported his discovery of a broadside ballad of 1775 that Burns radically abridges here, transposing it into lyric form. Burns's version is light and lilting, like its air (collected by Burns and first published in 1796). The stanzas see the '45 Jacobite rising from the perspective of Edinburgh lassies dazzled by 'Charlie and his men' during their brief but triumphant occupation of the city (September–November 1745).

It Was a' for Our Rightfu' King (*Tune: Mally Stewart*)

It__ was a'__ for our__ right-fu'__ king We left fair__ Scot-land's strand; It was a'____ for our right-fu'__ king, We__ e'er saw I-rish__ land, my dear, We__ e'er saw I-rish__ land.

Text and music: *SMM* 1796; unsigned. The date of composition is unknown, but probably 1795 or 1796. As JK notes, Burns usually did not sign his Jacobite songs (3, 1515). A holograph copy is included in the Cowie Collection, the Mitchell Library (Glasgow).

A chapbook ballad, 'Mally Stewart', supplied the imagery in stanza three; and a seventeenth-century English air, 'The Bailiff's Daughter of Islington', was altered slightly to supply the tune. Dick says, 'The rest of Burns's song owes nothing to the original, except the rhythm' (470). Burns alternates implied viewpoints (as his source did), but changes the tone from comedy to pathos. His despairing and defeated Jacobite soldier faces life in exile, while the woman he has left behind – and will never see again – lies awake and grieves. The authoritative, simple diction is well matched to a slow, pathetic air.

Oh Wert Thou in the Cauld Blast (*Tune: Lenox Love to Blantyre*)

Text: Currie 1801 (words only); his title ('Address to a Lady') has been changed. Music from Dick. The song, completed in the spring or summer of 1796 during Burns's last illness, was written for Jessie Lewars (1778–1855), sister of an Excise colleague and friend of the poet's. From January 1796, she helped to nurse Burns and also helped Jean (who was experiencing a difficult pregnancy) with the children. Following the poet's death and Jean's ensuing illness and grief, Jessie Lewars took all the Burns children except newborn Maxwell into her brother's house: nine-year-old Robert stayed with her for a year.

The poet, intent on a gesture of thanks for the girl's kindness, asked her to sing her favourite song for him: he then set new stanzas to it in her honour. (She must have had an excellent voice, for the range of 'Lenox Love to Blantyre' is nearly two octaves.) The silly original stanzas describe a robin's comic courtship of a coy wren. Burns's speaker likewise pledges faithfulness and a self-denying, chivalrous protection; but he does so in all earnestness: the arch whimsy of the original is changed to pathos. Like so many of Burns's best works, this touching song was inspired by a real-life relationship that the poet none the less stylizes and idealizes: for it was he who was receiving the affectionate care that his song pledges to young Jessie. Jessie Lewars married James Thomson, an attorney's clerk, in 1799; they reared seven children (*BE*).

Chronological Sketch: Scottish History and Literature Before Burns

1004	Feudal system is established by Malcolm II, whose victory over the Northumbrians at the battle of Carham (*c.* 1016) wins for Scotland the lands between the Forth and the Tweed.
1040	Duncan I is killed by his general, Macbeth, during a civil war.
c. 1080	Anglo-Saxon language is introduced through the influence of Queen Margaret.
1200s?	Poems and prophecies by Thomas the Rhymer.
March 1286	Alexander III of Scotland dies suddenly, survived only by his infant granddaughter, Margaret ('Maid of Norway'), who herself dies in September 1290 while travelling from Norway to Scotland.
1292	John Balliól and Robert Bruce are the closest legitimate heirs to Alexander III. Both are descendants of the Earl of Huntingdon, youngest son of David I (d. 1153). John Balliol is the grandson of Huntingdon's eldest daughter. (It was John Balliol's mother who founded the Oxford college.)
	Robert Bruce is the son of Huntingdon's second daughter. Rejecting primogeniture, Bruce argues that a grandson's claim to the throne is stronger than that of a great-grandson.
	(November) Edward I of England, intent on annexing Scotland, supports Balliol, but as his vassal. Within three years, Balliol rebels. In retaliation, Edward I claims Scotland.
1296	Edward I seizes the stone of Scone and carries it (and the Scottish muniments) to London.
September 1297	William Wallace (*c.* 1270–1305), outlawed – according to the metrical history of Blind Harry – for killing an Englishman following an insult, defeats Edward's army at Stirling bridge. Wallace becomes guardian of John Balliol; hence, of Scotland.
July 1298	Edward I defeats Wallace at Falkirk. Following the death at Falkirk of his comrade Sir John deGraham, Wallace resigns the guardianship of Scotland and resumes his raids on England.
August 1305	Wallace, captured and brought to trial for treason against England, is executed in London at Smithfield.

March 1306	Robert Bruce (grandson of the original claimant (d. 1295)) stabs John Comyn ('the Red'; current leader of the Balliols) during a parley in a Dumfries churchyard that ends in a quarrel. Despite his pending excommunication for sacrilege, Robert Bruce is crowned at Scone.
June 1314	Robert Bruce defeats the English army of Edward II at Bannockburn, the setting of Burns's 'Scots Wha Hae' and the most decisive military victory over the English ever won by the Scots.
1328	With the treaty of Northampton, England (led by the regents of Edward III), finally acknowledges Bruce's victory, re-establishing the sovereignty of Scotland.
1376	'Bruce', epic by John Barbour.
1388	Battle of Otterburn ('Chevy Chase').
1413	University of St Andrews founded.
1450	University of Glasgow founded.
c. 1475	Robert Henryson, a schoolmaster (probably in the Benedictine abbey school at Dunfermline), writes *Moral Fables, The Testament of Cresseid*, and other poems in middle-Scots.
1494	Kings College (Aberdeen) is founded.
1503	James IV of Scotland marries Margaret, eldest daughter of England's Henry VII, a union celebrated by the poet William Dunbar (c. 1460 – c. 1520) in 'The Thistle and the Rose'.
September 1513	James IV of Scotland, invading England, is killed at Flodden Field.
December 1542	Birth of Mary Stuart, whose father James V dies one week later.
1557–60	John Knox brings the Protestant Reformation to Scotland, decentralizing church governance: there are no bishops in the Scottish kirk. In August 1560, the Scottish Parliament repudiates papal authority and abolishes the Mass.
1561	Death of Francis II of France, Mary Stuart's husband. The Catholic queen returns to Scotland after thirteen years in France.
1563	Elizabeth I of England, Mary's first cousin once removed, commissions an inquiry into the number of Scots in London. According to Catholic thinking, Elizabeth – though the granddaughter of Henry VII – is illegitimate, being the child of a marriage subsequent to divorce: Mary, though a great-granddaughter, would to a Catholic have the stronger claim to the English throne. But local Scotsmen pose no threat to Elizabeth: her census locates only fifty-eight living in London in 1563.

1565	Ignoring the advice of her half-brother, the Earl of Moray, Mary Stuart marries her cousin Henry, Lord Darnley, who follows Mary in the line of English succession.
March 1566	Murder of David Rizzio, Mary Stuart's secretary.
June 1566	Birth of James Stuart to Mary.
February 1567	Darnley is assassinated.
May 1567	Mary Stuart marries the Earl of Bothwell, probable murderer of Darnley.
June 1567	After a defeat at Carberry Hill, Mary Stuart is forced to resign her crown to her infant son James (who will be reared as a Protestant). The Earl of Moray becomes regent.
1582	Edinburgh University founded.
February 1587	Mary Stuart is beheaded after almost twenty years of captivity. Burns's reading of Mary as tragic figure representative of Scottish history is offered in 'Lament of Mary Queen of Scots'.
1593	Marishal College (Aberdeen) founded.
March 1603	Union of Crowns. Probably the most significant date in Scottish literary history. James VI (Mary's son) becomes James I of Great Britain and the Scottish court moves to London. No Scottish king will again reside permanently in Scotland.
	This begins the decline of literary Scots, brought to perfection in the work of Dunbar and Henryson. In London, James turns from Scottish literature, becoming the patron of Donne and Jonson. In Scotland, the vernacular becomes increasingly associated with the provincial, the rustic: with those too poor to travel down to London with the court.
	The last of the court-sustained Scottish poets, William Drummond of Hawthornden (1585–1649), rejects the Scots almost entirely, turning to English and Latin.
1637	Charles I – son of James I (d. 1625) – is, as his father had been, intent on reinstituting the Scottish bishops. Jenny Geddes, an old lady of Edinburgh, speaks for most Scots when she throws her stool at the newly appointed 'Bishop of Edinburgh' during a service at St Giles. (One hundred and fifty years later, Burns names his horse 'Jenny Geddes'.)
1651	Scotland becomes part of the Commonwealth after Cromwell's victories at Dunbar and Worcester.
1661	Charles II, restored to the throne, re-establishes bishops in the Church of Scotland.
1688	James II, the younger brother who has succeeded Charles II (d. 1685), is forced into exile. A professed Catholic, James has (by a second wife) produced a male heir. Parliament, led by the Whig lords, rebels against a Catholic succession.

1689   William and Mary become rulers of Great Britain. Presbyterian Scottish Lowlanders largely accept the expulsion of Catholic James, for William and Mary are Protestants. The new Queen is a grown daughter of James by his first wife; King William is a Dutch warrior-prince. Many Highlanders, however, are Gaelic-speaking Catholics who join the armies of James II at the Boyne in Ireland. They are defeated by King William's armies. The Jacobite wars ('Jacobus' being Latin for James) begin.

        Burns's 'It Was a' for Our Rightfu' King' is set in Ireland after the battle of the Boyne and contains a vignette of a defeated warrior (perhaps James himself) riding down the shore to meet the boat that would carry him to exile: 'He turn'd him right and round about/ Upon the Irish shore,/ And gae his bridle-reins a shake,/Wi' adieu, forevermore.' Many other songs by Burns mention this war: 'Killiecrankie', for instance, describes the rout of a well-equipped Whig army by a small band of claymore-wielding Highlanders led by Viscount Dundee, who was, however, killed in the battle (July 1689).

April 1690   Establishment of the Church of Scotland; repeal of the laws requiring bishops.

February 1692   Massacre at Glencoe of nearly forty Macdonalds, in retaliation for the clan's delayed expression of allegiance to William and Mary.

1707   The Union of Parliaments with England; after the Union of Crowns, the event in Scottish history with the strongest impact on literature.

        The centre of political power and patronage passes from Edinburgh to London, and from 1707 an increasing number of Scotsmen move to London.

        Scotland's legal and monetary institutions remain distinct and continue to be based in Edinburgh. From this time, the most powerful residents of Edinburgh are often lawyers or judges: among literary figures, these include James Boswell (and his father), Henry Mackenzie, and Sir Walter Scott. University professors, clergymen, and gentleman scholars make up the other great class of Edinburgh's élite, the 'literati'.

1714   Queen Anne, the younger of James II's Protestant daughters, dies without an heir.

1715   James Stuart (James III and VIII; the Old Pretender) – in 1688 the infant heir who precipitated the Whig Revolution – invades Britain when Parliament names George of Hanover (the 'wee, wee German lairdie' of Jacobite invective) king. The Hanoverians are supported by most Presbyterian Lowlanders, who fear a Catholic succession. The Stuart cause, however, continues to find support among Highlanders, episcopalian Scots in the north-east, Catholics in all regions of Britain, and some Tories sceptical of the legality of Parliament's expulsion of James II in 1688. Scotland's Earl of Mar swears allegiance to James Stuart. The battle of Sheriffmuir, commemorated in one of Burns's best songs, occurs during this brief but bitter Jacobite conflict.

c. 1720   Allan Ramsay (*c.* 1685–1758), a wigmaker about to become a publisher, with William Hamilton of Gilbertfield (*c.* 1665–1751) initiates the eighteenth-century Scots vernacular revival.

Since shortly after the Union of Parliaments, Ramsay has been publishing poems in the Scottish dialect, largely to challenge the notion of its provinciality. Well acquainted with the work of London poets ranging from Matthew Prior and John Gay to Alexander Pope, Ramsay sees the Scots as a vigorous 'Doric' well suited to verse-epistle, pastoral, satire, lyric, and other Augustan occasional genres. The revival gains momentum following an exchange of lively vernacular epistles between Ramsay and Hamilton of Gilbertfield (1719), the publication of Ramsay's first collection of poems (1721), and the immense popularity throughout Britain of his songbook series *The Tea Table Miscellany* (1724–37) and his Scottish pastoral *The Gentle Shepherd* (1725), which, following the success of Gay's *Beggar's Opera* (1728), was recast as a ballad-opera.

1745–6   James Stuart's son, Prince Charles Edward ('Bonnie Prince Charlie') raises an army in Scotland. At first he is successful, but following his defeat at Culloden in April 1746, the Jacobite cause is crushed. The Highlands are fortified; the wearing of tartan is proscribed; the episcopal clergy are severely penalized. William Burnes, the poet's father, emigrates from Kincardineshire to Edinburgh in 1748, a casualty of the economic hardships in the north-east following Culloden.

'Charlie is My Darling', 'O'er the Water to Charlie', 'Farewell to the Highlands', and even 'Auld Lang Syne' are songs by Burns that echo the cultural impact of this final Jacobite war, which resulted in mass emigrations to North America and the Caribbean. In 'The Author's Earnest Cry and Prayer', Burns records his distaste for the postwar British policy that recruited starving survivors of the '45 into Scottish regiments of the regular army.

1750   Birth of Robert Fergusson (d. 1774), Burns's nearest and greatest Scottish vernacular predecessor. Fergusson's poems, despite their sardonic point and technical brilliance, never become popular: his dialect lacks the genial accessibility either of Ramsay or Burns.

In 1787, soon after arriving in Edinburgh, Robert Burns arranges for the monument and epitaph that still mark Fergusson's grave.

1759   Robert Burns is born.

Glossary

The language of Burns's songs presents few difficulties even for those unfamiliar with Scottish dialect. But readers new to Burns may be intimidated by the number of unfamiliar words in his satires and longer poems. Yet Burns's most distinctive stylistic trait may well be his repetition (often in compound phrases) of nearly equivalent words. Often, an unfamiliar Scots word will be paired with its English equivalent: 'kiaugh and care', 'furms and benches', 'decent, honest, fawsont' (fawsont means decent). Serial synonyms occasionally are in a single language, most often English ('insipid, dull an' tasteless'). With the occasional all-Scottish word-cluster, it is useful to remember that the grouped words are often similar in meaning, and that one or more of the dialect words will usually be cognate with (or very lightly disguised) English: 'brawnie and bainie'. In other cases, the sound of the words is a guide to their sense ('bickering brattle').

The words in this glossary fall into two basic categories. The core words are those Burns uses repeatedly: bonie and wee, but also such words as blink, glowr, lour (and many other words for varieties of eye-contact), braw, chiel, skelp, sonsie, callan, carlin, brae, etc. The words most often used by Burns refer to natural beauty and ugliness, physical activities and body processes, home-life and homelessness, weather and the landscape, food and drink, degrees of relationship (and friendship or enmity) within families and communities, and words for feelings and emotions: they soon become familiar because the poet introduces them repeatedly. The second group, on the other hand – and it comprises a high percentage of words in this glossary – is made up of words Burns uses only once or twice. These are words conjured up out of the exigencies of a particular rhyme-scheme, metre, speaker, or subject-matter, specific to that context and in some cases never again seen out of it. Examples are smeddum, kist (for tradesman's counter), studdie, foggage, braxies, gizz, fatt'rels, baws'nt, leister. This second group is made up largely of technical terms – names of tools or farming equipment or terms from animal husbandry; it also is comprised of words not at all rustic but drawn from eighteenth-century theology, fashion, law and finance, medicine, even ballooning. As with specialized words in any language, this second class of dialect words may well fade from exact knowledge and memory, and require occasional use of a glossary even among those familiar with Burns and the dialect.

Although the glossary clarifies what the poems say, readers themselves must still decide what they mean. Burns's dialect words in themselves are not difficult, but his use of them in context is often slyly 'sidelins-sklentin'. His word-clusters and parallel phrases, for instance, may set unlike things blandly together, as when Holy Willie prays he may continue to shine for 'gear and grace'. The glossary tells us only that 'gear' means worldly goods; the poet's meaning (once we know the definition of 'gear') comes in our sudden, comically horrified recognition of Willie's corrupted grammar and logic, which makes no distinction between saving money and saving grace.

Quotation marks around a definition in the glossary indicate that it was taken directly from *Poems* 1787 (Edinburgh), designed to be sold outside as well as within Scotland and so provided with a detailed glossary. (Burns seems to have been amused by the task: few of his entries are perfunctory.) Burns's own glosses are supplemented or (if the word was not glossed in 1787) supplied by several other glossaries, identified in brackets: [JK] for James Kinsley's edition of Burns's works, [Dick] for J. C. Dick's, [*OED*] for colloquial eighteenth-century English words requiring a gloss because they are no longer current, and, finally, [AR] for a 1721 glossary compiled by Allan Ramsay and appended to his *Poems*. Glosses not followed by a source in brackets are composites from the sources just named. The sources have been tapped selectively: entries for this volume print only shades of meaning relevant to this selection. For full references, seek the originals or the *Scottish National Dictionary*.

Some general guidelines for recognizing English/Scots cognates (words lightly veiled by differences in spelling) precede the main glossary. Burns prefaced his own glossary with brief comments on pronunciation, but they are somewhat inscrutable. The clearer directions provided below are taken verbatim from Allan Ramsay's *Poems* (1721), mentioned above – a work aimed (like Ramsay's later songbook series *The Tea Table Miscellany*) for an audience beyond as well as within Scotland:

Some general rules, shewing wherein many southern and northern words are originally the same, having only a letter changed for another, or sometimes one taken away or added.

I. In many words ending with 'l' after an 'a' or 'u', the 'l' is rarely sounded.

Scots	English
A'	All
Ba	Ball
Ca	Call
Ga	Gall
Ha	Hall
Sma	Small
Sta	Stall
Wa	Wall
Fou or Fu	Full
Pou or Pu	Pull
Woo or U [sic]	Wool

II. The 'l' changes to 'a' 'w' or 'u' after 'o' or 'a' and is frequently sunk before another consonant; as,

Scots	English
Bauk	Baulk
Bawm	Balm
Bow	Boll
Bowt	Bolt
Caff	Calf
Cow	Coll, or Clip

Fause	False
Faut	Fault
Fawn	Fallen
Fowk	Folk
Gowd	Gold
Haff	Half
How	Hole, or Hollow
Howms	Holms
Maut	Malt
Pow	Poll
Row	Roll
Scawd	Scold
Stown	Stolen
Wawk	Walk

III. An 'o' before 'ld' changes to 'a' or 'au'; as,

Scots	English
Auld	Old
Bauld	Bold
Cauld	Cold
Fauld	Fold
Hald or Had	Hold
Sald	Sold
Tald	Told
Wad	Would

IV. The 'o' 'oe' 'ow' is changed to 'a' 'ae' or 'ai'; as,

Scots	English
Ae or Ane	One
Aff	Off
Aften	Often
Aik	Oak
Ain or Awn	Own
Aith	Oath
Alane	Alone
Amaist	Almost
Amang	Among
Airs	Oars
Aites	Oats
Apen	Open
Awner	Owner
Bain	Bone
Bair	Bore
Baith	Both
Blaw	Blow
Braid	Broad
Claith	Cloth
Craw	Crow
Drap	Drop

Fae	Foe
Frae	Fro or From
Gae	Go
Gaits	Goats
Grane	Groan
Hait, or Het	Hot
Hale	Whole
Halesome	Wholesome
Haly	Holy
Hame	Home
Laid	Load
Lain, or Len	Loan
Laith	Loth [Loath]
Lang	Long
Law	Low
Mae	Moe
Maist	Most
Mair	More
Mane	Moan
Maw	Mow
Na	No
Naething	Nothing
Nane	None
Pape	Pope
Rae	Roe
Raip [Raep]	Rope
Rair	Roar
Raw	Row
Saft	Soft
Saip	Soap
Sair	Sore
Sang	Song
Saul	Soul
Slaw	Slow
Snaw	Snow
Staw	Stole
Stane	Stone
Strake [Straik]	Stroak [Stroke]
Tae	Toe
Taiken	Token
Tangs	Tongs
Tap	Top
Thrang	Throng
Wae	Woe
Wame	Womb
Wan	Won
War	Worse
Wark	Work
Warld	World
Wha	Who

V. The 'o' or 'u' is frequently changed into 'i' as,

Scots	English
Anither	Another
Bill	Bull
Birn	Burn
Brither	Brother
Fit	Foot
Fither	Father
Hinny	Honey
Ither	Other
Mither	Mother
Nits	Nuts
Nise	Nose
Pit	Put
Rin	Run
Sin	Sun

abiegh: 'at a shy distance'
aboon: 'above, up'
abread (abreed): 'abroad'
ae: one
aff: 'off'
aff-loof: 'unpremeditated'; offhand
afore: 'before'
aft: 'oft'
agley: 'off the right line, wrong'
aiblens (aiblins): 'perhaps'
aik: oak
ain: 'own'
airn: 'iron'
airt: point of the compass; to direct, direction
aith: 'an oath'
aits: 'oats'
aiver: 'an old horse'
amaist: 'almost'
ance: 'once'
ane: 'one'
anither: 'another'
a' run deils: through-going devils [JK]; all-round devils
asklent: askew, off the plumb, on the side, awry
aspar: aspread, with legs apart [JK]
aught: 'eight; possession, as *in a' my aught*, in all my possession'
auld: 'old'
auldfarran: 'sagacious, cunning, prudent'
aumous (aumos) dish: alms-dish or poor-box
ava: 'at all'
awkart: 'awkward'
awnie: 'bearded'
ay: always, ever; the word of assent
ayont: 'beyond'

babie-clouts: baby-clothes (including childbed linen)
backlins-comin: 'coming back, returning'
baiginet: bayonet
bailie (baillie): collection-agent for a landlord; also, a borough officer
    corresponding to an alderman [JK]
bair: bare, uncover, clear [JK]
bairn: 'a child'
bairn-time: 'a family of children, a brood'
baith: 'both'
bake: biscuit [*OED*]
ban': band (clerical collar)
bane: 'bone'
banie: 'having large bones, stout'
bardie: '*dimin.* of bard'
barefit: 'bare-footed'
barket (barkit): 'barked'
barm: yeast
barmie: 'of or like barm'; fermenting with ideas [JK]
batts: 'botts'; colic
bauld: 'bold'
bauldly: 'boldly'
bawbie (bawbee): a Scots coin, originally worth six pennies, later a half-pence
baws'nt: 'having a white stripe down the face'
bawtie: name given to a dog; cf. Fr. *baud*, white hound [JK]
bear (beir): barley
bear the gree: 'to be decidedly victor'
beese: vermin [JK]
beet: 'to add fuel to the fire'
belang: belong
ben: 'into the spence or parlour'; inside
benmost: innermost
bestead: placed, circumstanced [JK]
beuk: 'a book'
bicker: 'a kind of wooden dish; a short race'; a beaker or ale-pot; rush; flow
biel (bield): 'shelter'
bien: 'wealthy, plentiful'
bienly: comfortably, warmly, snugly
big: 'to build'
biggin: 'a building, a house'
biggit: 'builded'
bill: 'a bull'
billie: 'a brother, a young fellow'
birk: birch [Dick]
birkie: 'a clever fellow'; a conceited fellow
birsie: bristle, hair [JK]
bit: 'crisis, nick of time'; also (without 'of') a quasi-adjective indicating littleness,
    affection, contempt [JK]
bizz: 'a bustle, to buzz'
blastet (blastit): 'blasted'
blastie: 'a shrivelled dwarf, a term of contempt'

blate: 'bashful, sheepish'

blather: 'bladder'

blaud: 'a flat piece of any thing; to slap'; also specimen, piece [JK]

blaw: 'to blow, to boast'

bleezan: 'blazing'

blellum: idle babbler [JK]

blether: 'to talk idly, nonsense'

bleth'ran: 'talking idly'

blink: 'a little while, a smiling look, to look kindly, to shine by fits'; an amorous look, a glance, a short space of time [Dick]

blinkan (blinkin): 'smirking'

blinker: 'a term of contempt'; spies, cheats, flirtatious girls

blue-boram: *see* tipt you off blue boram

bluid: 'blood'

bluidy: 'bloody'

bluntie: fool; having a sheepish look, a stupid or simple person

boddle (bodle): 'a small old coin'

bogle: ghost, hobgoblin

bonie (bony): 'handsome, beautiful'

boord: surface, layer (of ice) [JK]

boord-en: head of the table

boortree, *pl.* boortries: 'the shrub elder, planted much of old in hedges of barnyards &c.'

boost: 'behoved, must needs'; must, ought

bore: crevice, crack [JK]

botches: 'an angry tumour'

bouk: bulk, the whole body, body, carcass

bouse (bowse): to booze, to drink heavily

brae: 'a declivity, a precipice, the slope of a hill'; the bank of a river

braid: 'broad'

braik: 'a kind of harrow'

braing't (braindg't): 'to run rashly forward'

brak: 'broke, made insolvent'

branks: 'a kind of wooden curb for horses'; wherewith the rustics bridle their horses [AR]

brash: 'a sudden illness'

brats: 'coarse clothes, rags'

brattle: 'a short race, hurry, fury'; noise, as of horse-feet [AR]

braw: 'fine, handsome'; brave, fine in apparel [AR]

brawlie (brawly): 'very well, finely, heartily'

braxie: the flesh of a braxy sheep; i.e., dead of disease or by accident yet still edible [*OED*]

breastet: 'did spring up or forward'

breef: 'an invulnerable or irresistible spell'

breeks: 'breeches'; trousers

brent: smooth, unwrinkled, high [Dick]; brought

brie: 'juice, liquid'

brier (breer): 'the brier, to sprout'

brisket: breast [JK]

brock: badger

brogue: cheat, trick (*OED* records usages throughout Britain from 1537 to 1791)
broose: 'a race at country weddings who shall first reach the bridegroom's house on returning from church'
brosse: raw oatmeal mixed with water [Dick]
brugh: 'a burgh', town or city
brulzie: 'a broil, a combustion'; hence, a hot debate or quarrel
brunstane: brimstone
brunt: 'did burn'
buckler: strap of a helmet [*OED*]
budget: leather workman's bag [*OED*]
buirdly: 'stout made, broad built'
bum: hum
bum-clock: 'a humming beetle that flies in the summer evening'
bumming: 'humming as bees'
bumper: a cup or glass of wine filled to the brim, especially when drunk as a toast [*OED*]
burdies: ladies, girls; *lit.* little birds, hens
bure: 'did bear'
burn: 'water, a rivulet; burnie, dimin. of burn'
burnan (burnin): burning
Burnewin: 'a blacksmith'
buskit: 'dressed'
bussle: 'a bustle, to bustle'
but: 'without'
butt an' ben: 'the country kitchen and parlour'
byke: a beehive, a crowd or swarm

ca': 'to call, to name, to drive'
caddie (cadie): 'a person, a young fellow'
cadger: 'a carrier'
caff: 'chaff'
caird: tinker, gipsy
calf-ward: 'a small enclosure for calves'
callan: 'a boy'
caller (callor): 'fresh, sound'
callet: a dirty woman, a trull, a drab
cam: 'did come'
can: a very large vessel, usually larger than a drinking vessel, for holding liquids [*OED*]
canie (cantie, canty): 'chearful, merry'
cankart (cankert): bad-tempered, soured; passionately snarling [AR]
canna: 'cannot'
cannie (canny): 'gentle, mild, dextrous'
cannilie: 'dextrously, gently'
cantan: canting, or use of pietistic phrases, hypocritical talk [*OED*]
cantharidian: 'made of cantharides'; spanish fly, considered an aphrodisiac [*OED*]
cantie (canty, canie): 'chearful, merry'
cantraip: 'a charm, a spell'
cape-stane: 'copestone, keystone'
care na by: do not care [Dick]

caressan: 'caressing'

carl: fellow, old man, churl, peasant; an old word for a man [AR]

carlin: old woman, shrew, witch

cartes: 'cards'

cauld: 'cold'

caup: 'a wooden drinking vessel'

cavie: a hen-coop

cess: to tax, the land-tax

change-house: small alehouse or inn [OED]

chantan: 'chanting'

chanters: 'a part of a bagpipe'

chap: 'a person, a fellow, a blow'

chapman billies: brother pedlars (purveyors of chapbooks)

cheek-for-chow: 'side by side'

cheel (chiel): 'a young fellow'

chimla: 'or chimlie, a fire grate'

chows her cood: 'to chew the cud'

chuck: a chicken, a dear, a sweetheart

chuffie: 'fat-faced'

cits: a pert low townsman; a pragmatical tradesman [Samuel Johnson]

clachan: 'a small village about a church; a hamlet'

claes (claise): 'cloaths' (clothes)

claith: 'cloth'

clap: 'clapper of a mill'

clark: scholarly

clarket: written up [JK]

clarty: sticky, dirty [JK]

clash: 'an idle tale, the story of the day'

clatter: 'to tell little idle stories, an idle story'

claut: clutch, grip, handful, lump [JK]

clautet: 'scraped'

claw: 'to scratch'

claymore: the two-edged broadsword of the ancient Highlanders [OED]

cleek: a large hook for catching hold of or pulling something; hence, to hook, snatch, pilfer

cleekit: to catch at hands or arms, or draw a partner close in a dance [OED]

cleg: gadfly or horsefly; a breeze [OED]; sexual apparatus (fig.)

clink: rhyme (fig.)

clinkan (clinkin): 'jerking, clinking'

clinkumbell: person 'who rings the churchbell'

clips: 'sheers' (shears)

clish-ma-claver: 'idle conversation'

cloot: 'hoof of a cow, sheep, &c.'

clootie: cloven-hoofed Satan, a devil

clours: 'a bump or swelling after a blow'

clout: patch

cluds: clouds

coble: fishing-boat

cockauds: cockades

coft: purchased, bought

cog: 'a wooden dish'

coggie: '*dimin.* of cog'

Coila: 'from Kyle, a district of Ayrshire, so called; saith tradition, from Coil or Coilus, a Pictish monarch'

collieshangie: noisy quarrel, uproar, confused fight [*OED*]

commans: commandments

coof: 'a blockhead, a ninny'

coor: cover

cooser: courser, a large powerful horse

coost: 'did cast'

cootie: 'wooden kitchen dish', a small tub

corn't: fed with corn [JK]

coulter: iron blade fixed in front of the share of the plough, making a vertical cut in the soil [*OED*]

countra: 'country'

cour: cower, duck down; also lower, fold

court-day: rent day

couthy: 'kind, loving'

cowe: 'to terrify, to keep under, to lop; a fright, a branch of furze, bloom, etc.'

cowpit: 'tumbled'

cowran: cowering

cowte: 'a colt'

crabbet: 'crabbed, fretful'

crack: 'conversation, to converse'

craft: 'a field near a house in old husbandry'

craig: a crag or rock, the neck or gullet

crambo-clink (crambo-jingle): 'rhymes, doggerel verses'

crankous: 'fretful, captious'

cranreuch: 'the hoar frost'

crap: 'a crop, the top'

craw: 'a crow of a cock; a rook'

creel: 'a basket; *to have one's wits in a creel*, to be crazed, to be fascinated'

creepie-chair: the stool of repentance, where fornicators sat during their public penance

creeshie: greasy, filthy [JK]

crood: 'to coo as a dove'

croose (crouse): 'chearful, courageous'

crouch: bend

crouchie: 'crook-backed'

croud: crowd

crowdie-time: 'breakfast-time'

crowlan: 'crawling'

crump: 'hard and brittle, spoken of bread'

crunt: 'a blow on the head with a cudgel'

curchie: 'a curtesy' (curtsy)

curler: 'a player at ice'

curmurring: 'murmuring, slight, rumbling noise'

cushat: 'the dove or wood pigeon'

daffin: 'merriment, foolishness'

dail: plank
daimen-icker: 'an ear of corn now and then'
daunton: to intimidate, depress, subdue
daur: 'to dare'
daurk: day's labour [JK]
dawd: 'a large piece'
dawt (daut): to fondle, caress, pet
dawtet (dawtit): 'fondled, caressed', petted
dead: death [JK]
deave: 'to deafen'
deil (de'il, deevil): devil
deil-ma-care: 'no matter! for all that!'
deil na: oath; expresses strong negation [JK]
deuck (deuk): duck
differ: difference
dight: 'to wipe, to clean corn from chaff; cleaned from chaff'
dine: dinner-time
ding: 'to worst, to push'
dinna: 'do not'
dinsome: noisy
dint: occasion, chance
dirl: 'a slight, tremulous stroke or pain'; a smarting pain, quickly over [AR];
    rattle [JK]
discover: to reveal a pregnancy
disrespecket: 'disrespected'
ditty: see gat our ditty
dizzen: 'a dozen'
dizzie: 'dizzy, giddy'
dochter: daughter
dockie: backside
doited: 'stupified, hebetated'; stupid as in frail old age [Dick]
donsie: 'unlucky'
dool: grief, pain
dorty: 'saucy, nice'; not to be spoke to, conceited [AR]
doup: the bottom, the arse, the small remains of a candle, the bottom of an egg-
    shell [AR]
doup-skelper: slapper (or stroker) of buttocks
douse (douce): 'sober, wise, prudent'; solid, grave [AR]
dow: 'am, or are able to, can'
dowff (dowf): 'pithless, wanting force'
dowie: worn with grief or fatigue; melancholy, doleful
dows: pigeons, doves
doxy: originally the term in Vagabond's Cant for the unmarried mistress of a
    beggar or rogue [OED]
doylt: 'stupified, crazed'; confused, silly
doytan: walking stupidly, shambling
drab: from Gaelic drabag, a dirty female, slattern [OED]
drap: 'a drop, to drop'
drappie: a small portion of spirits
dreeping: 'oozing, dropping'

dreigh (driegh): slow, long, tedious; keeping at a distance. Hence, an ill-payer of his debts, we call dreigh [AR]

driddle: to move slowly, more action than motion [Dick]

droddum: 'the breech'; the backside; dress your droddum: kick your backside

droot-rumpl't: 'droops at the crupper' (having sagging hindquarters or rump)

droukit: soaked, dripping, wet through

drouth: 'thirst, drought'

drouthy: thirsty

druken: 'drunken'

drumlie: muddy, discoloured, cloudy, thick-skulled

dub: 'a small pond'

duddie: 'ragged'

duds (duddies): 'rags, clothes'

dung: 'worsted, pushed, driven'

durk: dirk

dush't: 'pushed by a ram, ox, &c.'

dyke: a wall of undressed stones without mortar [Dick]

dyvor (diver): a bankrupt, to be bankrupt; a rascal

e'e: 'the eye'

een: 'the eyes'; also evening

eerie: 'frighted, dreading spirits'; frightened

eild: 'old age'

eldritch: 'ghastly, frightful'

ell: a measure of length: 37.05 inches in Scotland (45 inches in England)

Enbrugh (Embro'): 'Edinburgh'

eneugh: 'enough'

Erse: highland, gaelic

ettle: purpose, aim [JK]

ev'n down: downright

eydent: 'diligent'

fa': 'fall, lot, to fall'; lay claim to

factor: agent for an estate, steward

faem: 'foam'

faes: foes

failins: failings

fain of ither: fond of each other [JK]

fairin: souvenir of a fair, 'a fairing, a present'

fallow: 'fellow'

farls: 'a cake of bread'; a quarter of a circular oaten bannock [JK]

fash: 'trouble, care, to trouble, to care for'; vex [AR]

Fasteneen: 'Fastens-even' (Shrove Tuesday)

fatt'rels: 'ribbon ends'

fause: false

fausont (fawsont): 'decent, seemly'

faut: 'fault'

fauteless: 'faultless'

fawsont (fausont): 'decent, seemly'

fecht (fetch't): 'to fight'

fecht wi' nowt: bull-fight (nowt = cattle)

feck: value, return [JK] (the feck: the majority)

feckless: 'puny, weak, silly'

feg: 'a fig'

fell: 'keen, biting; the flesh immediately under the skin; a field pretty level on the
     side or top of a hill'

fen: a shift to get along [Dick]; fend

ferintosh: a peaty single-malt whisky, sometimes synonymous with whisky in
     Burns's day

ferlie (ferly): 'to wonder, a wonder, a term of contempt'

fetch't (fecht): 'to fight'

fey: fated, doomed

fidgean-fain (fidgin fain): to be fidgeting with eagerness; excited

fidgin: 'fidgeting'

fient: 'fiend, a petty oath'

fient haet: 'a petty oath of negation, nothing'

fier (fiere): 'sound, healthy; a brother, a friend'

fissle: 'to make a rustling noise, to fidget, a bustle'

fitt (fit): 'a foot'

fittie-lan': 'the near horse of the hindmost pair in the plough'; (rear, left-hand
     horse [JK])

flaffin (flaffan); flapping, fluttering [JK]

flainin: 'flannel'

flang: flung, capered

fleesh: 'a fleece'

fleg: 'a kick, a random blow'

fley: 'to scare, to frighten'

flichterin: 'stuttering'

flingin-tree (flingan-tree): 'a piece of lumber hung by way of partition between
     two horses in a stable; a flail'

fliskit: 'fretted'

flit: shift, move [JK]

foggage: rank grass [JK]

foord: 'a ford'

forbye: 'besides'

forgather: 'to meet, to encounter with'

forjeskit: 'jaded with fatigue'

fou: 'full, drunk'

foughten: 'troubled, harassed'

fow: 'a bushel, etc.'

frae: 'from'

fraeth: 'froth'

freaks: odd notions, fancies [JK]

fud: buttocks, tail

funny (funnie): 'full of merriment'

fur (furr), 'a furrow'

furm: 'a form, a bench'

fyke: 'trifling care; to piddle, to be in a fuss about trifles'

fyl'd (fyl't): 'soiled, dirtied'

ga': gall, pustule, sore [JK]

gab: 'the mouth, to speak boldly or pertly'

gae: 'to go'

gaed: 'went'

gaen (gane): 'gone,'

gaets (gate): 'way, manner, road'

Galston muirs: located several miles north of Mauchline

gangrel: vagrant, tramp [JK]

gar: 'to make, to force to'

gash: 'wise, sagacious, talkative; to converse'

gat: got, begot [JK]

gat our ditty: received our reproof [JK]

gate (gaets): 'way, manner, road'

gaun: 'going'

gaunted: gaped, gasped [JK]

gawsie (gawsy, gausy): jolly, buxom [*GS*]

gaylies: tolerably, adequately [JK]

gear: 'riches, goods of any kind'

geck: 'to toss the head in wantonness or scorn'

ged: 'pike'

Geordie: 'a guinea'

get: 'a child, a young one'

ghaist: 'a ghost'

gie: 'to give'

gied: 'gave'

gi'en: 'given'

gif: if

giftie: 'dimin. of gift'

giga: from 'gigue': a lively air that combines two different strains, each repeated
    [*OED*]; JK points out that *giga* is Italian for fiddle

gill: a Scots measure, a quarter mutchkin [JK]

gimmer: 'a ewe from one to two years old'

gin: 'if, against'; before [JK]

girdle: griddle (for scone-baking)

girn: 'to grin, to twist the features in rage, agony &c.'

girnan: 'grinning'

gizz: 'a periwig'

glaiket (glaikit): 'inattentive, foolish'

glaizie: glassy; 'glittering, smooth like glass'

glanc'd: could be seen, were visible

glaum: grasp, clutch

gleib: a piece, a portion; the land belonging to the clergy benefice

glen: a mountain-valley, usually narrow and forming the course of a
    stream [*OED*]

glib-gabbet: 'that speaks smoothly and readily'

glintan (glintin): 'peeping'

gloaming: 'the twilight'

glowran (glowrin): 'staring'

glunch: 'a frown, to frown'

gossip: a woman friend invited to be present at a birth, a godmother gowan: 'the flower of the daisy, dandelion, hawkweed, &c.'

gowd: gold

grace-prood: proud of their grace, sanctimonious

grain (grane): 'to groan'

graith: 'accoutrements, furniture, dress'; equipment, tools, harness, etc.

gree: 'to agree; *to bear the gree*, to be decidedly victor'

greet: 'to shed tears, to weep'

greetan (greetin): 'crying, weeping'

greive: a farm-bailiff; head workman on a farm

grip: spasmodic pain

grissle: 'gristle'

groanin malt (groanin maut): the lying-in drink for the midwife and friends; also used to ease the mother's labour pains

groat: a small coin

grozet: 'a gooseberry'

gruntle: 'the phiz, a grunting noise'

grushie: 'thick, of thriving growth'

gruttan: has wept

Gude: 'the Supreme Being', God

gude: 'good'

gudeman: 'master of the house'

guid: 'good'

guid-een: 'good evening'

guidfather: 'father-in-law'

guidwife: 'mistress of the house'

guid-willy: hospitable, kindly, generous good will [Dick]

gully: 'a large knife'

gulravage: horseplay, romp, uproar

ha'-Bible: 'the great Bible that lies in the hall'

haerse: hoarse

haet: *see* fient haet

haff: half

haffet (hauffet): 'the temple, the side of the head'

hafflins: 'nearly half, or partly'

hailstanes: hailstones

hain: 'to spare, to save'

hainch: haunch, hip

hain'd: 'spared'

hair on thairms: bow on strings

hairum-scairum: wild

haith: 'a petty oath'

hal': 'hall'

hald (hal'): 'an abiding place'; a holding or possession

hale: 'whole, tight, healthy'

hallan: 'a particular partition wall in a cottage' between the living room and the byre or between the door and the hearth

hallan-en: the end of the partition wall between the door and the fire

hallions: hellions, rascals, idlers

Hallow-mass: All Saints' Day

hame: 'home'
hamely: 'homely, affable'; friendly, frank, open, kind [AR]
hameward: 'homeward'
han-duark: handiwork
hangie: the hangman, or Satan
hangit: hanged
hanker: hesitate [JK]
hansel: a New Year's or good luck present
hap: 'an outer garment, mantle, plaid, &c.; to wrap, to cover; to hop'
happer: 'a hopper'
hap-step-an'-loup: 'hop, skip and leap'
harket (harkit): 'harkened'
harn: sackcloth, cloth made of coarse flax on tow [JK]
hash: a term of obloquy, applied to a person who 'makes a hash' of his words
    [OED]; a sloven [AR]
haud: 'to hold'; haud awa: see held awa
hauffet (haffet): the temple or side-locks of hair
hauf-mile: half-mile
haughs: 'low-lying rich lands, valleys'
havins: 'good manners, decorum, good sense'
hawkan (hawkin): 'digging'
hawkie: 'a cow, properly one with a white face'
hech: 'Oh! Strange!'
heckle: a flax comb; to cross-examine [Dick]
heeze: 'to elevate, to raise'; to lift up a heavy thing a little [AR]
held awa (haud awa): took (his, their, my) way [JK]
herd: 'to tend flocks; one who tends flocks'
herd-callan: 'one who tends flocks'
herriet: harried, plundered
het: 'hot'
heugh: 'a crag, a coal-pit'
hilch: 'to hobble, to halt'
hindmost: last, final
hing: 'to hang'
hingin: hanging
hirplan (hirplin): 'creeping'
hissels: 'so many cattle as one person can attend'
histie: 'dry, chapt, barren'
hizzy (hizzie): 'hussy, a young girl'
hoast (host): 'to cough'
hoddan: 'the motion of a sage country man riding on a cart-horse'
hodden (hoddin): a grey, coarse homespun of mixed black and white wool [JK]
hog-shouther: 'a kind of horse-play by justling [jostling] with the shoulder; to
    justle'
hoit (hoy't): 'urged'
hoolie: 'Take leisure! Stop!'
hoord: 'a hoard, to hoard'
hostan: 'coughing'
hotch: hitch, jolt, jerk
hough: to disable by cutting the Achilles tendon

houghmagandie: 'fornication'
houlets: owlets, owls
houpe: hope
hove: 'to heave, to swell'
howcket (howket): 'digged'; exhumed
howe: 'hollow, a hollow or dale'
howe-backet: 'sunk in the back, spoken of a horse, &c.'
hoyte: 'to amble crazily'
Hughoc: 'dimin. of Hugh'
hunkers: haunches
hurchin: urchin
hurdies: 'the loins, the crupper'; the buttocks, backside

ilk (ilka): 'each, every'
ingine: 'genius, ingenuity'
ingle: 'fire, the fireplace'
ingle-cheek: the side-piece of the fireplace
irie: eerie
ither: 'other, one another'

jad: 'jade, also a familiar term among country folks for a giddy young girl'
Janwar: January
jauk: 'to dally, to trifle'; to joke
jaup: 'to jerk, as agitated water'
jee (jee'd): stir, rock, swing sideways; to incline to one side [AR]
jimp: 'to jump; slender in the waist, handsome'
jinker: 'that turns quickly, a gay sprightly girl, a wag'
jirt: 'a jerk'
jo: sweetheart [JK], joy [Dick]
jouk: 'to stop, to bow the head'
jow: 'a verb which includes both the swinging motion and pealing sound of a
    large bell'
jowler: a dog with large jowls, a fierce dog
jundie: 'to justle' (jostle)

kae: 'a daw' (jackdaw)
kail: 'coleworts [cabbage], a kind of broth'
kail-blade: cabbage leaf
kail-runt: 'the stem of the colewort [cabbage]'
kain (kane): 'fowls &c. paid as in rent by a farmer'
kebars (kabers): rafters
kebbuck: 'a cheese'; kebbuck heel: rind of cheese
kecklin: cackling, giggling; to be noisy [AR]
keek: 'a peep, to peep'
keepet: 'kept'
ken: 'to know'
kend (ken't): 'knew'
kennin: 'a small matter'
ket: 'a matty, hairy fleece of wool'
kiaugh: 'carking anxiety'

kilt: 'to truss up the cloaths'; to tuck up the skirt

kimmer: 'a young girl, a gossip'

king's-hood: 'a certain part of the entrails of an ox'; second stomach of a ruminant [JK]

kintra (kintry, koontry): country

kirn: 'a harvest supper; a churn, to churn'

kirsin: 'to christen'

kirkton: a village in which a parish church is located

kist: 'a shop counter, a chest'

kitchens: seasons [JK]; 'anything that eats with bread; to serve for soup, gravy etc.'

kittle: 'to tickle, ticklish' (has connotations of sexual arousal); likely

knaggie: knobby, like points of rocks

knappin-hammer: 'a hammer for breaking stones'

knooz'd: drubbed; buffetted and bruised [AR]

knowe: 'a small round hillock'

kye: 'cows'

Kyle (Coil, Coila): Burns's region of Ayrshire

kyles: skittles

kyte: belly

lag: laggard, backward

laggen: 'the angle between the side and bottom of a wooden dish'

laimpet: 'a kind of shell-fish'; limpet

lair: grave, bed

laird: a landowner; a squire

laith: 'loath'

laithfu': 'bashful, sheepish'

lake (laik): lack

lallans: 'Scotch dialect'

Lammas: harvest-time

lane: see my lane, thy lane

lanely: 'lonely'

lang: 'long'

lang hame: 'grave'

lang syne: long since, long ago

lap: 'did leap'

last claith: shroud

lave: 'the rest, the remainder, the others'

laverock: 'the lark'

lay (lea): untilled ground left fallow [JK]

lear: 'learning'

least: lest, for fear that

lee-lang: 'live-long'

leeze me: 'a phrase of congratulatory endearment'

leister: 'a three-pronged dart for striking fish'

leugh: 'laugh'

leuk: 'a look, to look'

libbet: castrated

limmer: 'a kept mistress, a strumpet'

linkan (linkin): tripping
lint i' the bell: 'flax in flower'
lintwhite: 'a linnet'
loan: 'the place of milking'
loof: 'palm of the hand'
loot on: showed, disclosed (let on)
lough: lake (loch)
loun (loon): 'a fellow, a ragamuffin, a woman of easy virtue'
lour: look threateningly; impending, lowering
lowan: flaming
lowe: 'a flame, to flame'
lowping (louping): leaping [JK]
lowse: 'to loose'
lows'd: 'loosed'
lug: 'the ear, [or] a handle'
luggies: 'a small wooden dish with a handle'
lunch: 'a large piece of cheese, flesh, &c.'
lunt: 'a column of smoke, to smoke'
luver: lover
lyart: 'of a mixed colour, grey'; hoary or grey-headed [AR]

mae: 'more'
mailen (mailin): a farm or holding
mair: 'more'
mak: 'to make'
makin: 'making'
Mallie: 'Molly'
manteele: 'mantle'
mantling: the action of foaming or creaming [*OED*]
mark: a coin worth about 13 Scots shillings
mashlum: mixed corn
mattock: an agricultural tool for loosening hard ground [*OED*]
maukin: 'a hare'
maun: 'must'
mauna: must not
maut: *see* groanin malt
maw: 'mow'
mawing: 'mowing'
mealy bags: bags of meal
meikle (mickle, muckel): 'great, big, much'
melder: an order of meal ground by a miller for a customer
mell: 'to meddle'; to have sexual intercourse [Dick]
melvie: 'to soil with meal'
menseless: 'ill-bred, rude, impudent'
messan (messin): 'a small dog'
mickle (meikle, muckel): 'great, big, much
mim: imitative of the action of pursing up the mouth; affectedly demure and
    prim [*OED*]
mind: 'remembrance'; remember
minnie: 'mother, dam'

mirk: dark [AR]
mischanter: mischance, mishap
miska't (misca't): 'to abuse, to call names'
mislear'd: 'mischievous, unmannerly'
misteuk: 'mistook'
mite-horn: horn of the harvest mite [JK]
mither: 'a mother'
mixtie-maxtie: 'confusedly mixed'
mizl'd: confused, misinformed [JK]
modewurk (moudiewort; modiewort; modiewart), 'a mole'
moil: labour, drudgery [OED]
moistify: 'to moisten'
mony (monie): 'many'
moop: 'to nibble as a sheep'; to eat, generally used of children or of old people,
    who have but few teeth, and make their lips move fast, though they eat but
    slow [AR]
moorlan: 'of or belonging to the moors'
mottie: 'full of motes'
mou: mouth
moudiewort (modiewort, modiewart, modewurk): 'a mole'
mowe: crude Scots term for copulation
muckle: 'or meikle, great, big, much'
muckle house: Parliament
muir: moor
Murkirk: a village about nine miles from Mauchline
muslin-kail: 'broth composed simply of water, shelled barley and greens'
mutchkin: 'an English pint'
muve: move
my lane: when I'm alone [JK]

naething: 'nothing'
naig: 'a horse'
nappy: ale
near-hand: almost
neebor (neibor; nebor): 'a neighbour'
ne'er-a-bit: never a bit
negleket: 'neglected'
neist (niest): 'next'
New Holland: Australia
newk: 'neuk' (nook, corner, recess)
nice: refined, fastidious, dainty
nick: cut
Nickie-ben: Satan
niest (neist): 'next'
nieve: 'the fist'
nievefu': 'handful'
niffer: 'an exchange, to exchange or barter'
nit: nut
noddle: head, brain
norland: 'of or belonging to the North'

nowt (nowte): cattle

och!: expresses surprise, sorrow [JK]
Ochiltree: village five miles south of Mauchline
olio: a dish of Spanish and Portuguese origin with meat and fowl, bacon,
    pumpkins, cabbage, and turnips, stewed and highly spiced; any dish containing
    a great variety of ingredients, a hotch potch [OED]
onie (ony): 'any'
or: 'is often used for ere, before'
orra: extra, spare
ought: aught (anything)
oughtlins: at all, in any way
out-owre: beyond, above, across
owre: 'over; too'; excessively, excessive
owrehip: 'a way of fetching a blow with the hammer over the arm'

pack: 'intimate, familiar'
paidl'd: paddled
painch: 'paunch'; stomach
paitrick: 'a partridge'
pang: 'to cram'
pat: 'did put, a pot'
pattle: 'a plough-staff'; spade used to clean the plough [JK]
paughty: 'proud, haughty'
pawkie: 'cunning, sly'
pay't: 'beat'
peck: 2 gallons, 1/4 of a bushel [OED]
peghan (pechan): 'crop, stomach'
penny-fee: wages [Dick]
penny-wheep: 'small beer'
pet: 'a domesticated sheep, &c.'
philibeg: kilt
phiz: face
phraisin: 'flattery'
pin: skewer
pine: 'pain, uneasiness'
pirratch (parritch): porridge, an 'oatmeal pudding, a well-known Scottish dish'
plack: 'an old Scotch coin'
plackless: 'pennyless'
plaisters: medicinal plasters
pleugh: 'or plew, a plough'
pleugh-pettle: a small long-handled spade to clean the plough [JK]
pliskie: 'a trick'
pliver: plover
poind: distrained, to have one's goods seized and sold under warrant [JK]
pook: poke, bag
poortith: 'poverty'
poosion'd: poisoned
Poossie: 'a hare or cat'
pou'd (pou't): 'to pull'

pouk: 'to pluck'
pow: 'the head, the skull'; poll
pownie: 'a little horse'
preen: 'a pin'
prie: 'taste'
pu'd (pou't): pulled
pyke: pick at [JK]
pyle: 'a single grain of chaff'

quat: 'to quit'
quean: an attractive young woman
quier: choir

raep (rape): rope
raibles: 'to rattle nonsense'
rairan: roaring
rair'd (rair't): 'roared'
raize: 'to madden, to inflame'
ramfeezl'd: 'fatigued, overspent'
ram-stam: 'forward, thoughtless'
randies: sturdy, abusive, threatening beggars
rantin: 'ranting'
rash: 'a rush'
rass-buss: 'a bush of rushes'
rattlin (rattlan): 'rattling'; rattlin the corn: sowing the corn
ratton: 'a rat'
raucle: coarse, fearless, clever, stout, rudely strong
rax: 'to stretch'
reams: froths, foams
reave: 'steal'
reck: 'to heed'
red (rede): 'to counsel, counsel'
red-wat-shod: wading through blood, bloodshod
red-wud: 'stark mad'
reek: 'smoke'
reekin (reekan): 'smoking'
reekit: 'smoked, smoky'
reestet: 'stood restive, stunted, withered'
reif (reif): thieving
remead: 'remedy'
rief (rief): thieving
rig: 'a ridge'
riggin: roof
rigwoodie: term of abuse derived from a rig-woodie, the rope harness of a cart-
    horse; stringy, withered
rin: 'to run, to melt'
rinnin: 'running'
ripp: 'a handful of unthreshed corn'
rippels: shooting pains in the back and loins
risket: 'made a noise like the tearing of roots'

rive: break up
rockin: a spinning party, or winter evening party
roger: penis; coarse English term for copulation
rood: quarter-acre
roon: 'a shred, a remnant'; round circuit [JK]
roose: 'to praise, to commend'
roosty: rusty
roupet (rupet, rupit): 'hoarse, as with a cold'
rowe (row): 'to roll, to wrap'
rowte: 'to low, to bellow'
rowth: 'plenty'
rozet: 'rosin' (used as an insecticide)
rung: 'a cudgel'
runkl'd: 'wrinkled'
rupit (roupet, rupet): 'hoarse, as with a cold'
ryke: reach

sae: 'so'
saft: 'soft'
sair: 'to serve, sore'; also, surely
sair-won: hard won
sair-work (sair-wark): hard labour, hardship
sark: 'a shirt'; a smock
saugh: 'the willow'
saul: 'soul'
saumont: salmon
saunt: 'a saint'
saut: 'salt'
sautet: 'salted'
sawing: 'to sow'
sax: 'six'
scar: 'to scare'
scaud: scald
scaur: 'apt to be scared'
scho: she
sconner (scunner): 'a lothing, to loth'; to loath [AR]
scour'd: ran, ranged
scow'r: roister [AR]
scraich: 'to scream, as a hen, partridge, &c.'
screed: 'to tear, a rent'
screigh (skriegh): 'a scream; to scream'
scrieve: 'to glide swiftly along'
scrimpet: 'did scant, scanty'
scroggy: hill slopes covered with brushwood; thorny [AR]
shaird: 'a shred, a shard'
shaver: 'a humorous wag, a barker'
shavie: trick
shaw: 'a small wood in a hollow place'
sheep-shank: 'to think one's self *nae sheep-shank*, to be conceited'
sheugh: 'a ditch, a trench'

shog: 'a shock'; a shake [AR]
shool: 'a shovel'
shoon: 'shoes'
shore: to offer, to threaten
shouther: 'the shoulder'
sic: 'such'
sicker: 'sure, steady'
sidelins: 'sidelong, slanting'
siller: 'silver, money'
simmer: 'summer'
skaith: 'to damage, to injure, injury'
skeigh: 'proud, nice, high-mettled'; skittish [AR]
skellum: scoundrel
skelp: 'to strike, to slap'
skelpan: 'slapping, walking smartly'; to run – used when one runs barefoot [AR]
skelpet (skelpit): hurried, rushed
skiegh: 'proud, nice, high-mettled'; skittish [AR]
skinking: watery; to fill drink in a cup [AR]
skirl: a piercing sound, a shriek; to cry with a shrill voice [AR]
sklent: 'slant; to run aslant, to deviate from truth'
skouth: scope, liberty
skyrin: brightly coloured, shining [JK]
skyte: a sudden blow; fly out hastily [AR]
slade: 'did slide'
slae: sloe
slap: 'a gate, a breach in a fence'; a gap or narrow pass between two hills, a
    breach in a wall [AR]
slaw: slow
slee: 'sly'
sleekit: 'sleek'
sleest: 'slyest'
slypet: 'fell'
smeddum: 'dust, powder, mettle, sense'; fine powder used medicinally [JK]
smeek: smoke
smiddy (smiddie): 'smithy'
smoor: smother [AR]
smoutie: 'smutty, obscene, ugly'
smytrie: 'numerous collection of small individuals'
snash: 'abuse, billingsgate'
snaw: 'snow, to snow'
sned: lop, cut off
sneeshin mill: 'snuff-box'
snell: 'bitter, biting'
snick: 'the latch of a door'
snick-drawing: 'trick contriving'
snirtle: snigger
snool: 'one whose spirit is broken with oppressive slavery; to submit tamely; to
    sneak'
snoov'd (snoov't): 'to go smoothly and constantly; to sneak'
snowk: 'to scent or snuff as a dog, horse, &c.'

sodger: soldier

sonsie: 'having sweet, engaging looks, lucky, jolly'; sometimes used for large and lusty [AR]

sough (sugh): the sound of the wind moving among trees, or of one sleeping [AR]; sough for sough: *lit.* breath for breath

soupe: sup, drink, mouthful

souple: 'flexible, swift'

souter: cobbler, shoemaker [JK]

sowps: 'a spoonful, a small quantity of anything liquid'

sowth: 'to try over a tune with a low whistle'

sowther: 'to solder, to cement'

spails: splinters

spair: reticent, restrained

spairge: 'to dash, to soil, as with mud'

spak: 'did speak'

spavet (spaviet): 'having the spavin'

spavie: the spavin, a lameness (usually of horses) caused by inflammation or a tumour

spean: to wean by frightening the foal so that it refuses its mother's milk

speel: 'to climb'

speet: spit, transfix

speir: 'to ask, enquire'

spence: 'the country parlour'; an inner compartment of a house [OED]

spier: 'to ask, enquire'

spleuchan: 'a tobacco pouch'

splore: 'a frolic, a riot, a noise'

sprattle: 'to scramble'

springan (springin): 'springing'

sprittie: 'full of spirits'; n. (spirit) 'a tough-rooted plant something like rushes'

spunk: 'fire, mettle, wit'; tinder

spunkie: 'mettlesome, fiery, will o' wisp, ignis fatuus'

squatter: 'to flutter in water as a wild duck &c.'

squattle: 'to sprawl'

squeel: 'a scream, a screech, to scream'

stacher: 'to stagger'

staggie (staig): a young horse under three years

stane: 'a stone'

stang: sting

stank: pond, pool of standing water

stan't: 'did stand'

stap: 'to stop'

stark: strong, robust

startle: 'to run as cattle stung by the gadfly'

staukin: stalking, marching

staw: 'did steal, to surfeit'

steek: 'to shut; a stitch'; to close [AR]

steer: take one's way [JK]

steeve: 'firm, compacted'

stegh: to cram [AR]

stell: 'a still'

sten: leap, bound, to rear as a horse; to move with a hasty long pace
sten't: 'reared'
stent: 'tribute, dues of any kind'; to stretch or extend
steyest: 'steepest'
stibble: 'stubble'
stick-an-stowe: 'totally, altogether'
stilt: 'a crutch, to halt, to limp'
stimpart: 'the eighth part of a Winchester bushel'; a measure of grain ($\frac{1}{4}$ peck in
    JK)
stirks: 'a cow or bullock a year old'
stook: corn sheaves stacked two by two, in rows in a field
stoor: 'sounding hollow, strong and hoarse'
stound: a sudden pang [Dick]
stoure: 'dust, more particularly dust in motion'; hence storm, commotion, battle
    (AR glossary says *stoure* is dust agitated by horse-feet)
stow'd: crammed
stowp: 'a kind of jug or dish with a handle'
strack (strak): 'did strike'
strade: strode
strae: 'straw'
strae-death: 'to die in bed'
straik: stroke
strappan: 'tall and handsome'
straught: 'straight'
striddle: 'to straddle'
stroan: 'to spout, to piss'
strunt: 'spiritous liquor of any kind; to walk sturdily'
studdie: anvil
stumpie: '*dimin.* of stump'; the poet's worn-out quill pen
sturt: 'trouble, to molest'
suc like: such like
sucker: 'sugar'
sud: 'should'
sugh (sough): 'the continued rushing noise of wind or water'
sune: 'soon'
suthron: 'southern, an old name for the English nation'
swaird: 'sward'
swank: 'stately, jolly'
swankie (swanker): 'a tight strapping young fellow or girl'
swarf: to swoon away [AR]
swat: 'did sweat'; n. new light foaming ale
swatch: 'a sample'
swingein: 'beating, whipping'
swith: 'get away!'
swither: 'to hesitate in choice; an irresolute wavering in choice'
swoor: 'swore, did swear'
syne: 'since, ago, then'

taen: taken
taet: 'tuft, small handful'

tak: 'to take'

takin: 'taking'

tane: the one [JK]

tap: 'the top'

tapetless: 'heedless, foolish' (tap = head)

tapsalteerie: 'topsy-turvy'

targe: light shield [JK]

tarrow: 'to murmur at one's allowance'; to refuse what we love because of a cross humour [AR]

tarry-breeks: 'a sailor'

tauk: talk

tauld (tald): 'told'

tauted (tawted): 'matted together, spoken of hair or wool'

tawie: 'that allows itself peaceably to be handled, spoken of a horse, cow &c.'; tame

ten-hour's bite: 'a slight feed to the horses while in the yoke in the forenoon'

tent: 'a field pulpit, heed, caution; to take heed, take care'

tentie, 'heedful, cautious'

tentless: 'heedless'

tester: sixpence

teugh: tough

thack an' raep: 'cloathing, necessaries'

thae: 'these'

thairm: intestine; small tripes [AR]

thegither: 'together'

thiggin (thiggan): begging

thirl'd: 'thrilled, vibrated'

thole: 'to suffer, to endure'

thow: 'a thaw, to thaw'

thowless: 'slack, lazy'

thrang: 'throng, a crowd'; busy with many tasks

thrave: two stooks of corn; a measure of straw

thraw: 'to sprain, to twist, to contradict'

threap: 'to maintain by dint of assertion'

three-tae'd: 'having three prongs'

threteen: 'thirteen'

thrissle: thistle

throw'ther: 'pell-mell, confusedly'; *lit.* through each other [JK]

thy lane: on your own

tight: shapely, tidy

till't: 'to it'

timmer: 'timber'

tine: 'to lose'

tine your dam: to urinate involuntarily (lose control of your bladder)

tint: 'lost'

tipenny: twopenny; also an ale sold at that price per pint [JK]

tipt you off blue boram: given you syphilis ('blue boar'– a term inspired by London's infamous Blue Boar tavern at Oxford Street and Tottenham Court Road – was English slang for the initial venereal ulcer) [JK]

tirl: 'to make a slight noise, to uncover'
tirled at the pin: rattled the door-latch
tirlin: 'uncovering'
tither: the other [JK]
tit-ta (tyta): da-da; baby-talk for father
tittie: *colloq.* for sister
tittlan: 'whispering'
tocher: 'marriage portion'
tod: 'a fox'
toddy: whisky with hot water and sugar
todlan (todlin): 'tottering'
took the sands: fled [JK]
toolzie (tulzie, tulyie): 'a quarrel, to quarrel, to fight'
toom'd: emptied
toop (tip): 'a ram'
tother: the other
tout: 'the blast of a horn or trumpet'
tow: 'a rope'
towmond (towmont): year (twelvemonth)
towsie (towzie): 'rough, shaggy'
toy: 'a very old fashion of female head-dress'
toyte: 'to totter like old age'
tozie: cosy, tipsy, warm
transmugrify'd: 'transmigrated, metamorphosed'
trashtrie: 'trash'
trepan: trap or snare [*OED*]
trews: hose and breeches all of a piece [AR]; trousers
trottin: 'trotting'
trouth: 'truth, a petty oath'
trow: 'to believe'
tryst(e): assembly, meeting; appointment [AR]
trysted: appointed
tulyie (tulzie, toolzie): 'a quarrel, to quarrel, to fight'
twa: 'two'
twal: 'twelve'
twal-pennie worth: 'a small quantity, a pennyworth'
twa-three: two or three, a few [JK]
twin: separate from, deprive of
tyke: 'a dog'

unco: 'strange, uncouth, very, very great, prodigious'
uncos: news, gossip
unskaithed: unscathed
usquabae (usquebae): whisky

variorum: variation, a varying or changing scene [*OED*]
vauntie: vain, proud
vera: 'very'
vow: strange! wonderful!

wabster: 'a weaver'

wad: 'would; to bet; a bet, a pledge'
wae: 'woe, sorrowful'
waes me (waesucks): 'alas! O the pity!'
waft: 'the woof,
wair (war'd): 'to lay out, to expend'
wale: 'choice, to chuse'; the wale, the best [AR]
walie (waly): ample, large, handsome; chosen, beautiful, large [AR]
wallet: a beggar's bag [OED]
wame: 'the belly'
wamefu': 'a bellyful'
wan: won
wanchancie: 'unlucky'
wanrestfu': 'restless'
want ay: want for ever (better just than want ay: barely better than nothing)
wark: 'work'
wark-lume: 'a tool to work with' (work-loom)
warl (warld): 'world'
warlock-breef: charter conveying magical powers, charm [JK]
warly: 'worldly, eager on amassing wealth'
warsled: 'wrestled'
warst: 'worst'
wastrie: 'prodigality'
wat: know, be aware of, wet
water-brose: plain oatmeal (no salt, milk or butter)
water-fit: mouth of a river [JK]
wattle: 'a twig, a wand'
wauble: 'to swing, to reel'
waught: a long drink [Dick]
wauket (waukit): 'thickened, as fullers do cloth'
waukin (wauken): awaken [Dick]; 'to awake'
waur: 'worse, to worst'
wawlie (walie): ample, large, handsome
wean (weanie): 'a child'
weasan (weason, wyson): gullet
wee: 'little'
wee-bit: 'a small matter'
weel: 'well'
weelfare: 'welfare'
weel-gaun: well-going
weel-knooz'd: well-pummelled, drubbed [JK]
weel-stocket: well-stocked
ween: think [OED]
weet: wet
westlin: westerly
whaizle: 'to wheeze'
whalpet: whelped
whang: 'a leathern string, a piece of cheese, bread, &c.; to give the strappado'
whare (whar): 'where'
whase: 'whose'
whatna: on or by what
whid: 'the motion of a hare running, but not frighted; a lie'

whidden (whiddan): 'running as a hare or coney'
whiles (whyles): 'sometimes'
whin: gorse [JK]
whin-rock (whunstane); 'a whin-stone', any hard dark-coloured rock such as basalt; *fig.* hard
whipper-in: huntsman's assistant, whips stray dogs back into the pack [*OED*]
whisket: 'lashed'
whisht: 'silence! to hold one's whisht, to be silent'
whissle: 'a whistle, to whistle'
whitter: 'a heavy draught of liquor'
whittle: knife (used as a weapon or for surgery); to die upon a whittle: to die by surgical castration
whunstane: 'a whin-stone'; any hard dark-coloured rock such as basalt; *fig.* hard
whyles (whiles): 'sometimes'
wight: stout, clever, active: said of a man or person [AR]
wimplin (wimpling, wimplan): 'waving, meandering'
win: reach, gain, get
winkan (winkin): 'winking'
winna: 'will not'
winnocks: 'windows'
winnock-bunker: seat in the window
winsome: 'gay, hearty, vaunted'
wintle: 'a staggering motion, to stagger or reel'
wizen'd: 'hide-bound, dried, shrunk'
wonner: 'a wonder, a contemptuous appellation'
woodie: halter for hanging; the gallows [AR]
woor: wore out
wordy: worthy
worms: spiral tubes on a still
writer-chiel: lawyer
wud: 'mad, distracted'
wyliecoat (wylecoat): 'a flannel vest'
wylin (wyling): attracting by wiles, beguiling
wyte: 'blame, to blame'

ye: 'this pronoun is frequently used for thou'; you
yell (yeld): 'barren, that gives no milk'
yerket: 'jerked, lashed'
yestreen: last evening; 'yesternight'
yett: gate
yeukin: itching
yill: 'ale'
yird (yirth): earth
yisk: hiccough, belch
yokin: 'yoking about'; contest; sexual coupling
'yont: beyond
yowe: 'a ewe'

Index of Titles

Index of First Lines